Moses A[ustin]

Maria Austin

Emily

Stephen austin

James B Austin

J. Bryan

S.F. Austin

MOSES AUSTIN
HIS LIFE

MOSES AUSTIN
HIS LIFE

David B. Gracy II

Foreword by Mary Austin Perry Beretta

TRINITY UNIVERSITY PRESS

F
389
.A92
G73
1987

Trinity University Press gratefully acknowledges the assistance
of Mr. and Mrs. John W. Beretta and the Beretta Foundation in
making this publication possible.

LIBRARY OF CONGRESS
Library of Congress Cataloging-in-Publication Data

Gracy, David B.
    Moses Austin : his life / David B. Gracy II.
        p.   cm.
    Bibliography: p.273
    Includes index.
    ISBN 0-911536-84-1 : $24.95
    1. Austin, Moses, 1761-1821. 2. Pioneers--Texas--Biography.
3. Businessmen--Texas--Biography. 4. Pioneers--Southwest, Old-
-Biography. 5. Businessmen--Southwest, Old--Biography. 6. Texas-
-History--To 1846. 7. Southwest, Old--History.   I. Title.
F389.A92G73 1987
976.4'02'0924--dc19
    [B]   87-25551
                                                                      CIP

First printing 1987

Trinity University Press   715 Stadium Drive   San Antonio, TX 78284

DEDICATED TO

Professor Lawrence L. Graves
Texas Tech University
and
Professor Barnes F. Lathrop
The University of Texas at Austin

Your guidance, example, and encouragement represent scholarship at its
truest and best. You ignited in me an enthusiasm for learning and a joy
in the sharing of knowledge that will last a lifetime.

FOREWORD

The germ of the idea for this book, the life of Moses Austin, came from my husband, Jack Beretta, back in the early 1950s. Always vitally interested in history, and in particular Texas history, he felt both amazed and saddened that while much had been written about and tributes paid to the son, Stephen F. Austin, "The Father of Texas," very little information was available on the father, who had made the original plan to settle an Anglo colony in Texas and secured the permission to do so from the Spanish government. Jack decided that this omission should be corrected and that at a future time we would see to the necessary research and find the proper writer for a book on Moses Austin, my great-great-great grandfather.

Twenty years passed before we were ready to really start the ball rolling on the research. Through those years, while we raised and educated three children, we had made quick trips to the various places where Moses had lived. On our first visit to Durham, that serene village in the beautiful Connecticut countryside, we were delighted to find, on the main street, a two-story frame house with a historical marker denoting it as the birthplace in 1761 of Moses "who made the plan for the settlement of Texas, carried out by his son Stephen." We knocked on the door and were greeted by Mrs. Elizabeth Mansfield, the current owner, who had inherited it from her family, the owners since 1906. We identified ourselves and explained our great interest in this well-preserved house. She most hospitably invited us in and showed us the changes and additions that had taken place since Elias Austin, father of Moses, had built it in 1741. We drove out of Durham that day in a state of euphoric wonderment, excitement, and mostly silence, each thinking of the great man who was born there two hundred years earlier. I tried to picture Moses as a small boy who grew to the age of fifteen in that lovely spot which seemed to have changed little over the span of years. Did he dream of the adventures that would lead him ever westward? All in all, I think we both fell in love with Moses Austin. Later we made a quick stop in Potosi, Missouri, and saw the remains of a rock wall where he had built a large home for his family. We found also the old cemetery where his remains lie in peace.

In the early 1970s, the time had arrived to make definite plans to start research for this book that had become of primary importance to both of us. Through the instant interest and enthusiasm of Mrs. Betty Smedley, a delightful octogenarian dealer in rare Texana in Austin, Texas, we found a competent and knowledgeable researcher, Mrs. Gray Golden, also of Austin. Much to our delight, Mrs. Golden became a "Moses admirer" and over a period of a few years uncovered a wealth of information from the Barker Texas History Center, the Texas State Library, and the University of Texas Library. She made trips to Durham, to Philadelphia, Pennsylvania, Richmond and Austinville in Virginia, and Potosi, Missouri. At each place, she found more and more of interest, and it was she who made the statement: "The Grandfather of Texas was a giant of a man!"

While Mrs. Golden was involved and dedicated to her research, I began to give much thought to a writer of the book. It had been our good fortune in the 1960s to have made the acquaintance of Mrs. Rebecca Smith Lee of Lexington, Kentucky. Mrs. Lee had written and published a marvelous and, to me of prime importance, a very readable book on the life of Mary Austin Holley, niece of Moses and first cousin of Stephen F. In my search for just the right person to carry out the job of author, I had numerous talks via long distance with Mrs. Lee. It was her sound advice to "find someone who will fall in love with the Austins." My own determination was to find someone who would picture Moses as the very ambitious and intelligent man that he was but who would also see his faults, all of which made him the normal human being that Jack and I now pictured. The other "must" for me was that the book be readable and enjoyable – not a dull tome that one struggles through the first few pages and puts aside for an elusive "tomorrow."

I read a great many biographical books by contemporary writers, most of which I enjoyed and reviewed briefly with Jack, but I could not seem to find exactly the right person. Then, in the late seventies, Mrs. Golden sent us a small work written about Major George Littlefield by David B. Gracy II. An enclosed note said that she thought he might be what I was looking for as a writer. I sat down and started reading and became more elated with each paragraph. His style was what I wanted – warm and sympathetic to his subject, whom I later found out was David's ancestor. Jack read the piece and agreed that we must talk to Dr. Gracy. Through Mrs. Golden, we met our writer.

The book was underway in Dr. Gracy's capable hands. As the then Archivist of the State of Texas, he had contacts that led him to more and more information and involved travels to the various places following the trail of Moses Austin and even to archives in France and Spain.

Jack and I revisited Durham and enjoyed the enthusiasm and assistance of Mrs. Marjorie Hatch of Durham and Mr. Milton Whited of Meriden, Connecticut. So many people have encouraged us along the way, including Dr. Donald E. Everett of Trinity University and Miss Catherine McDowell, then Librarian of the Daughters of the Republic of Texas Library at the Alamo.

The book has taken a long time, but we knew that it would. We have not been concerned with the time element, however; not since the first chapters were sent to us and we knew the story would be told the way we had hoped.

Perhaps the most poignant moment to us was in Durham, standing on the crest of Old Burying Ground Hill by the crumbling gravestones of Elias and Eunice Austin, parents of Moses. Another marker identifies them as the grandparents of Stephen F. and the parents of Moses, and, oddly enough, the gravestones face west, where their youngest son was to plan and secure the site of what was to become the great state of Texas, with the city of Austin as its capital.

It is with a feeling of deep gratitude and emotion that I have written this Foreword to the book *Moses Austin: His Life.* With equally deep gratitude, I give thanks to my husband, John Ward Beretta (Jack), for not only the dream of this book but for making the dream come true; to Mrs. Golden for her help and constant interest and encouragement; and to Dr. Gracy for being the great writer that he has proven himself to be.

Mary Austin Perry Beretta

Mary Austin and Jack Beretta in front of the Elias Austin house. *Photograph by the author.*

ACKNOWLEDGMENTS

A biography may focus on the life of one person, but it represents the time, talent, and insight of a whole host of people whose various contributions greatly enrich the product.

To Mary Austin and John W. Beretta of San Antonio, she a descendant of Moses Austin, they benefactors of Texas history in a class by themselves, I am indebted for placing this unusually engaging and enjoyable project in my hands. Throughout my eight years of research and writing, they have been patient with my pace, encouraging of my work, and supportive of my seizing unique opportunities to enrich the project, including a fruitful trip to scour pertinent archives of England, France, and Spain. In a world so directed to the future as ours, the Berettas stand out by reminding us that the world did not spring into being with the dawning of the "information age" and that life can be lived more richly and profitably when we maintain knowledge of our roots—personal and national.

Mrs. Joe B. Golden of Austin, who has contributed greatly to the research, brought the Berettas and me together. Her almost off-hand question in October, 1977, "How would you like to write a biography of Moses Austin?" started it all. She thought I would have to mull over the matter and left my office precipitously without giving me a chance to answer. No indecision shackled me. I chased her down and told her that I was excited by such a possibility. No one has been more supportive, interested, and eager to see the finished product than she.

Frank and Helen Magre of Herculaneum, Missouri, introduced me to Moses Austin's Missouri as no others could have. Drawing on his life-long knowledge of the lead region, Frank took me to see the remains of several old lead smelters. He introduced me to Mrs. Norman A. Eshbaugh, who shared with me some of her precious cigarbox full of authentic drop shot, the product of a shot tower like the one Moses Austin established on the cliffs at Herculaneum, and to Mayford C. Warren, Lucille Basler, Susan E. Williams, and Ron Armbruster, who showed Ste. Genevieve, Missouri, to me in such a way that I could see the natural and built heritage of Moses Austin's day behind the structures of the twentieth century. Most important of all, Frank found William Saffell who could guide me to the remains of the homestead in which Austin had died and the cemetery in which he had been buried. Without Frank and Helen Magre, my understanding of the physical environment that governed Austin's world would have been restricted.

George W. Showalter, the historian of the Potosi, Missouri, region, and one of the most unselfish local historians I have ever known, shared his voluminous files unstintingly, his insight unhesitatingly, and his encouragement unreservedly. Paul R. Richeson of Potosi contributed his information on the Austin family, of which he is a part, on the Washington County region, and on lead mining, most particularly a brick of lead ore that has stirred in all who have seen it something of the same excitement that drew Austin and his contemporaries to the lead region.

Paul R. Austin of Wilmington, Delaware, a premier Austin genealogist, took me into his home for a highly valuable weekend discussing the heritage and characteristics of the Austin family. Mr. and Mrs. Gregor L. Lang, owners of the Anthony Austin House in Suffield, Connecticut, deepened my understanding of Moses' great grandfather, the patriarch, Anthony Austin, and his community. Elizabeth A. Mansfield opened her home—the Elias Austin House in Durham, Connecticut—to my full, inquisitive inspection. Thanks to her kindness, as I wrote I could picture the house as it was in Moses' day. Marjorie C. Hatch, Durham Town Clerk, not only gave me access to the Town records, but also introduced me to various persons whose information facilitated my understanding of Moses' birthplace, particularly Milton H. Whited who is knowledgable about the history of Durham.

Mary Medearis of the Southwest Arkansas Regional Archives in Washington, Arkansas, earned my warmest gratitude for sharing her extensive knowledge of the region with me and calling to my attention records with which I was unfamiliar, and for introducing me to several persons from whose knowledge of the history of the region I benefited greatly, particularly Grandison D. Royston, Jr. and Mr. and Mrs. William Etter.

I have never known an archivist who held back aiding a researcher. On this project, I found many who assisted far above and beyond the expected. Roland M. Baumann, then with the Pennsylvania State Archives, pointed me to the bankruptcy records that contained the file of Moses' brother, Stephen Austin, which answered questions about the Virginia mining venture answered nowhere else. The thorough, indefatigable work of Laura S. Bullion of the Western Historical Manuscripts Collection, University of Missouri, Columbia, saved me days, if not weeks, of searching. Peter J. Parker of the Historical Society of Pennsylvania, Edmund Berkeley, Jr., of the University of Virginia Library, Whitfield J. Bell, Jr., and his staff of the American Philosophical Society, Gary W. Beahan, State Archivist of Missouri, each in his own way contributed measurably to the content of this work. Other archivists who have helped me far more than they realize are: William G. Ray and Jane M. Pairo of the Virginia State Archives, Paul I. Chestnut, first at the Virginia State Archives and presently at the Library of Congress, Howson Cole and his staff (especially Mary Virginia Jones) of the Virginia Historical Society, Mike Soavedra of the Valentine Museum of Richmond, Judith A. Schiff of Yale University, Ruth M. Blair of the Connecticut Historical Society, John L. Ferguson, Elizabeth L. Cutcliffe, and Russell P. Baker of the Arkansas Historical Commission, Rosario Parra and her staff of the Archives of the Indies, Seville, Spain, and J. Bonnemains of the Museum of Natural History, Le Havre, France.

The expertise of several researchers enriched the sources available to me. Ricki S. Janicek devoted her expertise to searching the Spanish records of New Orleans, most particularly the notarial records, and found the data on which I corroborate Stephen F. Austin's often questioned, incredible story of the relationship of Moses Austin and the Baron de Bastrop. Sherrie S. McLeRoy, then Director of the Amherst County Historical Museum, and Jean O'Brien of the Missouri Department of Natural Resources turned up much in archives and printed sources of Virginia and Missouri respectively.

For their contributions in a variety of ways, I am indebted to professors Chester McArthur Destler (University of Connecticut, retired), Alwyn Barr (Texas Tech University), the late Walter Rundell (University of Maryland), and Donald E. Green (Central State University, Oklahoma); Mrs. Gifford E. Francis, Ellen Patterson, and Leland Seeton of Durham; Lucile G. Pregeant at the Virginia State Capitol; Nellie Severin, Henrietta Cragon, L. Wayne Bryan, and Paul E. Strickland of Austin, Texas; John R. Crowgey of Austinville, Virginia; James C. Martin, Director of the San Jacinto Museum of History; P. H. Bell of Houston; Pierre Ferrand of Evanston, Illinois; indexers Laura J. Adams, Robert Kelley Fair, Guy Hail, and Martha Richardson; and historians Robert M. Poss of East Haven, Connecticut, Margaret Smith Ross of Little Rock, Arkansas, Adan Benavides, Jr., of San Antonio, Andreas Reichstein of Ebeersreye, West Germany, Sue E. Sutton of Bishop's Stortford, England, the Reverend Charles F. Rehkopf of Webster Groves, Missouri, and Margaret Swett Henson of Houston.

For their thoughtful critiques of the manuscript, I am grateful to my mother, Alice Duggan Gracy, Jane Carlisle Maxwell, Jean Carefoot, G. Douglas Inglis, Carolyn Majewski, and my wife, Laura. The blue pencil and practiced eye of Lois Boyd and Joe Nicholson of Trinity University Press have turned my average-looking manuscript into a handsome book.

C O N T E N T S

Chapters

LIST OF ILLUSTRATIONS

PREFACE

Biographers live two lives. One is that of the researcher and writer. This involves, on the one hand, detective work to locate as much pertinent information — primarily the papers of the subject and his or her contemporaries — as possible. It requires, on the other, an open, multifaceted approach to writing. The writer whose work will be read has to find the drama, the story, among the facts. But, the writer whose work is to be relied on cannot let the telling of the story affect the reporting of the facts. Through it all, the writer whose work is to be appreciated must bring out poignant lessons to be learned from the subject's experience.

Every biographer, especially ones working in periods before the dictionary became a common reference, face decisions regarding standardization of spelling. The challenge is especially great in transcribing the writing of Moses Austin's wife, Maria. I have concluded not only to let each writer spell freely, but also to intrude as little as possible upon the style. Consequently, I have avoided the use of *sic* to note unusual spelling. The result is that many words appear in phonetic, not dictionary, spellings and that words in the process of being anglicized have substantially dissimilar spellings, because they received quite different pronunciations. "Mine a Breton" to the French, became "Mine a Burton" or "Mine a Barton" to the English speaker. Austin himself made little distinction between the period and the comma as proper punctuation at the end of a sentence. I have allowed him his way, especially since in some places the period could come at more than one point and thereby change the meaning of the sentence. The modern reader, as the contemporary one, must judge.

To heighten the continuity and speed the reading of the text, I have used end notes exclusively to present the authorities for my statements. Only in a handful of cases is information supplementary to the text included in the notes. Moreover, I have taken the prerogative of omitting in the notes the subtitles of the normally long eighteenth- and early nineteenth-century book titles. A sufficient title is reproduced so that no confusion will arise between two similar titles.

The other life of a biographer is a vicarious life of the subject. A biographer cannot delve far into the career of the subject without developing a conscious feeling for the biographee. It is a sympathetic feeling, else the biographer would give up the work. (I knew one would-be biographer who quit his project because he came to despise his subject.) The biographer maintains the feeling in his mind, because only in so doing can the biographer guard against becoming so sympathetic to the subject as to shade the story to reflect the person more favorably. The identification with the life of the subject normally should lead the biographer to those places in the world where the subject lived and died, worked and played, and is documented, so that the biographer can gain a real feeling for the environmental confines and releases that hampered and unfettered the subject, but which rarely merit mention in the letters, diaries, and other documents the subject has written. In the preparation of Moses Austin's biography, I have lived, struggled with, and enjoyed both lives. Austin's biography has been for me a labor of love at every turn.

MOSES AUSTIN
His Life

CHAPTER I

T WO DAYS before Christmas of 1820, Moses Austin, his slave Richmond, and two traveling companions rode quietly into San Antonio de Bexar, the sunbaked, 100-year-old capital of the Province of Texas on the far northeastern flank of the Spanish Empire.[1] Austin made his way through the dusty streets of the remote community of some 2,000 inhabitants to the government house in the center of town.[2] Weary from his journey through the nearly 400 miles of wilderness between Nacogdoches and Bexar ("Ba-har" the Spanish pronounced it. The Anglos compressed the two syllables into one: "bear."), Austin nevertheless pushed himself on. Fifty-nine years old, he had no time to lose.

Inside the *casa real*, Austin drew his short, stout frame to its full height before Governor Antonio María Martínez and began to speak. In French, the only language both understood, he told the Governor he wanted to bring a colony of Anglo Americans to settle in Texas. By all odds it was a bold scheme and a determined bid to recoup the fortune he had lost in Missouri, but the timing of his visit could not have been worse. Governor Martínez had explicit instructions from his superior, General Joaquin de Arredondo, Commandant of the Eastern Interior Provinces, to allow no foreigners, especially no North Americans, into his realm. For twenty years Anglo Americans had tormented the Spanish officials with a succession of armed forays into the country. At that very moment, "General" James Long was leading a band in East Texas bent on capturing the Province. Even were Martínez willing himself to consider Austin's plan, he would do nothing that might aggravate the strained relations between himself and Arredondo.

The Governor refused to listen. Preemptorially he ordered Austin to leave the town immediately and the Province as quickly as possible. Austin, who was not just another American, as he could prove with the old passport he carried that showed he once had been a subject of the King of Spain, thought to change the subject and, as his son later recounted, "give a favorable turn to matters by entering into a genial conversation." This tactic only agitated the Governor. Enraged, his voice charged with emotion, Martínez demanded Austin leave at once.

Moses Austin had failed. Disgusted and irritated, he left the Governor's office determined to abandon Bexar within the hour. Before him lay the grueling ride back to Missouri, a thousand miles through winter weather with no prospect for salvaging his fortune, without even the courtesy of one night's rest—the first in at least four weeks—under a roof.

As Austin crossed the plaza, one of those unaccountable twists of fate occurred that change history. He caught sight of the Baron de Bastrop, a Dutch adventurer of Austin's own generation, whom he had met many years previous, when the two chanced to stay at the same tavern. During the past fourteen years, Bastrop had lived in Bexar and, more importantly to Austin, had become a prominent and influential citizen.

Bastrop invited Austin to his modest quarters. As they talked, Austin elaborated his plans for bringing a colony of Missourians to Texas and showed Bastrop his papers. The Baron, recalling his own twenty-five years' experience trying, with little success, to colonize Spanish land, spoke frankly of the obstacles facing Austin, not the least of which was getting permission to bring the colony. Nevertheless, as Austin's enthusiasm returned, Bastrop caught the spark of the enterprise and decided to help.

Together, Austin and Bastrop retraced their steps through the plaza and waited upon the Governor. During their second meeting that Saturday, Austin and Martínez spoke in their native languages, leaving Bastrop to translate "well and truly." This time when the Governor asked Austin why he had come to Bexar, Austin replied simply that he sought "reauthorization to settle himself in...[the Province] with his family, inasmuch as he had already been a subject of the Government of Spain" in Missouri for two years, before Spain in 1800 had transferred the territory to France. Austin added, according to the Governor's official report, that he intended to support himself by raising sugar and cotton. Why, Martínez pressed, if he had been content as a citizen of the Spanish Empire, had he waited twenty years to apply for the settlement he wished to make? Austin talked around the question, then told the Governor it was "the new system of Government adopted by Spain," the constitutional monarchy reestablished the previous March, that enticed him to apply for permission to settle in Texas.[3]

After a few questions on other topics, Baron de Bastrop concluded the examination by gently reminding the Governor of his stern command that Austin leave San Antonio before nightfall. The old man, Bastrop said, was weak from exposure and fatigue. He could not endure the return trip without rest. Governor Martínez rescinded his order and allowed Austin to remain for awhile.

For three days, Austin and Bastrop worked on the colonization scheme. Finally, on December 26, they appeared before Governor Martínez again, this time with a formal document endorsed by the *cabildo*, the town council, outlining plans for settlement of a colony of 300 families. Martínez not only accepted the application, he forwarded it that same day to Arredondo in Monterrey with a ringing endorsement of both the proposal and the "worthy and well qualified subject," Moses Austin.[4]

Austin, with Bastrop's collaboration, had opened a new chapter in the history of North America. He cleared the way for the migration of Anglo Americans into Texas. Their coming would lead eventually to the birth of a new country and then to creation of the twenty-eighth state of the United States. Though Austin could not know the full significance of his accomplishment, he rode out of Bexar on December 29, 1820, on his way home exhilarated by the anticipation that he had laid the foundation for regaining his lost wealth. In whichever light his trip to Texas is viewed – as a personal venture or as a benchmark in history – it was without question a daring undertaking of a determined, driven man. It was characteristic of him and of his branch of the Austin line in America.

His great-great grandfather, Richard Austin, had been a man of unusual courage and will. In an age when families passed generation upon generation on the same plot of ground, or at least in the same neighborhood, he at midlife had been willing to uproot his from the familiar, comfortable ancestral home in Hampshire County of southern England and move 2,000 miles across the Atlantic Ocean to little known, barely inhabited Massachusetts. Richard did not do it for wealth. His father, Richard the elder, possessed a considerable estate at his death in 1622. He left £20 to his son Richard, an inheritance to each of his other six children, legacies for his eight grandchildren, and something as well for his son-in-law, three servants, and all his godchildren. By 1638, Richard the son, a successful tailor, could afford a servant whom he would take with his family to New England.[5]

Religious conviction drove Richard to ride the *Bevis* out of Southampton harbor on May 16, 1638. He did not go alone. Most of the sixty-one passengers about whom we know something advocated Puritan doctrine as did he. Indeed, the singular character of the little ship's passengers proved so noticeable that the King spotted it. Royal agents tried to prevent the sailing, but the ship had slipped away before they could act.[6]

Puritans believed that the Anglican communion retained too many vestiges of ceremony and hierarchy characteristic of the Roman Catholic Church, from which the Church of England had broken a century earlier. The Puritans based their convictions on individual reading and personal interpretation of the Bible, in which they found the blueprint of a stern existence governed by a harsh moral code. Though they believed the state should enforce that code, they maintained that each individual accounted personally to God. Each, therefore, worked daily and hard to be worthy of his convictions. "By self-imposed discipline, they endeavoured, in the very thick of worldly business, to preserve self-control and unquenchable devotion to the ideal of duty."[7] This did not mean that they withdrew from secular life. Far from it. The Lord rewarded those who showed responsible stewardship of the talents accorded them. Wealth, obtained the right way, was a sign of divine approval. In essence, the Puritan movement "brought seriousness of thought to thousands, and induced them to put that restraint on their luxuries and that vigour into the performance of their duties, which all religions enjoin, but which few enforce against the dead weight of social custom."[8]

The Stuart monarchs, who believed firmly in rule by divine right, thought the Church of England, if anything, not Catholic enough. The kings and their firm-minded subjects were traveling a collision course. Some 20,000 of the strongest-willed Puritans fled England during the 1630s for New England where they could practice their beliefs in both church and state. The Austins joined the stream only a few years before the conflict in England erupted into civil war.

Richard had hardly settled his family in Charlestown, across the Charles River from Boston, when his brother-in-law Edmund Littlefield broke with the congregation in Boston and moved his family away to the new settlement at Exeter in New Hampshire. About the same time, Richard died, leaving his widow to raise their two small boys.[9] The older son, the third in succession to be named Richard, would stay in Charlestown. In time he took up his father's trade and became active in both his church and community. Two of his descendants would make lasting reputations as pewterers in Charlestown in the late eighteenth and early nineteenth centuries, during the same years that their distant cousin, Moses, was developing the lead mines in Virginia and Missouri.[10]

Anthony was too young when his father died to have any memories of him. Yet in several interesting ways, Anthony followed in his footsteps. For one thing, he married late. Anthony was twenty-eight years old when he wed Esther Huggins on October 19, 1664, in Rowley, Massachusetts. The surviving records do not tell whether she, the second of eight children, and twenty-one years old at the time of her marriage, was a native of England or of New Hampshire. Whichever it was, both she and Anthony were Americans, and New England was the only land they knew.

In 1666, at the age of thirty, Anthony took his wife of two years and moved nearly thirty miles north to Rowley, a center of textile manufacture. Perhaps Anthony followed his father and brother into the tailor's trade, at least for a short time. Whatever occupation he pursued, he took full part in the life of the community, being first admitted to the church and then made a Freeman of the town on March 29 and May 19 respectively of 1669.[11]

It came as a surprise to the Rowley congregation in November, 1674, to learn that on the July 17 preceding, Anthony Austin received a grant of land—a homesite—in the Stoney Brooke Plantation one hundred miles southwest of Rowley in western Massachusetts. Anthony apologized to his friends in meeting for "his fayling that he had gone soe farr in ingageing himself to a remove to a new plantation before he had propounded his desire to the church that he might have their advice and Consent." The church members, mindful that he owned no property in Rowley, found "noe ground to disuade him from his undertaking...but wished gods blessing upon him and his."[12] A month later, he, his wife and three young sons left for the frontier.

In New England, the frontier was only a location, not a way of life. The word "plantation" to Anthony's contemporaries meant an area newly or recently opened for sale and settlement. None of the work of developing a plantation proceeded by chance or whim. Whether located on the east coast or on the inland frontier, the institutions of Puritan life were the same. The Puritan social order, rooted in towns, was too systematic, too structured to permit uncontrolled growth. With the permission of the General Court of Massachusetts, Major John Pynchon in 1671 established a committee and opened for settlement the heavily wooded, 22,000-acre Stoney Brooke tract he had purchased from the Indians two years earlier. The committee would direct the initial distribution of land, after which the plantation would become a town and the settlers—the "proprietors"—at last would govern themselves. The change in administration often was slight. The Puritans drew few lines between civil and ecclesiastical life. The authorities of church and of state reinforced each other. No one had a voice, not even in the town meeting in which civil offices were filled and the community governed, without being a church member first.

Theology even governed the distribution of land in a new settlement. A man obtained acreage according to "Quality, Estate, Usefulness and other Considerations, as the Committee direct."[13] This meant that the distribution was based primarily on one's acceptance in God's eyes. Faithful stewardship of God's bounty, as reflected in a man's wealth, deserved and brought a larger allotment. In Stoney Brooke Plantation, the committee directed that lots be created in eighty-, sixty-, fifty-, and forty-acre tracts. Anthony Austin, the twenty-second name on the roll, received a fifty-acre plot on the west side of Feather Street north of Stoney Brooke and next to a lot reserved for Major Pynchon.[14]

By the close of 1681, ten years after opening the plantation, the committee had completed its work. Instead of the twenty families originally called for by the General Court, the demand for settlement at Suffield, as the plantation became known, had caused the committee to settle 100 proprietors. Though the 100 represented a total population of some 300, only thirty-four held the church membership that afforded them a vote. These came together on March 9, 1682, the day after Sabbath, to establish a government to succeed the committee, or, in their flowing, artful words: "to order matters of General concernment for ye welfare of ye place."[15] They elected five Selectmen "by Papers" (ballots) and chose a recorder to keep the minutes. Forty-six-year-old Anthony Austin not only headed the list of the first Selectmen, but also, because of his legible and distinct hand, for which he had been employed as a letter writer in Boston years before, received the office of "Towne Clarke."[16]

Anthony's strong sense of public duty brought him a succession of committee responsibilities, over the following years, from searching for the town's boundaries to seeking a new minister. During the vacancy in 1693, he was even called to "officiate" in meeting "untill a minister be procured upon the place."[17]

The early years of the eighteenth century proved to be an anxious time in New England. The Indian presence, though considerably diminished by warfare during the 1690s, had not disappeared altogether. War in Europe inevitably resulted in conflict in the colonies, and this pattern repeated itself following the outbreak of Queen Anne's War on the continent in 1702. The next year in Suffield, the town meeting voted to fortify the pastor's lot. Armed guards watched over every gathering in the meeting house. The watch was no ceremony. The modern visitor to the two-story, English gambrel Anthony Austin House on old Feather Street,[18] whose construction dates to 1691, perhaps earlier, can see the head of a black flint arrow point recovered not many years ago from the back wall of the house. Thought to have been shot during Queen Anne's War, the flint penetrated two layers of chestnut clapboard siding, each one inch thick, and buried itself in the interior pine wall board.[19]

Through all these years, Anthony's distinct hand faithfully recorded the history of Suffield in the actions of its town meetings. On May 6, 1708, he was returned as Towne Clarke for the twenty-sixth consecutive year. But that time was the last. On August 22, seventy-three-year-old Anthony Austin died and was laid to rest in the burying ground near the meeting house.[20] The hand that entered the event in the town minutes was that of Anthony's son John.

Anthony had brought up his boys well. All made names for themselves in Suffield. Richard carried forward the martial renown of his father, who emerged from King Philip's War in 1678 as a sergeant and then rose to captain and command of the Suffield militia. Richard in time followed in both rank and command, an accomplishment probably of no surprise to those who knew the Austin Family motto: "Touch Me and I Sting."[21] Even so, it was no mean accomplishment in an age when military prowess and rank were a key to social standing, and social acceptance was linked to Godliness.

Like his father and grandfather before him, Richard married late. He was thirty-three in 1699 when he wed twenty-year-old Doritha Adams.

Her family, like Richard's mother's, came to Suffield in the 1680s from Newbury, Massachusetts, but arrived too late to be listed among the 100 first grantees. Hers was a hardy clan whose most distinguished sons would serve as the second and sixth presidents of the United States. The longevity of some family members attracted the notice even of contemporaries. Doritha's father would see eighty years, she nearly one hundred. In the space of nineteen of those years, she bore nine children, the last of whom, Elias, was born April 14, 1718.[22]

By the time Elias reached his majority in 1739, six years after his father's death, Suffield counted nearly 1,000 inhabitants, five times the number who lived there half a century earlier when his grandfather took his seat on the first Board of Selectmen. For its time, Suffield was a moderately populous settlement. The Austin Family contributed its full share to the growth. Captain Anthony's descendants in Suffield in 1739 numbered around fifty, at least a dozen of them as heads of households or soon to be.

Suffield could not provide for them all. Whereas five of Elias's six aunts and uncles lived and died in Suffield, his generation began an exodus that swelled a migration of the young occurring generally throughout Connecticut, the state into which Suffield was taken by a boundary change in 1749. It was sad in a way. When Suffield was established, the land within its boundaries had been a cohesive force. Each family could have some. Fathers like Anthony could even obtain lots for their sons. All, by virtue of their property, had an interest in the town and in each other. But within a generation, or two at the most, the vacant property had been taken up. By 1739, there were no empty places to absorb the younger sons. To get land of their own—to establish themselves—they had to leave. And so that same land that by its abundance in 1681 bound the townspeople together, by its scarcity in 1739 forced the young and ambitious out. At least three, perhaps four, of Elias's six brothers and sisters about whom a record exists left Suffield. Elias, who apparently left second, chose Durham, Connecticut, some thirty-five miles south of Suffield, to establish his home.[23]

Durham sat attractively on a ridge between hills to the east and low marshy Coginchaug Swamp to the west. At the middle of the town, Allyn Creek cut the ridge in two. The meeting house, the commons and a few fine residences stood south of the creek; the majority of the homes occupied land to the north. Along the mile-and-a-half length of Broad Street, one- and two-story white clapboard houses placed a discrete distance apart and back from the wide thoroughfare set a tone for the community. "Uncommonly elegant" one traveler recorded. Durham had an air of uncluttered spaciousness.

In some ways, Durham must have resembled the Suffield of Elias's youth. It had been settled at the turn of the century and was a generation behind Suffield in its growth. In 1740, its population totaled approximately 650, and, like Suffield at that age, it was growing rapidly, especially rapidly for a town off the beaten path. The only way in and out was by the road to Middletown, ten hilly miles away on the Connecticut River. Too, the economy of Durham rested on agriculture. Surplus farm products were taken over the road to Middletown, where they were sold locally, shipped to the trading centers of Boston and New Haven, or sent directly to the West Indies.

Despite its isolation, the town took an unusually deep interest in learning. In a day when the Holy Bible was the only book most persons read, or cared to read, twenty-five heads of households in Durham subscribed 20 shillings each to establish a private circulating library. The Book Company of Durham, created in 1733, was the first of its kind in Connecticut and followed by only two years the first one in all the colonies – Benjamin Franklin's Library Company of Philadelphia. Books circulated liberally. Even the President and Fellows of Yale College, eighteen tortuous miles away in New Haven, patronized the library. The influence of the library through the succeeding decades was great and reached families of all manner and means. It was this Library that gave a high character to the schools, and which created a taste of a liberal education, which for a long time characterized the town.[24]

Elias must have liked what he saw of Durham during the first weeks and months he lived there. On April 14, 1743, his twenty-fifth birthday, he gave Robert Fairchild, one of the founders of the Durham Book Company, £153 (a sum equal to two-thirds the annual stipend of the town's well-paid minister) for a little more than two acres of Fairchild's home lot on the west side of Broad Street, north of Allyn Creek.[25]

Apparently Elias built a house on his lot that same year. But the building that stands there today, identified by a roadside marker as the Elias Austin House, bears little resemblance to Elias's original frame cottage. The initial house followed traditional lines. Large square posts supported its superstructure and carried the clapboard siding. Like its neighbors, the building surrounded a massive central chimney to take full advantage, during the bitterly cold winters, of heat from the three fireplaces. Perhaps for the same reason, but out of harmony with his neighbors, Elias placed the house sideways on his lot, facing the building south toward Fairchild and away from the north wind, rather than east to Broad Street.[26]

Elias, who dressed typically in dark-colored coats, vests, and pants, their monotony broken only by silver shoe and knee buckles, likely used the parlor for a tailor shop. Judging by the assortment of shears, pressing irons, and other accessories listed on the inventory of his estate, he must have done a substantial business. In addition, like nine out of ten men in Connecticut in the mid-eighteenth century, he farmed. It was, to be sure,

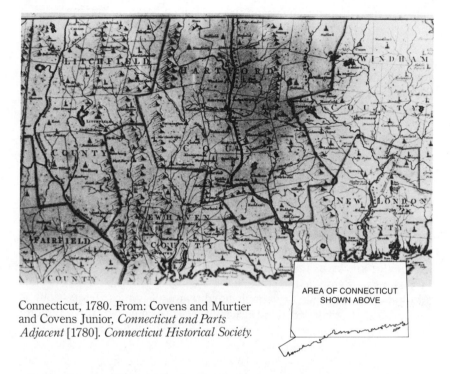

Connecticut, 1780. From: Covens and Murtier
and Covens Junior, *Connecticut and Parts
Adjacent* [1780]. *Connecticut Historical Society.*

AREA OF CONNECTICUT
SHOWN ABOVE

subsistence farming to provide basic food stuffs and raw material (wool
and flax) for clothing. If town records are complete, the tailoring and 2½
acres of pasture supplied his needs for perhaps twenty years.[27]

During those two decades, Elias established his family. About 1745,
before he passed a second year in the house by himself, Elias married
Eunice Phelps from Suffield. Their first child, Martha, came early in
August, 1746. Eight children followed at intervals of no more than three
years: Stephen in 1747, Martha, 1749, Elijah, 1751, Archibald, 1754, the
twins Hophin and Phineas, 1757, Gloriana, 1759, and little Moses on October 4, 1761. By the time Moses was born, three of his sisters and
brothers—the first Martha and the twins—had died.[28] Nevertheless, the
once ample four-room house had become snug with eight persons in it, six
of them children ranging in age from two years to mid-teens. Clearly the
family needed more room as well as more income.

In 1765, perhaps earlier, Elias more than doubled the size of his home by
adding two rooms on the north side, one upstairs and one down, with a cellar beneath them. These unheated rooms must have been cold in the winter, for their far corners lay a long way from the old central chimney that
remained the only source of heat. The family used the rooms above.
Downstairs Elias opened a tavern.[29]

Tavernkeeping for many made the difference between staying solvent and falling victim to the rampant inflation of the day. The business fed on both the increasing urban population and the growing numbers using the colonial roads. Though Durham's population rose by a third in the twenty years before the Revolution, Elias probably intended to rely on travelers for much of his trade. A good road finally had been pushed south from Durham to open direct communication with New Haven, a seat of the General Assembly and one of the colony's principal ports. Mail traveled over the road on a 2½-day round trip between New Haven and Hartford every weekend. Sometime afterward, the New York to Boston stage line changed its route between New Haven and Hartford and sent its coaches through Durham. By one act, Durham forever lost its quiet isolation.[30]

Perhaps the idea of opening a tavern had come to Elias through his family. His brother, Moses, and then his nephew, Jesse, both of whom had moved to Durham from Suffield a decade earlier, operated the inn at the northern edge of town. Moses bought the twenty-four-year-old establishment (later known as the Swathel Inn) in 1754. The place became a regular and popular stop on the stage line. Passengers had time to stretch and take refreshment while drivers changed teams of horses. Jesse acquired the inn soon after he settled in Durham in 1757. And he was the proprietor on that long-remembered day in 1775 when General George Washington stopped at the inn for a meal.[31]

However clear the economics of the matter, the decision to open a tavern could not have been easy for a churchman as devout as Elias. He had to disregard the rebukes of those in sympathy with a Middletown minister who railed against "covetings to have licenses for selling of drink."[32] His mind once set, though, Elias erected a signpost on Broad Street and laid up in his cellar casks of wine, rum, cider, brandy and beer. Considering the stock and fixtures recorded in the inventory of his estate, he must have enjoyed a very satisfactory business.[33]

Moses, Jesse, and Elias all three played active roles in the life of their adopted town. Each had a vote in the town meetings and filled offices by election of that body. Elias served once as a grand juror, twice as a hayward to enforce the town ordinances regulating swine on the highway and commons, and three times as a tythingman. This official had "liberty on Sabbath and other Days of publick worship to sit in those pews or seats where they shall judge most convenient to preserve good order."[34]

Elias had completed the last of his six terms in office by the time his youngest child, Moses, was old enough to begin to remember. Of Moses' early life little can be known. No family documents have survived from these years, and, if Moses ever reminisced about them to his own children, his words died with them. But there is no reason to think that he grew up in a home out of harmony with the ways of mid-eighteenth-century Connecticut. During this period, fathers ruled households. Mothers and fathers together, as ten of Elias and Eunice's neighbors pledged in writing with their minister, accepted as their duty to "Keep our Children and servants in subjection, Instruct them in the principles of our Holy Religion, and Endeavr to Restrain them from all Profaneness and Immorality."[35] Children in this strictly ordered society were considered young adults, and when they grew up, "the firm hand of authority, structuring all of life, framed steady and resolute personalities, sure of the world in which they lived and as stern in exercising authority as their fathers."[36] The system bred patriarchs.

The instruction in religion, central in the pledge and so basic to traditional New England life, came both at home and in school. Elias must have been proud and gratified during his lifetime to watch two of his children formally accepted into the Durham congregation. His youngest, Moses, received classroom instruction—possibly all he would ever receive—in the schoolhouse that still stands on Durham's meeting-house Green. The plain white frame building was more than forty years old by the time Moses studied his primer, psalter, and perhaps other religious texts during the eight-month annual terms prescribed by the town meeting.[37]

Elias's family not only reflected Connecticut society, it also typified the Austin line. The eight living members made it of average size. And since several males in each generation—all six in Elias's—had children, the Austin clan after four generations and 150 years numbered in the hundreds. When Elias's mother died in 1772 at the age of ninety-nine, the small, weekly *Connecticut Courant* of Hartford took note. She, its readers learned, was the "mother of 9 children, 73 grand children, 118 great grand children, and 5 of the fourth generation, in all 205." Combine the numbers in each family unit with the fourteen (in Elias's case) or more years over which the children were born, and the Austins had considerable overlapping and intermingling of generations. Moses' closest confidant and personal secretary in Missouri would be his first cousin once removed, Jesse's son James. A generation separated James and Moses on the family tree, but only 1½ years on the calendar. Their closeness would be cemented and reflected further when the two married sisters.

Death, never far away, particularly for the young, contributed to forcing family concern inward. Elias lost three of his children and used the name "Martha" twice. His brother Richard gave the name "Elizabeth" to three separate babies. In these tragedies, the Austins shared with their neighbors. At least they were spared the triumph and tragedy of the Sykes Family of Suffield, whose two sons carried the names "Victory" and "Posthumous."

In their name-giving, the Austins followed Puritan practice. They took male names from the Old Testament or, less frequently, chose them from

traditional English names. Elias introduced the name "Stephen" into the
family, but it was his grandson, Stephen Fuller, who would make it
famous. Girls received biblical names, too. Or they were named for virtues
considered in women: "Devotion," "Thankful," "Submit," "Mindwell,"
"Mercy." The Austins preferred the biblical names with one exception.
Elias struck a second note of independence from family tradition, perhaps
even from the solemn Calvinist philosophy, when he gave his tenth child
the happy name "Gloriana."[38]

Happy was the way Moses must have remembered Durham, his father's
house, and his childhood. A quarter century later and half a continent
away, he would name his new, grand seat "Durham Hall" in memory of his
early, good years and of the spacious town on the ridge which, once he left,
he never saw again.

MOSES HAD just turned nine years old when John Forbes submitted his first notice to the *Connecticut Courant*. Actually nothing about the small announcement in the issue for October 30, 1770, made it stand out from any other advertisement. Forbes, who recently had moved to Hartford from Philadelphia, simply invited patronage of his clock and watchmaking business. But Elias Austin and his family twenty-five miles away in Durham, if they saw that issue, surely read the little block of print with unusual interest. Forbes had set up "at the shop of Mr. Stephen Austin, Taylor in Hartford." And the announcement put Stephen's new business in the public print for the first time as well.

Barely three weeks shy of his twenty-third birthday and the oldest of Elias and Eunice Austin's six living children, Stephen had been the first of the brothers and sisters to leave home. If Elias's children repeated the pattern set by their father and his brothers and sisters, then by the end of the decade most would be gone from their parents' home on Broad Street, the boys to seek their fortunes, the girls married and rearing families. Moses, the youngest, of course would remain at home with his parents for several more years, during which he might follow in Stephen's footsteps and learn the tailor's craft from his father. If not that, perhaps he would move to Hartford to live with his brother and learn the business of a merchant. It seemed to be the nature of the Austins to think ahead, to try to be ready for whatever life had in store. It was a good trait, for time and events rarely follow the course marked for them.

Though Stephen began his career as a tailor, his heart lay elsewhere. He never advertised himself in the newspaper as a man proficient with needle and thread. The first notice he placed in the *Courant*, on November 16, 1771, offered dry goods for sale: chamois leather for linings, cloth and needles, leather breeches "of the best kind" and "just received from Philadelphia." His association with Forbes evidently opened commercial contacts to him in the country's largest city. Stephen took advantage of his opportunity, and in so doing found his calling.[1]

From the first, Stephen prospered. Forbes's little notice shows that young Austin already had learned the fundamental secret of success in the business world — put your property, and by extension, the toil of others to work for you. From the earliest record, rents supplemented what he earned from creating clothes and handling merchandise. Three years later, with Forbes gone, Stephen had filled his place with Thomas Hilldrup, another watch repairer. For his day, Hilldrup gorged the *Courant* with announcements. Using twenty-six of the weekly issues in all, he advertised more than any other merchant in 1773, and every notice carried Stephen Austin's name gratis as the address of Hilldrup's business.[2] By 1774, Stephen had expanded his own enterprise by adding a shop in which his workmen manufactured, as he termed it, leather "in the best manner."[3] Where the amassing of material goods one hundred years earlier in great grandfather Anthony's day proved God's favor, by Stephen's generation grace no longer motivated men of enterprise. Wealth alone offered reward enough for industry. Shrewd dealing and a passionately independent spirit increasingly characterized the business world of late eighteenth-century Connecticut and New England.[4] First Stephen, then Elias's other boys, became caught up in the tide.

After Stephen had gone, it was in the order of things that the next oldest, Martha, would marry and leave. And soon thereafter, in 1771 it appears, she did. Within the same year, on December 11, Moses' mother died. Elias tried to compensate for the loss the following year by marrying twice-widowed Sarah Akins. In 1774 the next two children to come of age, Elijah and Archibald, left to establish themselves in New Haven. If they departed to become tailors, soon they, like Stephen, abandoned their father's occupation and began trading in dry goods. In any case, by 1775,

Elias and Eunice Austin tombstones. *Photograph by the author.*

only Elias, his wife, his daughter Gloriana, and his son Moses remained. Within four short years, the eight Austins in the home on Broad Street had been reduced to three, plus Elias's new wife.[5]

Then two years later, on October 12, 1776, a weak Elias summoned the Reverend Elizur Goodrich to prepare his will. Dr. Goodrich, during his thirty years of ministry to the town, had been with Elias through good times and bad, baptizing four of his children, burying his first wife, and marrying him to his second. Elias expressed but two wishes. One-third of his personal property should go to his wife, the remainder of his personal effects and all of his real property he directed to be divided equally among his children. Contemporaries estimated his entire estate, consisting of the home and barn on two acres, just under three acres of pasture land, his household belongings, tavern stock, and personal effects, to be worth nearly £450. When divided out, Elias bequeathed to each of his six children a modest inheritance of about £70. The old man labored to scrawl a shaky signature to the document. Two days later he died.[6] They laid him to rest beside his first wife near the top of the slope in the picturesque old burying ground overlooking Allyn Creek and, in the distance on the other side, the familiar meeting house and meeting house green.

Moses had barely turned fifteen when his father died. Someone could have tried to comfort him by pointing out that Elias, the youngest in his generation too, had been the same age when his father died. But there the consolation and the coincidence ended. Elias's mother survived her husband and reared her children. Moses' mother was dead, and his stepmother appears not to have developed a close relationship with her husband's children. By 1782, she had left the family and married for the fourth time. That summer the Austin children bought out her interest in Elias's estate for £30, and her name never came up among them again.[7]

Moses had little time to dwell on this end to his youth. His eyes were fixed firmly on the future. On October 9, less than a week after his twenty-first birthday, he borrowed $320 from his brother Stephen, took whatever capital he had of his own, and formed a partnership with his brother-in-law (Martha's husband), Moses Bates, in a dry goods business in Middletown. Two months later, on Christmas Eve, the Bates and Austin enterprise took space in the *Connecticut Courant* to advertise a stock that included cloth, buttons, utensils, shoe and knee buckles, spectacles, teas and tea accessories, and "a wide variety of other articles." Such an assortment typified the merchant of the period. Few specialized. Shopkeepers normally could replenish their stock only when the opportunity presented itself, which, in a port city, often meant when a ship arrived. By the same token, of course, merchants had to keep up with a large selection of otherwise unrelated goods. To survive, they needed an innate sense of quality—quality of both the goods they obtained for sale and of the produce and wares they took in barter for their merchandise. Grades of goods were not then so clearly distinguished as they later would become. Merchants needed good intuition, too, in granting credit, the grease on which commerce ran in that day of slow communication. And in a place like Middletown, shop keepers had to be more than casually knowledgeable of various circulating coinages and currencies, for the sailors of the ships that docked there brought diverse money.[8] Moses Austin apparently enjoyed it all: the trading, the building of financial arrangements, the judging of people and products and exchange.

The two Moseses – Austin and Bates – could have been contemplating forming their partnership since July, the earliest date that records place them in Middletown. Or the idea could have come earlier, if Moses lived with his sister's family during any of the six years following the loss of his father. Austin could have been attracted to his brother-in-law because Bates, more than others, must have understood how Moses felt after the death of Elias. Bates never knew his own father. Samuel Bates had died a month before his last child was born.

After their marriage, apparently in 1771, Moses Bates and Martha remained in Durham. They were admitted to the Durham congregation on February 23, 1772, the same day their first child, Clarissa, was baptized. Dr. Goodrich baptized two more in their turn: Elias in 1773 and Parsons in 1775. If sister Gloriana lived in the Bates household as well, they must have continued in Durham some years more, for the faithful Dr. Goodrich recorded her admittance to the Durham congregation in 1781. Gloriana then married Dr. Aaron Eliot of Killingworth in January, 1782, six months before the date of the first record that places the Bates Family and Moses Austin definitely in Middletown.[9]

Family tradition suggests, however, that Moses Austin and all the Bateses moved to Middletown shortly after the death of Moses' father. The baptism of the Bates's fourth child, Henry, does not appear in Dr. Goodrich's book. The tradition holds, too, that in Middletown young Austin first became acquainted with the mining, smelting, and marketing of lead. An outcrop of lead along the Connecticut River, $2\frac{1}{4}$ miles east of town, constituted the largest body of ore in New England. It had been known and worked from time to time since the first Europeans had settled the area 140 years before. But for some years it lay dormant until the early rumblings of the Revolutionary War recalled it to life in 1775. For three years, the committee responsible for the mine spared no effort to push production. Yet for all the labor, only a pitiful 15,563 pounds of lead came from the single vein that lay in an unyielding granite seam. Even during wartime, the mine could not pay the cost of working it, and the operation was abandoned in 1778.[10]

That Moses Austin gained his first exposure to the lead business in this mine seems highly unlikely. There is no indication that either the Austins or the Bateses knew the prominent men on the Middletown Committee that ran the mine. Hence there probably would have been no avenue for young Austin to observe the operation other than from the end of a shovel. But that was back-breaking labor a teen-aged boy would not seek unless he had to. Moses did not have to. His brothers and sister all could provide a home for him. His brothers, moreover, could give him jobs in their stores where he could anticipate learning a more prestigious occupation than digging ore.

Whenever they moved to Middletown, Bates and Austin had made a smart move. Most local merchants in 1782 saw bright prospects with peace and the young decade.[11] All outward signs indicated that the Bates and Austin store had been established in the right place at the right time. But Moses Austin thought he saw even richer opportunity elsewhere. He had fixed his eyes on Stephen and Philadelphia.

Of the Austin brothers, Stephen, with the head start, had built up the most prosperous trade. As the years had passed, his business had grown steadily. From needles, cloth, and clothing, he broadened his stock to include hardware, household utensils, crockery, wine, and sugar on which he prided himself as the British blockade curtailed the supply. To wares from the colonies he added merchandise from the West Indian commerce, then goods from Europe. At war's end, Stephen ranked both among the very few whose business continued uninterrupted throughout the conflict and among the most successful of the some 150 or so merchants then in Hartford.[12]

Stephen's success rested in part on his wisdom in settling in Hartford — Connecticut's seventh largest town, set in a rich agricultural region, its commerce favored by its location on the banks of the broad Connecticut River—in part on his native ability, and in part on one stroke of blind good fortune. Directly across Queen Street from him, Jeremiah Wadsworth chanced to open his store. Four years older than Austin, the son of a minister, Wadsworth had learned his business in Middletown in the store of an uncle, then had gone to sea in command of one of his uncle's ships in the West India trade. During the war, he rose rapidly to become Commissary General of the Continental Army. By 1781, Wadsworth had built the largest fortune in Connecticut and had established business connections throughout the new nation and Europe.[13]

Wadsworth profited by the war, and Stephen profited by his association with Wadsworth. Business flowed to Austin that otherwise might not have. In April, 1780, Stephen closed a substantial deal to obtain merchandise from Barnabas Deane & Co., of which Wadsworth was the principal, though secret, backer. Indications are that Wadsworth became directly interested in Stephen's little company. Later in 1780, when Stephen traveled to Philadelphia to buy goods for his store and to scout the market for

Connecticut wares he could sell in exchange, he left his shop in Wadsworth's charge. During this and subsequent trips, Stephen corresponded with his colleague about prices, goods that would sell, and rates of exchange. The two traded in whatever articles they found in demand. In a day of many and unregulated currencies, speculating in the exchange rate afforded further opportunity. Probably the lucrative arrangement they shared through the years, and could share the more if one of them located in another place, motivated Stephen to uproot his family, when his second child was but a year old, to move to Philadelphia. Though Hartford emerged from the war as the outstanding business center in Connecticut, thirty-four-year-old Stephen sold both his shop and house in Hartford to Wadsworth and left Connecticut, probably in October of 1782, to establish Stephen Austin and Company in the capital of the new United States.[14]

Philadelphia in the early 1780s meant business activity and prosperity. The largest, it may have been also the busiest and most dynamic city in all the thirteen states. Its population spread along the Delaware River bank where more than two miles of docks received hundreds of ships a year engaged in both coastal and transatlantic trade. Philadelphia was a center of communication and information. New York City lay but three days away by stage, and mail passed between the two a wonderful three times a week. News of the world arrived every day that another merchantman docked. Perhaps most importantly of all, however, the materialistic, practical philosophy of life that pervaded the city nurtured "a growing, grasping, expanding society [that] offered to individualism a degree of free play seldom exceeded."[15] Philadelphia beckoned the opportunistic, the energetic, the risk taker, the person on the make. And they came. From its approximately 23,000 during the war, the population shot up by 60 percent in the first half of the 1780s to 37,000 in 1786. In Dock Ward, where the marine trades and merchants like Stephen clustered, the tax list nearly doubled during the decade after 1779.[16]

Stephen took to Philadelphia from his Hartford enterprises a tidy capital of $11,500 and evidently invested it promptly in foreign trade. After all, what goods could an American merchant expect his countrymen to want more than the English wares that had been so scarce during the six years of war? Stephen, who from the earliest record characterized himself as an "English Merchant," anticipated correctly. Hardware, woolen cloth, figured cottons, hosiery, haberdashery, and earthenware from Britain indeed poured into the United States following the peace in the spring of 1783. For the rest of that year and into the next, the lively British trade rivaled its prewar levels.[17]

No one had to wonder long whether Stephen had made an advantageous move. The answer stood out in the first city directory. Stephen Austin and Stephen Austin and Company occupied two structures at 613 and 615 Second Street respectively. Employing separate buildings for residence and business proclaimed success in the most obvious way. Philadelphia's economy rested on the one-man shop, which the proprietor, sometimes assisted by a clerk or two, operated from a single room of his home. Only the very prosperous could afford, or needed, a building devoted solely to business.[18]

If through the winter of 1782-1783 Moses Austin thought Philadelphia an even better place than Middletown for a young businessman to make his mark, he was right. If he contemplated going to the new capital because so many others were making the move and maybe they knew something he did not, then he heeded a sound impulse. If he based his decision on Stephen's recommendation, he accepted good advice. Whichever it was, sometime in 1783, no one can know for sure just when, Moses Austin left the Bates Family and the business in Middletown and moved to Philadelphia.

He found a place on Market Street between Front and Second streets and opened a store. That location put his shop in the heart of the business district, within a stone's throw of the Old London Coffee House, one of the two principal establishments where traders and businessmen met daily to talk prices, conditions, markets, and to make deals. The site lay two blocks north of Stephen's store. A few months later, in February, 1784, Moses took in a partner, Manning Merrill, in order to go into, or to expand his interest in, the lucrative English trade. Merrill may have been a friend of Stephen's and come from Hartford where George and Daniel Merrill, like Stephen, traded in leather goods and English wares and Hezekiah Merrill dealt in books and drugs. Though Moses did not admit it in his autobiography, Stephen had a substantial interest in the firm, perhaps to the extent of two-thirds. (Actually, he may have supported Moses in the original Market Street store. But no records survive to show, and by the time Moses wrote about his life in Philadelphia, he and his brother had fallen out with each other. Moses gave him credit for nothing.) Three months later, they expanded by opening what Moses later called "a whole sale store" two blocks south on Front Street between Chestnut and Walnut. In those days, every merchant retailed his wares; few thought in terms of what we have come to know as a wholesaler.[19]

As the Austin and Merrill enterprise grew, the British trade felt the first faint shudders of trouble. In November, 1783, one prominent Philadelphia merchant sold his English merchandise below cost on credit in order to dispose of it. Joseph Poultney shortly afterward put his finger on the problem: "There has been a great glut in the market of European goods," he wrote, "many of which have been sold to loss, and but a few I believe will yield much profit to the speculators."[20] The market neared saturation. Goods moved more slowly than before. Merchants consequently required larger credit and for longer periods. For many, time simply ran out. Alexander Hamilton, a few years after to become the first Secretary of the Treasury in George Washington's cabinet, could not help but remark on the "number of adventurers without capital, and in many instances without information, who at that epoch rushed into trade, and were obliged to make any sacrifice to support a transient credit."[21] In the course of a year, the tremors deepened into depression when Americans vented their rage at British government policy by avoiding English goods. In November, 1784, Benjamin Fuller, one of the city's most substantial merchants, advised "having little to do in the purchase way particularly *Dry Goods —* "[22] To another correspondent he warned that "Trade is in a most wretched State, and I am convinced many Bankrupcies must take place in the Course of a Year or Two."[23]

Where others worried and retrenched, the Austins and Merrill continued to expand. In August, 1784, barely half a year after they had formed their association, the partners sent Moses to Richmond, Virginia, to open a branch of the company. Evidently he did not at first plan to make Richmond his home. But about this time, it seems, Merrill died. Moses cut his umbilical cord, left the Philadelphia operation to his brother, and in September, 1784, took permanent charge of the operation in Richmond.[24] Soon, if not from the first, the Richmond enterprise operated under the name of Moses Austin and Company. Philadelphia was so far away, several days by either land or sea, that for all intents and purposes Moses had become an independent businessman simply connected by agreement with his partners in Pennsylvania. Moses Austin had come a long way in a short time. In only two years he had risen from junior partner in his first mercantile interest to be the master of his own business. Rarely afterward would he take a subordinate role to anyone in any business enterprise.

Although Moses liked being on his own in Richmond, he missed family companionship. For the first time in his life, he had settled where he had no relations nearby. He knew, however, how he wanted to resolve the situation. "For heavens sake," he pled with Mary Brown on January 25, 1785, in the oldest document surviving in his own hand, "tell me what is the matter why dont you write me am I forgot so shortly— no it shall not be so . . . I cannot endure the Idea of being forgot by my Maria."[25] During his year or so in Philadelphia, Moses had met and fallen in love with the attractive great-stepniece of Benjamin Fuller.

Mary, born on New Year's Day, 1768, in Sharpsborough Furnace, New Jersey, and the oldest living child of Abia and Margaret Sharp Brown, descended from substantial, proud stock on both sides of her family. Her maternal great, great grandfather, Anthony, a Dublin merchant, had business dealings with William Penn at least as early as 1676 and had bought land in New Jersey by 1682. Records do not show whether Anthony came to America, but there is no question that his son, Isaac, did. Isaac Sharp served his adopted land in several capacities, including Judge of the Court in Salem, New Jersey, Proprietor of East Jersey, and Colonel of the Salem Regiment of Foot. Through distaff lines, Mary's heritage could be pushed back to Robert Turner, one of the twenty-four proprietors to whom the Duke of York released East Jersey, one of the original purchasers of West Jersey, and a member of the Governor's Council, first in New Jersey and later in Pennsylvania. The Browns traced their heritage to Mary's great, great grandfather, Abraham Brown, an original patentee of Shrewsbury, in Monmouth County, New Jersey, ninety miles northeast of Sharpsborough Furnace. Mary's ancestors included both devout Anglicans and commited Quakers whose roots by her time burrowed deep into southern New Jersey and eastern Pennsylvania.

Little is known of Mary's father, Abia Brown. He must have been well educated, as he wrote a beautiful, angular but flowing signature. In 1772, he served as a county justice. Perhaps he achieved greatest notoriety for membership on the Council of Safety in 1774, and for service as a deputy in the Provincial Congresses in 1775 and 1776. Brown amassed fairly substantial real estate holdings in connection with an iron mining and smelting business in which he held an interest with the Sharps. When twenty-two years old, in 1765, he married Margaret Sharp, who bore him eight children before she died at the relatively young age of thirty-three in 1780.[26]

Brown either fell on hard times at this very juncture or became so distraught over his wife's death that he could not properly care for his seven children. (One son had died in 1779, a year before Brown's wife.) Whatever the cause, in 1780, he journeyed to Philadelphia to see Benjamin Fuller, the husband of his dead wife's aunt Rebecca. Fuller, a native of Dublin, Ireland, had come to Philadelphia early in his life. Through the years he built up his contacts in European, West Indian, and American ports until he numbered among the city's leading importers and dry goods merchants. He enjoyed an enviable reputation "for his correctness in business transactions."[27] As the Revolution approached, Fuller abandoned Philadelphia to live in the country and did not return until the British evacuated the city in 1778. Though his fortune shrank considerably during these years, still in 1780 he could subscribe £2,000 for the support of the army. Primarily a man of business, Fuller did accept public service in 1778 under the Supreme Executive Council of Pennsylvania. Abia thought Fuller would be sympathetic to him because Rebecca Fuller maintained close ties with her relations and because Fuller already had given financial assistance to his wife's family. He had made one loan to Isaac Sharp a dozen years earlier, which Fuller well remembered since the note had yet to be redeemed.[28]

When Abia called on Fuller, he took his children with him and evidently asked the aging Irishman to board at least one of them. Fuller "Spontaniously & freely," he later wrote, took in the oldest, thirteen-year-old Mary, whom he called "Polly." Fuller, the men agreed, would provide bed and board in his fine home on Front Street in the heart of the city. Brown would supply her clothing. As Fuller would take only one child, Brown put Mary's ten-year-old sister, Rebecca, in school in Philadelphia "with a request to Mrs. Fuller that she would have Motherly care over her—"[29]

By placing his daughters with the Fullers, Brown meant in no way to relinquish his interest in them. "I am Anxious for your Happiness and am in hope that your own Prudence will prevent you from Running too much into the Fashions and follys of this World," Brown wrote Mary in July, 1780, in a letter not unlike that which her future husband would send to her children a quarter century later. "Remember my Dear Child that one Vice brings on another, and the more a young Person gives way to them, the worse they want to."[30] Brown never could uphold his end of the financial bargain, and Fuller supported the two girls completely. The burden troubled the old man little, for he came to love both, but Mary especially. In fact, he named one of his ships the *Polly and Becky*, doubtless after them.

Before Abia Brown could reclaim his children, he died on April 15, 1785, in his forty-second year. Polly, seventeen years old, "is now an orphan indeed," Fuller wrote a family friend. She visited her old home in New Jersey for a while after her father's death, then returned to Philadelphia sometime early in the summer.[31]

Moses Austin must have felt keenly for Mary. His teen-aged years had been not so different from hers. He pressed his court until she consented to marry. They wed on the evening of Wednesday, September 28, in Philadelphia's grand (Anglican) Christ Church, where her grandmother and great-grandmother had been married before her. The next day, Moses and Maria, as he and her descendants called her, boarded the packet boat for Richmond and a new life.[32]

Behind Moses lay the difficult, unsettled years without parents, living in someone else's home. Behind him, too, lay the trials of learning an occupation and getting on his feet. Moreover, he had found a mate who, as much as he, wanted to establish her own home and enjoy a strong, close family, and who would see him through the rest of his life. On his twenty-fourth birthday, less than a week after his marriage, Moses Austin must have been very satisfied with his life and his prospects.

CHAPTER III

To HEAR ROBERT Hunter tell it, the Austins had gone to the end of the earth. He scorned Richmond as "one of the dirtiest holes of a place I ever was in."[1] The red dust that swirled above the streets when the sun shown turned to red mire when it rained. At intervals, piles of cinders and ashes offered footways across the streets. But the piles served none too well at best. One misstep during wet weather and the unfortunate pedestrian sank into puddles of mud and water.[2]

Like the fruit of a cornucopia, Richmond's homes clustered in and fanned out down the valley of Shockoe Creek, a substantial stream that cut a deep swath between Shockoe and Church hills on its way to the James River. "Tenements" the future Mrs. John Marshall derided the houses, echoing Hunter. The one her father, soon after to be Treasurer of the State, procured for his family was "the only decent tenement on the hill," she told a friend, "though our whole family can scarcely stand up all together in it." With but 280 dwellings total in the town, the oldest of which outdated by only a few years the house Moses Austin had grown up in, no new arrival enjoyed much selection. "It is indeed a lovely situation and may at some future period be a great city," Betsy Ambler summed up her early impression of the community, giving Richmond all the credit she could, "but at present it will scarce afford one comfort in life."[3] Richmond in no wise resembled polished Philadelphia.

For all that it lacked, Richmond did possess great promise. Commercially, it must become an entrepot of commerce, because its location at the head of navigation on the James River insured that it always would have the business of transshipping goods around the falls. The most tangible symbol of that promise, however, stood on the brow of Shockoe Hill. There, barely two months before Moses and Maria arrived, the cornerstone had been laid for the new state capitol. Richmond had been the seat of government only since 1779, when the General Assembly voted to abandon Williamsburg, a capital vulnerable to "the insults and injuries of the public enemy." The lawmakers chose Richmond for their seat because it was "more safe and central than any other town situated on navigable water." They convened there for the first time in May, 1780, using a "clumsey looking," plain, single-story frame structure northwest of Shockoe Creek but below Shockoe Hill. The totally undistinguished appearance of the barn-like building actually saved it when the British under Benedict

Arnold overran the town in 1781. The soldiers failed to recognize the structure for what it was and destroy it. After the war, Virginians looked forward to having a suitable state house and called upon Thomas Jefferson, an accomplished architect and former governor, for plans. With the capitol cornerstone in place, Virginians awaited the plans coming from France where Jefferson served as the American ambassador.[4]

Idleness did not characterize Richmond in 1785. The town was entering a period of rapid and dynamic change. Signs appeared everywhere. All could see the land development spreading north and west of the old town. After Shockoe Hill had been selected for the capitol, wealthy Richmonders acquired blocks – often of one or two acres – and built their seats on the hill behind the site. As they moved, business establishments followed them. Most had relocated on the Shockoe Hill side of the creek by 1785.[5]

The capitol explained some of the activity, but not all. The population was growing, too. From 1,800 in 1781, half of whom were slaves, it would double before the first United States census takers made their rounds in 1790, and continue climbing to 5,737 in 1800. More important, its composition was changing as well. In 1780 the observant Miss Ambler recorded that "with the exception of two or three families this little town is made up of Scotch factors" who came to conduct the business of their British houses, then return home. But after the war, American merchants from the North and East – "adventurers" near-contemporary historian Samuel Mordecai termed them – arrived to challenge the longstanding supremacy of the foreign firms.[6]

They came at the right time. Virginians had begun to realize that they could not build their state on a tobacco economy presided over by a broker who set both the price they received for their staple and the price they paid to buy goods in return. In four counties around Richmond residents formed societies to discourage extravagance and encourage home trade. The combination of the new trade routes to the north and the new spirit at home weakened, then finally broke, the strangle hold of the direct trade with Britain. Richmonders saw the results of their efforts as the town's trade expanded and specialized shops sprang up to challenge the dominance of the tobacco companies in the import and retail business. By 1785, the capital boasted at least three new ventures.[7]

Richmond's future greatness clearly lay ahead, and perhaps not far distant. But the next two years brought economic misery. Two months after the Austins arrived in Richmond, young Thomas Rutherford, who, like Austin, had come to Richmond in 1784, informed his Scottish suppliers that "Trade has been verry bad here this fall, that I cannot say there is any one article w[oul]d now command cash to a profit – With regard to farther under taking next fall I know not at present what to say. The prospect is by no means agreeable."[8] Soon after, he added his certainty that "much money has been lost, in the course of last year, both by Sales & remittances, by a great number in Richmond."9 The 1786 season proved no better. "Trade has in general been very dull this fall: the planters most wretchedly poor, numbers of them not able to purchase necessaries for their negroes," he lamented. "Business is carried on here with amasing trouble...altho few have better success than myself it is with great regret I see myself so much behind hand—"10

Moses Austin, who ran a diversified operation buying his own merchandise, handling goods from paintings to hats on commission, and trading in tobacco, echoed the sentiment in June of 1787. "As to Business," he wrote associate George Westcott in Philadelphia, "nothing can equal it for Badness Puter [pewter] is as good an article as any I know of at this time but such is the state of Business hear that nothing will command cash."11 Indeed, there was little cash to be had. The General Assembly had been forced to pass a measure accepting tobacco in payment of taxes "in order for a little to relieve the clamours of the people, who all declare they cannot pay their Taxes specie."12 More than half of all the cases for collection of small debts brought by Moses Austin and Company in Richmond's Husting (municipal) Court were filed that year. "I have ma[n]y times wished my self out of this place," he summed up his frustration. "Nothing hear is pleasing except the Joy of making money and that chance seames to be *over*."13

What sustained Moses through his depression, he told Westcott, was Maria. "Was it not for the best of *wives* life would be a burden but after retireing from the vexing sceans of Business the sweet society of a worthy and loving *woman* makes amend for all one smile changes the though[t] all is harmony & *order*...its Heaven to be with her and Hell to be alone." Now, though, he worried for Maria who "is very unwell." Her affliction, however, was not illness. The next day, June 29, she gave birth to their first child, Anna Maria. The baby lived slightly more than a month and died on August 1, 1787.14

Although 1787 bore hard on the Austins, they were far from being down and out. On the Richmond City Land Tax roll for that year (the first for collection of the tax) Moses Austin declared property yielding a substantial £115 per year in rents. On the personal property list he rendered his first slave. Perhaps most important of all, he, his wife and home, and his business all survived unscathed the great fire of January 8, which before daybreak reduced more than one-sixth of all the homes and businesses in the town to smoldering ruin.15

Moses Austin stayed in Richmond, with better times to follow. In 1788, he purchased the southwest corner lot at Main and Fourteenth streets, a block from the temporary capitol in the heart of the merchants' quarter of a recovered Richmond. The home he built there drew praise more than a half century later as "the most imposing structure of its day." Of its design and construction we know nothing beyond Philadelphia brick, handsome woodwork, beautiful marble and an "elaborate cornice" that provided a nesting place for martins for more than sixty years. Truly it must have been impressive to have outshone the simple elegance of the John Marshall House that still stands but a half-mile away behind the capitol on Shockoe Hill.[16]

"Crowds" of friends came to visit in the new house. During one of Moses' absences in 1789, Maria complained mildly of them, and of one person in particular who stayed for two weeks. That, a minor dispute with a neighbor over the boarding up of some small windows, and finding chores to occupy their now half-dozen slaves constituted the matters that troubled her most as their fourth wedding anniversary approached. Truly, things were going well for them, and she knew it. "I am Sensible," she apologized, "of the Impropriety of letting such trivial matters affect me."[17] Moses worried little over them or her. Maria was a capable, steady woman. He knew that she, though sometimes moody, could handle any trials she met. Besides, he had far more urgent matters on his mind.

The year 1789 opened broad, new horizons all around. Barely a year earlier Stephen had summed up the exasperation of American business when he told Jeremiah Wadsworth that he could "See no use to Imbark in Business in a Cuntry whose Law & Government are so Insufficient to Secure the advantages of it."[18] But on April 30, 1789, when George Washington stood on the balcony of the Federal Center in New York City and took the oath of office as the first President of the United States of America, the country completed a thoroughgoing change of government. After nearly a decade under the weak Articles of Confederation, America at last had a strong national government whose constitutional power to regulate trade and to administer the affairs of the country gave a fresh spirit of energy, hope, and anticipation to the business community. On top of that, the commercial revival that had begun after mid-decade reached full tide.[19] In short, 1789 presented the best time in years for striking out in new directions.

Moses Austin had a venture in mind. What he needed and wanted was the partnership and resources of his brother Stephen. He could not have found a better time to approach him. During Stephen's years importing and retailing dry goods, his obligations and those due him had become exceedingly complicated and geographically scattered. The situation, though hardly unusual, weighed on Stephen until finally it drove him to conclude his importing business, liquidate his store, and close his accounts. At the end of April, 1788, forty-one-year-old Stephen set out on a two-month, 1,100-mile journey through Maryland, North Carolina, and Virginia to meet his debtors face to face, most of them being "Store Keepers in the Cuntry." "I have a good hors," he told Wadsworth, probably his most important creditor, "& Shall not Leave a Man untill I have Settled or Secu[re]d his acct by Bond & Mortgage in my own name—"[20] During his odyssesy, Stephen obtained little cash. But he secured his obligations well, and through the succeeding months the debts due him reached Philadelphia. Early in 1789, even before all accounts had been closed, Stephen discovered that during his seven years in Pennsylvania "he had more than doubled the capital with which he began."[21]

As he worked on his books, Stephen considered ventures in which he might invest some, if not most, of his newly liquid worth of probably $25,000. Though he sought Wadsworth's advice on at least one idea, he seemed in no hurry to act. Sometime late in 1788, or more likely in early 1789, Moses approached him with his idea that the two form a partnership to mine and manufacture lead.[22] They would begin by acquiring rights to the old Chiswell mine some 250 miles due west southwest of Richmond. Though anyone could find it—labeled simply "Lead Mine"—on one of the maps tucked inside Jedidiah Morse's contemporary, pioneering *American Geography*, the place was remote, especially remote in that day of poor transportation and rutted clearings that passed for roads. "Around us are mountains of every conceivable shape," wrote a visitor there years later, ". . . mountains lapped and dovetailed within mountains, range above and beyond range, in seemingly endless succession." The New River, a tributary of the Great Kanawha, itself a tributary of the Ohio, skirted the mine tract, flowing "silently . . . but with a subtle force, between banks lined with sycamores, which trail their branches in the water in many instances."[23] Though alluvial lowlands of moderate richness stretched back from the river here and there, the banks generally rose to "terrible cliffs, and toppling precipices of solid limestone, often hundreds of feet in height, and inaccessible to any foot save those of the bird and reptile."[24]

For years the mine anchored the edge of civilization. In 1768, it had been named in the important Treaty of Hard Labor as one of the handful of fixed points mooring that formal boundary between English settlements on the east and Indian lands on the west, and few whites then knew what lay to the west. Daniel Boone's first venture into Kentucky would not occur until the next summer. Even after later agreements pushed the treaty line farther west, the Lead Mine area remained the jumping off point where immigrants to Kentucky "reached the borders of the great wilderness. The wild, rough, dangerous part of the journey commenced when New River was crossed at Inglis's Ferry, and travellers turned squarely toward the setting sun."[25]

If Stephen had inspected the property, he might have turned his brother down abruptly. The place "was not only unimproved, but absolutely wild." Trees and brush had overgrown the diggings. The warehouse and other couple of buildings, as well as the furnace, stood deteriorating.[26] They could hardly be distinguished from the wilderness crowding in upon it. Looks could be deceiving, however, and the history of the mine suggested great potential for a profitable operation. The diggings actually were comparatively fresh. The outcrop had been discovered by Colonel John Chiswell only thirty-three years before in 1756 as he made his way along one of the steep banks near Bald Hill, his life in the balance. In the vicinity he had spotted a party of hostile Indians. When Chiswell came to a cave a hundred or so feet above the river, he ducked inside and was trapped there as long as the Indians remained nearby. To pass the time, he examined the rocks in the dark hole. From his experience in mining iron, he knew enough to recognize that among the stones he found was lead ore of substantial purity. Lead in commercial quantity would be discovered in but a few locations in that part of the country, and Chiswell, intent only on saving himself, had stumbled upon the richest of them.

To exploit his find, Chiswell formed a partnership that brought three of the colony's most prominent men into his venture: Governor Francis Fauquier, Colonel William Byrd of Westover, the founder of Richmond, and John Robinson, Chiswell's son-in-law and a former Speaker of the House of Burgesses. The partners bought up the prior claims of speculators to the area, then used their political influence to obtain the right to survey their tract as waste and unappropriated land. In 1761, the year Moses Austin was born, Chiswell laid formal claim to 1,000 acres in a bend of the New River at Bald Hill, known ever since as the Lead Mines Tract.

The associates at first worked the cave, but soon abandoned "Chiswell's Hole," declaring it inaccessible for mining. Thereafter their men explored the surface of Bald Hill, and each time the hands struck a promising show they dug a trench following it into the earth. Some veins disappeared "suddenly and totally," others continued deeper into the ground than the open trench could follow. Never did the work become easy. Wherever they found ore, it was imbedded in rock, sometimes mixed with earth, "which requires the force of gunpowder to open it."[27] No one knows how much lead Chiswell's three dozen slaves extracted during the fifteen years before his death in 1776, but of the richness of his Lead Mines Tract there was no question. The mines yielded an average of 60 pounds of lead for each 100 pounds of ore delivered at the furnace.[28]

After Chiswell's death and as war with England made the mines more prominent, the government of Virginia took charge of the property, appointed Charles Lynch, Jr., superintendent, and directed him to move against those unfriendly to the American cause. In his early forties, a former Burgess, and an independent, no-nonsense patriot, Lynch accepted the mission with pleasure. When he caught suspected Tories, he convened an informal military court, with himself as judge and jury, and tried them on the spot. The guilty were sentenced to shout: "Liberty Forever!" and given thirty-nine lashes on the bare back. Those who refused to shout the patriot slogan were strung up by their thumbs, then lashed. Lynch executed no one, but his quick, decisive, summary justice became widely known and contributed to the English language the term "lynch law."[29]

Lynch found the mines easier to defend than to manage. By 1780, his output of lead had become so small that in some parts, window lead and shop weights had to be melted down to meet demand. And the situation went from bad to worse. Seven months before the decisive Battle of Yorktown, a correspondent told the chief executive that the poor condition of the lead mine and the desperate scarcity of lead demanded his attention. Governor Thomas Jefferson could do little, however. A year later "the works at the Lead mines are so entirely out of repair" that both the back country settlements and the army of General Nathaniel Greene soon could be "critically in want of ammunition."[30]

Lynch and his managers, it must be said, faced troubles beyond their making. One was supply. The mines were so remote that in Chiswell's day, and probably still, the most convenient source of provisions lay not in Virginia at all, but at the Moravian settlement in North Carolina (at modern Winston-Salem). Even it could not satisfy all the needs. The shortage of meat became so critical, word of it reached the governor, too. For their daily bread, the miners had to grow their own corn, which took time away from mining. That Lynch and his deputies drove the men as if the hands had nothing to do but dig lead sparked serious discontent. The core of the thirty-man work force appears to have been Welsh. Some, if not all, had been at the mines since Chiswell's day, and may have been brought over by Chiswell, whose father had immigrated from Wales. Tensions rose until Lynch fired some and the rest went on strike in sympathy. The mines might have been less productive had it not been for the "public negroes," government-owned slaves sent out from their confiscated Tory plantations, who had no choice but to work the diggings whatever the conditions.[31]

Through it all, the mine produced an average 20-25 tons of lead each year and recorded 60 tons during one twelve-month. In his catalog of the state's resources—*Notes on Virginia*—published in 1784, Jefferson speculated that 50 men could work the veins profitably and that the tract could produce even more than 60 tons in a year.[32]

Perhaps two-thirds more hands could have nearly tripled the annual output, but in so doing they would have taxed their inefficient system of production to its limits. Since Chiswell's Hole had been abandoned, the miners had recovered only surface ore. They dug down no farther than they could heave the ore and dirt out of their trenches, about ten to twelve

The maps in Jedidiah Morse's *The American Universal Geography* were among the most accurate of their day. This one shows the location of Chiswell's lead mine and may well have been the map Austin used in plotting his trip in the winter and spring of 1796–1797 from Austinville to the Lead Mines of Spanish Upper Louisiana.

feet. Other men then loaded the ore into wagons, hauled it a quarter of a mile or so to the bank of New River, shoveled it into canoes, and paddled it across. The furnace for reducing the ore, that is, for separating the lead from the earth and rock in which it was imbedded, had been located on the other side of the river to take advantage of a lively stream for washing dirt from the ore before smelting. The cleaned ore was roasted in the furnace to recover the pure lead. Over a period of several hours the molten metal drained out an opening at the base of the furnace and into molds, often no more than gashes in the earth. The finished product was roundish, oblong bars called "pigs" because each resembled the body of a hog. The modern pig, now trapezoidal in shape, weighs a standard 100 pounds. The bars of Chiswell's and Lynch's day weighed anywhere between 60 and 150 pounds.

Actually, producing the pigs represented only half of the undertaking. The other half was transporting them. The pigs were loaded into wagons and hauled the tortuous 250-plus miles over the mountains and through the Piedmont to Richmond. Some were taken 130 miles east northeast through the rough country to Lynch's ferry (modern Lynchburg), where John Lynch, Charles' pacifist Quaker brother, operated a crossing of the upper James River. These pigs were transferred to batteaux—long, slender, shallow-draft, canoe-like boats that transported cargo on the James above the falls. Another 130 miles east down the James lay Westham, the landing at the head of the Falls, about six miles above Richmond. There men sweated over the bars again, loading them into wagons to be hauled to the landings at Richmond for shipment aboard seagoing vessels. Without substantial demand, the return from the lead could not recoup the cost of its freight. In 1785, some thirty-seven tons of lead, almost two years' production, sat at the mines. And there it remained as the Robinson and Byrd heirs struggled with the State over ownership of the property and the amount of rent due them from the government. While they argued, the mine—both diggings and buildings—deteriorated from neglect.[33]

After four years, the State and the heirs agreed that the mine should be leased for the revenue it would bring. Moses Austin, though neither he nor his brother had any experience in the lead business, sensed a golden opportunity. This mine had been the largest and most productive in the United States. It could be again. He talked to Stephen with all the persuasiveness he could muster. And Moses could be persuasive. By late spring, Stephen had been "induced by the solicitations of his brother . . . to engage in the lead mine business." In Richmond in May, 1789, he and Moses signed a ten-year lease for the Lead Mine.[34]

Before the ink had dried—long before they took possession in October—the brothers began shaping their new venture. On May 22, they wrote the Governor outlining their ambitious plans. First, they told him, they intended to work the mine "in as extensive a Manner as Possible," which would require rebuilding or replacing the run-down "Buildings, Furnance, Mills, etc." To manufacture "the large production of Lead which these Mines will afford," they would "Establish a Shott Manufactory in this place [Richmond], Buildings &c. for which we have already contracted for." Theirs would be more than a work of local note, however. If all went as they hoped, "we have reason to flatter ourselves that not only the Interest of this State but the United States in General, & More particularly this city is interested in the Success of our undertaking." The produce of their mine and manufactory, they believed, would be sufficient "to prevent the importation of a considerable part, if not all those usefull articles of Shott & Lead from Europe to this country and thereby retain the Large Sums of Money which is yearly drawn from those States for those articles." They intended, in other words, to try to supply the entire American demand for lead.

To help them launch their worthy enterprise, particularly to provide them working capital to repair the mine works, "the compleating of which will be attended with considerable expence," they asked the loan of 30 tons of lead belonging to the State. It "has for Seven years past and Still continues to Lay at these works," they pointed out to the Governor, and "in the first establishing this Business, will rinder us very Essential Service."[35] The Governor and Council granted their request.

In August, Moses left for the mines, where he spent all of September establishing the Austins' control. When he and Stephen met again in Richmond in November, Moses' report glowed. He had put ten men to work digging ore. From old trenches they were producing 1,000 pounds of lead a day, far above the output of Lynch's miners. More exciting yet, they had found a rich new vein yielding 75 pounds of lead for each 100 pounds of ore. Fifty tons of lead bars already sat stockpiled on the ground. Initial production more than met the partners' hopes.[36]

Anticipation soared yet higher, Stephen reported before he left Richmond, when on November 26, 1789, the manufacturing plant that the brothers had set up in the city produced its first shot. No record survives to tell how the lead balls were made. Their men could have poured molten lead into individual molds. Or, to obtain small sizes of shot, they could have followed Colonel Henry Bouquet's instructions. Take "a round wooden Box with a wooden cover nicely fitted to it," and coat the inside with chalk. Pour molten lead into the box, shut and "shake it violently, so that the metal within may be agitated forcibly against all parts of the box." As the metal cooled during the shaking, it formed granules of various sizes. However the Austins made their shot, they thought it of high quality, "much better than the British drop shott," Moses boasted.[37]

Stephen left Richmond exhilarated. Considering the abundance of the ore and the pace at which the pigs were being produced, he believed that a force of fifty miners could supply the United States. By the time he arrived back in Philadelphia, he had determined to raise "a Brigade of Men" to unleash on the Lead Mine. A hundred men, he told Wadsworth, working "at the Same Rate as those Imployd 4 months past will Produce us Ten Thousand lbs per day—"[38] The mathematical computation of the possibilities of the diggings staggered his mind.

Stephen set to work with unrestrained enthusiasm and resolve. By January, he had become "a perfect Serjt Kite Recruting Men for the Lead Mines—& my house full from morning to Night."[39] He proved a shrewd judge of men, for many whom he brought served the partners well and remained in the area as respected settlers long after the Austins had departed. Robert Percival and Nathaniel Frisbie each would manage the mines for a time. Thomas Jackson, a twenty-seven-year-old bachelor and a skilled mining smith from Westmoreland County, England, not only later acquired the entire tract, but built a shot tower downstream that is one of only three still standing in the United States.[40] Both Austins worked at fever pitch. While Stephen in Philadelphia recruited his force to increase production at the mines by three-, four-, or five-fold, Moses in Richmond worked to secure a new and lucrative outlet for their lead. He sought the contract to roof the new capitol.

Jefferson's plans for the capitol building arrived in Richmond late in

Thomas Jefferson, architect of the Virginia capitol, sent from France this plaster model of the Maison Carrée, the Roman temple after which he took his design for the capitol. *Virginia State Library Picture Collection.*

1785. They called for a structure modeled closely on the building that he unreservedly called "the best morsel of ancient architecture now remaining"—the Maison Carrée, a Roman temple in Nimes, France. With appropriate adaptation in size and floor plan, the building he proposed met perfectly, he thought, his charge from the Directors of the Public Buildings to "unite economy with elegance and utility."[41]

Three years after construction began, before the brick walls had been faced with stucco and the portico put up, the building had been finished sufficiently to be occupied. The General Assembly moved up the hill from the temporary capitol in October, 1788, followed by the Governor the next year. Other offices moved during the spring as arrangements expired on the quarters they had occupied. Unhappily, they found the building not fully ready for them. The roof leaked.[42]

Jefferson intended that the building, like its model, have a pediment roof. But in February, 1787, the Directors had accepted the offer of Samuel Dobie, their architect, who had directed construction from the laying of the cornerstone, to put on a flat roof instead. The change would trim the cost of the roof to a mere £170. But, "after much labor in honestly endeavoring to fulfill his contract," Dobie gave up. The hot sun melted the pitch waterproofing he used. It ran into the gutters and away, leaving the boards that formed the roof exposed to the rain, which soon soaked through. When Dobie could not stop the leaks, the Directors concluded that "for the preservation of the building from ruin" a pediment roof must be put on at once. And to insure that it be perfectly tight, they wanted it covered with lead, a not uncommon covering for churches and other major buildings in Europe.[43]

Edward Carrington, chairman of the House Committee that received the Directors' recommendations, took the floor on December 14, 1789, and announced to the House his committee's concurrence with the Directors' proposals. For the lead, he continued, the committee recommended that "the said Directors be authorized and requested to give preference to such as is the production of this Commonwealth, if the same can be procured in season at a rate not exceeding five per centum higher than other lead would cost." Both the House and Senate concurred and appropriated the £3,476 the roof was estimated to cost.[44]

Two and a half weeks after Carrington spoke, Moses Austin obtained the contract to cover the roof with lead. He could not pass up a bonus of 5 percent on the price of his lead. The authorities doubtless considered Austin, though new to the lead business, a satisfactory contractor, he having done acceptable work repairing the Governor's House. At the signing Moses received an advance of £600. But he could not begin work for six months until the framework of the new roof, under a separate contract, had been erected.[45]

In the meantime, Moses pushed production at the shot factory. Before the end of January, 1790, no more than two months after the factory began operation, he sent his first shipment of more than eight tons to market in New York. A month later, he followed it with another consignment, this shipment more notable than the first. Through his brother Elijah, still in New Haven, Moses carried in his store Josiah Burr's New Haven osnaburg and linen. That second shipment of shot, Moses wrote Wadsworth with unrestrained pride, consisted of "the first shot made in America with american lead & bagged in American linen."[46]

Proud though he was, Moses had a firmly practical motive for writing the New England businessman. In 1790 Jeremiah Wadsworth sat in Congress representing a Connecticut district. The Austins, as they had hinted to the Governor in May, wanted the United States to encourage and protect their infant home industry with a tariff on imported lead. Wadsworth's support for the duty would be invaluable.

The seven-month-old first tariff of the new United States admitted lead duty free. Since the country still manufactured little and used its agricultural output to purchase manufactured goods, the act had been designed in the main merely to raise operating revenue by levies on commerce. But subsequent public reaction to stiff European duties created a congenial atmosphere in which to seek a duty on lead that would raise the price of the imported product to make it easier for the domestic lead to compete. "Have you any Doubt but Congress will Lay at Least one Cent duty on Shott & Sheet Lead – if Not on Barr Lead – when we made it appear our daly Production is Eaqual to the Consumtion of this Cuntry – " Stephen inquired of Wadsworth on January 17, 1790.[47]

The answer did not matter. When the facts had been gathered, the Austins discovered that imported tonnage exceeded their output substantially. In June, they took a different tack and went back to the Governor, and to other friends of the nation's leaders, emphasizing the expenses they faced in competing and the exertions they were making to expand production of their mine.

> In the prosecution of this business [they wrote Governor Beverley Randolph] we find it impossible to bring our lead to market and stand on an equality with the importer of it, as we cannot vend the quantity we could wish nor obtain a price sufficient to repay us. . . . The many difficulties we have to encounter from the long distance inland which is attended with a very expensive Transportation makes it necessary to ask the aid and assistance of the Public who we flatter ourselves will view our exertions in the manufactory of so usefull and necessary an article in a favourable light.[48]

The Governor lost no time in providing letters of introduction and solicitation to President Washington and Secretary of State Jefferson. The Austins, he wrote his fellow Virginians in mid-July, sought from Congress "some encouragement in order to enable them to furnish this Country with manufactured Lead in all its various Forms."[49]

"I believe you are well acquainted with the Fertility of these Mines," Randolph added in his letter to Jefferson. Nevertheless he enclosed a report on the mines that the Austins had supplied him to show the improvements and exertions they had made. Prepared by three prominent, long-time residents of Wythe County, the report documented a five-fold increase in the force at the mines. The nearly sixty men worked seven excavations, rather than the two when Jefferson compiled his information for the *Notes on Virginia*. Where the former miners dug only shallow trenches, the Austins took their excavations down some seventy feet into the earth following the veins, and in consequence were retrieving six to eight tons of ore a day. They had introduced (an unspecified) "very simple, but improved manner of beating and washing the ore," had repaired the old furnace and were recovering a ton and a half of lead per day, "sufficient [the three believed] for the Consumption of the United States." Whether or not it was enough might not be the most important question. "We . . . wish to remind our Rulers, that the time has been that much depended on the preservation and success of the same manufacture: That similar Occasions may happen in the course of future Events that will show the good policy of being independant of all the World for so necessary an article."[50]

Having prepared their way, Stephen and Moses went to New York City, seat of the federal government, to lay their case personally before the nation's leaders. On July 23 they called on the Secretary of State. He was unswayed. Jefferson remained both unreconciled to the concept of protective tariffs and fearful of the precedent established if Congress favored a private venture. Stephen apparently received a similar reception from the President. Undaunted, the Austins approached members of Congress. John Brown, from the Kentucky District of Virginia and a former law student of Jefferson's, agreed to introduce the bill they wanted providing a duty of "one cent per pound on bar and all other lead imported." Congress readily concurred in the measure, and within a month of the Austins' arrival in New York, the bill had been enacted. Subsequently on March 2, 1791, the lawmakers expanded the coverage of the duty to include all manufactures of lead and products in which lead constituted the chief article.[51]

The Austins had achieved a sweeping success. Not even Secretary of the Treasury Alexander Hamilton, a strong proponent of protective tariffs as a means of stimulating manufactures that would liberate the American economy from its dependence on European production, could suggest improvement. After the duty had been in effect for a year, he reported to Congress that "The duties already laid upon the importation of this article, either in its unmanufactured or manufactured state, ensure it a decisive advantage in the home market, which amounts to considerable encouragement."[52]

The Virginia legislature offered incentive, too. In June, before Moses had left for New York, he and the Directors of Public Buildings agreed on the terms by which he would roof the capitol. Austin would "cover the roof, cornice and balustrade of the Capitol with lead at the rate of 52 *l.* per ton, the total cost of which exclusive of the completing the cornice (which for want of funds was necessarily suspended) amounts to the sum of 2,873 *l.* 5 *s.* 2 *d.*"[53] And he guaranteed the work against leaks for a year after completion. Then, "In order that there may be no Delay in the completion of his contract," the Directors gave Austin £200,[54] work began, and Austin left for New York.

Although everyone expected the work to be completed in two months, it was not. Henrico County's representative in the General Assembly blamed "the rise of grain and the impossibility of procuring wagons to transport the lead in consequence thereof, but more particularly . . . the smelting furnace (which at the formation of the contract there was reason to believe would have continued fit for use at least till the execution of their contract) and the consequent necessity of erecting a new one, before they could proceed further in their business."[55]

Austin's reasons mattered little to the Directors, whose work with the capitol already had fallen behind schedule. Besides, the continuing leaks every time it rained only hurt the building more. On August 11, they agreed that "to obviate the damage the house was daily suffering," and to make possible work on the interior that could not proceed as long as the roof leaked, they would, after the 15th and at Austin's expense, hire the shingling of the unfinished portion of the roof and the portico.[56]

Four months later Austin still had not finished replacing the shingles with lead. "There is yet a good deal to do to the Roof," Director William Hay wrote the State Treasurer on January 4, 1791. "The late high wind has turned up a sheet, which has remained so many days," Hay wondered whether Austin still had a plumber competent to repair it. Nonetheless the Directors, the House concurring, recommended payment in full to Moses Austin and Company for the leading of the capitol roof.[57]

After 1789, the lead business occupied more and more of Moses' time. But the name Moses Austin & Company in Richmond still meant in part dry goods: Hyson tea "of good quality," book muslin, soap, paper hangings, candles, and paintings. For brother Elijah in Connecticut, Moses during the summer of 1791 even handled tickets in the New Haven Wharf Lottery.[58]

In all these lines, Moses — as every shopkeeper — watched carefully the money tendered in payment. "Evil minded Persons," the merchants branded them, shaved silver coins, reducing their true worth, then offered them at face value. Exasperated Richmond businessmen — Moses Austin's bold signature prominent on the petition – begged the General Assembly to substitute copper for silver. Though both the federal government of the Articles of Confederation, led by Jefferson on this issue, and the State of New Jersey had established precedent for it, the Virginia legislature offered no remedy.

For the problem of bank paper, which circulated at varying discounts and could be totally worthless, Secretary of the Treasury Hamilton proposed a solution in December, 1790, when he submitted to Congress a plan for a Bank of the United States. Hamilton's bank would provide a circulating currency uniform throughout the country that would significantly control the paper issues of state banks. Hardly had the President signed the bill than 116 progressive merchants and community leaders of the Richmond area, Moses Austin among them, petitioned to have a branch established in Richmond, an important trade center whose exports in 1791 would reach $1.2 million. Most Virginians, however, despised the concept of a national bank, fearing both that it placed too much power in the new central government and that it would work to the advantage of commercial and business interests alone. A group arose to charter a state bank in opposition, which killed the national bank branch for Richmond.[59]

Moses, vigilant of the money he took in payment, had to mind his competition as well. In addition to the other stores offering dry goods, in 1791 two new firms took space in the *Virginia Gazette* to advertise lead products. Warmington & Keene offered "their usual well selected assortment of. . .powder, shot and flints."[60] The competition of former London plumbers Emery and Swingle appeared to be more serious. These men carried lead in all its forms – shot, bar, and sheet – as did Moses Austin & Company, and also like Austin, they drew their supply of lead "from our own Mine (situate on the river French-Broad)."[61] If Austin had a real advantage over Emery and Swingle, it was that his mine lay a good 125 miles nearer Richmond than theirs. The additional mountainous miles Emery and Swingle had to freight their lead would make it difficult for them to charge the same prices as Austin. Was it coincidence then that two weeks to the day before Emery and Swingle first advertised in the newspaper, Moses Austin & Company reduced prices three shillings per hundred-weight across the board "in consequence of receiving their lead now by water from Lynchburg"?[62]

By the fall of 1791, competition or no competition, the Austins had fashioned from scratch an operation to be envied. They had won a protective tariff to support the price they needed to make their venture profitable. They had acquired substantial contracts and outlets for their product. And they had built a reputation for a business from which, Supervisor of Virginia Revenue, Edward Carrington, wrote Alexander Hamilton, "new Manufactures are daily coming into practice, such as sheet lead for roof-

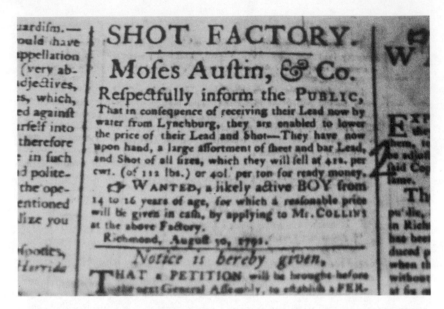

Moses Austin & Company Advertisement, 1791. Advertisement from the *Virginia Gazette and General Advertiser,* August 31, 1791, for the product of Moses Austin's Richmond lead works.

ing, shot &c."[63] Moses and Stephen Austin in two years had achieved stunning success. But success is a restless spirit. After a time it builds a momentum of its own, feeds on itself, and pushes relentlessly, blindly for more. The Austins soon found they could not rest with their good fortune.

If they wondered what more they could do to strengthen their business, the *Virginia Gazette* of December 14, 1791, brought an answer. Tucked among its advertisements appeared a notice that the lead mines and the 1,400-acre Lead Mine Tract they held under lease would be sold at public auction at the door of the Eagle Tavern in Richmond on Monday, February 20, 1792. The Commonwealth of Virginia and the pre-war owners finally had come to terms in their protracted dispute over ownership and rent payments. Under the agreement, the State granted the tract to Charles Lynch as Trustee for the Lead Mine Company, a firm apparently consisting only of the heirs of the original owners, who by this time had taken each other to court feuding over their individual interests in the property. In November, they decided it would be easier to divide money than to partition the property.[64] According to the *Gazette*, no bid under £5,000 would be accepted. Nor would the sale affect the eight years remaining on the Austins' lease, which would yield the purchaser £150 in each of the first three years and £200 in all of the remaining five.[65]

In January, Stephen traveled to Richmond to discuss their opportunity with his brother. And "being persuaded," he later testified, "that the purchase of these mines was essential to the advantageous improvement of the business, they entered into a negotiation. . ."[66] First they came to agreement between themselves, the terms of which they signed on January 18, 1792. They would bid up to £10,000 for the tract, Moses Austin and Company holding a two-thirds interest, Stephen Austin one-third. Since the purchase price would allow credit for the monies due under the lease, the partners agreed to continue the lease, paying the annual rental to themselves in proportions commensurate with their interests. Curiously, despite their uneven interests, they decided to split all expenses, profits, and losses equally.[67]

The agreement struck, they sought three sureties. Two who agreed to stand behind the Austins' note were prominent businessmen: Samuel Paine of Richmond and John Field of Philadelphia. For the third, Moses secured a man already interested in the mines, an insider whose influence in the Austins' behalf could be invaluable—Charles Lynch.[68]

On February 20, 1792, Moses Austin went to the Eagle Tavern, near his grand home, and purchased the mines with a bid of £6,505, half payable in two years, the other half in three.[69]

What appeared as an innocent transaction proved far from it. The ramifications of Moses' successful bid directly changed the course of both his and Stephen's careers, not to mention those of Paine and Field. They could see some of it that day. "Having thus become the proprietors of these mines," Stephen recalled years later, he and his brother went largely into the mining and manufactoring of lead."[70] But that was only the beginning.

CHAPTER IV

RICHMOND PARLORS must have buzzed with the news of Moses Austin and the mines. Not the word that the Austin brothers had acquired the property, for most thoughtful persons probably anticipated that they would make the successful bid. The news was that the prosperous, well-established Moses was pulling up stakes, leaving his magnificent house with the memorable cornice, and moving to the mines to manage them personally. As the majority owner of the operation, he determined to redouble his efforts to make his investment profitable.

Personally, the decision to move could not have been easy. Neither he nor his polished wife were people of the frontier. Maria had never been west of Richmond, as far as any record shows. To the contrary, she had grown up surrounded by eighteenth-century luxury in Benjamin Fuller's house, a lifestyle her husband approached, if not duplicated, for her in Richmond. Luxury, being relative, in their time meant a larger, more elegantly appointed home, and in the South, it also meant having more slaves than real chores to occupy them. But the actual routine of living varied little from Philadelphia to Richmond to far southwestern Virginia. Two circumstances, however, would make life in Wythe County different from anything they had known: its remoteness and the ever-present menace of Indians. "It is uncertain when hostilities may be committed on the inhabitants of this County," Colonel Walter Crockett wrote in one of the steady flow of letters and petitions that besieged the governor through the 1790s, "but I think we are in as emenent danger as any people can possibly be exposed to."[1]

Moses surely knew the risk, but reasoned that if his direct attention could make the property and the men more productive, then he would move into the wilderness. Actually, additional men at the mines would help to protect the place from attack. More importantly, they could further expand production. The brothers still hoped to supply the needs of the country. In December and January, 1791-1792, Moses called through the *Virginia Gazette* for fifty to sixty laborers—enough to double again the already record force at the mines—to contract for one, two, or three years' work.[2]

The American laborers could provide muscle, but no special expertise in the mining or working of lead. And any competitor could easily increase production to the same degree as the Austins simply by adding the same number of laborers. To forge ahead in the business, Moses and Stephen realized that they needed to make substantial improvements in the work at the mines. But men with the knowledge and experience they wanted could be found only abroad.

If the Austins read more of Treasury Secretary Hamilton's *Report on Manufactures* than the part that mentioned their mining operation, they would have been encouraged. With "the disturbed state of Europe inclining its citizens to emigration," Hamilton told Congress, "the requisite workmen will be more easily acquired than at another time."[3] It did not prove so for the Austins. The "liberal wages" they advertised to attract American laborers could not have approached the sums required to secure hands from England. To induce some to cross the Atlantic, Stephen recalled, the Austins had to give salaries ranging up to $1,000, a phenomenal figure for those days.[4] To support such outlays, the foreign experts would have to work a revolution in mining, smelting, and manufacturing lead.

More than good pay alone, Moses knew, was necessary to produce a truly stable work force and avoid the troubles that plagued Lynch. "Men with families who have nothing but their day labour to depend on will find it to their interest to engage with the subscribers," Moses' *Virginia Gazette* advertisement said, "as they are allowed many advantages they cannot obtain in towns, which enables them to support a family comfortably on their wages."[5] But in a day when families averaged five to eight members, hiring between fifty and a hundred heads of households meant an onslaught of between 250 and 800 people. There was no place for those numbers at the mines. The partners literally had to create a town. "To accommodate the number of workmen employed," Stephen reported later, the brothers "were obliged to build houses, stores, mills, furnaces, potters, blacksmiths, and hatters shops," as well as "shops for the manufacture of almost every instrument and utensil."[6] To facilitate transportation, they obtained authorization from the legislature to establish a ferry across the New River. Out of it all, a new community emerged. By the end of 1794, one businessman could describe it as "a great place of Trade & business."[7] It took on a new identity as correspondents began dropping the old address of "Lead Mines" in favor of the new "Austinville."

Increasing production meant more frequent or larger shipments, all the more reason to haul the lead to the James River and float it to Richmond. If the river passage did not shave time from the month required to freight the lead more than 250 miles by wagon to Richmond, it did reduce the cost of the haul by about one-third. The company needed a place to stockpile pigs at the river and on November 11, 1792, purchased lot 19 in Lynchburg. On the quarter-acre just above John Lynch's ferry, Austin put up "a good frame house, stable and Smokehouse."[8] The brothers also thought they needed additional manufacturing facilities. By late summer, 1792, Stephen had established his own "Lead-Warehouse, two doors south of Walnut Street Wharf, adjoining...[the company's] new factory." In this Philadelphia plant he produced sheet and bar lead of all sizes and "equal in quality to any manufactured in Europe."[9]

This sudden, feverish physical expansion rivaled in ambition and achievement the Austins' earlier success obtaining favorable tariffs and lucrative contracts. Its cost was quite another matter. The huge and persisting expense of their expansion staggered even the well-heeled Austin brothers. Undaunted, they sank virtually every dollar they had into the enterprise. Together they poured in $50,000 of "proceeds of the lead made and sold at different times." Stephen personally gave $30,000. First he invested "all the property...made in the dry good business." Later he "was obliged to sell two houses he owned in Philadelphia, for which he received about 7000 dollars."[10] No records remain of the sums Moses contributed. But if he paid proportionate to his interest, his investment should have totalled near $60,000. Quickly Moses and Stephen saw that they could not support all the expenses alone. They borrowed thousands of dollars to meet regular outlays. Perhaps more typical for that time before banks and other lending institutions became common, they took in another partner. On November 2, 1792, for $15,000, they sold Thomas Ruston of Philadelphia a one-eighth interest in the mines and properties at Austinville, Lynchburg, and Richmond.[11]

The Austins and their backers could easily see the fruits of their investment. The Englishmen introduced technical improvements, the exact nature of which was never recorded, that merited Stephen's mention more than a decade later. Evidently they streamlined the operation as well by relocating the washing and smelting of the ore to a site near the mines. To this day one stream near the center of the old mining area bears the name "Buddle Branch" after a box used in the washing process.[12]

The Austin investors could see, too, a large and expanding market. Their lead in wholesale quantities went to New York City. Though records are sketchy, the Austins apparently had direct outlets in New Haven, Connecticut, and in the Southern states. With Jefferson's blessings, they likely contracted with the federal government to supply its magazines around the country. To the west also lay a mushrooming new field. Two of the three great routes to the West—the road from Philadelphia down the Shenandoah Valley and the road west from Richmond—converged at old Fort Chiswell. So many people streamed down the road that the Southwest Territory was created in 1790, and Kentucky, with the requisite 60,000 inhabitants, entered the Union as the fourteenth state in 1792. The mines were ideally located to supply the western market. Indeed, so much Austin lead traveled into Kentucky, one contemporary observed, that, combined with the product of the Spanish deposits near Ste. Genevieve, it squeezed the profit out of the local lead mines at Lexington, and they were abandoned.[13]

Moses Austin could afford to leave Richmond and devote himself to the mines because he had men in whose hands he trusted his business. To superintend completion of the work on the capitol roof, he turned to his nineteen-year-old, Durham-born nephew, Elias Bates. The roof had been laid and Austin paid more than eighteen months before. But contrary to Austin's warranty against leaks, rain continued to seep through cracks and crevices marking, then loosening, the plaster ceilings. The leaks directly through the roof, according to one investigator, resulted from Austin's use of slabs "of such immense weight that the nails heretofore intended for that purpose could not prevent...[them] from sliding down and leaving a chasm [of several inches] between this and the sheet next above..."[14] Moreover, his men had laid the sheets of lead endwise from bottom to top, "folding" them together rather than overlapping them. The worst leaks, though, occurred in the gutters, from which water soaked great supporting timbers which could not easily dry.[15]

For more than a year the Directors of Public Buildings called the failures to Austin's attention and "have been uniformly amused with Promises of Complyance..."[16] Their patience had worn thin by May 8, 1792, when Austin's competitor, John Emery, proposed to complete the roof and repair the gutters to meet the terms of Austin's contract. The Directors wrote Austin threatening to accept Emery's offer and to file suit for damages, the proceeds of which would be used to pay the new contractor. Nothing happened. A month later the Governor summoned Director William Hay to see for himself the damage caused by the defects in the roof and to demand a full report. No alternative remained, Hay responded two days later, but to recover Austin's bond and employ someone else to finish the work. Austin would have three days to satisfy Hay that he would make his contract good.[17]

On the very morning that Hay submitted his report, June 14, Bates informed him "that as soon as the weather permits they will set about the work." Unimpressed with the latest promise, Hay closed that portion of his report on the roof saying that "In the present State of the Roof the Directors conceive that some decisive Measure should be taken & get the advice of the Board therein—"[18]

Austin's men worked on the roof, but still could not make it tight. Six months to the day after Hay wrote, on December 14, 1792, the House of Delegates took up the matter. The facts at hand led the representatives to conclude that Austin was at fault and that his bond should be collected. Two days later, the General Assembly voted out a measure appropriating Austin's bond money to finishing work on the building.[19]

Even legislative action did not settle the matter, however. A year and a half afterward, in July, 1794, the Directors sent Samuel Coleman onto the roof to make another inspection. Recent heavy rains had "rendered the Council Chamber...unsafe from the great probability of the plaster falling."[20] Coleman looked. "It appears to me impracticable to keep the roof tight with the lead put on as it is now," he reported, "even with the most faithful workmanship, which I do not believe from present appearances has been practiced upon it."[21] And because of the manner in which the slabs were laid, he could see no way to make the roof serviceable.

When it met at the end of 1794, the House of Delegates considered Coleman's report, concluded that the lead roof had been a failure, and resolved to try slate for the covering. Presumably the change would cost the State nothing, as sale of the lead ought to cover expenses. But the State had yet to collect the eighteen-month-old debt passed against Moses Austin and Company, and it owed workmen $1,000 in wages to have been paid from Austin's bond. The General Assembly instructed the Directors "to use their utmost endeavours to collect the monies" due.[22]

This was the last time Austin's name appeared among the records concerning the capitol roof, even though the rains continued trickling through the cracks for nearly four years more. Records do not show whether the State ever collected the bond, but the root of the problem finally was eliminated in 1798 when the lead slabs at last were taken up and replaced with slate, making the third complete roof on the capitol in ten years.[23]

The nagging, unsettled situation hurt Austin, for he could ill afford the drain of the continuing unsuccessful work on the capitol roof. Combined with outlays at Austinville, at Lynchburg, and in recruiting his work force, it taxed to the limit his and the company's dangerously overextended resources. Even before the July rains agitated the roof matter in 1794, Moses and Stephen knew that something had to be done to strengthen their financial condition, and they agreed that no further stop-gap measures, no more borrowing, would do. The situation called for a bold move. Stephen should go to England to sell the mines. Early in June he sailed with a box of ore and high hopes.[24]

Stephen no sooner stepped from the boat than trouble dogged his tracks. He was arrested and clapped into debtors' prison for a ten-year-old, $4,321.20 debt that he and Moses had incurred in their former firm of Merrill and Austin. Somehow Stephen obtained his release on bail. But it was a small victory. Two thousand miles from home and his sources of income, he had to raise more than $4,000. Moreover, he could not leave the country until he had settled the old obligation. Furthermore he still needed to pursue the original object of his trip, the sale of the mines.[25]

As time passed, Stephen in England received encouraging nibbles from prospective purchasers. But nearly a year after he had begun his mission, the mine property remained in his hands. Disappointed, nevertheless "he seems in good spirits," Blanchard informed Moses in May, 1795, "and is determined to do something great before he quits."[26] Stephen thought that perhaps his initial failure could be traced to the uncertain relations between Great Britain and the United States. Ministers of the two countries were at that time hammering out an agreement. "Should the Treaty be Receivd & a good understanding between the Two Country I have no Doubt of Sucsseding—" Stephen prophesied to Wadsworth.[27] And so it apparently happened. Jay's Treaty, satisfactory to Great Britain, was signed, and Stephen did arrange a sale of the mines. The £8,400-deal hinged, he said, on Moses incorporating the company.[28] That never occurred, and the sale was lost.

Eventually, Stephen gave up. He had sold several thousand acres, it was true. But "finding himself by his inability to dispose of the [mine] property compelled to continue this concern, he obtained credit in England for £5000 sterling in goods which he brought with him to this country which goods were sold to pay debts, and furnish the works."[29] Actually, while his negotiations still flickered, Stephen began obtaining the merchandise. In May, 1795, he dispatched nearly £1,000-worth of musical instruments to Philadelphia. When Blanchard learned they were addressed to him, he was stunned. "I could wish I knew what to do with them when they arrive," he scrawled lamely to Moses.[30]

Admitting failure, Stephen was ready to leave. Late in 1796, two years and four months after he arrived, he finally pulled together enough cash, some apparently earned by handling business for colleagues, to pay off the Merrill and Austin debt. The day after he settled that matter, he arranged for a London house to accept orders for shares in the mines, left them his box of ore, then boarded a ship for the United States, never to leave home again.[31]

The failure of Stephen's mission clearly left the Austin brothers in a bad situation. They had overextended and drained their resources trying to meet their commitments, but worse, all those loans so easily accepted in the halcyon days at the beginning of the decade were coming due. Robert Gamble, a successful dry goods merchant of Richmond, who had sold Moses the lot on which he had built his grand house, presented his account with the reminder that it was payable in "May 1795 suppose the time it may best suit you to pay." Most ominous of all, though, the financial affairs were woven into an interdependent, almost hopelessly tangled web. Gamble's single note represented "cash advanced Mr. Chas. Hay for you to pay Valentine pr. your Bond pr. Richd Smith."[32] If part of the structure collapsed, what would happen to the rest? Moses soon found out. That same spring of 1795, partner Ruston's credit evaporated, and banks refused to honor his paper.

Shortly, notes both of George Lauman and of Stephen Austin and Company stalled, too, but fortunately, not for long.[33]

The most nagging of the debts was that to the State for the lead borrowed to help put the mines back into repair. Austin through the years had repaid approximately one-third of the obligation. Though State authorities had lost track of the exact amount, the debt remained on their books. For two years, even the Governor blustered and threatened Austin about it, with no result. Finally, in December, 1795, the State's attorney filed suit. The very day he learned of it, December 12, Moses responded, begging an opportunity to explain his delay in retiring the six-year-old obligation. Persuasive as always, Austin obtained the extension he sought yet one more time.[34]

Though at times it must have seemed that the financial structure would come crashing down around him, Moses Austin held to his course. Characteristic of the Moses Austin who had survived the business depression of the 1780s, and the Moses Austin who had conceived and with his brother built the lead venture, he thought to overcome his economic woes by expanding his business interests. In the spring of 1796, he agreed, for one-third of the profits, to put the building housing his shot factory on Carey Street in Richmond, plus a stock of lead, into a firm to manufacture pewter buttons. Parsons Bates, the third of the four Bates children and now twenty-one years old, would head Parsons Bates and Company, in which Austin and Thomas Norvell, for years an agent of Moses Austin and Company in Richmond, shared interests. By May 20, 1796, a month after the deal had been struck, the firm was "making all kind of WHITE HARP METAL BUTTONS, of the most fashionable figures." Local retailers should find the buttons especially appealing, the company advertised, because by saving transportation costs on the heavy product, they could sell Bates' buttons cheaper than any others. Unfortunately, it must have worked out differently. The last record of Parsons Bates and Company is its advertisement in the *Virginia Gazette* a month or so after the first white harp buttons appeared.[35]

This was the second time one of the Bates men found an opportunity in the lead business with Moses Austin. It would not be the last. Moses had discovered that his own younger kin could be the most faithful, loyal, and helpful of employees and partners. He never forgot the lesson.

It was not surprising that Austin made the discovery, because he enjoyed keeping up with his relatives. More than that, he took pleasure in looking after them, too. "You cant conceive what pleasure it has given me that you have taken up this affair [settling Abia Brown's estate and securing the inheritance of his wife, her brothers and sisters] & intend to prosecute it with Spirit," Benjamin Fuller wrote him once. "In my opinion it is the only thing that can be done to recover or save any property for the

Orphans— It may be troublesome, but God will bless you & yours for your goodness."[36]

With Benjamin Elliott, Moses formed a friendship so strong that Elliott a few years later would follow Austin to Missouri. The two, only a year apart in age, had gained a family connection in 1782 when Austin's sister, Gloriana, had married Elliott's brother, Aaron. Benjamin, a physician, had become a prominent figure in Manchester, across the James from Richmond, by early 1786 when he was elected first senior deacon of the newly chartered Manchester Masonic Lodge.[37] Elliott and Austin could have been acquainted at least since 1782, especially if Gloriana, the Bates, and Moses lived in Durham until Gloriana's marriage. And if Austin and Elliott had become friends, then, it is just possible that Elliott had been the first of the two to settle at Richmond, had told Moses of the business opportunities there and thus was the catalyst behind Moses' move to Virginia. However that may be, it clearly is true that not only did Moses enjoy his relatives, but also something drew them to him. He was emerging as a patriarch.

In one way Moses already had taken up the role. On November 3, 1793, in Austinville his first son had been born. Named Stephen Fuller, undoubtedly for Moses' brother, Stephen, and for old Benjamin Fuller, the boy actually was the third child of Moses and Maria. Their second, Eliza Fuller, had died in Richmond in December, 1790, not quite eight months old. Then, on June 22, 1795, twenty-seven-year-old Maria bore their fourth child, Emily Margaret Brown.

By 1796, Moses' neighbors in Austinville and Wythe County, like his nephews and cousins, had begun to look on him as more than just the owner and director of the lead mines. On March 8, the County Court recommended him to the Governor for appointment as an officer in the local militia. Governor Robert Brooke put aside his long and unsatisfactory correspondence with Austin over the lead owed the State and issued the commission in July. By the time the appointment arrived, Moses had accepted the additional office of a justice on the local bench.[38]

That fall of 1796, Moses Austin passed his thirty-fifth birthday. Thirty-five can be a reflective time when people step back and review their lives to reassess their goals and the means by which they expect to achieve them. Moses would have had much to contemplate. During the preceding few years he had been to the heights, and seemingly to the depths, in his business pursuits. Moreover, he had developed a new facet of his character. To the driving businessman had been added a patriarchal element, fulfilling the upbringing of his traditional Congregationalist father. A close observer might have suspected that a new foundation had been laid, and wondered whether change was not imminent.

CHAPTER V

THE WINTER of 1796 struck the West with a fury. The temperature plunged to uncommon lows. For days on end clouds blocked the sun and blanketed the country with freezing rain and snow. Roads froze fast. Men and animals without shelter suffered terribly.[1] This was a winter, more than most, to stay near home and a comforting fire. But that, Moses Austin could not do. No longer would he remain at the mines watching events run their tortured course. It was time, he had decided—he, a maker of events, not a follower—time for bold action, time to seek new opportunity.

Moses had heard of fabulously rich lead mines across the Mississippi River in Spanish Upper Louisiana (modern Missouri). He first learned of them, his son Stephen later wrote, from a chance encounter "with a person who had been in the mining district to the west of Saint Genevieve...and who gave a favorable account of the prospects in that country..."[2] Surely, though, Moses must have known of them from the competition the Spanish lead gave his product in Kentucky and throughout the West. Moses' friend, Henry Schoolcraft, thought Moses said he learned of them through his association with Dr. Jedidiah Morse, America's first geographer. Even if true, Morse had not seen the mines with his own eyes, had no firsthand information, and in his book could only quote Sibley that Upper Louisiana "is a country equal to Kentucky, or any part of our western territory; and the lead and iron mines contained in it, render it a country of vast importance."[3] Until the fall of 1796, whatever Moses knew of the Spanish mines came to him secondhand at best.

That fall he came across a short description of Upper Louisiana written by a man who lived in and knew the country well. Writing for Americans and with the blessing of the Spanish authorities, Chevalier Pierre De Hault Delassus Deluzieres painted his country as a land of milk and honey: fertile acres, bumper crops, teeming forests, gurgling streams and "so far blessed, as to be exempt from chicanery & lawyers." Almost half way through the text Moses read the passage that captured his attention:

> There is in this country a great quantity of iron, lead and copper ores, and of stone coal; lead ore in particular, is so very abundant, that where they work it, they are generally at no other pains than to pick it up on the surface of the ground; this is about a day's journey from St. Genevieve.[4]

The description had to be faithful. It had been written only a few months before, in May, 1796, and had been endorsed by François Valle, Commandant of Ste. Genevieve. DeLassus Deluzieres's few words cemented Austin's determination to gamble his life on a trip of 2,000 miles through little-known country, much of it uncharted wilderness, all of it in the grip of this harsher than average winter, to see the mines for himself, as he later told Spanish authorities, "with the object of forming a big establishment there."[5]

Delassus Deluzieres's work may have appeared in newspapers in the United States before it was printed as a pamphlet. If Austin saw only the pamphlet, not published until October, it could have done no more than confirm his determination to visit Upper Louisiana. By that time, his plans for the trip were well advanced. On November 7, he thanked the widely connected Virginian John Preston for "Sundry letters" of introduction to gentlemen in Kentucky, including Isaac Shelby, a former governor.[6]

A month later, on the evening of December 8, 1796, Moses rode away from Austinville. Accompanied by Joseph Bell, one of his men from the Austinville mines, and a pack mule, Austin followed a route westward along the Wilderness Road and through the Cumberland Gap into Kentucky. Aside from the cold, the first few days passed routinely. To get relief from the biting temperatures, the travelers stopped at whatever accommodation appeared along the road at the end of the day, usually a private house. Some residents readily invited them in and offered to replenish their provisions. Others only tolerated them. Then, on their fifth day out, the snow falling heavily, they came to the cabin of Benedict Yancy at the head of a rugged road into Powell's Valley in Kentucky.

> The badness of the weather had made me Determin not to go any Further, . . . however I found it was not so Easy a matter to bring the old Man and Woman to think as I did; For when I demand.d or rather request.d leave to say, they absolutely refus.d me, saying, that we could go to a Hous six miles Down the Valley. Finding moderate words would not answer I plainly told Mr Yancy that I should not go any further, and that stay I would. Old Mrs Yancy had much to say about the liberties some Men take, and I replied by observing the Humanity of Others, and so end.d our dispute.

Once it had been settled that the travelers would remain for the night, "we soon Found ways and means to make the rough ways smooth." After a good supper, the weary Austin and Bell spread their blankets on the floor, stretched out with their feet toward the fire, and enjoyed a good night's rest.[7]

During the succeeding days the weather turned colder, or so it seemed. The two men were as prepared for it as travelers on horseback in a thinly settled country could be. Not everyone was. On the night of December 17,

after an especially unpleasant day during which Austin and Bell had
crossed several frigid streams, they stopped at a filthy hut measuring only
twelve feet square in which seventeen men, women, and children huddled
against the darkness and the elements. Moses slept little, unable himself
to get comfortable and uneasy for their mounts unprotected in the second
night of distressing cold. The people he encountered in the cabin and on
this stretch of his journey continued to crowd his memory until, three
months later, he poured out his wonder in what has become one of the
classic passages in the literature of the American frontier.

> I cannot omitt Noticeing the many Distress.d families I
> pass.d in the Wilderness nor can any thing be more distressing
> to a man of feeling than to see woman and Children in the
> Month of Decembr. Travelling a Wilderness Through Ice and
> Snow passing large rivers and Creeks with out Shoe or Stock-
> ing, and barely as maney raggs as covers their Nakedness,
> with out money or provisions except what the Wilderness
> affords, the Situation of such can better be Imagined then dis-
> cribed. to say they are poor is but faintly express'g there
> Situation, — life *What is it, Or What can it give*, to make Com-
> pensation for such accumulated Misery. Ask these Pilgrims
> what they expect when they git to Kentuckey the Answer is
> Land. have you any. No, but I expect I can git it. have you any
> thing to pay for land, No. did you Ever see the Country. No but
> Every Body says its good land. can any thing be more Absurd
> than the Conduct of man, here is hundreds Travelling hun-
> dreds of Miles, they Know not for what Nor Whither, except
> its to Kentucky, passing land almost as good and easy obtain.d,
> the Proprietors of which would gladly give on any terms, but it
> will not do its not Kentuckey its not the Promis.d land its not
> the goodly inheratence the Land of Milk and Honey. and when
> arriv.d at this Heaven in Idea what do they find? a goodly land I
> will allow but to them forbiden Land. exausted and worn down
> with distress and disappointment they are at last Oblig.d to
> become hewers of wood and Drawers of water.[8]

Hardly rested, Austin and Bell left the small house at daybreak and
trudged on. Over the next few days the numbing cold made it impossible
to maintain their pace of at least thirty miles per day. Stopping in Stanford,
a place of twenty-one houses, three stores, and four taverns, Austin found
several former friends from around Austinville, whose conversation light-
ened the burden of the trip. More importantly, he delivered his letter of
introduction to former Governor Shelby, who entertained him at dinner.
Before they parted, Shelby passed on the favor, giving Austin a letter of
introduction to Señor Argotee, the Spanish consul in Frankfort.

The bitterly cold weather made travel so difficult that it took Austin and Bell two days to cover the short distance to the capital. Upon their arrival, Austin went directly to Señor Argotee's house and laid before the consul his plans and hopes for the mines of Upper Louisiana. Austin's vision captured Argotee's imagination. The consul encouraged him by giving him strong letters of introduction to both Commandant Valle of Ste. Genevieve, who had endorsed the little pamphlet Austin had read, and to Zenon Trudeau in St. Louis, the Governor of Upper Louisiana. That single letter John Preston wrote Isaac Shelby had paid handsome dividends.

Likely Argotee explained to Austin, if the traveler had not learned already, that while Louisiana belonged to the King of Spain, the local officials whom he would meet, like Valle and Trudeau, all were of French extraction and actually had altered their ways and their local government imperceptibly since Spain had taken over the territory in 1763. French was the language Austin would need, not Spanish. That mattered little to Austin who knew neither.

On December 27, almost three weeks out of Austinville, Austin and Bell crossed the frozen Kentucky River, leaving Frankfort behind, on their way to Louisville. Moses would be glad to be out of the state, whose architecture offended his refined taste. The town of Shelby, where he spent the night of the twenty-seventh, was to his eye "small and like all the towns in Kentucky badly built." Louisville had potential and "By nature is beautifull." But, he continued, "the handy work of Man has insted of improving destroy.d the works of Nature and made it a detestable place."[9]

No sooner had they left Louisville and crossed the Ohio River, itself frozen nearly solid, than the weather turned yet worse. "A Very heavy snow fell in the night" and "so obscured the Trace" that the next morning "not a foot Step could be seen." The travelers were stymied. Finally someone told them that still they could find their way to Vincennes by following the blazes on the trees along the road. Progressing from mark to mark, they reached Vincennes on the 1st or 2nd of January, 1797, having survived the exposure of the journey of more than 140 miles from Frankfort in weather so cold they and their animals crossed every river but the Ohio on foot.

Vincennes pleased Austin as Louisville had not. Indeed, the practical Austin waxed poetic: "The God of this Comely land has been lavish in finishing his Work, for notwithstanding that the Sovereign hand of Winter had extended its Terrific Influence over all the face of Creation Yit inexpressable charmes could be discover.d which the severety of Winter could not change."[10]

Soon after he arrived and told the purpose of his trip, Austin was directed to the home of Monsieur Dubois, and his house guest, Mr. Henry, who, like Moses, was making his way toward the Mississippi River. Austin found Dubois, Henry, and friends eating. "I was unfortunate in not having letters to any Gentlm in Vincennes," Austin wrote later, "however the imbarisment I felt on this Account was soon remov.d by the Politeness of Mons Dubois who without ceremoney took me to the Table and placed me beside the Roman Priest."

Austin and Henry talked through the afternoon about the trip they wanted to make. As they conversed, more snow fell. The two knew full well that it "made the road not onely disagreeable but dangerous." Nevertheless, "Mr. Henry as well as myself came to a resolution, to undertake the Journey." Their companions at the table and those with whom they talked that evening at a ball all tried to dissuade them from their foolhardy plan. "The good people of Vincennes...said such a Journey with such a Debth of snow and such severe weather, had not been undertaken by any man, that the Open Country we had to pass was such as to render it Impossible to Keep the road with so large a body of Snow on the Ground." Neither man wavered. "Notwithstanding all that was said," Austin scrawled later, "I was fully determin.d to go forward." He had not come this far to spend the winter in Vincennes or to "think of returning with out Executing the plan I had in Vew."[11]

Austin and Henry used the next few days to recruit their strength, rest their animals, and make their preparations. Neither knew the way, but a Monsieur Basidon turned up saying he could pilot them through. Basidon looked like a guide: short, even by the compact Austin's measure, dressed half in European clothing, half in Indian, and carrying handy on his saddle-horn an old pistol and scalping knife. The travelers provided themselves "with such things as we thought we should want." Five days' rations under normal circumstances would be sufficient. Of course, with the snow cover they could not count on foraging and would have to carry everything they expected to need. Perhaps because Basidon was so confident of his abilities, perhaps because the going would be difficult enough for the animals in the deep snow without extra weight, they decided to pack only minimal provisions.[12]

On the morning of January 5, the party rode out of Vincennes and across the frozen Wabash River with Basidon on the point, Bell and the mule in the center, and Austin and Henry bringing up the rear. They made a scant six miles that day to the far bank of the Embarrass River, where "the great Debth of snow made some Trouble in fixing our Camp." But "after removeing the Snow and makeing a large fire," Austin recorded in his journal, "I found notwithstanding the Severety of the Night I rested well." They made thirty miles on the Sixth. But the farther they went, the deeper the snow became and the harder the going. They warded off the "pinching Cold" of that night with a blazing fire and bolstered their good spirits by eating. "As we had a plenty of provisions we thought it well to improve our time in eating as well as Travelling." Near noon on the Eighth,

Basidon announced that they had covered half the distance to Kaskaskia.[13] They were approximately on schedule.

There, as Austin saw later, "our good luck left us." Throughout the day as they crossed a broad plain, the wind pelted them with snow and sent thick waves of flakes cascading across the path before them and over the tracks behind them. They lost the road. Confident they would find it once they reached woods, they pushed on. But when they came to the trees, they found no way through. The four rode back and forth along the timber line, but could locate no trace of a road anywhere. Soon the day had been spent, and nothing more could be done than make camp. To make matters worse, at dinner they consumed the last of their provisions. With Basidon's anemic pistol the only firearm among them, they knew they had no hope of bringing down any game, the only available source of food that Austin could see. The men passed the darkness thinking about their suddenly serious situation.

The next morning, January 9, they decided to push forward. Basidon maintained adamantly that he knew their approximate position (though they had traveled only a third of their way, not half as he supposed) and insisted that he could make his way to Kaskaskia without any road. When the Frenchman set his course in a northwesterly direction, however, Austin objected. Kaskaskia, he contended, lay to the southwest of Vincennes, and as they had been traveling west and northwest, it had to be southwest of them yet. Austin, though correct in his belief, lacked the confidence of his conviction. They decided that Basidon must know best where they were and how to get where they were going. Austin's timidity very nearly cost him his life.

For two days they followed the guide's course, and for two days they appeared to get nowhere. All the while they became more conscious of their rising hunger. On the morning of the Eleventh, they came to a river, frozen over as all the others, that they took to be the Kaskaskia, and turned to follow its southwesterly course. Two days more they trudged along its bank, the depth of the snow steadily increasing until it reached an average of three feet.

For four days they had been without food. For four days they had seen no sign of a road – any road – or of a settlement, Indian or otherwise. "Our Situation became Truly distressing," Austin recalled. "About Sun Down it began to rain freezing as it fell. about 12 O Clock it turned to snow." To the four travelers, "this night Prov.d more disagreeable than any we had experienced." The light of morning revealed snow to "such a Debth that it was almost impossible to move. our Horses which suffer.d as much as ourselves was also doubley distress.d. the bushes was frost.d in such a manner that they could git nothing."[14] Austin's companions despaired.

Austin "did not like the state of things" either, but he maintained his composure. After all, they had their animals, if worst came to worst, on which they could subsist. But before they were reduced to that, he thought they could reach civilization. The terrain had changed. They had left the seemingly endless succession of prairies and groves of trees through which they had passed since departing Vincennes. Lately they had come into a country laced with small ridges. Most significantly, he thought, the creeks uniformly ran west. The Mississippi River must not be far. The four struggled to move and had not gone a mile when Whitesides Station appeared on the horizon. "Had the Everlasting Trumpet Sounded our Eternal happiness," Austin recalled his elation, "I do not think It would have been more Agreeable."[15]

At the little village, they learned just how lost they had been. Whitesides Station lay near Cahokia, across the Mississippi from St. Louis, and nowhere near Kaskaskia, sixty miles to the south. That being the case, and since Austin had Argotee's letter to Governor Trudeau, he decided to go to St. Louis first, then to the mines. The four left Whitesides in time to reach Cahokia before nightfall. The next morning, January 15, 1797, they would cross the River to meet the Governor.

Moses knew the value of a good first impression and prepared carefully for the meeting, Henry Schoolcraft reported Austin telling him in 1818. After crossing the river, Austin robed himself "in a long blue mantle, lined with scarlet and embroidered with lace." Taking the best horse among their mounts, and positioning his companions behind him, he entered St. Louis, a town of barely 900 residents, with "as much parade as possible." As he wished and expected, "so extraordinary a cavalcade, in a place so little frequented by strangers, and at such a season of the year, could not fail...to attract the particular attention of the local authorities." Trudeau sent an orderly to ascertain Austin's "character and rank," after which the Governor invited Austin and his party "to take up their residence at his house, observing, at the same time, in the most polite manner, and with characteristic deference to the rank of his guest, that there was no other house in town that could afford him suitable accommodations during his stay." And, Schoolcraft concluded the story, "the favourable impressions created by this entree, which Mr. Austin, in after life, related to his friends with inimitable glee, led on to his ultimate success."[16]

No doubt Moses did scheme to capitalize on the character traits of officials who valued pomp and circumstance and whose support he needed. No doubt, too, as Schoolcraft wrote, Austin placed "his chief reliance for success upon his own personal address—a qualification which he possessed in no ordinary degree."[17] But the tale Schoolcraft spread did not relate incidents recorded in Austin's journal of the trip, which Schoolcraft also had read.

After sunup on January 15, Austin wrote two months subsequently, he and Henry crossed the River—on the ice, as they had crossed every other stream since Vincennes. They left Bell and the mule behind, "beeing told there was not any Tavern" in St. Louis. They should not have been surprised. Taverns were hardly known in Upper Louisiana. In fact, Austin himself almost found no place to stay. "I beleave I should have been oblig.d to have returned to Kahokia the same Day had I not meet with a man by the name of Drake who spoke English and went with me to a Mons. Le Compt, who politely Took Mr. Henry and Myself into Hous."[18] Settled, the two travelers changed clothes, then paid their respects to Lieutenant Governor Trudeau to whom both had letters of introduction. Trudeau, forty-nine years old and one of the few American-born government officials in Upper Louisiana, did treat them politely "and promisd us all the assistence the Nature of our business Demanded." To start with, he gave Austin a letter to François Valle, asking Valle to provide Austin a guide to the mines. Afterward, Austin sought out Charles Gratiot, a leading merchant of long standing in St. Louis, to whom he also had a letter of introduction. Fortunately for Austin, who knew no French, Gratiot spoke English fluently. Moreover, he took the time to talk with Austin at length about the trade of the community.[19]

On January 19, Austin finally met François Valle in Ste. Genevieve, a settlement older and slightly larger than St. Louis. Two or three years Austin's senior, the firstborn of the wealthiest family in the area, Valle was confident of his position, though he had been civil and military commandant less than a year. After Austin explained his mission, Valle placed at his disposal "a *Carry all* and Two Horses" with which he left for the mines on Saturday, January 21.[20]

Beside Austin rode a new traveling companion, John Rice Jones of Kaskaskia. Of Valle's age, small like Austin, and dignified, Jones had been in the Illinois-Louisiana country for more than a decade. With a quick mind and a forceful manner, he had no peer in any courtroom west of the Allegheny Mountains. Unquestionably he was among the most cosmopolitan figures on the frontier, being Welch-born, an Oxford graduate in both medicine and law, and fluent in English, French, and Spanish. It was true, too, that Jones had an uncanny knack for forging strong acquaintances with the prominent men of his time and place. How he and Austin came together—whether while both lived in Philadelphia in 1784-1785; or through mutual acquaintances in Vincennes, where Jones lived for some years; or by a chance encounter in Kaskaskia, where he resided in 1797; or simply because Jones could converse with Austin and translate—may never be known. However it was, they struck up a quick and long-lasting friendship.[21]

The two men took two days to travel the forty miles to the mines through the tree-covered but otherwise desolate hills. If the snow were not

John Rice Jones. *Missouri Historical Society.*

too deep, Austin's anticipation would have been especially aroused as he neared the end of his long journey. In the last twelve or so miles of the approach to the mine region, he wrote a few years later, the land "exhibits strong appearances of mineral."[22] As they topped the last ridge, Austin and Jones would have looked out over a "delightful valley, of small extent," bisected by a meandering "stream of the purest water." In a large open field on the other side of Breton Creek lay the mines.[23]

The creek and the mines both bore the name of François Azor dit Breton, the French soldier and hunter who had discovered the lead deposits a quarter century earlier while stalking a deer. Running after his quarry, Breton, as he had become known, tripped on a rock and fell. Gathering himself, he looked carefully at the rock and realized it to be a block of lead. Or, so the other story goes, he discovered the mineral when he noticed that what he took to be a tree root beside his camp fire melted.[24]

However he discovered it, Breton had happened onto one of the richest lead deposits in the world. Delassus, Austin found, had been accurate in his description of the place. Large pieces of lead did lie scattered on the ground. What was better, immediately below the surface and in a strata perhaps four feet thick, lay a "gravel mineral" with chunks of lead "in pieces from 1 to 50 pounds weight of solid mineral." A distinctive sand rock strata five to six feet thick beneath the gravel held "mineral nearly of the same quality." And below that, at a depth of approximately ten feet and for how far down no one knew, Austin found a third strata—a bed of red clay—that contained "mineral of the first quality...in pieces from ten to five hundred pounds weight."[25] In the valley, the bluish-gray mineral lay so shallow that heavy rains and freshets washed it up. "It is not uncommon," Austin wrote some years later, "to find in the draughts leading to creeks and rivers, and in gullies made by the spring rains, mineral in pieces from ten to fifty pounds weight brought down by the torrents."[26]

Austin marveled. Unbelievably abundant, the ore in these mines was, moreover, of "better quality than any I have ever seen either from the Mines in England or America."[27] With such good mineral so easily obtained, every miner worked his own excavation. Each dug a circular hole around himself straight down, recovering chunks of lead as he went. When, at a depth of about ten feet, the tailings began to fall back into the hole on him, the miner scrambled out, moved to another site, and began again. In the twenty-five years since Breton discovered the place, holes, one beside another, had been sunk over an area of about forty acres.[28] The field must have looked like it had been the target of an intense artillery barrage.

Around the area Austin found twenty stone furnaces, similar in appearance to limekilns, that the French miners used to extract the lead from their ore. As Schoolcraft pictured them, these box-shaped, stone structures had three sides, a floor, and were built on a slope so that the molten lead would run into a groove in the floor of the furnace, out an opening at the front, and into molds formed in the earth. When a sufficiency of ore had been accumulated—usually 3,000 to 5,000 pounds—the men covered the floor of the furnace with the largest logs they could find, shoveled the mineral onto the logs and surrounded the pile with wood. The pyre was then set ablaze and kept burning "until the mineral is entirely smelted, burnt or lost in the ashes." From 1,000 pounds of ore, about 350 pounds of lead drained into the molds. The process was crude and wasteful, but, with ore so plentiful, no one thought about the loss.[29]

It was the smelting process that Austin focused on particularly during his visit to the mines. His workers could dig the ore no more efficiently than the French miners. But if he could improve the smelting and recover a greater quantity of lead from the ore, then he could realize more product from the same amount of work. Austin conducted an experiment which, "If I was rightly informed as to the quantity of Ore they Took to make a 1000 lb Lead in the Logg fires," showed that by his methods three times as much lead could be obtained from the same amount of ore. In addition, Austin tested the ashes discarded from the furnaces. He found the slag so rich in lead that as much again could be obtained from it by his process as the French had realized from the original ore.

Austin's stay on Breton Creek ended abruptly when the weather suddenly turned warm. He and Jones thought it best to return to Ste. Genevieve without delay. Nevertheless, from his couple of days in the valley, Austin had "found the Mines Equal to my Expectation in Every respect," and he rode away "Satisfied...as to the Object I had in vew."[30]

The very day he reached Ste. Genevieve, January 26, Austin went to work to secure the mines for himself. He composed a lengthy memorial to the Governor General of Louisiana, the Baron de Carondelet in New Orleans, asking that the mine property be granted to him. "Great and incalculable advantages," Austin told the governor, "will result from a methodic and more fruitful working of the lead mines." From intense development of *these* mines alone, Austin prophesied, he could supply His Catholic Majesty, the King of Spain, with "all the lead in rolls which he will need for the service of his navel forces in his colonies." Moreover, Austin would bring to Louisiana the Englishmen who had so greatly improved his Virginia operation. These miners were "the only ones of their kind which exist in the United States of America." Fully capable of manufacturing lead "following the ordinary method," they also could produce Watt's Shot "as in England,... a process very well thought of in all Europe and known exclusively by said Watt's Company and the supplicant." (Reduced to its simplest terms, Watt's process produced shot by dropping molten lead through a sieve and letting the friction of the air form it into balls.) Finally, in time, of course, some of Austin's men would leave his employ and establish works of their own. By spreading his methods to other mines and combining their output with his, Austin concluded, the lead manufactured in this single colony "will amply fulfill the needs of Spain."

For his part, Austin asked to be given sixteen leagues, approximately 70,000 acres, in a square centered on the mines, so that he could "establish, on a large scale, the manufacture of lead in all of its branches, such as in sheets, in shot, in rolls, white lead and black lead." Since the Spanish government, to encourage actual settlement, normally granted only one league to one person in one place at one time, Austin told the governor that "three powerful considerations" required this extensive domain for him. First, the smelting fires consumed huge quantities of wood, which only a large expanse could sustain. Second and third, Austin needed land he could distribute precisely to attract actual settlers: farmers, millers, and various other artisans to sustain the miners. Austin knew from his experience in Virginia that to work mines intensively in an isolated place, he must develop a complete, virtually self-sufficient settlement.[31]

Unfortunately, the sixteen leagues encompassed several small parcels already granted to French miners. Several of them had built cabins along the south bank of Breton Creek in a cluster large enough to be known as "The Village." Among the structures stood quite substantial buildings,

such as Basil Valle's five-year-old, two-story dwelling and office. Frenchmen had been mining the Breton discovery for a quarter century and considered their tenure permanent.

Austin harbored no motive "to injure the rights of others," he declared.
But he did "have the formal intention of peacefully dispossessing the
grantees of their said lands unless it can be arranged in a friendly and vol-
untary manner with them."[32] To him, it was a matter of developing the
potential of the mines. Despite the richness of the lead deposits, few of the
French were interested: only 17 of the 125 families in Ste. Genevieve in
1791 engaged in mining. Many of those 17 were merchants who hired others to do the digging. Since the employers had to supply provisions as well
as wages, the enterprise yielded a poor return, a return all the more modest because the French normally worked the mines only four months of
the year. The 40 to 50 seasonal miners came around the end of August,
after harvest, and stayed until December when winter drove them back to
Ste. Genevieve. Nor were the French likely to do more at the mines,
because the fierce Osage Indians, who still controlled the back country,
discouraged the thought of greater activity.[33]

The Governor General had a clear choice, as Austin saw it. He could
reject Austin's bid and achieve "no other result than absorption of a real
loss of a large quantity of mineral."[34] Or he could grant the territory and,
on Austin's enterprise, with lead from Upper Louisiana, supply the needs
of the King's Caribbean fleet, and later of all Spain.

Weighing in Austin's favor in 1797, as would not have been the case even
a year earlier, was Spain's fear of England. In 1795, Spain had concluded a
peace with France and, in return, incurred the wrath of Great Britain, her
former ally. Spain feared retaliation. Upper Louisiana, so close to the
English in Canada, appeared especially vulnerable. The most effective
deterrent to attack, Governor General Carondelet decided, was a sizeable
population. And the best, quick source of people was the United States,
with whom Spain had recently signed a treaty particularly popular west of
the Appalachian Mountains. Thus, not a year before Austin submitted his
memorial, the Spanish had reversed themselves and begun encouraging
immigration from the United States. They offered a special inducement to
Americans: land for the settling at no greater expense than minimal fees
and taxes. It was a far more liberal arrangement than the $2 hard cash per
acre that the American government demanded for its public domain.
When Carondelet visited Upper Louisiana in 1796, he instructed Delassus
"to invite inhabitants of the United States, not hunters, but those who had
families and great means, to settle in his district, and to grant them as
much land as they wanted." Thus Delassus wrote his pamphlet.[35] Whether
or not he knew it, Austin had come at the right time.

What he did know full well was that he more likely would get what he wanted if people with contacts took an interest in his venture. Once again the timing was perfect. Two of the most prominent men of the region needed someone like him just then. In 1793, Delassus, a personal friend of Carondelet, had contracted to furnish 30,000 pounds of lead to the Spanish military in New Orleans for five years. In 1795, Commandant Valle and his brother, Jean Baptiste, joined Delassus in the contract. But when their first shipment arrived in New Orleans in 1796, the new Intendent, Don Juan Ventura Morales, insisted on weighing it by the larger Spanish scale, not the smaller French measure they had used. The quantity fell short, and this unexpected turn of events "made the contract difficult to fulfill."[36]

François Valle must have told his colleague Delassus of Austin while the Virginian toured the mines, for Austin found both men waiting when he and Jones returned to Ste. Genevieve on January 26. All four talked and readily concurred. Contingent on the granting of the memorial Austin already had prepared, they would form a partnership under the name of Moses Austin and Company, with Moses holding a half interest and managing the firm's affairs, "to exploit the said mines and to establish therein the manufacture of lead."[37] Austin agreed to bring 3,000 piastres-worth of goods and his miners as part of his half of the 8,000-piastre capital. Jones's and Valle's 2/10ths interests each and Delassus's 1/10th apparently represented operating capital. At least the men were to reimburse Austin's expenses in proportion to their interests in the company. Austin made his partners promise to have no other mining interest as long as they participated in his company. Agreed, they wrote it down and signed the document that same day.[38]

The deal was completed the following day when Commandant Valle gave Austin a paper promising land to the thirty families of farmers and tradesmen Austin planned to bring. Austin probably did not know that Valle lacked authority to make such awards of lands. But then, the entire arrangement hinged on the action of the Governor General anyway. The value of Valle's certificate would be cosmetic in stirring families to come with Austin, if Austin came.[39]

His work done, his hopes riding on the memorial he and his partners had drafted to send to Carondelet, Austin paid a social call on his new associate, DeLassus, in New Bourbon, two miles south of Ste. Genevieve,[40] then crossed the Mississippi River to Kaskaskia to confer with Jones before leaving for home. For some reason he had not before heard a translation of the partnership agreement as it had been committed to paper in French and signed after the four men reached verbal accord on the Twenty-sixth. Jones translated, and Austin listened in vain for a statement that the lead-rich ashes from the French furnaces would belong to the partners. Austin lost his temper. He had been "thinking that if the mineral digging should not turn out profitable he should . . . be able to save himself" by smelting the ashes. Indeed, he told Jones sternly, those ashes had been his "principal reliance, his only inducement. . . to make the arrangement." It was for them that he risked "property to be employed without any obligation on the part of the other partners in case of loss before it should arrive at Ste. Genevieve, to indemnify him—and to give up a part of the profits that might arise from the said property." Jones replied that the other two partners had not believed the ashes of much value and had omitted mention of them. He promised to remedy the misunderstanding, and Austin left on February 8, no doubt wondering whether the arbitrary action of his colleagues, and his failure to find it out on the Twenty-sixth, would haunt him later.[41]

By the time Moses reached Austinville a month later on March 9, 1797, he knew that he had done something historic, had seen two thousand miles of country as it would never be seen again. During the succeeding two weeks, he wrote a thirty-eight-page journal of his trip "for the Use of my son, should he live to my Age, Not Doubting but by that time the Country I have pass.d in a state of Nature will be overspread with Towns and Villages, for it is Not possible a Country which has with in its self everything to make its settlers Rich and Happy can remain Unnotice.d by the American people."[42] Keen-eyed and prophetic, Austin produced a document that stands as one of the premier records of the great westward surge of the American people in which he participated.

Two months after he arrived in Austinville, Moses left again, this time with Maria for Philadelphia to arrange affairs with Stephen. Without delay the brothers disengaged from their partners, in particular from Thomas Ruston whose disheveled accounts presaged his total collapse and bankruptcy four years later, and from John D. Blanchard, who staved off bankruptcy two years longer than Ruston. This may have been the juncture when they severed connections with partner John Field, who followed Blanchard by only a month into bankruptcy court. It would take far more than separation of interests, however, to calm the restless financial situation around the Austins. Their account with Ruston showed just how precarious their own financial status remained. Poor sales combined with substantial expenses on improvements during the preceding three years had resulted in losses totaling not less than £3,312. "The State of the Companys finances here," Stephen wrote from Philadelphia in June, 1797, "are such as demand the greatest Exertion. . . by Every Possible Means to Raise Money. . . to Discharge Several Most Pressing Demand for Cash."[43] Stephen's own accounts, weighed with debts from former business transactions, only intensified his anxiety. To raise the badly needed capital as quickly as possible—"to Induce Purchasers to come forward," as Stephen phrased it—they advertised lead delivered anywhere in the country for cash at prices cut by as much as half.[44]

Despite it all, they maintained confidence in their future, and justifiably so. Not only did they anticipate a most lucrative venture in Upper Louisiana, but their operation in Virginia "had attained to such excellence," Stephen said later, "as to flatter...[him] with a prospect of complete success."[45]

In this spirit, the brothers on June 15 dissolved their former separate businesses to create "the firm of Stephen and Moses Austin" to conduct the two ventures. Moses, of course, would take charge of the Spanish mines. They agreed, too, that whatever lands he "or any other person of his family" might obtain would be counted as property of the concern. He was to leave the Virginia works "under the direction [of] Confidential Persons," and drawing on his family circle, as could have been expected, he selected their cousin James, Jesse Austin's son, for the job. Completing the arrangement, Moses and Stephen decided to liquidate this partnership and divide their assets two and a half years later, on January 1, 1800, at the dawn of the new century.[46]

The work done, Moses and Maria planned to leave Philadelphia during the first week of July. But sometime after the brothers reached their accord, they turned once more to their financial situation and shortly fell to quarreling over their strained accounts. The longer they talked, the more tense their conversations became. On June 24, Stephen presented Moses with a litany of unsettled accounts Stephen held against him. Dating to their first transaction—that loan in October, 1782, which Moses took to get into his first business—and including expenses on furniture, clothing, and carriages, gilding a watch, monies paid on Moses' bills, and, finally, interest Stephen had been calculating over the past fifteen years, Stephen computed that as of June 24, 1797, Moses owed him £762 15s 10p. The brothers argued for a month. By July 20, when they signed an understanding, they could agree only to adjust their balances of monies actually spent. The accumulated interest lay completely beyond accord. Even accounts of actual expenses could not be finally settled, because essential books were at Austinville. Consequently they decided that Moses would deed to Stephen two tracts at the Virginia mines valued at $3,666. Unless Moses sent Stephen sufficient money (an amount unspecified) within nine months to discharge the debts, Stephen could then sell the land and apply the proceeds to the obligation. Should the property sell for less than book value, Moses would owe Stephen the difference, and vice versa. The deal offered a way out of their dispute, but, as they must have known, only postponed the reckoning. The quarrel was bound to simmer over whatever sum the tracts commanded and thus over who owed whom. If by the time they dissolved their partnership two and a half years later they still could not agree between themselves, they would submit their dispute to arbitration. The once close brothers cemented their now hostile distrust of one another by binding each other "in the Sum of Six thousand Dollars to be paid by the Party who Shall not Comply with the Spirit and Interest of this agreement."[47]

We can only surmise what triggered their bitter falling out in July, 1797. To some extent it probably began brewing as they stretched their financial resources to make the exceptionally heavy investments in personnel and improvements at the mines. Likely it was aggravated by the recession in 1796-1797. Perhaps, though, it was then, for the first time, they glimpsed that more than likely they could never pull themselves out. On June 14, the day before they finished shaping their new firm, Congress suddenly dropped the duty on all lead and lead products. Without protection, the price of American lead was bound to fall. Rescinding the tariff "gave an opening to such large importations of those articles," Stephen recalled, "that they fell from 180 to 100 dollars per ton." The effect on the nation's largest lead producer of this 45 percent drop in prices, though it material-ized over a period of time, was devastating. "This unexpected event," said Stephen, "blasted" their promise in Virginia.[48]

Through July and August, Moses awaited news from Upper Louisiana. Finally in September, it came in a letter from Commandant Trudeau. The grant had been awarded, but for one league only – about 4,250 acres – covering merely one-third of the mines. Under his circumstances, Moses decided that would do.

The Governor General, Trudeau continued, required Austin to establish his lead works within a year of the time Trudeau's letter reached him. Since the grant had been made in March, six months before he learned of it, Austin took steps to claim his new property as quickly as possible. In early December he dispatched Judather Kendal and Elias Bates with at least three wagons of goods and supplies, seven men and a crude map to take possession of the property, to lay out the settlement he planned, to construct a furnace, mills, and other buildings, and to begin sinking a mine shaft. There would be no question that he had met the deadline.

Thereafter, during the first months of 1798, Moses devoted himself to assembling the supplies, equipment, and provisions he would need both for the trip and to establish his community on Breton Creek. Some items he would take from Virginia, but he bought $4,600-worth new. In May, as wagons lumbered back and forth taking his goods to the Boat Yard on the Kanawha River, Moses concluded his tenure in Virginia by disposing of several tracts, as well as of his right to operate the ferry over New River.[49]

On June 8, 1798, Moses left Austinville for the last time, with a caravan of a coach and four horses, nine loaded wagons, and forty men, women, and children. He, his wife, five-year-old son, and three-year-old daughter; his brother-in-law, Moses Bates, with his wife and two sons; plus workers and slaves – all boarded a flatboat on the Kanawha to float to Ste. Genevieve.

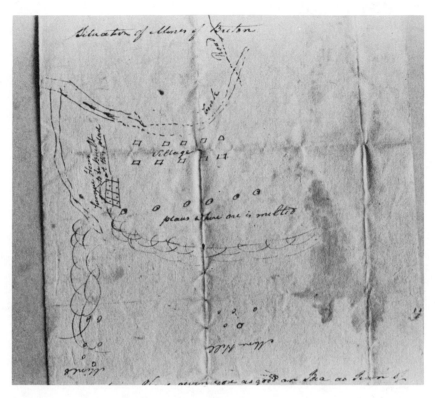

Mine a Breton, 1797. Austin gave this rough sketch of the Mine a Breton location to Judather Kendal and Elias Bates in December, 1797, to guide them in taking control of his grant. *Austin Papers, Barker Texas History Center.*

The three-month trip proved hard and costly. Moses Bates lost his entire family. Son Henry drowned as they passed the treacherous falls of the Ohio River at Louisville. His wife, Martha (Moses' sister), and their son Parsons "paid the debt of Nature," as Moses phrased it, elsewhere along the way. Of the seventeen persons remaining on board on September 7 when the barge nosed into the mud at Kaskaskia, only two could walk ashore. For twelve days they recuperated. Finally, on October 1, 1798, four days before his thirty-seventh birthday, Moses moved them across the Mississippi River to take up their new life in a new land and a new country.[50]

CHAPTER VI

M OSES AUSTIN chafed to push the work at Mine a Breton. He had given his advance party under Elias Bates and Judather Kendal lengthy instructions for occupying and preparing the concession for his arrival. He directed the men to begin building the structures needed both to carry on the lead business and to provide for the colony Austin would plant on Breton Creek to sustain the miners. At the same time, Moses wanted the crew to secure all the lead slag they could for smelting in his furnace. Finally, he ordered the men to inaugurate the mining operation by sinking a shaft past the customary ten- to fifteen-foot level. As quickly as Moses could settle his household after all reached Ste. Genevieve, he left for the mines to take personal charge of his men and their industry.[1]

Much had been accomplished in the six months since Bates and Kendal had led their party into the Breton Creek valley to establish Austin's settlement – the first permanent white settlement west of and back from the banks of the Mississippi River within the present State of Missouri. On April 5, 1798, the very day they took possession of the place, the half-dozen men went to work, Bates wrote later, cutting timber for a furnace house and mills and beginning to make brick with which to build the furnace itself. They worked feverishly through the summer to prepare the site for Austin and the rest of his followers.

The furnace house, the most important single business building at the mines, was to be located, by Austin's explicit instructions, "at the lower end of the [French] Village. . . at the point of the Road that goes to the Mines."[2] Moses directed his men to make the structure nearly square, its dimensions approximately 30 by 38 feet under a 12-foot ceiling. He wrote nothing of the design he preferred for the building, but one way or another Bates and Kendal knew that Austin meant for his community not to be plain, dull, and "badly finished," as were all those other isolated, frontier settlements he had passed through on his trip a year earlier. Austin must have expected something special in the furnace house in particular, since it would shelter the facility that would set his mining operation apart from all the others in Spanish Louisiana. What his men produced was a work of art. On the well-proportioned building, they placed a gable roof dressed with a cupola, itself crowned by a flowing bird-shaped weathervane. The furnace house probably had been completed by the time Moses arrived in October, though the furnace itself would not be ready for two months more.

Mine a Breton, 1799. This earliest drawing of Austin's settlement, prepared in August, 1799, shows a frontier community remarkable for the cultivation of its architecture, not "badly finished" as all those others of which Austin had complained. In the ramshackle sketches of the sturdy French cabins, the plat exudes the contempt in which the Americans held the French. *Mapas y Planos #198, Archivo General de Indias.*

Austin's men built a manager's house, probably occupied first by Kendal, and a house for the workmen. They started, or at least located sites for, buildings to house a blacksmith shop, saw and grist mills, a shot factory, and a distillery that two of them were to fashion in Kaskaskia and bring to the mines ready to operate. If all the structures had not begun to rise by the time Austin arrived in the fall of 1798, construction began soon after, for all had been completed by the summer of 1799.[3]

Likely the crew awaited Austin's coming to commence work on the building that would serve him as both home for his family and headquarters for his business. It would be no ordinary house. Moses Austin meant to make a statement to all who beheld the place. For the site, he chose a location across Breton Creek from the French village and almost directly opposite the furnace house. Because the ground on the north side of the stream fell at a significant angle down to the water, he made a level place large enough for a house and yard by creating a huge fill fronting on, and rising six or eight feet above, the bank. Around the fill he put a wall two feet thick, perhaps more, of stones so carefully dressed and laid that, without mortar, one section remains in place to this day. On his eminence, Austin positioned his house to look out over the French village to the south and the furnace house and mines to the southwest.

In a country in which people clustered in settlements and huddled behind palisades for protection against the marauding Osage Indians, most men building on his scale would have built for defense. Not Moses Austin. He erected a mansion. Two rooms deep and three wide, two-and-a-half-stories tall, the frame house had large sash windows, was buttressed by a pair of chimneys on the back, and sported a circular window in the front gable. Styled in the tradition of genteel, settled Virginia, the tasteful manor house replaced the furnace house as the architectural gem of the settlement, indeed, of the Mississippi River watershed above Natchez. No line of the design resembled the New England house in which Austin had been reared. But Moses remembered Durham, and when, like the aristocrats of Virginia, he named his seat, Moses called it "Durham Hall."[4]

Everything about the house, including the staff of slaves to maintain it, testified that during his ten years in Virginia Austin had adopted the ways of the Southern upper class as his own. The slaves were a clear sign. Moses had bought his first, for the luxury of having house servants, less than two years after he settled in Richmond. Soon after he acquired the Virginia mines, he put blacks to work there as well.[5] If Moses' taste explained the style of Durham Hall, his manner answered for its being raised on a coarse frontier. By all measures, an elegant house like Durham Hall was out of place on this rawest edge of civilization. But in his house, as in his bearing, Moses Austin exhibited an audacity and a brazen self assurance pronounced even for Americans of that day.

Durham Hall, 1799. This sketch was drawn two months after Austin and his family occupied the house. It is enlarged from a drawing of Mine a Breton made in August, 1799. *Mapas y Planos #198, Archivo General de Indias.*

The brashness and audacity that Austin cultivated, his new neighbors scorned. Temperamentally the French and the Americans had little in common. The vivacious French, who had established their ways in Upper Louisiana more than half a century before the Americans came, lived more to enjoy life than to make money. "The want of industry" and "indolence" are what the Americans called it. To the French it was working enough to provide a sufficient livelihood. Most lived by the land. To those few who worked the mines, lead never provided more than a small supplement to their agricultural or mercantile living. As a people, they valued neatness, refinement, and culture, paid great deference to men in positions of power, and were "never more happy," observed the first American governor after the Louisiana Purchase, "than released from apprehension of a legal process." A strong sense of pride and vanity, he continued, combined in them into "a high sense of honor, to render them honest in their dealings...."[6] Many, like Commandant Valle, embraced the ideals of the American Revolution and supported the American cause. Most, also like him, later recoiled at the impatient and uncouth Americans who swarmed across the Mississippi in the closing years of the eighteenth century.[7] The seeds of conflict lay everywhere. Avoiding a collision called for tolerance and understanding on both sides. Moses Austin might compromise on some things, but not on his concession.

A portion of the wall around Durham Hall. This section of the original wall, from below the porch, still may be seen in Potosi. *Photograph by the author.*

By the time Moses reached the mines in the fall of 1798, trouble was brewing. He wanted the lead slag discarded from the French furnaces. Since the grant had not mentioned the scoria, his partner, John Rice Jones, was to have obtained official blessing for Moses having it. Moses presumed Jones had succeeded, but directed Kendal, nevertheless, to "Demand of the Commandant to Know if I am not to have all I finde on the ground." Whatever the answer, Kendal was to "give all the Hands absolute Orders not to say a word as to the Value of the Ore about the Old Workings for If they say much about the Value of the Ore It may make trouble for me."[8]

Perhaps one of them talked. Jones accused Valle. However it happened, by the time Austin arrived, the previously useless lead cinders at Mine a Breton had become valuable, at least to the extent that the French miners went out of their way to keep them from Austin's men. On September 27, 1798, fourteen Frenchmen signed an agreement donating their slag to Pierre Vial. A trailblazer who made his mark in history by opening routes between Santa Fe and San Antonio, Natchitoches, and St. Louis, Vial came to Upper Louisiana for the third time in 1797, disaffected by the ingratitude of the Spanish government in New Mexico.[9] He was a good blacksmith, but lacked both expertise and facilities to produce lead from the scoria. The local miners had bested Austin by giving the appearance of

François Valle. *Missouri Historical Society.*

legality to their action.

Moses wanted to see Valle. Jones agreed to accompany him since Valle could not converse in English. Austin understood little of what his two partners said, but there was no mistaking that they disagreed. The longer they talked, the more heated they became. Nothing was settled by the meeting. Jones and Austin left for the mines, where, on Jones's advice, Austin informed Baptiste Valle, the commandant's brother, that he claimed the cinders and "should contend for them."[10]

Then fate presented Austin a second opportunity to talk with Valle, when Dr. John Watkins of St. Louis, to whom Austin confessed his plight of feuding partners, offered to translate. During the meeting, Valle blamed Jones for the misunderstanding about the cinders. Jones had mentioned something about the ashes to him, Valle admitted, but never had made their possession a condition of the partnership. Valle had no reason to consider them of value, he contended, and consequently "had thought no more on that subject."[11] Had Jones only impressed on Valle the importance of the scoria, he would have secured it for Austin.

Valle then loosed his wrath on Jones. The reason Valle had reserved the right to withdraw from the partnership, he declared, was because Jones had been brought in. The French community despised Jones, and if Austin were wise, Valle continued, he would dissolve his connection with him.

Vehement, Valle announced that he intended to remain in the partnership no longer and, furthermore, that "no confirmation of the grant...could ever be expected so long as an alien [Jones] was concerned."[12] The Commandant could afford to indulge his anger and threaten Austin, because he had nothing to lose. The Napoleonic Wars had frustrated his and DeLassus's plans to sell their lead in Europe, and DeLassus had lost his contract to furnish lead to the Spanish government. By the time Austin arrived in Spanish Louisiana, Valle no longer needed him.[13]

Though the meeting apparently ended after Valle's angry outburst, his mention of Austin's grant no doubt touched a raw nerve. Austin felt betrayed by his partner. When Bates arrived in April, 1798, he found "all sorts of people [being allowed] to work in the mine at Breton and to deplete it of the Best it contained Without paying any attention to the Concession" granted Austin. Bates protested to Valle, but to no effect. The next month he appealed to Lieutenant Governor Trudeau "for an extension of his [Austin's] acreage with an order to stop the Plundering made daily On the Petitioner's Concession." Still nothing was done. When Austin arrived in the fall, he was shocked to find the French still working sites on what he considered his property. "It is impossible," he wrote in the third person, "...to express his astonishment when he found that Even though the honor of the Government was committed to put him into the immediate possession of the property Granted...,the Commander of St. Genevieve allowed" the illicit digging to continue.[14] To Austin this was not just a breach of contract. In Philadelphia, on July 13, 1797, he had obtained a passport signed by the Spanish Ambassador to the United States, and "from that very moment I considered myself as Spanish citizen," Austin wrote his partner DeLassus.[15] The violation of his concession was in Austin's eyes a breach of faith with a loyal citizen.

The problem was that the concession did not specify boundaries for Austin's league. "I do not Know," Valle confessed, "Whether or not this concession can be granted to him [Austin] in the places occupied by the living miners, who have been exploiting the said mine for 15 or 20 years."[16] The French miners thought not. Before Austin came, they could mine and smelt ore almost wherever they pleased. Some based their right to mine on the act of settlement—building cabins and cultivating gardens for their support while digging. Others had obtained formal concessions. J. St. G. Beauvais obtained a grant in 1788 for 60 feet in radius from every hole he might dig at Mine a Breton. Austin's partner DeLassus concurred that the French, by prior occupancy, had the better claim and told Austin he never interpreted Austin's original petition otherwise. Unless Austin agreed to a clear line separating his concession from the long-established common mining ground, DeLassus addressed him bluntly, "I foresee some very great difficulties...Think about that which my friendship and my attachment to you and your interests have me tell you here disguisedly."[17]

Austin stood firm. His concession, as he understood it, gave him a league to be located wherever he wished at Mine a Breton, and he claimed the rich public land where all had been digging. Austin might be a Spanish citizen, but he still thought like a New Englander. Moses, as his forebears, believed it a simple matter that those who were of greater economic benefit to the country should have a larger share of the property. And he felt in his own mind that he would make better use of the property than all the French put together.

The increasingly bitter dispute fed on the inability of Moses and the French miners to communicate. Because of the language barrier, Austin told DeLassus, "One had no difficulty at all to convince them I was greedy man who wanted to invade everything and depossess them from their properties. How could I have suspected such circumstances, since I had no other intentions than to enjoy what had been promised to me without giving trouble in the property of anybody."[18]

Conceding no ground to Austin, the French miners showed their contempt initially by disregarding his claim. They dug where they always had, and they dug on new locations within the boundaries he asserted. Shortly the dispute turned mean. The French began cutting the saplings around Austin's mills to deprive him of wood for his furnaces. Reminiscent of their ploy with the cinders, they marked off plots and sold them to each other. Even Americans who had come to the country after Austin's concession had been granted, men with no stake in the province, Austin complained to the lieutenant governor, joined in the buying and selling. Finally, the French petitioned the Governor General to revoke Austin's grant on the grounds that he "had attempted to deprive the people of Ste. Genevieve of the employment of their long established privileges" at Mine a Breton.[19] The only way to resolve the dispute was to survey Austin's concession and mark his boundaries. Governor Trudeau on January 14, 1799, ordered that the survey be run. Two months passed. The vandalism continued. Trudeau then promised the work in April.[20]

In March, Jones convinced Austin that they should talk with Valle about his participation in the partnership. Valle had been a partner for more than two years but had paid nothing toward his share of the capital. On March 13, 1799, after Austin had recovered from a bilious fever that had confined him to his house for weeks, he and Jones went to see the Commandant. The meeting must have been stormy, for it ended when Valle withdrew from the partnership.[21] April passed without a survey.

The unpleasantness probably made Austin all the more eager to rush completion of Durham Hall and move to the mines. For more than a year, he and his family had been living in Ste. Genevieve in a cabin that Moses had bought for $200 in 1798, not long after they had arrived. The property was well located, only a stone's throw south of Commandant Valle's home on the other side of the main road between St. Louis and New Madrid. The clear, cool South Gabouri Creek gurgling in its limestone bed marked the south boundary. Austin occupied the place for a few months before he recorded his purchase. But two years elapsed before he discovered to his dismay that Amable Partnais dit Mason, from whom he had acquired the property, never had obtained a concession to the land. Austin had no valid title. He asked Valle to grant the concession to him, which apparently the Commandant did. Though the incident cost Moses nothing more than the energy to rectify it, he never became accustomed to the lackadaisical attitude toward land titles that characterized his new neighbors.[22]

By the time he had cleared his title, Moses no longer occupied the cabin. In June, 1799, with the boundaries of his concession at Mine a Breton still unsettled, but Durham Hall at last finished, Moses moved his wife and children—Stephen, five-and-a-half years old, and Emily, then just turning four—into the grand mansion overlooking the creek. Events suggest that this only provoked the militants among the French miners. Three, including Vial, moved onto Austin's property near his house, put up "a hut to live in, as it has been practiced by all the other miners," and built a furnace to smelt lead ashes.[23] Not content with that, they "wronged and threatened him and blocked his roads." Austin complained over Valle's head to the lieutenant governor and obtained his order to protect Austin against the abuse. But there was a stipulation. With his boundaries still in dispute, Austin must agree "that those who are there may stay there until they have completed the work which they have begun."[24] Neither side was satisfied.

Moses turned to Jones. Though John Rice repeatedly denied Valle's assertion that his connection with Austin was the cause of Austin's troubles, Moses had concluded that, for the sake of his grant, Jones must leave the partnership. They agreed, however, that after the title to Austin's concession was securely in his hands, Jones could be reinstated as a partner. Moses had the dissolution acknowledged in August before a notary in Kaskaskia, then publicized it by taking the paper to the lieutenant governor.[25]

If Moses Austin thought that Jones's expulsion would expedite his survey, he was sadly disappointed. Actually, the lieutenant governor himself may have been partly to blame for the continuing delay. In July, 1799, Trudeau had left office and been replaced by Carlos DeHault DeLassus DeLuzieres, the son of Moses' partner Pierre. The new lieutenant governor found himself in an awkward position with Austin. On the one side was young DeLassus's father, for whom he felt such loyalty and affection that he had abandoned a promising military career in Europe to come to America to be near him. On the other was the Spanish Governor-General

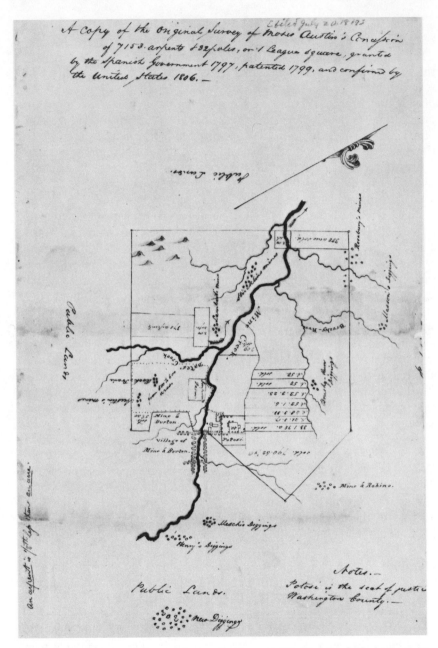

Moses Austin's Mine a Breton Grant. Austin sent this sketch of his property to Henry Schoolcraft in 1819 to use in trying to sell enough of the domain for Austin to pay off his debt to the Bank of St. Louis. *Henry R. Schoolcraft Papers, The Library of Congress.*

Manuel Gayoso de Lemos in New Orleans, who had blunted Carondelet's warm invitation to Americans. Lieutenant Governor DeLassus apparently procrastinated. Six months after he took office, in February, 1800, he simply referred Austin to Valle and Surveyor General Antoine Soulard to carry out the survey.[26]

Those three men did not finally meet at Mine a Breton until May, a year and a half after Trudeau ordered the survey. During that interim, Spanish land laws had been revised to require that the surveyor and landowner be accompanied in marking the bounds by the commandant of the district and two neighbors of the land owner. Without the agreement of all to the lines, the survey could not be certified as correct and in conformity with the concession, an essential step in obtaining title.[27]

No one could have expected Austin's survey to proceed smoothly. Austin meant to include much of the rich old mining area within his boundaries, and the French knew it. Valle advised Beauvais in particular of the date of the survey, and probably he told others who could be directly affected as well. To guard their interests, the French miners delegated an extra representative.

Soulard cautioned Austin to mind his temper during the survey. The surveyor general of five years had much personally at stake. He liked Austin. But, a native of France broken in fortune, and a man who had abandoned both a commission in the French Royal Marines and command of a naval vessel rather than return to fight in the revolution engulfing his country, Soulard risked his reception in the French community by his friendship with the stubborn American. Writing on May 1, "not in an official but in a more familiar way and Consequently easier to tell you my opinion," he quoted a French proverb "that flys are not Caught with Vinegar[.] Kindness with people with whom you Live if you mean to Do one Day as you please[,] Speak to Day as they Do Speak Bad people Can nether take off from you the Superiority of your talents nor your industry Sacrifices I say it again establish yourself in a Solid manner expect every thing from your perseverance and time."[28] For the restless Austin, sacrificing and waiting would be easier said than done.

The six-man survey party gathered on the morning of May 26, 1800, to pore over a map and plot the lines before marking them on the ground. Austin began. From a point in front of Durham Hall he drew the first line southerly to divide the mine field. After protecting his furnace house, mills, and other buildings, he angled it several times so as to separate the French village from the old diggings. None of the segments were drawn, Valle wrote for the record, "without violent debates between the inhabitant[s] and Mr. Osten, who did not cease being demanding and claiming." But after the boundaries had been agreed to and the calculations completed, they discovered that rather than taking in the traditional French

Original survey point on Austin's grant, 1800. This small granite shaft, put in place
in May, 1800, marked the corner by the spring shown on the August, 1799, map
(see page 72). In 1987, the shaft survives as the oldest survey point in Washington
County. *Photograph by the author.*

diggings, the line placed Austin's mines west of them.

After lunch, the party worked on the north side of Breton Creek, where
the bulk of the concession would lie. Austin wanted the line to commence
at the morning's starting point and run easterly, more or less paralleling
the creek. If permitted, Valle noted, "it shuts down the village in its depth
and also puts the inhabitants further away from having wood." The Commandant objected, and the six men argued until Valle recessed the proceedings for the night.

Before morning, Austin offered a compromise line. But it evidently varied little from his original, and the villagers rejected it outright. Wearying
of the conflict, Valle suspended the survey and forwarded the dispute to
the lieutenant governor to settle. In the meantime, Austin asked, could the
line they had run and the lines he proposed stand provisionally until the
lieutenant governor rendered his decision? Austin's boundaries encompassed only one-third of the mines, and Valle assented.[29]

Austin had foiled the villagers this time, for with the Commandant's
acquiescence, Soulard could complete his official return. The surveyor
general presented it to the lieutenant governor in mid-June, 1800, and
DeLassus, conscious of the months upon months Austin had been waiting
for the survey, accepted the boundaries that Valle had agreed to. "I confi-

dentially say," Soulard wrote Austin after presenting the paperwork to DeLassus, "that the Survey which has been made, will stand as it is without any alteration, 'till the decision of the Government General. and the business [dispute] cannot be brought there, unless the Inhabitants concerned can prove in writing that the manner in which your Land was Survey'd is prejudicial and ruinous to them."[30] Austin rejoiced, and in August, 1800, wrote his brother, Stephen, in high spirits and anticipation "of obtaining full possetion of the Lead Mines and the Lands as by the Grant and the Prospects of the advantage resulting from it."[31]

Full title to the mines and land, as Moses would soon learn, was far from his yet. But the prospects for lead production hardly could have been more flattering. With surface mines yielding as munificently as they were, the potential for rich seams underground appeared limitless. Austin had been impatient to find out how extensive the veins were and had directed Kendal and Bates, as quickly as they could spare the hands, to sink a shaft past the customary shallow depth of the French miners. The ore his men found between ten and seventy feet below the surface proved so incredibly rich that Austin believed "15 Acres of Common Mining land would last 20 hands for an age."[32]

The work required by the deep mining, however, turned out to be far more difficult than anyone had anticipated. The miners encountered strata hopelessly intermingled and jumbled, "in *no* Wise the same as in regular beds which gives the Miner a tolerable Knowledge how many stratas he has to pass before he may expect the Mineral...." This discovery was the more discouraging because the digging would be largely prospecting. "It is... impossible to fix on any given rule when you are to expect *Mineral* or when spar, sand gravel or limestone for in many places you find Valuable beds of Mineral immediately after passing the *Sod* and at Other immense Masses of gravel spar and sand and limestone before any Mineral is obtained - and all this variation Within fifty yard *Square*...." As if that were not frustration enough, the technical costs of burrowing in earth so haphazardly structured, Austin knew, would be great.[33] Water alone, however, according to the knowledgeable Timothy Flint, caused Moses to abandon the idea of deep shaft mining. More water "came in upon this digging" than Austin thought worth fighting.[34] But Flint looked too deep for a reason. In truth, as long as mineral remained plentiful near the surface, the wealth of the deep lead could not compensate for the expense and trouble of digging it out.

So much lead had yet to be recovered from the surface that, by contracting the right to dig on his property, Austin could realize a fine income without the expense of maintaining a mining force of his own. Moses made every contract with care. He permitted the miner to select the location he wished to excavate and granted him exclusive rights within a radius of fifty feet of his hole. Each miner could hold but one plot at a time, which he could sell only with Austin's consent. To insure his profit from the wealth of his land, Austin required that all mineral dug on his leases be delivered to his furnace house for smelting.[35]

Austin had both a "common furnace" to reduce raw ore and an ash furnace to roast the precious lead cinders. Both were reverberatory furnaces, the concept of which the English miners had introduced to him, and he, in turn, had brought to Spanish Louisiana. A reverberatory furnace worked on the principle of an oven, reducing the ore with hot air, not by direct contact with the fire. Because each furnace was, in effect, a fire box with a long flue, the draft that passed through it could be regulated to intensify the fire and raise the heat substantially above that which could be achieved in a log furnace. As a result, the smelterer recovered more of the lead from both the raw ore and the scoria.

A good common furnace produced about 2,300 pounds of lead a day, about 50,000 in a normal blast of 15-20 days' duration. Since only 60 percent of the lead in the ore melted in the first firing, however, Austin had his men transfer the chunks of partially roasted ore to the ash furnace, where they recovered another 15 percent.[36]

The efficiency of Austin's reverberatory units was awesome. Obtaining

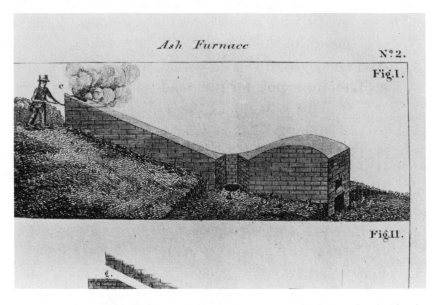

A reverberatory furnace. Henry R. Schoolcraft included this drawing in his pioneering book on the lead mines, a work written in Durham Hall. From Henry R. Schoolcraft, *A View of the Lead Mines of Missouri.*

75 percent of the lead in the ore better than doubled the production of any log furnace. Not six months after Austin put his first unit in blast, independent miners began bringing their ore to him for smelting. Austin required them to supply the wood for their smelt and gave them only 50 out of every 100 pounds smelted, after saving for himself the first 10 pounds. Still, the 50 pounds he gave each customer represented a 15 percent higher yield than the miner could ever get in his own log hearth. Austin quickly developed a thriving business in contract smelting. One by one the French smelterers gave up the competition and abandoned their log furnaces. Of the twenty log hearths in use in 1798 when Austin arrived, only one remained in 1802.[37]

Figures for both ore raised and mineral smelted during Austin's early years in Spanish Louisiana, though fragmentary at best, show how accurate Austin had been in reckoning the potential of the mines under his direction. Lead production shot up after 1798. For Mine a Breton alone, Austin estimated that between 1798 and 1803 the 40 to 50 French miners raised annually between 550,000 and 600,000 pounds of raw ore, which yielded about 366,600 pounds of lead, a quantity greater than the entire production of the best year before he arrived. The output from all the mines combined pushed the figures beyond any comparison. Moses, indeed, had expanded output as he had promised in his petition, and, according to two separate French observers, Spanish authorities took great satisfaction in the record production.[38]

By all measures Austin had struck it rich. Even the total loss in the spring of 1799 of his furnace house and its contents, including stocks of lead belonging to his customers, proved only a temporary setback. "I [was] left a beggar and with out property, four horses three Mules and three negros excepted,"[39] he recalled dramatically the charred ruin. But with productive mines, efficient methods, and good management, Moses recovered quickly. At Austinville in Virginia, by contrast, the prospects continued to deteriorate.

Before Moses left Virginia, Stephen had begun writing their superintendent, nephew James Austin, directing his work and pleading for "the greatest Exertion" to raise cash. Stephen sent his twenty-four-year-old son, Charles, to help, but for the first year after Moses left, little changed. "We still continue to go on but not well our Money matters are very pressing and how to relieve them can't say," Charles reported. "Trust to Providence and our Good luck."[40] As cash disappeared, they bartered lead for supplies. Stephen directed them, where they could, to obtain goods on credit. The notes only added to the burden, however. "Mr Sayers Cant Want his Money," Stephen wrote James in anguish. "Cant you Put him of a little longer by Promising to pay him the Intrest on what is due this we had better pay than be so Pushd—"[41]

The Austins' finances stood precariously like a house of cards. One exceptional demand for payment would bring the whole structure down. It came early in 1799 when Stephen's business colleague and good friend, Theo Hopkins, suddenly called for payment of £2,200 Stephen had borrowed years before in London. Actually Hopkins had long intended to write off the loan as his legacy to Charles, but serious reverses forced him to grasp for every dollar he could and to resurrect the old obligation. The only way Stephen could see to raise so much money was to sell slaves, animals, and lands at Austinville. In March, 1799, he wrote James that he had disposed of "All the Property of S and M Austin on New River Except the Lead Mines."[42]

The sudden sale could not help but inflame the tension between Stephen and Moses as soon as Moses learned of it. Even more than that, James feared for the future of the Virginia operation in the hands of the new owner. Stephen had sold to Charles, in whom James had seen no talent for management. At first, Stephen rented the slaves from Charles to work the mines, but soon he simply turned the mines over to his son for half the proceeds.[43] The fate of the Austins in Virginia lay squarely in Charles's hands.

Stephen labored under no delusion of the perilousness of the financial situation at the mines. He warned James to secure his salary by "Constantly taking Either Lead or Something that is within your power on the Place," for Stephen already doubted that he could meet any large demand. As the months passed, prospects dimmed. The Austin lead sold poorly in the saturated markets of New York and Philadelphia, throwing it entirely on the weaker Virginia outlet. Stephen then looked to the crops they raised at Austinville to make up their losses. "I [k]no[w] not what to Say at this Distence but that you must exert yourselves and do the best you can," he told James in July, 1799. "Unless the People can be Imployd to good advantage you know all is Ruin . . . for Gods sake see what you can do – "[44] James could do little. Lead production dropped within nine months to a pitiful 72,000 pounds a year. "Charles has made Every possible Exertion to try to get some thing from the Mines but the more he struggle the Deeper he is," Stephen confided to Moses a few months later. During his son's tenure, the mines had cost Stephen some $3,000 he could ill afford to lose.[45] Creditors grew restive. The State filed suit against surety Samuel Paine for the purchase money of the mines, which, James warned Moses in April, 1800, "would ruin him if there was not a stop put to it."[46] The Austins' former partner, Thomas Norvell, went to court to settle his account with Moses. Though "well Satisfied M Austin dont owe him one shilling," Stephen instructed James nevertheless to sell Charles all the company animals and equipment at the mines which Norvell might attach.[47] "Your profest friends," James wrote Moses, "became enemies after your departure." Responding in kind, James took morbid pleasure that "Old Percival," a third creditor, "is gone to hell the Devil catched him noding at his Poarch door and he had no time to prepare for his journey."[48]

As Moses' sanguine letter of August, 1800, worked its way toward Philadelphia, Stephen, pressed on all sides, addressed his brother with gloom. The suit against Paine appeared destined for execution later that fall. The State, at the same time, had begun demanding repayment of the lead Moses had borrowed in 1791. Four months Stephen had advertised the mines throughout the country for sale, but no one had responded. The situation further deteriorated when Charles decided not to renew his rental arrangement for 1801. Like Theo Hopkins, Stephen grasped at every apparent opportunity. With Peleg Sanford, husband of his brother Elijah's widow, he took an interest in a gristmill in Milford, Connecticut. He had seen no return by September, 1800, and three years later still would be waiting. "As to our own affairs," Stephen scrawled to Moses, "I know not what is to be the Event, nothing but my Ruin which appears Inevitable."[49]

For more than a year, Stephen wrote his brother long letters describing his plight. In some, he browbeat Moses with litanies of their tangled accounts, extending back to his first loan to Moses in 1782 and leading up to the substantial sum he calculated that Moses owed him. In one letter the amount totaled upwards of $12,700, "a sum every Dollar of which I have actually paid out of my private Pocket and it is a sum justly due me from M A for the statement I have made is in Equity and Good Conscience and as God is my Judge I have made it as if under the most Solem Oath to do justice between M A and myself."[50] Moses, Stephen believed, had abandoned him to his fate with "the wreck you Left at the Mines the whole of which will not pay me 8 shillings on the Pound."[51] Having squeezed every dollar he could from the mines, and finding the amount insufficient, Stephen on one occasion bitterly denounced Moses, writing that "If M Austin has a farthing of any thing left in which he has a Claim, I want it as I have not the Most distant hope that he will Ever pay me the Just Balance due me on his obligation."[52] In September, Stephen submerged his ill feelings to beg Moses for help. "For Gods sake," he pled, "Send me at Least 3000 Dolls from New orleans in good Bills On this Country."[53]

Moses responded initially with compassion, giving Stephen "hopes of being saved from the Ruin which has some time awaited me as well as your Self." But later, after learning first of the sale to Charles and then of the valuation of the property remaining in Virginia, which he considered too low, Moses changed his mind. He had, he contended, left at the mines far more property than Stephen credited to him, enough, indeed, to answer Stephen's needs. In December, 1800, Moses' temper had cooled, and he wrote of sending money to his brother following a trip to New Orleans in 1801. But a week later, after James Austin had arrived in Spanish Louisiana to give Moses a report on conditions and chronicled Charles's mismanagement and Stephen's appropriation of company resources, "all is again Reversed and you write while agitated by Violent Pashions." James also reviewed entry by entry Stephen's latest claim—for $14,000—and concluded that Moses could justly owe no more than $803.83.[54]

Throughout their correspondence, Stephen viewed the reversed fortunes at the mines as a continuing responsibility of their partnership. Moses disagreed. Their connection had been dissolved as of January 1, 1800, he maintained, and their agreement of July, 1797, governed their financial relationship. Each succeeding letter from James describing events at the mines further hardened Moses' heart, until the letter of October 15, 1801, exhausted his compassion. James wrote that Charles, unable to succeed at mining, had sold most of the property to the credit of his own account and then rented the mines to two men who were "makein lead very fast."[55] Furious, Moses promised his brother he would do "nothing for me unless I will Become a Banrupt etc and by this Exonerate My self and you from all my old affairs."[56]

Stephen addressed Moses once more at the end of February, 1801, "now actually [in] Distress," and without "Property on which I Can Command one Dollar." Living from day to day, he expected at any time "to be arested and Imprison'd."[57] Moses apparently did not reply. Stephen gave up on April 25, declared bankruptcy, and assigned his property to his creditors. "Stripd of Every thing," he informed Moses, only "my Health and Spirits is Left to work with my hands...[to keep from being with] my Helpless family...a Beggar on Earth."[58]

James stayed at the Virginia mines for another year, trying on the one hand to obtain the wages due him and on the other to avoid being pulled down in the maelstrom. In March, 1802, he quit the company, but "my Body was attachd" along with the company's books. "It is very hard upon me that I should be troubled for the Compy Debts when there was lead sufficient here to settle the demand and Charles and his father should apropritate it to their use and make away with the property and leave every thing unsettled."[59] As soon as he could, James took his wife, Peggy, a sister of Moses' wife Maria, and their children, and left for Spanish Louisiana.

To save himself, Paine, along with former Austin associate John Field, who soon would plunge into bankruptcy, and with plaintiffs from the case that had opened the Chiswell mines to public auction in 1789, obtained a court order setting aside the sale to the Austins. No payment ever had been made to the State for the property. The mines would be exposed to public auction again. Sadly for Paine, the sale failed to realize enough to cover the Austins' obligation. His bond remained in force, and slightly more than a year later he found himself in court obliged for the £6,505 principal, plus interest accrued since the first payment fell due in 1794, a total, Stephen reckoned, of more than $21,500.[60]

Paine apparently could meet the obligation no better than the Austins could. In 1806, the property again went on the auction block. This time, a satisfactory sale resulted, one of the purchasers being Thomas Jackson, a miner whom the Austins had brought from England. Though the Austins—Moses, Charles, and the partnership of Stephen and Moses—continued through 1811 to be assessed for, and apparently to pay taxes on, some 2,800 acres in seven parcels in Wythe County, and though some 2,000 acres remained in Moses' name until 1831, the Austin period at the lead mines of Virginia had ended.[61]

As Stephen's finances and Charles's management sank toward collapse, Moses in Spanish Louisiana struggled to solidify his position. Surveyor General Soulard had predicted in August, 1801, after handing his papers on Austin's survey at Mine a Breton to Lieutenant Governor DeLassus, that none of the French miners would protest the lines. The lieutenant governor waited six months, then ordered Soulard to issue Austin a certificate of survey. After that, only one step remained for Austin in the process of obtaining title, a process that already had consumed three years. Austin must present the certificate in person in New Orleans. "I Would recommend to you not to alter the folds and to take the best Care not to Spoil it [the certificate] any way untill you arrive at New Orleans," Soulard cautioned, "for as the Deed of Grant which Shall be Delivered to you is to be written underneath[,] if it was not in a Good order there might arise Some difficultys."[62] Soulard, who knew that Austin still struggled with the languages of the country, graciously suggested names of influential men in the Spanish capital who spoke English.[63]

A journey of two thousand miles, riding the Mississippi's current to New Orleans and fighting it on the return trip, constituted a venture of major proportions that would take no fewer than four and a half months. As important as the title was, Austin would not make such a trip solely to obtain it. He would take lead to his factor (agent) and bring back stocks of supplies for his family and little colony at Mine a Breton. The preparations consumed two months. Finally, on April 12, Moses left Ste. Genevieve with two flat boats loaded with lead. Austin kept a journal of the trip, but not, as in 1796-1797, because he expected this journey to be a historic trek. Instead, he recorded his experiences navigating the river for reference on future expeditions.[64]

In New Orleans on May 15, Austin went to see William Stephens, his factor for at least a year, and settled accounts. That same day, at Stephen Austin's suggestion, Moses called on John Francis Merieult, a former member of the New Orleans Cabildo (city council) and a merchant reputed to be worth a half-million pounds, to see if Merieult would handle Austin's business. Merieult, Stephen wrote, momentarily setting aside his bitter differences with his brother, should be able to help Moses in dealing with the unfamiliar Spanish bureaucracy, because his "interest and influence is Equal to the Gov't."[65] Stephen knew this only by word of mouth. He had never met the New Orleans merchant himself, but had learned of him through a man Stephen had encountered during his trip to England.

Moses and Merieult got along well. Merieult invited Austin to stay with him, agreed to act as his factor for a five percent commission, and began by receiving the two boatloads of sheet lead and shot. Ten days later, Austin bought from his new colleague $2,000-worth of goods of all descriptions, from writing paper to wine, women's fine stockings to hardware, to take back with him to Mine a Breton.[66] With the Spanish government, Moses could only wish for similar good fortune. Though he stayed in New Orleans more than two weeks, he failed to obtain the precious title he had come for. Early in June, he gave up on being able to accomplish it himself, appointed Merieult his attorney in fact to press the case, and returned home.[67]

Despite his reputation, Merieult worked no miracles. Nearly a year passed. In April, 1802, Moses sent Elias Bates on the spring trip to New Orleans to deliver lead and buy supplies, and to talk with Merieult about the title. But Merieult had done all that he could. Indeed, Surveyor General Soulard, not Merieult, brought Austin's title to completion. Soulard had journeyed to the capital on business unconnected with Austin. But as long as he was in town, the authorities solicited his observations on Austin's improvements, industry, and the nagging boundary dispute. Soulard told them that, besides putting up improvements and providing employment for many, Austin "has given permanency to . . . [the settlement at] the mine, has excited an emulation among the miners who had no regular method of working, Since before the arival of Mr. Austin they were ignorant of the manner of melting the Scoriae, which every one now works up to a considerable advantage." The dispute, Soulard asserted, had no more foundation than "Mutual ambition . . . betwixt him and the most noted of those who pretended a claim to the productions of the mine."[68] Soon after Soulard testified, Spanish Intendent Juan Ventura Morales, on July 5, 1802, granted Austin title to 7,153 arpents,[69] 32½ feet adjoining the mine and village.

The four-year struggle to obtain formal possession of his grant took no toll on Moses' business. Only a scattering of accounts have survived, but they reveal an extensive trade. Moses sent lead to at least two factors in Kentucky, as well as to the two in New Orleans. He was pleased when Merieult wrote that he intended to contract for Austin to supply lead to the Spanish garrison in Havana. Almost everywhere Austin's lead went, so too did his trade in hardware, liquors, pipes, textiles, and foodstuffs, because Moses meant to make money everywhere he could find it. His business grew so large that by 1802 he had to employ his own crews to pilot barges regularly on the Mississippi. And it was lucrative enough to endure occasional loss to pirates and sinkings.[70]

The Osage Indians, angered by the tide of advancing settlement carving up their territory in eastern Missouri, actually presented a greater menace than the hazards of the river. Well-proportioned, good-looking, graceful and quick, the Osage roamed the country at will, stealing horses and plundering supplies. As a consequence, the typical house in Ste. Genevieve stood behind a seven-foot-high palisade of stout timbers driven into the ground upright. The outlying mines for years had offered inviting targets. The new settlements built by Austin and other Americans both stirred frustration in the Osage at the invasion of their country and provided additional opportunities for attack.

The Osage had struck Austin's settlement at least as early as 1799 and continued to harass the place annually. Each attack proved to be but a prelude, however, to the assault of May 12, 1802. Thirty Indians fell on Mine a Breton, according to Stephen F. Austin, then nine years old, intending both "to plunder my father's house and store, and to kill the Americans, or Bostonians, as they called them."[71] Outnumbered three to one, Moses Austin and nine of his men made their stand behind the walls of Durham Hall and repulsed the onslaught. The mines settlement sustained one person killed and one woman kidnapped. More than that, it lost whatever goodwill existed between the Americans and the French. Because the French gave no assistance in the battle and left Austin to his fate, Moses never forgave them and years afterward still recalled this with unreserved bitterness. Even Commandant Valle reprimanded his countrymen for refusing to fight. "I took on the responsibility," he informed the lieutenant governor, "to tell the miners not to let the Indians take advantage of them like that. I also told them that they should have used their weapons immediately to defend themselves against such robbers...."[72]

Austin went to Valle soon after the fight and appealed for a detachment of soldiers to protect the settlement. The Commandant refused, saying that he could not authorize it, that the inhabitants must defend themselves. Austin then requested a three-pounder cannon "which I found in the streets of... [Ste. Genevieve] filled with Clay & half in the Ground."[73] Valle gave him the gun with the understanding that the government would repay his expenses in preparing it for service. To support his field piece, Moses asked to establish a gunpowder factory. Local officials favored his plan, but permission never came from the authorities in New Orleans. Nevertheless, the gun evidently served its purpose, for during the remaining years of Spanish control of the territory, Moses never fired it in hostility.[74]

That same year of 1802 in Louisiana, the transfer of the territory from

Spain to France consisted of no more than rumor. Official word had yet to be received that on October 1, 1800, the King of Spain, indeed, had retroceded the land to France. United States President Thomas Jefferson had not learned of it until 1801, after which he sent representatives to Emperor Napoleon to try to purchase New Orleans and West Florida. By the time the American minister arrived in Paris, Napoleon had dropped his plans for colonial expansion and offered to sell all of the Louisiana territory to the Americans. The deal was completed quickly in the spring of 1803 and the treaty ratified and proclaimed the following October. In the meantime, on June 5, 1803, Commandant Valle in Ste. Genevieve posted on the church door the official communique announcing cession of the territory to France. Two months later unofficial word reached Upper Louisiana that France had relinquished the territory to the United States. All the while, until the end of 1803, Napoleon left the Spanish authorities in power. On the fringe of the territory, in St. Louis, the agent of France did not occupy the government house until March 9, 1804, and turned it over to the representative of the United States the following day, a brief formal conclusion to a long and unsettled period.[75]

With rumors abundant and the future uncertain, Moses Austin learned in November, 1802, that Merieult had received the title to his grant the preceding July. "In the present Situation of things," he wrote with relief, this "is of the Greatest Consequence to me."[76] He would not know for some years just how right he was. On July 18, 1802, the King of Spain in Madrid took steps to halt the wave of Americans flowing across the Mississippi River into Louisiana and proclaimed that from that date forward no grants of land would be made to Americans. Austin's grant had been completed not two weeks before. Moreover, only a handful of grants ever were completed—but four in the lead district—because of the enormous expenses of surveying, travel, and fees, not to mention the extremely long time it took for the process to be completed.[77] From the day Austin submitted his petition, more than five years elapsed before his grant had been confirmed by the Spanish.

As the actual change of government approached in the fall of 1803, men jockied to position themselves for the new order. Moses, having lost his friendship with Valle and being on poor terms with the French at Mine a Breton, evidently did not look forward to the sovereignty of the French. In August, he wrote James Richardson, one of Soulard's deputy surveyors and a resident of the country eleven years longer than Austin, suggesting that the Americans take special steps to ingratiate themselves with the new government. Wishing "to render the Americans in this country as respectable as possible," he wrote, and since "in my opinion the first impressions are always the best," Austin proposed that they, in typical American fashion, form a committee to approach the new high officials.

"Stating the many advantages that would accrue from a proper encouragement of *commerce* and agriculture, it would have a good effect, and I think
it would bring the Americans into notice." Moreover, he concluded, "by a
well timed union of opinion and *measures* the situation of the Americans in
the country may be changed."[78] If Richardson responded, there is no
record of it. But two weeks after Austin wrote, he learned from friends in
the United States that America, not France, would take permanent charge
of the territory. Richardson's opinion no longer mattered, because Austin
soon would be back under a familiar government.

Since under the Spanish system few landholders completed titles to
their property, the changes of government brought a rash of speculation in
land by those hoping that the new authorities would accept the claims
advanced under the old. In his original petition to the Spanish, Austin had
requested land to distribute in smaller parcels to persons who had followed
him from Virginia. Five of them had yet to ask for the acreage to which
they were entitled, when, in June, 1803, Valle posted the notice of the cession to the French. Austin and Soulard both claimed that they then acted
to protect the rights of Austin's negligent companions. The Surveyor General obtained eight blank concessions predated to the period of Trudeau's
administration and signed by Trudeau. Austin was to put up money
enough to cover Soulard's fees. Whether their dispute over the fee Austin
still owed from the survey of his concession in 1800 or over some other
cause dissolved their mutual trust, the deal fell through. In January, 1804,
Austin returned the concessions to Soulard, disgusted "that I have had a
part in this business by which I have... recd from you a Charge of Conduct of which I always shall Declair myself Blameless."[79]

Austin told Soulard that he believed "your intentions have been always
to give Sattisfaction to Evry man yet your unbound'd confidance in [dep-
uty surveyor Thomas] Madden and his friends has induced you to look on
me as a man unworthy of belief—and Capable of many improper thing."[80]
If Austin was extending his hand to Soulard, the surveyor slapped it. Early
in February he sent Madden himself to survey a tract in Bellevue for Pas-
cal Detchemendy. Far from being vacant, the land was occupied by William Reed, a friend of Austin. Soulard must have known that trouble likely
would result, because Austin had complained to him five months earlier of
Madden, calling the deputy an opportunist detested by the Americans and
warning that "difficulties... might Arise unless some man Other then
Maddin" marked the tracts Soulard and Austin intended to reserve for
Austin's men.[81]

Soulard sent Madden anyway. The deputy and his crew arrived at
Reed's place but could not finish the survey before nightfall. While they
waited for daybreak, word of their presence spread to neighboring houses.
The next morning ten armed men prevented the deputy from completing

his work. Lieutenant Governor DeLassus reported that the rioters, as he called them, shouted "Viva Gifferson" as they obstructed government business, and he blamed Austin for the incident. Austin and Soulard never regained their former friendship. Nor did the dispute die. Three years later and a thousand miles away in Philadelphia it flared again when, on April 18, 1806, the *Farmer's Journal and Philadelphia Advertiser* carried Austin's statement blaming Soulard and the Spanish officials for the apparent speculation with the eight blank concessions.[82]

By the time the Spanish officials were ready to leave Upper Louisiana, in November of 1804, Austin held no respect for them. In gathering property of the Spanish government for shipment, Carlos DeLassus asked Austin for the three-pounder cannon Valle had given him. Austin, never having been paid for rehabilitating it, refused to hand it over and taunted the Lieutenant Governor that if "the Spaniards wanted the cannon they could get" it. What "ungratefulness," DeLassus responded, in a man who "had been greatly favored by the Spanish Government."[83]

What the Spanish thought no longer mattered to Austin. He had fulfilled his obligation to them. Moses had introduced the mining innovations he had promised. He had dramatically increased the lead production of the territory and had supplied the king's forces with lead. Moreover, his intensive mining and his efficient method of smelting, as he had predicted, had been catalysts for the spread of mining and the development of the country. Within a radius of twenty miles of Mine a Breton, more than a half-dozen mines had been opened or reopened between 1799 and 1803, most of them by men who had worked for him. For himself, Moses had secured the grant he had sought. He realized that the change of government would open new doors, and the prospect brightened his outlook. This country, he wrote his brother-in-law Aaron Eliot, in August, 1803, "will present the grea[test opportunity for] a Young man of any in the [world]. If you have any Intentions of [ever coming out?] this fall will be the time."[84] Moses Austin looked forward to the new day.

CHAPTER VII

THE CHANGE of government in Upper Louisiana catapulted Moses Austin without warning into public prominence. He knew more about lead, the principal industry of the country, than anyone else, and he had prospered more handsomely than any other American already resident there. Moreover, though officially a citizen of Spain, he made no secret that he was an American at heart. Who more than he should the new government look to for leadership?

The first sign of Austin's new role came early in 1804 from Captain Amos Stoddard, then on his way to St. Louis to establish the American government in Upper Louisiana and to assume the duties of its first Civil Commandant. Captain Stoddard carried the injunction of President Jefferson to provide him with as much information as Stoddard could obtain on the new territory. Without question the lead mines should be the subject of a full report. A communication submitted to Congress the previous November had described them in glowing but unspecific terms. The Captain asked Austin to prepare a dissertation giving concrete facts. "From his education and experience," Stoddard wrote the President, "I conceive him to be better calculated to give correct information on the subject than any other man in this quarter."[1] Austin worked quickly and completed his manuscript on February 13, more than a week before Stoddard reached St. Louis and nearly a month before the Spanish relinquished the territory.[2]

Austin described specifically "the number, extent and situation of the Lead Mines in Upper Louisiana, with an estimate of the average quality [quantity] of mineral produced, and the number of hands employed at each mine."[3] Shrewdly he seized his opportunity to tell the future Civil Commandant, and through him the President, his view of the needs and prospects of the country. "The time cannot be far distant," Austin wrote, renewing the theme he had struck with the Spanish authorities seven years earlier, "when this country will furnish lead sufficient, not only for the consumption of the United States, but all Europe."[4] To support his contention, he included figures on "the probable quantity which may be annually produced, when the country becomes populated so as to afford workmen sufficient to occupy the mines to advantage." Combine the discoveries waiting to be made in the fabulously lead-rich country with a considerable immigration from the United States and the production, Austin concluded, must skyrocket. To encourage this increased output, Austin recommended the United States embrace the Spanish policy of awarding four acres to the discoverer of a mine. But at the same time, he continued, the government should impose a tax on mineral raised on public land so as to realize for itself some of the wealth of its new domain.

President Jefferson found the report so satisfactory that he remarked on it in his State of the Union message on November 8, 1804. "The lead mines in this territory," he told Congress, "offer so rich a supply of that metal as to merit attention," and he called on the legislative branch to provide for "immediate enquiry into their occupation and titles."[5]

Jefferson's partisans in the House of Representatives enthusiastically received the report, which the president had appended intact to his message, and moved with dispatch to give him the inquiry he wanted. Federalist Simeon Baldwin opposed the idea, scoffing that "the attention of the gaping Democrats gazing at the wonders of Louisiana is turned from the splendour of the mountain of salt to streams of Lead flowing from Austins mines."[6] But he could not stem the tide. On November 21 the House authorized the president to appoint an agent to investigate the occupation of and titles to both lead mines and salt springs in the Louisiana territory. Baldwin's colleagues in the Senate, however, mustered the strength to thwart the Democrats.[7]

The second sign of Austin's new role came about six months later. Late in the summer of 1804, Governor William Henry Harrison, Stoddard's successor, appointed the forty-two-year-old Austin one of the five justices on the first Court of Common Pleas and Quarter Sessions for the Ste. Genevieve District. Moses had seen the inside of a courtroom only as a litigant, but, excluding possibly François Valle, his credentials for the position compared favorably with those of the other appointees. All were prominent and respected citizens.[8]

Totally aside from the quality of his appointments, Governor Harrison's administration never satisfied the majority of his constituents west of the Mississippi River and lasted less than a year. The discontent focused on the act of Congress which established his caretaker government. The Act of March 26, 1804, grated on several raw nerves, but two in particular. First, it rested on the assumption that the inhabitants of the newly acquired territory were incapable of governing themselves. The bill contained no provision for eventual self-rule. Second, it declared null and void all of the Spanish land grants made after the Treaty of San Ildefonso of October, 1800, the agreement by which France acquired the country, excepting grants of small extent to actual settlers who occupied their tracts prior to December 20, 1803.[9]

Congress heard the objections and responded with two new measures. On March 2, 1805, it revived the House's November authorization of an agent to investigate titles to mineral deposits and incorporated it into a bill creating a Board of Land Commissioners to review and validate all claims in the territory. Three days later Congress provided a new government for the region. The Law of March 5, 1805, established the Territory of Louisiana within the framework of the familiar territorial system of government created by the Northwest Ordinance of 1787. Under this system, the region received its own governor, three judges, who with the governor served as the legislative body of the Territory, and secretary. Further, as the population grew, the Territory would progress through clear stages to eventual statehood.[10]

Creation of the Board of Land Commissioners would, Congress hoped, provide a ready and easy solution to a new, nagging, and dangerous situation. The United States never before had obtained territory from a foreign power with an unfamiliar land system. It groped for the best way to distinguish real from pretended claims. Most agreed that the actual settler on the land before the United States took control of the Purchase could and should be confirmed in his possession, and so read the Law of March, 1804. At issue lay grants larger than the Spanish normally made, blank— or floating—concessions that could be located anywhere, particularly located fraudulently on a known lead mine or on someone else's newly discovered outcrop, and permissions to settle or orders of survey written after, but dated before, acquisition by France.

The problem was widespread, because fewer than a half-dozen concessions in the lead country ever had completed the entire Spanish process and been confirmed by the highest officials in New Orleans. Thus, permissions to settle and orders of survey existed in some numbers and could be easily disputed. In addition, everyone knew that the lieutenant governor, for his own enrichment, had sold antedated concessions, blank forms dated prior to French acquisition of the territory. Complicating the issue, however, was the fact that not all blank concessions were fraudulent. Some were legitimate, having been prepared for followers of men like Moses Austin. Those who came with Austin had been entitled to small grants of their own. But not all had claimed them. On request in cases such as these, the lieutenant governor would sign and date concessions, allowing the name and location to be filled in later.

The situation was ripe for speculation. The fortunate could anticipate obtaining either valuable mining tracts, or land that would rise in value quickly, or both. The laws of the United States at that date gave no land for free. The last free acreage was that held under Spanish rights. People knew that property values would rise; no one could foretell by how much. It proved to be substantial, for by the end of his administration, Governor Stoddard had noted an inflation of approximately 400 percent. As for the claims, he identified twenty-three fraudulent grants made on antedated paper, among them claims to the best mines. Austin asserted that he knew of 30,000 acres covered by bogus paper in early 1804. More than sixty spurious claims were advanced within a few miles of Mine a Breton.[11] Speculation in Spanish land rights, whether for lead mines or resale, became big business.

For the three years before the land board began to take up the claims one by one in June, 1806, the gambling raged unchecked. The high stakes enterprise, carried on in a society of hard-working, hard-playing miners, attracting opportunistic and desperate men willing to spare nothing to have a part, insured that life in Louisiana Territory would be raw, dangerous, and unsettled. "The mines soon became the scene of every disorder, depravity, and crime, and a common rendezvous for renegados of all parts," observed Henry Schoolcraft, who knew many of the contemporaries.[12] No one but outsiders flinched when, at dances, knives or pistols crashed to the floor from their concealment in the clothes of the revelers. "The mine country is a very unpleasant place of residence," traveler Christian Schultz judged, "as the continual broils and quarrels among the workmen, as well as the proprietors, keep up a constant scene of warfare. You would certainly feel yourself in very suspicious company, were you to discover, that most of those around you wore a concealed dagger, and sometimes even two, one in the bosom, and the other under the coat; while others have a brace of pistols in the girdle behind the back. I have heard of a number of quarrels since I have been here, and of two or three being wounded by pistol shot, but no lives were lost; which has rather been owing to the precipitancy of firing, than want of inclination to kill."[13]

The volatile condition of Louisiana Territory called for the best appointments President Jefferson could make. The new government needed leaders who could settle disputes without taking sides, could govern with a firm but just hand. Moreover, the president had little time to ponder his choices if the appointees were to be in the Territory when the March Act became effective on July 4, 1805. For governor, he chose the handsome, gentlemanly, agreeable, well-educated James Wilkinson. The forty-eight-year-old Wilkinson brought impressive credentials to the position. Allied by marriage to the prominent Biddle Family of Philadelphia, he had risen to the office of clothier general during the Revolution, then in 1797 been given command of the entire United States Army, a position he continued to hold.

Jefferson picked Wilkinson, a military man, for a civil office, because of his deep concern for the defense of the country's western flank against the Indians, Spanish, and English. "St. Louis," he explained to one Senator, "is too important to be left in a state of anarchy, or placed in nerveless hands."[14]

Wilkinson was hardly nerveless, but the loyalty of the army's com-

Moses Austin's Missouri, 1796-1821.

mander extended no farther than his financial interests and his unbridled ambition. The wise President George Washington had glimpsed the traits in Wilkinson fourteen years earlier. But neither Washington nor Jefferson conceived that at the time each tendered appointment to Wilkinson, the officer was receiving a pension from the nation's uncertain friend, the government of Spain. Since the mid-1780s, Wilkinson had been cleverly preying upon the fears of both the United States and Spain, playing each country against the other and accepting pay from both to defend the one and control the other.[15]

General Wilkinson reached his capital late in June, 1805, seemingly with a clear understanding of the work before him. "Placed here to promote the happiness of this People," he wrote one of his commandants, "it becomes our duty to resist, as well the sympathies as the antipathies of the restless, Interested and ambitious, and by a deportment dispassionate, conciliatory and inflexibly impartial, to foster a spirit of forbearance, liberality and mutual concession, among all ranks and descriptions of the Inhabitants."[16]

That was easier said than done, but the general soon had an opportunity to set an example. The week before Wilkinson took office, Major Seth Hunt, commandant of the Ste. Genevieve District, ordered one John Smith off the public domain near Mine a Breton. An employee of Smith's had discovered lead on the public land and begun establishing a permanent settlement to exploit the find. Smith sought to secure the tract for himself by locating a Spanish floating concession that he had bought from Hunt barely two weeks earlier. Major Hunt, who had been appointed by President Jefferson and who had assumed his office with the change of government the previous October, issued his ultimatum to Smith under the long-standing directive of the Secretary of War to remove intruders from the public domain. Smith approached Hunt, who directed him to the new governor.[17]

John Smith of Tennessee, slender, with a handsome, youthful face, looked the well-bred, enterprising man-on-the-make that he was. Thirty-five years old, nine years younger than Austin, he, like Austin, represented the fifth generation of his line in America. Smith, however, descended from piedmont Virginia stock so imbued with the southern ideal that they had moved as a group to the Georgia uplands to maintain their aristocratic style undisturbed. Young Smith grew up on the Georgia frontier, but obtained his education at William and Mary College in Williamsburg, Virginia. As a young man, he found doors open to him in land and public life in East Tennessee. Even after moving to Upper Louisiana, he maintained his interests there. Smith may have arrived in the Ste. Genevieve district, attracted by the lucrative lead mines, as early as 1798, but he remained politically active in Tennessee as late as 1801 and first appeared in public records in Ste. Genevieve only in 1802.

Those who knew nothing else about Smith knew he was a crack shot. He went nowhere unarmed. Moreover, he carried the finest pistols in all of Upper Louisiana, each one made on his place to his specifications. Normally he carried four pistols, two in his belt and one in each side coat pocket, plus a dirk at his bosom and a rifle by his side. Anyone who crossed him did so at his peril. Smith never ducked a challenge and never lost a duel. "When aroused," wrote one Missouri historian, "he was one of the most dangerous men in the history of the state."[18] John Smith is credited by another historian with being the greatest of the speculators and claim-locators in the mineral district. To insure his hold on locations and to intimidate the timid, he recruited a private army of indigent miners with which he occupied the sites he wanted, particularly lead mine tracts discovered in the few years following cession.[19]

Smith was a proud man, too. Few things came to anger him more than being mistaken for someone else with the same name. To put an end to it once and for all, he took the letter "T" from "Tennessee" and attached it to his name. After 1805, *he* was John Smith T; everyone else was just plain John Smith.[20]

Wilkinson received Smith T on July 5, the Governor's second day in office, and heard Smith T's side of the story. The previous summer, Smith T explained, his agent had taken possession of a small tract of vacant land

John Smith T. Taken from a portrait painted while he was a student at
William and Mary College, ca. 1790. *Photograph by Frank Magre.*

on which he had discovered lead. Smith T claimed the place under the
Spanish four-acre discoverer's right honored by the United States, he
thought, during Captain Stoddard's administration. In addition, he
intended to locate that floating concession of 500 acres beside the four
acres in hopes of acquiring a major mining area. When Smith T asked the
surveyor general to mark the tract, he was told that Major Hunt had for-
bidden further surveys of old grants, even though, according to Smith T,
Governor Harrison had expressly permitted them under the president's
order to maintain the Spanish system until Congress could provide a government.

The stories of Hunt and Smith T bore significant differences. But while
telling his, Smith T established a strong friendship with Wilkinson. The
governor needed nothing more. Surely, he told Smith T, "the Major may
be deceived in point of fact, which will be most acceptable to me, because
it is my warm wish that no occasion may occur to make it necessary to
exert the arm of the law against an individual, much less one of Captain
Smith's respectability."[21] The governor then gave Major Hunt's letter to
Smith T for Smith T to prepare a written reply.

We cannot know for certain what attracted Smith T and Wilkinson, but
Smith T's mother was a Wilkinson. More importantly for the general and
governor, no doubt, two of Smith T's brothers were serving in the army

and a brother-in-law held a seat in Congress from Georgia. Probably most significant of all, however, Smith T was an adventurer. Wilkinson one day soon might use an army of such men as he.

For his part, Smith T must have sensed in Wilkinson what many others already knew: an enemy of a friend of the general was an enemy of the general as well. This presented Smith T an opportunity not to be missed. In closing his exoneration, he gratuitously named the man and the motive he saw behind Major Hunt's action. "I have reason to believe," Smith T confided to Wilkinson, "that Moses Austin wishes to add my little possession to his own, and that Major Hunt so partial to him would readily attempt to deprive me of Character as well as property."[22]

In less than a month, word of Smith T's indictment reached Austin, who professed ignorance of the offense he had evidently given Smith T. "What have I done to this *monster* in Society?" Austin inquired of his friend Rufus Easton. "He never had a moments conversation with me in his life I have said nothing about the fellow. I have had nothing to do with his business Directly or indirectly."[23] Frustrated ambition was the only motive Austin ever could suggest for Smith T's attack.[24] Smith T apparently never revealed the injury. But soon the original provocation no longer mattered.

When Austin learned that Governor Wilkinson had given Major Hunt's letter to Smith T, his indignation exploded. "Did you Ever know of such steps in an Officer," he wrote Easton, who, as territorial judge, held one of the highest political appointments in the Territory. "What compensation is equal to being thus Exposed to Every Offender. . . It is my Opinion and (believe me my friend I am not alone) in saying that an Official Communication from one Officer to an Other ought to be as sacred as the chastity of his Wife."[25]

In July, 1805, Austin's opinion mattered little to the governor, and it would take more than a handful echoing his sentiments to make any difference in the administration of the Territory. Yet few observers could fail to be surprised that Major Hunt's seemingly nonpolitical effort to defend the public domain had produced an apparently significant shift in the political balance in the Territory in three ways, none of them satisfactory to Hunt and his friends. First, Major Hunt received a stern rebuke from the governor, who had reversed the commandant's ruling and allowed Smith T to stay on the property. Within two months, Wilkinson would have Hunt arrested and replaced. Second, Austin, whom Wilkinson had never met, lost his entrée to the inner circles of government. Third, and most important, Smith T gained an unassailable position of influence. Smith T saw his opportunity and pressed it.

Having the governor's ear, Smith T poured in more vituperation against Austin. On July 22 Smith T taunted Austin that he intended to obtain his removal from the Bench of Common Pleas and Quarter Sessions and had begun circulating petitions, particularly among the French. Austin's Achilles heel, Smith T saw, was the French community. The French remembered Austin's clash with the villagers at Mine a Breton over the boundaries of his grant. Moreover, with the change of government, Austin had so identified himself with the American sympathizers that by July, 1805, the French were "violently prejudiced agt. you on account of your public communications—"[26] Though the French population numbered no more than a third of the approximately 12,000 inhabitants of the Territory,[27] Smith T knew that the governor had taken a special interest in them, particularly the wealthy of St. Louis. Wilkinson would have no sympathy for a man rejected by the Chouteaus, Gratiot, and Soulard among others.

Moses responded to Smith T's taunt that "Men holding public Functions must Expect to Undergo Examination, and at this moment of party madness I aught not to Expect to Escape. When called on," he added contemptuously, "I shall be ready to meet my opponents at the Bar of Justice."[28] Measured by the number of his supporters, Austin, indeed, was ready. A petition signed by 200 of them already rested somewhere in Governor Wilkinson's office. Executed in late June, it called on the governor to retain Austin as chief justice of the court, "confidently believing that [he] is from his correct information, inflexible integrity and rigid adherance to principle & justice, the person best qualified to fill" the post.[29]

To the governor, Austin wrote that he had "Ever wish'd a harmony and union of Opinion might take place between the French and Americans and with confidence do I Declair that Its not my fault there exists a Difference."[30] After asking to see the charges of his accusers, Moses closed by commenting on the campaign against him in words that could only inflame the governor. "Few men in public Stations escape the milignant tongues of the restless members of society," he scrawled, alluding pointedly to Wilkinson's new favorite. "I am marked Out As a Victim to disappointed ambition."[31]

Though playing with fire, Austin still thought he could regain control of events. The same day he wrote Smith T, Austin sent Easton the letter he had written Wilkinson and asked the territorial judge to deliver it to the governor in person. Easton met regularly with Governor Wilkinson on administrative matters and obliged Austin on July 29, 1805. Wilkinson read the letter, "smiled at one passage, but appeared somewhat agitated," Easton reported afterward. "They must, said he [Wilkinson], be greatly mistaken who think that I shall decide and decree upon such attacks—" Clearly, Easton told Austin, the governor "is greatly chagrined at the cabals [raised by] the *factious* party spirit which prevails through out the District." And "he will very properly take every means to quell that spirit and restore harmony to social intercourse—" Austin had nothing to fear,

Easton thought, however, as Wilkinson, as Easton saw him then, is "a fine
man and one who will do justice—"[32]

Exercise moderation in dealing with General Wilkinson, Easton counseled, specifically warning Austin to control his fury. "If you will excuse
the freedom I take as a friend...you have been rather too much heated
from the abuses you have received, and...from too great a violence[,] you
may have given your enemies more advantage over you than otherwise
they would have had—" But, Easton continued, "your enemies will not be
able to injure you with the Govr....By a cool, calm & temperate conduct
with a firm resolution you will" survive the attacks.[33]

The "Insults I have rec'd," Austin conceded, "has at times led me to
express myself freely." But, he complained, "all my conduct is so watched
and represented that what is of little consequence in any other man is considered as an offense in me."[34]

Austin had no time to lick his wounds. The newest and sharpest attack
came shortly and from an unexpected quarter, the governor himself. Austin learned on good authority that at a public meeting at Housleys settlement Governor Wilkinson said that Austin's "conduct as an officer of
Justice was a proof that he was also a V-l [villain?] highly finished...[and]
should be immediately discharged from Office with Disgrace. Mr. Heart
asked Callaway whether he believed the Govr had said any such thing he
said he did & that It was believed in the Village." Austin rankled first at
the charges and then at their effect. "Many of the people said that If the
Govr thought them [Austin and Sheriff Israel Dodge] D-m V-l they must
have don something that Deserved his Displeasure."[35] Austin had been
declared guilty without a trial and been convicted on innuendo.

Not more than two weeks later, sometime early in August, 1805, Governor Wilkinson summarily dismissed Austin from the court. If Wilkinson
wrote Austin giving a reason, the letter has disappeared long since. But
the governor did write at some length to Secretary of State James Madison justifying the action.

> We have here some scintillations of faction, emitted from the
> collisions of a few ardent discontents, who having failed to
> inlist me in oposition to an ideal French party, would turn their
> Batteries directly against me, if they could do so with effect,
> and as is not uncommon in such cases, will probably endeavour
> to carry by sap, what they cannot accomplish by open
> assault— I infer from a variety of strong indications, that a Mr.
> Moses Austin, has been the prime mover of these discords—
> this gentleman whom I have not the pleasure of knowing,
> became a voluntary subject of Spain about nine years since,
> and having under the patronage of that Government, from
> small beginnings secured a large fortune; now alledges that he

has been cruelly persecuted for his americanism, and on this ground lays claim to extraordinary patronage from the United States: it is to be regretted that this gentleman should have been able to seduce, several of the junior Territorial Officers, to make common cause with him, in the excitements, which have agitated the District of St Genevieve—Yet I am pursuaded Sir, these agitations cannot affect the concord and tranquility of the Territory, and I venture to intrude this detail on you, to prevent any uneasiness which might be produced by misrepresentation—[36]

Wilkinson then replaced Austin on the court with John Smith T.[37]

Moses thought of possible responses. The course that most appealed to him was simply occupying the seat by force of arms. He suggested the idea to his attorney, William C. Carr, who served also as the first United States Attorney in Ste. Genevieve and who cared for Wilkinson and Smith T no more than he. Carr, a twenty-three-year-old Virginian, respected the law far too much, however, to encourage such action, yet knew he had to evaluate the idea carefully to cool Moses' rage. On August 12, Carr advised Austin to think long and hard before he used force. "This is certainly an affair pregnant with important consequences both of a public and private nature—and deserves well to be weighed, before you proceed to

Rufus Easton. *Missouri Historical Society.*

carry it into execution. Will it not produce a riot? Can Smith yield to it peaceably? I fear not I fear he would proceed to some outrage If so it might tend to very pernicious effects." The courts, Carr thought, provided Austin's best remedy.[38]

Easton, too, discouraged reckless action. "I admitt you are Justifiable in such advice," Austin acknowledged and dropped the idea. "But my Dear Sir," he asked bluntly, "how am I to answer my family & friends who are Daly branding me with a want of resolution to meet the abuse Daly offered to myself and friends."[39]

Bide your time both attorneys answered. For a while he did. Austin knew that many did not accept the governor's unsubstantiated denunciation. Following that meeting in which Wilkinson had labeled Austin a villain, the "thinking part of the Americans said that if the Govr was capable of making use of such Expressions about men in office without a trial no man of consideration would hold an Office under him, that If the Official Communication of an Officer [Hunt's to the governor about Smith T's encroachment on the public domain] was to Draw him into Disputes for doing his Duty, that If the first Judge of the County with the sheriff are to be call D-m V-l by the Govr without hereing them in Defence but because John Smith of Tennessee says so, little can be expected from our Change & New Government." With that in mind, Austin told Easton he would "not allow my confidence in the Govr to diminish until I have *reason* from some further favours to Smith & party."[40] But resentment continued to fester in Austin nonetheless.

For perhaps a month Austin held his frustration in check. But in late September or early October he cast aside the advice of Carr and Easton and demanded an interview with the governor. "After suffering myself to be calumniated out of all reason," he told Easton afterward, "I made my appearance at St Louis not doubting but I should be able to convince Gov. Wilkinson of the fallacy of my calumniators." Austin overrated his powers of persuasion. Instead of clearing his name with the governor, he found himself subjected to a new charge. General Wilkinson asserted "that a combination was formed against him & that Majr. Hunt, Judge Easton, Moses Austin, I. Dodge & Wm. C. Carr was at the head of this combination in short that the above Gentlm. were the life and cause of this combination." Austin was dumbfounded. "I immediately declared to the Govr *the Truth* which was that the information he gave me was the first I had heard of this strange business. The Idea of a combination was to me new and ridiculous. I stated to the Govr. that I would not say what cause Judge Easton had given him to Justify such an opinion, but the letters I had recd. from the Judge would prove the Injustice of his suspicion. The Govr. answered I [Wilkinson] may be mistaken in my opinion."[41] After Israel Dodge heard of the charge, he dissociated himself from the alleged junto, but not without first pointing his finger at the other four.[42]

Even before Dodge wrote in November, the governor hardly acted like he thought he might be mistaken. The next thing Austin knew, Wilkinson reportedly had said that, during their meeting, Austin "had sunk Majr. Hunt as *low as MUD*. I am unwilling to believe," Austin gasped, "Gov Wilkinson capable of such an expression sunk as *low as mud*. What language for a Gentlm in Gov Wilkinson's situation and station in life." Austin believed, instead, that "This is a fresh step of our Enemies to plunge us into new Difficulties. I shall not believe untill like Thomas I have thrust my finger into the Hole. *I solemnly* protest that nothing passed between the Govr & myself that can justify his saying I had sunk Majr Hunt as *low as mud* the general dispute between Majr Hunt & Govr Wilkinson was not brought into view nor did the Govr say a word that would have wounded the feelings of Maj Hunt's nearest connection before mentioned." On the other hand, Austin thought, "If the Govr has made use of expressions tending to a belief that I have sacrificed Maj Hunt to obtain his friendship he says it without foundation be the man who he may that says I have expressed myself unfriendly toward either you [Easton] or Hunt that man tells an Untruth."[43]

Was there a pattern in the charges, countercharges, rumors, innuendo, factional discord, and political unrest? More than one person thought so. The first was Major James Bruff, commander of United States troops in St. Louis before General Wilkinson's arrival. Major Bruff suspected it could be traced directly to General Wilkinson, and in particular to his relationship with Vice-President Aaron Burr.

> The first hint I had of a connection between General Wilkinson and colonel Burr was drawn from two paragraphs in Kentucky newspapers, in the Spring of 1805, before General Wilkinson reached St. Louis: the first alluded to the old plan to form a separate government west of the Allegany, and ascribed it to General Wilkinson and associates, and doubting whether that scheme had yet been abandoned; the next was an extract of a letter from Fort Massac, published in the papers, which states that Colonel Burr had been several days there with General Wilkinson, probably giving General Wilkinson lessons on government.[44]

To this day, no one knows for certain what plans Burr and Wilkinson might have made. Perhaps they intended to separate the West from the rest of the United States. Maybe they designed to attack the Spanish provinces and establish a new nation. Some believed they planned to do both. No one who failed to join Wilkinson unreservedly ever received more than hints of the scheme. Of those who apparently gave themselves completely in support of the project, none evidently told all that he knew. In the hindsight even of contemporaries, however, it became abundantly clear that something was afoot, that it was the project of two well-placed government officials but not of the government itself, and that the Territory of Louisiana was to be a major source of men and lead.[45]

Observers eventually saw, too, that the "grand scheme," as Wilkinson sometimes called it, governed not only Wilkinson's personal affairs, but also his dealings both with his subordinates, civil and military, and with the citizenry in general in Louisiana Territory. Early in his administration, Wilkinson approached Major Bruff about the scheme. When, after four meetings, Bruff failed to warm to Wilkinson's suggestive, but inexplicit statements, Wilkinson showed him the door and later found cause to have him court martialed. Major Hunt, commandant of the district richest in lead, took no interest in the plan either. Within a month, the general not only refused to support him in the dispute with Smith T, but administered a stinging rebuke. A few weeks later, in September, 1805, Wilkinson had Hunt arrested for insubordination and replaced him as commandant of the Ste. Genevieve District.[46]

Rufus Easton came next. On the recommendation of Vice-President Burr, whom Easton had supported in the New York election of 1804, Easton had been appointed a territorial judge. Close observers saw clearly the political deal. Jefferson openly despised Burr, but the president wanted a conviction in the impeachment trial of Judge Samuel Chase and removal of the senile old Federalist from the Supreme Court. The vice-president, as presiding officer of the Senate, conducted the trial. To dispose Burr, the president gave him the appointment of both Easton as territorial judge and Dr. Joseph Browne, Burr's brother-in-law, as secretary of the Territory. (Some contemporaries, thinking it exceeding strange that a president with the democratic credentials of Jefferson had appointed a soldier on active duty to a civil office simultaneously, wrote off the naming of Burr's friend, General Wilkinson, to the governorship as one more manifestation of the foul pact.) Wilkinson knew that Burr thought highly of Easton. Yet when Easton failed to express interest in the scheme, even after Wilkinson brought Easton into his intimate counsel in governing the Territory, Wilkinson turned against Easton and had nothing more to do with him, even refusing to permit his mail to pass through the St. Louis post office, which Easton directed as postmaster. Not stopping there, the governor went out of his way to alienate the young judge by denouncing him to Austin.[47]

Smith T, by contrast, took an active interest in the plot and had much to contribute to it. He could recruit and command men, as well as fight himself. Moreover, with his various claims and interests, he could provide lead in abundance to the army Burr and Wilkinson would raise. Wilkinson rewarded him handsomely. He placed Smith T on the Court of Common

Pleas and Quarter Sessions and named him a justice of the peace, commissioner of rates and levies, and lieutenant colonel in the 2nd Regiment of militia for the Ste. Genevieve District. Perhaps his greatest favor, Wilkinson advanced Smith T's designs in the Territory by undermining the standing of his chief rival, Moses Austin.[48]

Over and over the pattern repeated. Those who joined Wilkinson in the grand scheme received appointment and preference from the governor. Those who did not, or who opposed men favored by the governor, suffered Wilkinson's wrath and indignation. The pattern of reward and reprisal could succeed, however, only so long as a few men, and even fewer in high places, were attacked. Wilkinson did not know when to quit. Whether or not a conspiracy had developed on its own in opposition to him, his treatment of Austin, Hunt, and Easton, among others, had the effect of raising significant opposition. By late in the fall of 1805, the situation in Louisiana appeared to attorney Carr to have slipped beyond the governor's control. On November 14, he wrote the secretary of the treasury that "Party spirit continues to rage here, & with redoubled vigour . . . There is probably no part of the United States so much torn to pieces by dissention and partyism as Louisiana and whose government is so unsettled . . . It is generally believed," he concluded prophetically, "that the parties have gone to such extremities that one or the other must fall."[49] As the year closed, Easton left for Washington, one of the first of a stream of men to make the long trip to lay their fears for Louisiana Territory before the country's leaders and try to bring a quick end to the malignant administration of Governor Wilkinson.[50]

Easton could also discuss with government leaders a proposal to raise revenue from lead mines on public land. The preceding January he had laid before the president a two-part plan calling for a tax on the mineral dug and an agent to both lease mines and collect the duty. With the revenue, raised at the rate of twenty-five cents per hundredweight, the agent would buy mineral, smelt, and sell it. By Easton's figures, the United States would realize some $2,500 annually. As only one person had a furnace sufficient to handle the work, the choice of the agent was obvious. "I venture to say," Easton offered, "that the Executive branch of the Government could not select a more capable and trusty character than Moses Austin Esquire who is now extensively engaged in that business and who would readily accept the proposition from the Government." Perhaps most significant of all to money-conscious administrators, Austin would take the job "without a Salary or any other reward than the exclusive privilege of purchasing in the mineral which would belong to the United States."[51]

Easton evidently received no encouragement for his plan and dropped it. That might have been the end of the matter had not Governor Wilkinson in September, 1805, revoked the privilege of the French miners to dig mineral on public land. The outcry against his sudden prohibition of a right long established under Spanish rule forced Wilkinson to rescind his order. But the unrest led Carr to address the secretary of the treasury in November with a version of the Easton plan. Carr made a strong case, pointing out that actually all the lead produced in Louisiana Territory came from public land, "those parts of the mines covered by private claims, being preserved by the owners, who carry on the manufactory of lead by purchasing the mineral obtained by the people from the public land." The secretary should understand, too, that the quantity of mineral raised, lead produced, and profit realized all were immense. Individual miners commonly made between $50 and $100 for a single day's labor, an incredible sum for that time. Such a figure represented months of labor for most men. "This was done at the Mine a Barton[,] part of which is claimed by Moses Austin esquire," Carr assured the secretary, "and serves to discover the fertility of the mines & what might be done by miners who had a proper stimulus applied to induce them to labour." More than the mere $2,500 per year that Easton estimated, Carr envisioned that within a few years the income could substantially repay the cost of the entire Louisiana Purchase – nearly 15 million. As Easton had proposed, the plan would cost the treasury nothing, since the government agent could take his profit from the smelting.[52]

Some have suggested that the plan really was Austin's to control the entire lead production of the Louisiana Territory.[53] Perhaps it was. Certainly it was characteristic of Austin to use well-placed men to promote his ideas and plans. Moreover, he was an early, if not the first, proponent of a tax on mineral dug from the public domain as a means of raising revenue for the government.

To put the plan into operation, Austin surely would have had to enlarge his plant. In 1805, as subsequent records would show, his mine and smelter entered their period of peak production under his ownership. Austin received an estimated 800,000 pounds of lead per annum for four straight years. The monetary value reached astronomical heights, amounting to $50,000-worth of lead that summer alone, with demand still exceeding supply.[54]

Austin's operation dominated the mining country in part because of the richness of his mine and in part because he would modernize his methods. James Austin, for example, brought an exciting new way to wash lead that two of the Englishmen had developed at the Virginia mines. It was "done with a machine that can be worked by a boy of 12 years old Mr. Rugles has look at it and can fix one in the same way for very trifling expense it workes as fast as two hands and much cleaner which may be of some advantage in the lead makeing business."[55]

Moses Austin, alone among all who smelted ore, utilized the reverberatory furnace. No other smelterers considered the $5,000-6,000 cost worth the expense. The open hearth furnace that cost but $50 to construct had begun to reappear by 1807 when Christian Schultz visited the mine country. Lead ore remained so plentiful and in such great demand that miners could realize a satisfactory profit using that far less efficient, but also far less expensive hearth. For Austin, a satisfactory profit was not enough. The reverberatory furnace gave him a share in the profit of other miners through his contract smelting business.[56]

Austin's best markets appear to have been along and south of the Ohio River, and in the eastern United States. If his product proved poor for the market, as did a shipment of sheet lead too soft for the common use in Philadelphia, he could do nothing but accept the lower price it brought. On occasion, where demand was strong, he set the retail price for his product. But the slow transportation and communication of the day put him at the mercy of the jobbers. In Nashville in 1805 he ordered a load of shot sold at ten cents a pound. Through a third party he learned that the store ignored his instructions and sold the shot for more, intending to charge him interest and commission on the sum, "an Irish trick equal to any Yanky trick," Thomas Westcott growled.[57] Nevertheless, in spite of these irritations, Austin profited handsomely from his business.

Profit bred envy, and in the spring of 1806 Smith T broke the uneasy peace that had separated him and Austin. Smith T had decided that he wanted for himself the rich Mine a Breton tract. To get it, he would take several tacks. One was to plant rumors that would cause questions to be raised concerning Austin's title to the property. In late April or early May, he let Austin know that James Maxwell, the popular Catholic priest of long residence in Ste. Genevieve, was saying that Austin had mortgaged his grant. Outraged, Moses demanded an explanation "to remove the injurious impressions made on the Public mind, as to the solvency of my Situation." Maxwell denied ever having made the statement Smith attributed to him, but as the priest and Smith T were friends, Moses doubted he told the truth.[58]

Next, Smith T planned to humble Austin. He would take the three-pounder cannon Austin still had. Moses had used the little gun only to fire alarms and to celebrate the anniversary of the country's independence. What better day for Smith T to make his move than July the Fourth? That morning Austin followed his customary procedure of firing the first salute at daylight. At sunrise he touched off a second salvo as he raised the fifteen-star flag on the pole he had erected three years earlier beside his house. About this same time, at a house in the village, a group of men had gathered in preparation for the customary militia muster later that morning. "Several persons were in the drinking way," a contemporary recorded, and two had stripped to fight when John Smith T, Lieutenant Colonel of

Militia and Justice of the Peace, arrived and "commanded the peace."
After Smith T said he would send Thomas Scott to jail, his brother John
Scott suddenly pushed or grabbed Smith T by the collar. The two already
that morning had argued after Smith T announced his intention to take
Austin's cannon, and "said with three of his own choice he could have the
peace of ordinance taken and have austin hanged." When Scott laid his
hand on Smith T, the lieutenant colonel, some said, drew his dirk and
growled that he feared neither of the Scotts. But Smith T must have
decided to save his fight for later, and the two men parted without coming
to blows.[59]

About 10 o'clock, two companies of militia mustered at a distance from
Durham Hall and began parading. A half-hour later, a detachment of a
dozen men marched to Austin's residence with a letter from battalion commander Smith T ordering Austin to turn over the cannon, claiming it to be
the property of the United States. Austin replied that he had no public
property, hence could hand over none. He had dug the cannon out of the
mud in Ste. Genevieve, had fitted it for action, had been promised reimbursement but had never received any. Thus the cannon was his. Shortly
word came back that Smith T "had Determined on take[in]g the *Cannon*
by force," and called for fifteen volunteers to make the assault.[60] Austin
pulled the gun back within the compound of his front yard, the same compound he had held against the thirty Osage four years earlier, and prepared for the advance.

In hopes of avoiding bloodshed yet, Austin hastily appealed to Andrew
Henry, Judge of the Court of Common Pleas of Ste. Genevieve, who was
present as a soldier in muster.

> I have this moment been Called on by Colo Smyth to give up
> a three pounder in my possession and as I have been told that
> my House is to be forced to take it from me I pray you to make
> use of your Authority as a piece officer and I demand that pro-
> tection the laws of my Country give me—[61]

Then Austin waited.

Henry's reply repeated the demand for the cannon. He urged Austin to
be reasonable and pledged his own honor to return the field piece if Austin
would let the battalion borrow it for the day. Austin knew better than to let
the gun out of his hands and into Smith T's and refused. "This is not a
moment to speek of reason," he answered Henry with fire in his words,
"since reason appears Not to be the Order of the Day." After reciting his
right to the gun, Austin told Henry that he, Austin, was "always dispo'd to
meet my fellow men on friendly terms to arrange misunderstandings with
temper and reason but Mr. Henry do you Expect I am to be forced into
measures No Sr. I now tell you that If my House is forced by armed men
so be It, I can only stand on the Defensive." He ended by reminding Henry

of his office on the bench and by placing responsibility for the outcome of the confrontation squarely on the Judge. "Reason is and shall alway be my guied [guide] and on Reasonable terms only am I to be Your, O[bedient Servant]."[62]

Austin waited again. Instead of an attack, he watched his ranks begin to swell. One by one, soldiers unsympathetic with the confrontation deserted the muster and took up positions within his perimeter. Around one o'clock, word reached Austin that "Colo Smith had relinquished his Intention of takeing the gun by force" on account of both the desertions and "a general determination on the part of the Citizen[s] not to support" him. Austin had won the war of nerves. After the muster, the militia captains gave the traditional dinners for their companies, and Austin, following suit, feasted his supporters.[63]

Two days later, Moses Austin addressed a long letter to Territorial Judge John B. C. Lucas, the most outspoken opponent of Governor Wilkinson, recapitulating the events of July 4, "because I think an outrage of so dareing a nature in violation of all law requires legislative Interference, & because the officers under Smith have Imbibed an Advice that they are bound by the Militia Law to Obey the Colo, altho his Orders Extend to the ruin and life of a Citizen, & lastly because I have reason to beleave representations will be made Calculated to Injure my reputation in society."[64]

Not a month after Austin wrote, Smith T, just as Moses predicted, resumed the attack on his standing by announcing that Austin's Mine a Breton grant was invalid. Moreover, Smith T said that he would pick up the property with the large St. Vrain concession he had acquired. Austin thundered that he would prosecute any case of trespass and would protect those digging on his land with his permission. "Should the said John Smith T. make any attempt to molest or give any hindrance or to interfear in any wise with the people now Digging on my Land, Either by writing, personal action or by agent, I will take on myself to Answer the consequence that may arise by treating said notice with silent neglect—"[65]

About the same time, Mine a Breton resident William Perry went to Durham Hall on business. As he and Austin discussed Moses' boundary in "the pinery" where Perry had cut some house logs, evidently for Smith T, Austin flew into "a passion" and called Smith T "a Liar rascal & murderer,...guilty of the basest action."[66] Perry reported the words to Smith T, who filed suit against Austin for slander and demanded damages of $10,000. Austin retaliated with a suit of his own, setting a pattern for suit and countersuit for the next year.[67]

On August 7, 1806, Austin sent Smith T a scathing letter denying Perry's report of Austin's words, and responding to a letter from Smith T.

> [The] unbounded and unprovoked abuse I had rec'd from
> you could not be justified on any grounds what Ever. the

attempt to ruin myself and famely which was reported by *your-self* and *Maxwell* have not to this day been sattesfactory Explained[68] Your unwarrantable assault on the 4 of July and the report by you that I am depriv'd of my lands and that I had not a tittle to an Acre are all things calculated to produce the same consequences, *ruin. If in you[r] power*, to ruin me, and which you told me in presents of sundry Gentlm. are proofs of your Determenation to continue the same line of conduct towards me.... your conduct to others I speak not of, its your conduct toward me which I now say is and has been Such as no man can Justify.

Moses had, he said, "don What Every man of Honor ought to have don on such an occation I have manafest'd a wish by my treatment of you that no remembrance of the past should ever be recalled, but has that been your conduct toward me No unless one fourth of the reports are incorrect, you take Every Oppertunity to do me injury—"[69]

Moses evidently prepared for all-out war. In response to the militia appointments of Governor Wilkinson, so some said, a group of men at Mine a Breton formed themselves into a company. In mid-August, 1806, they gathered in front of James Austin's house and began "exercising as militia commanded by persons acting as officers." As Sheriff Henry Dodge, accompanied by John Smith T, rode up, the ranks shouldered their weapons, aimed over the heads of Dodge and Smith T, and fired. Smith T's horse reared and threw him. But he remounted and asked what they were doing. "Mustering," they responded. As Justice of the Peace, he then charged several with riotously disturbing the peace and ordered all to disperse, which they evidently did.[70]

Moses Austin's Durham Hall surely was a prize worth fighting for. As Moses' interests expanded, so had the complex around his home. In 1802 and 1803 he erected a log kitchen, two years later a barn, stable, and blacksmith shop, smokehouse, and henhouse. In the middle of the decade, he put up a two-story frame structure behind Durham Hall for his growing dry goods business. And to insure that Mine a Breton, a thriving village of nearly forty houses, continued to be the trading center for the surrounding mines country, he put in roads to Old Mines five miles northeast, the oldest diggings in Louisiana Territory, and to Mine a Renault, six miles north, the second oldest. In addition, he threw a bridge across Breton Creek in front of his house.[71]

The investments paid off. The store, with its varied stock, prospered. Young Stephen Austin recalled particularly the Indians that came to trade for both dry goods and liquor. Moses had been doing business with them for years, initially under license from Commandant Valle. "My father has had hundreds of them at his home at the Lead Mines in Missouri,"

Stephen wrote years later. "He traded with the Shawnees and Delawares and was their friend I was then a little boy and have often played with the Shawnee children."[72]

Stephen F. Austin, as he approached the teenage years, was a young-looking boy, erect, with a well-proportioned head and smooth, handsome features. His countenance betrayed no effects of growing up on the frontier, which was as his father would have it. Moses wanted his son accepted into the highest circles of society. To prepare the boy, Moses and Maria sent him East, out of the culturally barren mines country, to receive a proper education. Early in the summer of 1804, not yet eleven years old, Stephen left in the company of Daniel Phelps, a second cousin, on a thousand-mile pilgrimage to New England. His education began as soon as he left home, for, as his father told him, "Your troubles on your Journey will learn you a little of what you are to expect to meet with in life."[73] The first lesson, no doubt, was to conquer homesickness. Stephen would be gone for four years.

From Louisiana Territory, Moses had little way of selecting the right school for his son, but he still had family in Connecticut. Consequently, Stephen, who could not possibly have remembered any of them, if he had ever met them, carried a letter for young Phelps's father in Suffield asking the gentleman to place Stephen "at the best school in your Country."

Stephen Fuller Austin, 1805. Moses Austin's oldest son at age 12.
Item 750-4, Texas Memorial Museum.

Moses meant a school known for the morals it inculcated, as well as the academics it offered. "Great Care...must be taken," Moses instructed Phelps, "that he formes no Improper Connections that may have A tendency to Corrupt his Ideas of propriety I wish him to be furnished with such masters and Connect himself with such Society as becomes a Young Gentln in his Situation." Moses also asked his cousin by marriage to outfit the boy in "Clothing proper to appear as becomes a Gentln." Always conscious of his prominence and his station, Moses wanted Stephen both to reflect it and to prepare himself to continue it. Moses would pay the cost, whatever it was.[74]

Phelps, fifteen years Moses' senior, had physical and financial troubles that prevented him from accepting the role Moses had thrust upon him, apparently without warning. Thus he placed the boy in the care of the Penniman family, who in time enrolled him in Bacon Academy in Colchester. The Academy had opened only in 1803, but under its first principal, John Adams, quickly had built an outstanding reputation. It enjoyed a substantial enrollment of around 200 students and offered a curriculum emphasizing Latin, Greek, and religion.[75]

Though the school promised to polish Stephen to the highest social standing, Moses nevertheless outlined explicitly and at length to Professor Adams the education he expected his son to receive. "I have a dispossition that Stephen should go through the Classicks," he wrote. "In short I wish to make him a scholar yet I must confess I have for many years disapproved of spending month and year on the Greek and Hebrew. I have thought neither of those languages of much advantage to a man of business, and as I do not wish my son to make devinity his study, [I should like] as little time spent in Greek and Hebrew as is consistent with the regulations of the Acady." The career Moses wished for Stephen, if the boy's talents inclined in that direction, was law. Realizing, however, that Stephen had his own life to live, Moses added that "I have so many times in my life blamed Fathers for pressing on their sons a profession nature never intended them for that I shall make of him what Nature has best calculated him to be."

Whatever work Stephen might choose, however, Moses believed there were certain things every young man must learn. "A Correct mode of thinking both Religious and Political is of consequence and aught to be early implanted in the mind of man," he wrote the Principal. "I do not wish my son a Bigot in Either, but correct Moral principles is of the first consequence such I trust you will impress on his mind."

To Stephen, Moses wrote equally explicitly, but far more tenderly, a letter worthy of any father. "I hope and pray," he scrawled, that "you will improve Every moment of time to the utmost advantage and that I shall have the sattisfaction of seeing that my expectations are not Disappointed.

remember my Dear Son that the present is the moment to lay the foundation for your future greatness in life that much money must be expended
before your Education is finished and that time lost can never be recalled,
therefore be studious and attentive to obtain full information of all matters
given to you to learn—"

Stephen would receive adequate spending money, his father told him,
but must take care with it. "I do not expect you will expend money
unwisely," Moses instructed, "Yet I do not wish you to render yourself Disagreeable to your young friends to avoid expending a few Dollars when it
appears necessary for you to forme company pay readely your part of all
expenses that may arise but Never lett yourself be imposed on by an
improper Demand and If you finde a Disposition in any of your young
friends to do such an Act, I charge you, have nothing more to Do with
them, Keep not there Company and promptly tell them the Cause, that is,
that you will never keep Companey with a Boy disposed to impose on you,
nor allow yourself to make an improper Demand on your friends to save a
Dollar these are things many suppose of Small moment, but I do not. its
small things that stamp the disposition and temper of a man and many
times, Boys lessen there greatness in life by small things which at the
moment they think of little or no Consequence."

In October, 1804, with Stephen gone but a few months, the Austins sent
Emily, then only nine years old, to Mrs. Beck's Boarding School in Lexington, Kentucky, to begin a four-year course of study.[76] With Stephen and
Emily gone, the sounds of only one child echoed through Durham Hall.
"Jacque Elias," as the name was entered in the baptismal record of the
Catholic church in Ste. Genevieve, "James Elijah Brown" as he was called
in the earliest letter to mention him, had been born on October 3, 1803,
one day short of Moses' forty-second birthday. Since the boy went by his
third given name, "Brown," the confusion whether his second honored his
grandfather or his uncle evidently was forgotten.[77]

By Brown's third birthday, the political balance in Louisiana Territory
was shifting significantly. General Wilkinson had been ordered to military
duty at the southern end of the Mississippi River and had left St. Louis,
never to return as governor. What an apparent good fortune for Aaron
Burr that was, since his designs focused on the New Orleans area as either
the center of a new country or a staging ground for an attack upon the
Spanish dominions.[78]

Burr began his move. His flotilla of fewer than a dozen craft conveying
some 100 of the 1,200 men he had hoped to raise, reached New Madrid on
New Year's Day, 1807. It was then that John Smith T misplayed his hand.
Early in January, with Henry Dodge and a load of lead, he started down
the Mississippi from Ste. Genevieve to join Burr. Smith T and Dodge,
however, never caught up with the former vice-president. When, some-

where on the River, they learned that President Thomas Jefferson on
November 27, 1806, had proclaimed Aaron Burr a traitor to the United
States of America and ordered his arrest, they turned around and paddled
home as fast as they could.[79]

They could not reach home in time to avoid facing treason charges of
their own. Smith T refused to let the warrant against him be served.
When the coroner, acting for the indicted sheriff, arrived at Smith T's
house to take him into custody, Smith T met him at the door. "I know what
you have come for," Smith T said calmly. "You have come with a writ to
arrest me. If you attempt it you are a dead man; I will not be arrested."
Then, in as much as dinner had just been prepared, Smith T invited his
would-be captor to join him for the meal. The guest ate with a pistol laying
on the table, aimed at him and cocked, insuring that he made no
unfriendly move. After they finished, Smith T rode with the official into
Ste. Genevieve to respond to the accusations. But never was he a pris-
oner.[80]

Smith T's actions displeased the new political leaders of Louisiana Territory. Meriwether Lewis, famed for his part in the Lewis and Clark expedition, whom the president on March 3, 1807, named to replace Wilkinson,
ordered his colleague and militia commander, William Clark, to remove
from office "without partiality favor or affection" all those clearly involved
in the Burr affair, particularly the "highly implicated" Dodge and Smith
T.[81]

The new territorial secretary, Frederick Bates, occupied his office on
April 7, 1807, and a month later, his investigations completed, he moved
against the Burrites. "Justice and the dignity of the Government," he, as
acting governor, wrote the president on May 6, "required that a few of the
most conspicuous of the disaffected should be dealt with in an examplary
way. Colo John Smith (T) of whom so much has been said, on various occasions, has been removed from all his offices civil and military." Among the
reasons Bates gave Smith T–"that rash and impatient man"–was Smith
T's contempt for the law in resisting arrest.[82]

Moses Austin had survived the Wilkinson years, all in all, quite well. His
businesses prospered. His family made him proud. Best of all, no doubt,
he had seen John Smith T brought to heel, at least politically. Moses could
begin working to restore his own influence in the highest political offices
of the Territory. He set his sights in particular on the judgeship that
Wilkinson had taken from him.

CHAPTER VIII

M OSES AUSTIN lost no time making the acquaintance of Frederick Bates, the new acting governor. At the end of April, 1807, before Bates had completed a month in office, Austin entertained him at Durham Hall for two days. Moses, who understood the value of first impressions and knew how to charm new acquaintances, especially those in positions of importance, meant to get the jump on his rivals for the friendship of the incoming administration. But if Austin was observant, he saw from the fact of Bates's trip to familiarize himself with the Territory, if from nothing else, that Bates bore no resemblance to his predecessor.

Twenty-nine-years-old, sixteen years Austin's junior, and unrelated to Austin's brother-in-law, Moses Bates, Frederick Bates came to Upper Louisiana with a reputation for uncompromising honesty. Integrity, sobriety, diligence, and attention to his business had characterized Bates from his first job as assistant to a Virginia county recorder, and he took pride in it. Bates first came to public notice in Detroit, where, after his successful dry goods venture burned to the ground, his passion for politics and law led him to seek and accept appointment to public office. As land commissioner and associate justice of Michigan Territory, Bates soon distinguished himself by remaining above the corruption that tainted his colleagues. For President Jefferson, after the debacle of James Wilkinson as governor of Louisiana Territory, which he had followed with the appointment of Meriwether Lewis strictly in reward for his service on the Lewis and Clark Expedition, it was essential that the new territorial secretary in St. Louis be a tested administrator free of all suspicion of bias and faction. Jefferson could have found no one more appropriate for the demanding job. Bates would do what he perceived to be best for the Territory as a whole, regardless of friendship.[1]

From their first meeting, Bates liked Austin. Austin showed him the mining operation and dazzled him with figures of profits. A slave, who would do the real work, Austin told him, could repay his $400 purchase price in one year or less. Bates began considering buying a few slaves and a place of his own in nearby Bellevue. But aware already of the tangle of disputed land claims festering in his new territory, he was too wise to jump in rashly.[2] Bates in fact did nothing precipitously, and especially not in his new position. Instead of returning Austin to the bench, he investigated. At the bottom of the political unrest in the Ste. Genevieve district, he discovered not only Smith T, as Moses no doubt had warned him, but also Austin himself. Smith T and Austin, Bates told the secretary of state, "have kept the District of St Genevieve in continual ferment." And the warring had gone on for so long, he added, "the opinion pretty generally prevailed that the administration of the territorial government must *Sink*, if not sustained by a *Party*."[3] Bates would have none of it and "disappointed the expectations of *all* by refusing to strengthen either of the contending Cabals with the executive patronage."[4] Having removed Smith T from the court, Secretary Bates declined to appoint Moses Austin in his place.

Moses was <u>disgusted</u> (Bates underlined the word in writing Secretary Madison). Timothy Phelps, a brother of the widow of Moses' brother Elijah Austin, who had settled in Louisiana Territory and got along well with Moses, saw the anger too and offered his friend some unsolicited advice. "If you could form one other resolution and carry that also into effect," Phelps wrote, "I think—your days in future, would pass in peace and quietness—that is, under all circumstances and in all situations do your duty and command yourself, if things work ever so contrary and perverse, dont give way to your Passions, but make the best of it—every thing can be effected by resolution—this mode of conduct is the most satisfying you may depend—I know by experience—"[5]

If Frederick Bates sincerely thought that withdrawing government patronage would snuff out the contention and rivalry between Austin and Smith T, or that he thereby could extricate his office from their fighting, he was sorely mistaken. By December, 1807, he realized it, when he confided to his brother that the men he found in the Ste. Genevieve District "who emigrated prior to the acquisition, are, with few exceptions industrious, intriguing, turbulent and avaricious, Mean and fawning when it suits their purposes, and insolent Bravos when they drop the mask, on a disappointment of their hopes."[6] Indeed, he concluded, "it is our own refractory countrymen with whom all my unpleasant contests have arisen."[7]

The bad blood between Austin and Smith T ran so deep that the loss of political preferment hardly dampened the wrangling. Indeed, not even their friends could stop it. Joseph Ficklin, one of Austin's business associates, begged him, for his own benefit, to end his feud with Smith T. "It was counted Good policy in the Ky Hunters," he advised Moses from Kentucky, "not to disturb a buffalo when he had recvd a mortal wound because if they did he would give them much heap of trouble whereas if he was left to himself he would soon die— it so with many of your enemies— they have receivd a vital wound in the infamy of Genl W and A Burr and if you suffer them to rest they will soon cease to disturb you on the Contrary you may be attending to everything you hear [and] for ever have trouble yourself and your friends too."[8] Ficklin must have been alone in his views, however, for the friends of Austin and Smith T, Bates stormed, "would quarrel

with Heaven for dispensing its sunbeams on their enemies."[9] With government beyond their control, they carried on their struggle in the murky
waters of disputed land claims.

Speculating in land claims in American Louisiana brought out the worst
in men, as they jockied to position themselves to reap large returns from
small investments. All with money to spend acquired, then schemed to
substantiate, claims to known or suspected lead properties. Few hands
were clean. Austin's were not. During an early meeting of the Board of
Land Commissioners, surveyor Thomas Madden, whom Austin's forces
had thwarted two years earlier, obtained his revenge when he produced a
letter from Austin professing surprise at Camille DeLassus's attempt to
acquire a tract to which Austin asserted a prior claim. "This letter," Will
Carr told Austin, "al tho apparently produced to benefit the U S in proving
the date of C's survey, were nevertheless produced to injure you; by she-
wing in the first place your intention to defraud Luzierre out of the land or
to prevent him from obtaining it; or secondly to manifest your disposition
and desire of obtaining concessions which must have been antedated; and
also much land."[10]

If this unpleasant disclosure prompted Austin to want to bridle his
acquisitiveness, Smith T revived Moses' contentious nature. The smooth
Tennessean, known even to Treasury Secretary Gallatin for the property
he had taken through political corruption and vigilante force, boldly
repeated his claim to Austin's Mine a Breton. Acknowledged at first by the
federal government as a complete title, Austin's claim had been reopened
when later laws of Congress recognized only grants made before October,
1800, the date the country passed from Spain to France.[11] Austin was far
too solidly entrenched in 1807 for Smith T to hope to unseat him, but in
their struggle, harrassment brought satisfaction of its own.

Two could play Smith T's game, of course, and within a few months,
Austin turned the tables at Mine a Renault, about six miles north northwest of Mine a Breton, where Smith T in 1806 had located a portion of his
St. Vrain claim. Situated on government land, Mine a Renault long had
lain abandoned because, Austin speculated in his report to the president in
1804, rich mines had been opened nearer the settlements, not because of
inferior ore. Smith T held the place unchallenged for a year. In the spring
of 1807, however, the federal government, heeding the urgings of U.S.
land agent William C. Carr, Austin, Secretary Gallatin, and others,
adopted a comprehensive measure controlling both settlement on and digging lead from public lands. Specifically, the act opened the land for leasing. Austin quickly sent William Mathers and Michael Hart to obtain Mine
a Renault. After they secured the lease, everyone felt there would be trouble. "From the temper of the present occupants," Bates confided to Gallatin, "I have no reason to anticipate a peaceable compromise."[12]

It appears to be no coincidence that near the same time that Mathers and Hart took the lease, Austin at the head of seventy men (many of whom had been in the muster that Colonel Smith T had confronted not a year earlier) offered their services to the territory as a "Military School." Secretary Bates accepted the company,[13] perhaps because, lacking a sufficient militia, he might need it to maintain order at the mines, or perhaps, to gain a clear measure of control over the potentially unruly band.

As it happened, Austin caught Smith T at a vulnerable moment. The colonel, Bates wrote at the end of May, 1807, lay in bed recuperating "from several severe wounds, received in a late Recontre, in which it is said that he acted on the defensive. He will *recover* altho he has one Rifle Ball, thro' his body and a deep gash in the thigh. His antagonist was dreadfully mangled and expired on the spot."[14] Or perhaps Smith T disregarded Austin's challenge, believing leasing to be no threat to his claim of ownership.

Whatever the case, Smith T could not ignore the news early in 1808 that his and Wilkinson's old enemy, Major Seth Hunt, had turned up with a claim to Mine a Renault as good, if not better, than Smith T's. Major Hunt had acquired the claim of the mine's discoverer, Philippe François Renault himself. The claim dated from 1723, when the government of France made four grants to Renault for his services to the Company of the West, a firm formed to mine gold and silver, but which succeeded in finding only lead. Spain in its turn recognized all the French concessions made prior to Spanish occupation. Major Hunt acquired Renault's interest from a granddaughter of the Frenchman. To substantiate the validity of the claim, Hunt produced for Secretary Bates documentation from the Recorder's Office in Kaskaskia showing that similar claims had been acknowledged by American authorities. Bates received the information but committed himself only to submit the Major's documentation to Secretary Gallatin.[15]

Few reacted as calmly to Hunt's news as Secretary Bates. The claim has "excited much alarm among those Persons interested in similar speculations," Bates told the treasury secretary, "and a general curiosity among all descriptions of People."[16] Smith T flew into action. He knew that neither his nor Hunt's claim had been marked on the ground, an essential step in establishing any title. Consequently, in January, 1808, he dispatched a crew to survey his claim at Mine a Renault, including the lease of Mathers and Hart within his boundaries, and sent men to occupy the property. Mathers and Hart held their ground. When Smith T's representative, Edward Cheatham, arrived to recover mineral dug on the lease, Hart barred his way and warned that he moved for the lead "at his peril, for if he took the Mineral away there would be some blood spilt." Cheatham growled back that "he could spill as much blood as any man,"[17] but finally left without a fight and empty-handed.

Bates recoiled at "the rapacious extremes into which he [Smith T] is hurried by that Mineral-Mania, which appears totally to have disordered the understandings of his faction."[18] From Durham Hall, Austin exhorted the acting governor to protect the lease holders. "Colo Mathers deeply feels the outrages lately committed on his property & the insults offered his person," Austin wrote, "& depends much on you to see him remunerated for his losses."[19] That was not enough for Mathers and Hart, who eventually gave up the struggle and quit their lease. But by that time Austin could afford to lose them. Harassment no longer motivated him. He had bought from Major Hunt a substantial $6,800 interest in Mine a Renault.

Following his own interpretation of the Golden Rule – "do as he would be done by. give unto others what he *expects* others will give to him"[20] – Moses Austin looked forward to the fight he had bought into. "I have always been of opinion that we should have a contest," he said to Wingfield Bullock on July 16, 1808, "not only with the Government but also With sundry others say a Mr John Smith and Joseph Brown[e]" the former territorial secretary and Smith T's partner. Moses chose as the ground for the fight the meeting room of the Board of Land Commissioners and set about to assemble as much testimony as possible to substantiate the Renault claim. "Its of the utmost consequence that a strong and firm stand should be made and every circumstance brought forward to prove to the commissioner the authenticity of the original concession," he told Hunt. "If the Claim is Established its a fortune for us all independant of every other."[21]

The thought of sharing in the riches of Mine a Renault braced Austin as he watched business conditions deteriorating around him. His troubles had begun two years earlier when "The Situation into which this Whole Country was placed in all the year *1806* in consequence of Burr Expedition delayed my shipment to New York twelve month – "[22] By June, 1807, when he finally sent two boatloads of shot to market, the price had fallen by 40 percent from its zenith of $7 per hundredweight in 1806. More disturbing, after the cargo, which Moses valued at $9,000, reached New York, it sat unsold. Moses had shipped the shot under the charge of nephew Elias Austin Elliott, namesake of his father, who put it in the hands of factors, then committed suicide. The New York agents refused to release the lead without a power of attorney from John Rice Jones, Moses' partner in the venture.

The slow, uncertain communications of the day compounded Moses' frustration in settling the business. After finishing his letter of July 25, 1808, to cousin Henry Austin in New York, brother Elijah's son, who was trying to help him, Moses gave it to a friend on his way to Kentucky "to be put into the [post] office in that State I hope to God it may reach you."[23]

As Moses took stock that summer, he saw his situation worsening still. "Losses have become customary to me and disappointment common," he told Charles Elliott in mid-June. "Such has been my late losses and treatment that I find nearly all the funds I possessed last year are out of my hands—"[24] In Kentucky, not only had the bottom fallen out of the market, but also a load of his lead sat marooned in Louisville. Worse, in New York City, the federal government had purchased all lead on the market except his, which the recalcitrant factors steadfastly continued to withhold.[25]

Fear that fighting would erupt in defense of American shipping prompted the government demand. As Napoleon's armies marched across Europe and Britain struggled to hold them back, the carrying trade of the neutral United States became caught in the middle. Proclamations and counterproclamations by the belligerents against trade with the other, punctuated by blatant, unremorseful British attacks on American vessels, had to be answered. Before resorting to war, President Jefferson, with Congressional approval, imposed an embargo on all foreign trade. Far from affecting only foreign shippers, the measure brought business to a standstill even in landlocked Louisiana Territory and thus further compli-cated Moses' situation.[26]

Always the diversified entrepreneur, Austin looked for ways to turn the situation to his benefit. Early in 1808 he noticed that stocks of English goods stood severely depleted and that merchants delayed replenishing inventories while awaiting resolution of the unsettled conditions. Antici-pating a strong demand in the fall and sensing a real opportunity, Moses formed a partnership with Seth Hunt for the major to travel to England and, for a 12½ percent commission, purchase goods for shipment to Aus-tin. Hunt left Louisiana Territory in midsummer, but never managed to leave the United States.[27]

Moses thus had to continue to rely on his lead mines. Happily, not long after Hunt left, Austin's prospects took a dramatic turn for the better. His hands discovered a rich new mine on his land, and within six weeks, 100 men had produced more than 200,000 pounds of mineral. It is hard to tell which pleased Moses more: the wealth the new mine represented, or the torment his good fortune gave Smith T. "To make use of the language of our Louisiana bucks it put my Enemies, up a *stump* Smith and Co are down in the mouth."[28]

Of course, the lead brought cash only after it had been shipped down the Mississippi River and sold, normally in markets far from Louisiana Terri-tory. The costs of freighting his lead the forty tortuous miles from Mine a Breton up high ridges, over steep hills, and across narrow valleys to the Mississippi River at Ste. Genevieve easily added up to be one of Austin's largest outlays in the marketing of his product. If he could shorten the trip, he could reduce the expense. Moses had been thinking for nearly a year about establishing a shipping point on the Mississippi closer to Mine a Breton. Records suggest that in 1807, he and Samuel Hammond, former commandant of the St. Louis District, four years Austin's senior, and a man who, for his humanitarian compassion, had suffered the wrath of James Wilkinson, formed a partnership to establish a town and port. They traded a pair of field slaves to Austin's former point man, Judather Kendal, for 400 acres at the mouth of Joachim Creek. A distance north of Ste. Genevieve, the property lay about five miles nearer Mine a Breton than did the old town, and it included established landings on both the creek and the river. The site improved on Ste. Genevieve as a shipping point in one other, very important respect. "The Banks of the Mississippi are generally insecure, and the village of St. Genevieve has retired at least 1 1/2 miles to avoid the inundation of the Spring-Freshet," Frederick Bates wrote as Austin made plans for the town. Austin's location, by contrast, "is more elevated, and occupies the intermediate space between two rocky Promontories which will forever prevent a waste of the Banks."[29]

The English traveler G. W. Featherstonhaugh saw the natural beauty of the place, set as it was in a semicircular cove where the edges of weathered limestone strata called to mind the image of rows upon rows of seats in an amphitheater. Austin had seen it, too, Featherstonhaugh understood, and it had inspired him to name the place "Herculaneum" for the ancient Roman city buried by Mt. Vesuvius.[30] If true, Moses' personal reading had taken him deep into classical literature, a further expression of his refined taste that already had raised the stately Durham Hall on the raw mining frontier.

Samuel Hammond. *Missouri Historical Society.*

Late in 1808, Austin and Hammond laid out a square grid of seven streets north-south and seven east-west. Emphasizing the importance of river commerce to the town, they platted the streets running to the river a full 60 feet wide, while drawing the others only three-quarters as broad. Austin took for his property a half-block fronting Water Street, the thoroughfare paralleling the bank of the Mississippi. Only a block and a half separated his place from the mouth of Joachim Creek.[31] From his location, Moses could survey the landings and all the river traffic.

Austin held high expectations for his town. Its situation, he wrote Hunt, "will make it rise."[32] And it did gain at least local distinction quickly when John Maclot, a refugee from the French Revolution and a son-in-law of Charles Gratiot, who had helped Moses find his way in St. Louis on that frigid January day in 1797, built a shot tower in 1809 on the bluffs to the south. Maclot advertised his establishment in the young *Missouri Gazette* as "the first shot tower in the West." The next year, Austin built his own shot tower on the north bluffs. His proved the better location, because wagons could haul the raw lead up to the tower. Indeed, the ruts left by the heavy conveyances still can be seen in Dunklin Park along the brow of the promontory.[33]

Through both the good years and bad since 1802, when James Austin arrived from Virginia to join his uncle in Spanish Louisiana, at least if the surviving records give a true picture, Moses had not spoken the name of his brother Stephen. It was not because Moses cut himself off from his family in the East. Moses attracted family. By 1808, no fewer than eight relatives, and relatives of relatives, had moved to Louisiana Territory to seek their fortunes around him. In addition to Elias Bates and James Austin, who had come before cession to work for Moses at the mines, his brother-in-law, Aaron Eliot, and Aaron's brother, Benjamin Elliott (the brothers spelled their last names differently), arrived in 1805 and 1804 respectively, both to practice medicine, Aaron in Ste. Genevieve, Benjamin in Mine a Breton. Aaron's son and namesake of Moses' father, Elias Austin Eliot, Horace Austin, son of Moses' brother Elijah, and Horace's cousin, Timothy Phelps, all had arrived by 1807. Horace went to work clerking in Moses' store in Ste. Genevieve, while Timothy rented Moses' house on South Gabouri Creek in the old French settlement to set himself up in business. Henry Austin of New York, Elijah's young, handsome, and already wealthy son, came in 1806, but only for a visit.[34] Among them all, Henry complemented Moses best. They shared a perseverance and a knack for making money. But Henry possessed one trait that Moses lacked. He was a healer. Early in 1808, Henry set it as his business to heal the wounds between Moses and Stephen, or at least to settle the disputed finances.

Perhaps Henry took an interest in the plight of his oldest uncle after the

Henry Austin. *1969/19-1, Estelle H. Folk Collection, Prints and Photographs Collection, Archives Division, Texas State Library.*

bankrupt Stephen abandoned Philadelphia, moved to New York, and took any job he could find to support his family. Whatever Henry's reason, Moses appreciated his initiative. "I feel real pleasure," Moses encouraged him, "and much gratification that you have undertaken to bring the business of my unhappy Brother and myself to a close you have my thanks for your good intentions." Even so, Moses harbored reservations of Stephen's demands, for "I am not the rich man some suppose what I have has been obtained by long suffering and much self denial."[35]

During the month between mid-April and mid-May of 1808, Moses dispatched five letters to Henry—all of which arrived on July 4—outlining his position. On the bottom line, he offered to pay $5,000 over three years to liquidate Stephen's claims, on condition that should war break out and force Moses to abandon his property "on an extreem frontier," he would not be clapped in debtor's prison for failing to fulfill his promise.[36] Henry Austin worked fast, and on July 7, 1808, informed Moses that Stephen had accepted the terms. In the satisfaction of his triumph, Henry became a party to the settlement by advancing Stephen the capital to open a tea store and agreeing to accept in repayment the obligation due from Moses.[37]

Moses would find it hard to cover his notes as economic conditions continued to deteriorate. By May, 1809, he had become alarmed. "Money in this Count[r]y is of Great consequence and I may say greater than in any I have been acquainted With[,] there being no such thing as accomodations in the money Way—" he told factors in Kentucky.[38] Characteristically, but dangerously, he chose to meet the challenge by expanding. Through Major Hunt, Moses borrowed $7,000 from John G. Bond of Boston and gave the investor a substantial interest in the lead business.[39]

The move apparently helped little. From September, 1808, to February, 1810, though he operated one of but three manufactories of shot and colors of lead in the United States, Austin sold only a pitiful 89,000 pounds, mostly in bars. If the lead brought as much as ten cents per pound, Austin should have received approximately $8,800, far from the income of the halcyon days a few years previous. In July, 1809, he could not meet obligations, including two of Bond's for $1,100.[40]

Definitely hurt, Moses still was far from financially crippled. In 1810, he drafted a memorandum of his estate, which showed his basic financial strength. He valued Mine a Breton at $150,000, the Renault claim at $20,000, property in Ste. Genevieve, Herculaneum, on Grand River and at Bellevue at $10,000, and his moveable goods at another $10,000, for a grand total of $190,000. Though excluded from the accounting, his interests in the contract smelting and in his stores in Mine a Breton, Ste. Genevieve, and Herculaneum continued to provide income. Hardly in a mood to consolidate, Moses, who had traded in peltry for years, acquired a tanyard and currying shop, which James Austin, who had bought into it first, operated in a partnership arrangement. Later in the spring of 1810, he sold a single load of lead for nearly $8,000, a sum duplicating his income of the past two years.[41]

With English goods no more plentiful in 1810 than in 1808, Moses' hopes for the successful conclusion of his venture with Major Hunt rode high. Hunt, long stymied, first in reaching England, then in making profitable arrangements for goods, had at last dispatched a shipment due to reach New York that summer. Unable to contain his anticipation, Moses traveled to New York, his first trip East in almost fifteen years, to meet the cargo. He waited and waited, but it never arrived. Moses had to content himself with the purchase of textiles, hardware, and medicines from New York and Pittsburg to stock his stores.[42]

In Louisiana Territory the maneuvering over the Renault claim continued unabated and expensive. During 1809 and 1810, Austin paid out more than $1,200 in attorney's fees, surveying fees, and costs of attending court in Illinois to prove the validity of the claim, all to good effect, his colleagues thought. "I am strongly of opinion that the Claim now stands on a better footing than ever and that we shall eventually succeed," Jones encouraged Austin, "notwithstanding the Strong phalanx, which will shortly be broken that is opposed to us."[43]

Others must have thought so, too. Evidently unaware that Austin had been called out of town on business, a person or persons unknown approached Durham Hall unnoticed on the evening of January 23, 1811. As Maria Austin, her children, and several friends sat talking, four shots crashed into the house through a window. One bullet lodged in the sash, and the other three shattered the glass and buried themselves in a door immediately opposite the window, narrowly missing several of those in the room. For four weeks Austin offered $500 through the newspaper for information leading to the capture and successful prosecution of the attackers. "Against the assassins of life, or the violators of my property, it is my determination, as it is my duty, to defend myself and family," Austin thundered, "and what I cannot do for myself, I trust, with a becoming confidence, that the LAW will do for me." But no one ever came forward.[44] Austin and his associates believed their position so stout in the Renault matter that they filed several suits "to *stay waste*, and for the recovery of damages against a great number of persons."[45] The refusal of the judge to grant their injunctions seemed a vexatious but temporary setback.

It paled, however, against the sudden and unexpected news that the government had entered the struggle directly by pressing a claim of its own to the tract. "An accidental concurrence of circumstances," Bates wrote Gallatin on June 20, 1811, "has enabled me to gain possession, without the employment of force, of a Lead Mine, which promises to be abundantly richer than any yet discovered in Louisiana." Smith T's brother, Reuben, had located 1,000 acres of the St. Vrain claim at Mine a Renault in 1808, found no rich seam, and left. Subsequently Bates acquired the tract for the United States. By October, 1811, the rents due the government from the Renault area amounted to no less than $6,000, and conniving for possession of the Mine reached fever pitch. "A strange contest appears to have arisen," Bates informed Gallatin, "whether the *Agents* of *Renaut, John Smith (T)* or the *Government* shall receive them!"[46] The turn of events proved more than Smith T could stand. In December, he lost his composure and challenged Bates to a duel. Bates declined it, of course. Furthermore, he and the government appeared to be emerging the surprising victors in the battle for control of Mine a Renault.[47]

Moses Austin's energetic mind almost always kept him a step ahead of a loss. By the time the Renault scheme escaped him, Austin already had his sights focused on another design. In 1810, he had conceived a plan to incorporate his operation at Mine a Breton by act of Congress. His work, he thought, as anyone who read the petition could see, met a national need.

"In a free Country," he admitted "it is doubtless, a good general maxim, to leave most of the objects of human pursuits to individual Enterprize, and individual Industry." But there are "objects of primary necessity, which are placed by Circumstances, beyond the Range of individual Exertion, beyond the limits of individual Attainment.—In this situation, your Petitioners presume to say, the mining and manufacturing of lead in the Territory of Louisiana, is placed." And that being so, Congress should act. Lead was essential to the national defense. Yet while lead sufficient to satisfy world demand lay at Mine a Breton, the petition asserted, the United States in 1810 had to import the metal. The Louisiana Lead Company could reverse that dangerous situation and provide the permanent and reliable supply of lead necessary to render the country truly independent.

To Louisiana Territory, incorporation would bring "a portion of that prosperity, which, by the Influence of chartered Immunities, is rapidly pervading the Union at large." Such a happy object could be realized because the new firm must draw funds from eastern investors. The $300,000 capital would allow the company to pay for lead with specie, creating a medium of exchange and putting the business of the Territory on a sounder footing than it presently was. In addition, incorporation would stabilize the always volatile mining population. "To recommend an Occupation to Americans," the petition read, "it is necessary, that it may be pursued without any considerable diminution of personal Independence; that it would be reputable; and that its recompense should be certain and prompt.—That such would be the Effects produced by the Institution contemplated, your Petitioners, presume to believe, will not be questioned." Finally, by incorporating Austin's company, Congress could "rescue" the lead business from the depression into which it had fallen and "elevate it to that Rank which its Importance merits."[48]

A treasury department report, of which Austin probably was unaware, concluded without reservation that the lead mines of Louisiana Territory not only were the richest in the country, but also were not being wrought to their potential. Though the manufactories of Philadelphia and Louisiana were satisfying the country's demand for shot and colors of lead, about 600 tons per year, for other needs the United States imported more than 2,500 tons annually.[49] Clearly the government's facts supported Austin's case.

What the petition did not tell was the real reason Austin sought incorporation. And Henry Austin advised Moses to be cautious in revealing it. They both understood, as Henry wrote, that "the Property will be greatly enhanced in value" by incorporation. The place "will certainly yield double in this way than any other," he added. "Nothing will be wanting if the Charter is granted but good management to make it a Princely estate—" Moses himself would receive half of the capital for his interest at Mine a Breton—$100,000 in cash and $50,000 in stock, which led to Henry's warning. "I must again mention the necessity of avoiding any remarks that look like a wish to get rid of the Property the property will speak for itself when examined by such as wish to take stock, but should it be as well known to many as it is to some that your object is to dispose of the property there would be an end of sales. men would be fools to Purchase of another at his own price property which he shows such anxiety to get rid of— as yet those who know anything about it think favorably of it but the thing must be managed adroitly to succeed well."[50]

Fully cognizant that good people associated with an enterprise counted for as much toward its accomplishment as good reasons, Moses enlisted the Governor of Illinois, Ninian Edwards, for the Board of Directors. From Louisiana Territory, he took his widely respected partners Hammond and Jones, his trusted associates James Austin and Elias Bates, and one James Bryan. Thirty-five-years-old, Bryan had come to Upper Louisiana soon after cession, if not earlier, to work as a store clerk. Within a couple of years, he had acquired stores of his own, bought lead property, and by August, 1810, established a thriving settlement on Hazel Run, a short distance above its confluence with the Terre Bleue River, about twenty miles east-southeast of the lead mines. Finally, Austin included his geographically well-placed and financially respected cousin, Henry Austin of New York.[51]

A bill to incorporate the Louisiana Lead Company passed first reading in the Senate on January 21, 1811, moved to committee, and stalled three weeks later when postponed to the next session. The people of Mine a Breton raised their glasses in contempt on the fervently patriotic day of July 4, 1811, when they toasted "The lead-mines of Louisiana, may they increase and multiply in wealth, and merit the name of the Potosi of the United States, and prove to the general government how much they have neglected their best interests, and the happiness of this people." A booming cannon salute and six cheers sent the sentiment echoing through the hills.[52]

Through the summer and fall, Henry Austin spent weeks in Washington lobbying for the measure. He succeeded in getting it reported out of committee on January 17, 1812, in spite of the fact that he could not produce for the lawmakers documentary evidence of Moses' title to Mine a Breton. Until he had it, however, the bill would progress no farther. Everything waited for John Rice Jones to deliver the papers. When he had not come by February 23, 1812, and consideration was postponed until sometime in March, Henry worried that the delay might jeopardize the bill. Maria turned bitter. "It appears as though their was a fatallity attending all those whome you put Confidence in," she seethed. "When I reflect how often you have beene deceived by mankind & how much money you have lost in Consequence of those repeted Deceptions I assure you my Dr it gives me a poor Opinion of the hole Race, & if your Charter falls through from Mr. Js. neglect, I feele as if I never could forgive him."[53]

The rapport between Austin and Jones had been deteriorating for years. When Moses reorganized his original partnership in 1807, the year the agreement expired, only Jones of the first five partners remained. Although Austin observed to him that his contribution to the capital had been niggardly, Austin agreed to continue the partnership nevertheless. By 1811, the two men, in Henry Austin's words, were "getting at variance" to the point that they spoke of concluding their relationship. But if they parted then, the Louisiana Lead Company scheme, started in the partnership, would be lost.[54]

Jones finally arrived with the documents near the beginning of March, 1812, and Henry Austin left him to conclude the matter. "It will now be Jone's falt if the businiss falls through," Maria wrote, "but he [Henry] thinks their is no Possibility of that."[55] The Senate adopted a number of amendments, none of which compromised the basic purpose of the bill, and sent the measure to the House on March 26. Henry was jubilant. His confidence soared further a few days later when the mail from Washington brought news that on March 31 the bill had breezed through its first two readings in the Lower Chamber. The report swept from his mind every lingering doubt of the success of their efforts to incorporate the Louisiana Lead Company.[56]

The House, resolved into a committee of the whole, brought the bill to debate three weeks later, on April 13, and, by a majority of three, voted it down. The Austin forces were stunned. "I can Judge of your Disappointment by my one [own] feelings," Maria consoled her husband from Philadelphia. "When H. Austin left Washington he had no doubt but it would be granted & he blames Mr. J. Altogether for its falling through. Had Mr. J. been their with the necessary papers at the Commencement of the Business it would have been granted without the smallest Difficulty, but in Consequence of his Unpardonable Detention H.A. could do nothing & it was Procrastinated from time to time & finally those friends who he knew would vote in favour of the Charter Obtaind leave of Abcence & when it was brought forward for the last time, & had gown [gone] through every prior difficulty, it was lost by a Majority of three against it."[57]

Moses took the disappointment stoically, as his Congregationalist upbringing taught him to do. To his daughter Emily he confided his "hope that . . . establishing the charter at Washington would have made such a change in my situation that my stay in this Country would be short, but like all Other events in this World, they have terminated differently and I must submit to my disappointment."[58]

Her father's desire to abandon the mines, the location of the only permanent home Emily had ever known, probably came as no surprise to her. For months, maybe a year or more, her mother had been begging her father to leave Louisiana and move them back to Pennsylvania or Connecticut or somewhere they could live out their lives in the pleasant company of old friends and relations.

Life on the frontier had not been good to Maria. She had lost weight and by 1811 endured nearly constant pain. A change of climate, she and her husband decided, might do her good. Moreover, a trip to the East would give her the joy of renewing acquaintances with her kin, none of whom, save her sister Peggy, James Austin's wife, had she seen since before she left Virginia thirteen years earlier. Moses and Maria agreed, too, that she should take their two youngest children. Seven-year-old Brown, born in Louisiana, needed to meet his relatives on both sides, as he knew only those few of his Austin relations who had come to the mine country to work. For sixteen-year-old Emily, it was time to enter a good Eastern school where she, like her older brother before her, could finish her education. "I am satisfied that my Emily should lay up a store of information," her father told her. "Its Riches that cannot be taken from her, and should dame fortune turn her heel against you she cannot touch your store of Information It is a treasure no reverse of situation can deprive you of — therefore drink deep at the fountain of knowledge. It prepares you to discharge the duties of a child, a friend and wife."[59]

Moses asked the homesick Elisha Lewis, third husband of the widow of Moses' brother Elijah, to escort Maria and the children on the two-month journey to Philadelphia. After trading for perhaps nine months with Indians along the Mississippi River, Lewis had become desperately anxious to return to New Haven. Taking advantage of this opportunity, Moses also engaged him as part owner of a shipment of 900 pounds of feathers, various peltry, 104 venison hams, and a quantity of lead for delivery in New York. Part, if not all, of his proceeds from the consignment Moses earmarked to support Maria and the children.[60]

After disembarking in Baltimore, ninety miles from Maria's destination, Lewis deserted the Austins to expedite his own return home. First angry, Maria then realized her unreserved relief. Where Moses confided in her on business matters, Lewis "is one of those kind of men that thinks women has nothing to do with mens Business, and when I asked him upon what turms Chew and Ralph had taken his lead to ship and how much money theay had advnacd him, he just turnd it of[f] with a laughf, and begged I would not give myself any uneasiness about it, that he had don every thing for the best boath for him and yourself, that I should have what money i wanted and that was sufficient for me to know."[61]

Maria went first to the home of her sister, Rebecca, in Camden, New Jersey, across the river from Philadelphia. The women so reveled in each other's company that Maria put Brown in school and decided to stay for an extended period. But when she and her son both caught an ague and fever, she changed her mind abruptly and fled to Connecticut to escape Camden's suddenly unhealthy atmosphere. To her pleasant surprise, Maria delighted in New Haven even more than in Camden. Friends called on her constantly. "I expect to be Ingaged, all next week in returning Visits," she bubbled to her husband. "In Short the Coming Week will be nothing but one Continued scean of Visiting & Amusements." Moreover, the town itself she found "by far the Handsomest place I ever was in." Emily agreed, and "Joines with me in praying, that the time is not far distant when it will be in your power to leave Louis & settle down in pease & quietness in a town like this where you could injoy life. it tis pleasing to anticipate the happyness we might spend the remainder of our days in, providid you had money sufficient to satisfy your wishes. god grant, that this pleasing dream may sooner or latter be reallized is my sincear wish—"[62]

Barely a month back in the East, Maria was ready to settle there permanently. But level-headed and practical, she could neither wish nor dream without thinking first of the money required. It is curious, then, that, bold and outspoken, she apparently avoided confronting Elisha Lewis, the source of her financial discomfort. He never gave her a penny from Moses' shipment, perhaps because, Maria found out elsewhere and reported to Moses, "He has goon quite Contrary to your Ordors." Lewis had consigned Austin's lead to merchants of his own, not Austin's, choosing, who sold it for $2.00 per hundredweight less than it could have brought. Moreover, he answered none of the letters Moses' agent wrote him trying to settle discrepancies in accounts.[63]

Clearly it was Maria's character to focus on financial matters. Highly capable of handling money and directing economic developments, she tolerated no less in those around her. "I am very sorry to say," she castigated Rebecca's husband, "Mr B. is . . . Ignorant in every kind of business except his trade & that he is two lazy to cary on. Yes my dear, I have seen sufficient to Convince me that my poor sister has made a very Imprudent Choise."[64] Evidently she convinced Rebecca of it, too. Three months after Maria left Camden, when Rebecca thought herself dying, she sought to arrange with Maria for Moses, a thousand miles away, not her own husband, to receive her family inheritance and "take Charge of her boy & bring him up. She thinks he would receive a plain Education in Kentuck on the Interrest of the money she would place in your hands."[65]

For her own children's schooling, Maria placed Brown with the Reverend Whittlesey and his family in Washington, Connecticut, and the slender and graceful, fair-complected Emily in Miss Hall's school near New York. Definitely pleased with the academics she anticipated, Maria nevertheless winced at the $100 per quarter basic cost. "My dear Compannion & best friend will be Surprised when he reflects on the Emence expence attending the Education of our Ofspring," she wrote apologetically. "The only thing that can Reconsile a parent to those Expenditures is the pleaseing hope that theay [the parents] will in the end receive a Compensation in the Improvements their Children will make by paying close Attention to their Studdys & giveing, by so doing, Sattisfaction to their Instructors."[66]

Emily blossomed in school. "She has Arrived at that period of life," her mother wrote, "which points out the necessity of strict Application to study & I have no doubt but that she will acquir more Usefull knoledge in six Months with Miss H. than she would in twenty with Mrs. B[eck]" in Lexington.[67] Maria was right. The trip and school had opened a new world for the girl. "You are doing just as you should do," Moses encouraged his only daughter a few months later as she prepared to visit Philadelphia.

> Now is the time to examine well the things of nature and art, every thing you see will teach you the duty and obligation we are under to our god and society—it will prove to you how much man is capable of doing, when his mind is properly improved. it proves to you the great and unbounded Works of Nature. its the strongest proof that all things in this life are under an all wise Creator, who has ordered all things to answer his great intentions. no place exhibits man in a more striking point of View, then in a large City—[68]

Moses stressed to Emily, as he had to Stephen before her and as his Congregationalist father must have stressed to him, the obligation they had to society. "One of the greatest duties enjoined on man," he admonished her, "is to do as he would be done by, give unto others what he expects others will give unto him. the rule strictly & frankly adheared to, will always produce friends and admirers in every country and among every Nation. it also produces an internal Sattisfaction which nothing can take from you— let me recommend the rule of conduct to you my Emily—" Ever mindful of the privileges and responsibilities of their station in life, Moses added that "the pillars of a female character are Truth and *Virtue*, with a modest deportment to *all* but especially towards her inferiors—let your Deportment always be courteous to such whose situation in life has rendered them unequal in, information or personal acquirements—"[69]

With neither husband nor children to care for day by day during the winter of 1811-1812, Maria immersed herself in a whirl of social activities in Philadelphia. She delighted in the engagements and the old friends. But she wrote particularly of the expense. "I think the Philadelphians are much more Extravagant in dress & Entertainments than theay formerly was," she complained. "Fashonable Articles of dress are very high. I find the few things I was Oblighed to get in order to appear something like fasscion has nearly Exausted the Hundred dollars I have received from Mrs. Westcott since I arrived in the City."[70]

Maria curtailed her hectic social pace sharply in the face of her mounting expenses and filled the lonely void with worry. Even before she could have received one letter from her husband the previous July, she had written him that she would "hope for the best and pray god to protect you and eneable you to get the better of all your bloodthirsty Enimys."[71] Four months later, her worst apprehensions materialized when Emily showed her a letter in which Stephen reported that "Lyd had Attempted to poison hur Master & that she & John Camp was to be sent down the river. Let me beg my dear Husband to ship the wretches of[f] as soon as he possibly can. I always was affraid of Camp, but I never should have suspected Lyd of so bace an Act."[72] Beside herself with torment, Maria saw only one solution. "Oh let me Intreat you to Arrange your Affairs as soon as possibly so as to leave the Country," she begged Moses. "You have had so many hare breadth Escapes of your life that it Appears like a Warning from Above and I sincearly hope you will view it in that light."[73]

Despite her anxiety, and even with all the activity, perhaps because of it, Maria's health actually grew stronger. "You can have no idear how she has improved boath in looks, and health, and is grown very fleshy," Emily marveled to her father in December, 1811.[74] Maria could feel it herself. "Beleive me it tis with sincear Gratitude to an all wise and Mercifull Providence, that I am permitted to Inform you that I injoy at this period a much greater portion of health than I ever flatterd myself I should in this world of pain & tryal," she told her husband in mid-March, 1812. "Your, nor any of my friends never knew how much I suffered for many years with pain & Debility. I ever felt a reluctance in Complaining as it only Created Uneasiness to my friends."[75]

Maria could not restrain the serious apprehension she felt in the spring of 1812 over the real and growing threat of war with Britain. In April, 1812, she reported to Moses with great foreboding that "In Several places the war fever appears to be very high. All these Desperate Characters that have nothing to loose are very Violent in favour of war with England & theay are the Democrats. Heaven forbid that such fellows should have Influence Sufficient with the Government as to Envolve America in Ruin. By all Accounts their will be fighting Enough to be done on the frontiers with the Indians, without going further."[76] Because of it all, she longed to be with her husband.

Maria could undertake such a journey only with money and an escort. If Stephen would come with a load of lead, he could take her home. Moses had planned for months to send his son on the young man's first major business trip, and Stephen was as ready as any eighteen-year-old could be. He had left Bacon Academy in 1808 with a diploma from Principal Adams certifying that "As a Scholar he has been obedient and studious; as a boarder, unexceptionable. Having passed acceptably the public examinations, and having during the whole period sustained a good MORAL character, he is judged worthy of this honorary testimonial."[77] Rather than matriculating at Yale University in comfortable New Haven, however, Stephen enrolled next at Transylvania University in Lexington, Kentucky, where Horace Holley, the husband of his first cousin, Uncle Elijah's daughter, Mary, served as president. In the spring of 1810, after two and a half sessions in the Presbyterian institution studying the liberal arts, the sixteen-year-old boy heeded his father's call, apparently over his mother's objection, to return home, apparently to take charge of his father's store at Mine a Breton. Save for a likely brief study of French in 1812, his formal schooling had ended.

During the two years working for his father between 1810 and 1812, Stephen proved no coward in standing up for himself and no fool in affairs of business. Hence in the spring of 1812, Moses looked to him to take a load of lead to New York. Stephen could have been given no more important job, as the proceeds of the cargo were to discharge all his father's obligations in New York, settle his account with James Bryan in Louisiana, pay his wife's bills, and provide the wherewithal to bring her home.[78]

On April 28, 1812, Stephen stepped aboard a barge laden with lead and began his trip. Moses wanted to tell his son so much as he left—to advise him on the trip, to wish him well, to bid his speedy return—"but the fullness of my heart and mind drove all most Every thing from my thoughts." After Stephen had floated out of sight, Moses sat and wrote a long letter to make up for what he had been unable to say. "A Young man must always remember that his appearance is greatly Noticed by Strangers," the father counseled. "You will therefore immedeately on your arrival obtain in Orleans such a Suite of Clothes as will be agreeably to the place a Black Coat you will find not only in tast in Orleans but also in Philadelphia in Orleans White Janes for Overhalls and Vest but in new York and Philadelphea they would be out of the Order of Dress, and to avoid unnecessary Baggage and Expence provide only what will answer for your stay in Orleans for you will not use them in the Cities to the North, you have been so long in the Woods that you will finde an Attention to your Dress indispensable this you will attend to—" Manners, of course, told the calibre of a man as well as clothes, and Moses instructed his son to mind them, too. "Always informe yourself of the rules of the table and conform to them these little attention are absolutely Necessary. with out them you will be Deficient in breeding."[79]

About the time Stephen left, Maria exhausted her purse. The always generous Henry Austin stepped in to cover the expenses of the children in school and advanced Maria $30 for her own living. "This I must make answer till my dear son Arrives," Maria declared bravely, having no idea when Stephen might appear.[80] Then she began to worry. "Oh, how truly Mortifying will it be if all is lost & you are not Able to pay him [Cousin

Henry] the money he has advanced."[81] Her anxiety was well placed, for
Moses had no cash in his hands with which to pay him. "Collections have
been nothing," he confessed to creditor Bryan, "and all the lead that was
on hand I have sent of[f] for Herculaneum so that every thing depends on
collection."[82] By early June and three weeks behind in her board, Maria in
Philadelphia had been reduced to sharing $17 from the winnings of a lot-
tery ticket. But even the entire ticket would not have covered her
arrears.[83]

For Maria, sincerely glad in her belief that Stephen had left with the lead
that would rescue her, but frightfully anxious that along the way some terrible incident would befall her oldest son, the worst possible news came on
June 21, 1812. Sinking into the chair at her writing desk, she scrawled for
her distant Moses, "It is with heart felt sorrow I take up my pen to Inform
my dear Husband that, *War*, is Absolutely declared. the Express arrived
from Washington last Evening...I have always dreaded a war so
much...but it tis two true—and my fears for my Dr friends in louisianna
is now greater than theay ever have beene." In anguish beyond anything
since she had left Moses eleven months before, Maria knew more than
ever that she would "not know what happyniss or Comfort is, till I am
Restord to the Society of my Husband and famaly—"[84]

NEWS OF the declaration of war roused strongly conflicting emotions in Moses Austin at Mine a Breton on the far western flank of the United States. For his wife and children, he felt pain. Maria, Emily, and Brown were caught half a continent away, separated from each other, in financial distress, and in a part of the country more likely than others to see invading British troops. For his ailing business, on the other hand, Moses anticipated a new and strong demand for lead. If Stephen's trip, whose timeliness was uncanny, went well and he were able to sell his lead at a good price, the war could be just the stimulant Austin's business needed to rebound from the previous lean years. Moses waited for news.

From Philadelphia, Maria reported the price of bar lead at a very satisfying $11 to $12 per hundredweight, almost double the normal figure. "If you can but push on the lead boath up the Ohio & by the way of N.O.," she urged him, "I have no doubt but you will make money fast while the war lasts."[1] After watching the price climb by fifty percent during succeeding weeks, and fearing that delay might result in her husband's lead arriving too late to realize the phenomenal prices, she implored him a second time to "push on lead as fast as you can up the Ohio."[2] The price might not hold for long if the war truly were short. But, she noted soberly, "the ruller of the Universe only knows that."[3]

What she did know for a fact was that her husband's outspoken temperament could bring him trouble in times of strong passions, passions like those she already had seen the war stir in Philadelphians. Consequently, Maria could not close without cautioning Moses to mind his often explosive conduct. "I beg & Intreat you will be silent on the Measures of Government," she pled. "These are perilous and dangerous times & many here are Affraid to speak their Sentiments. I hope my dear Husband will stand Nuturel & let all parties Alone. Strive to send on plenty of lead for them to make balls to fight their battels with & let boath partys pursue their one [own] measures Unmolested by you."[4]

From New Orleans, Stephen reported that word of the declaration threw commerce "into confusion. Business is almost annihilated Cotton fell in one day from 9.50 to 5 and 4.50 There are a great many Vessels in port all loaded and redy for sea they are now Striping and laying them up—" The market for lead alone skyrocketed. One buyer offered the young man an astounding $17 per hundredweight for sheet lead. Neither

Stephen nor Moses could have wished for a better opportunity, but, to his anguish, Stephen could not deliver. Less than sixty miles above the city, his barge had foundered on a sandbar and still lay with its cargo in ten feet of water. He had gone on to New Orleans merely to make arrangements to return home to await a fall in the river, which would ease the work of raising the lead. The astonishing prices, however, combined with the new imperative to bring his mother, sister, and brother home before any fighting should erupt, changed his mind. Stephen raised his lead as quickly as he could, but not before the bottom apparently fell out of the market. Through September he lingered in New Orleans with his cargo searching vainly for a buyer at the price that had eluded him in July.[5]

At the mines, Austin saw business conditions follow the pattern of the New Orleans lead market. After a promising start in July, trade slowed dramatically in late summer. "Its much more difficult to obtain either lead or money at this time then in the Spring," he reported to James Bryan. "For the last two months almost every man in the Country has Either been out on the frountier or are held in requisition to march at a moments notice this as you may suppose, has put a full Stop to all business and all Collection, . . . Very little lead has been made this summer and not much will be made this fall and Winter." Indeed, "If I can collect half the debts now Due," Moses admitted in October, "Its more than I Expect."[6]

Times were bad, but Austin had faced hard times before. Characteristically he had pulled his business through by acting uncharacteristically – by expanding when others consolidated, by moving when others held firm. This time he had greater basis than usual for optimism. Present and anticipated stocks of lead, he calculated, could not possibly supply the country's wartime demands. Consequently, taking advantage of Stephen's presence in New Orleans, Moses put more lead on the river to him and instructed him, while he sought a buyer, to look into purchasing ten or a dozen slaves. "I wish I had 50 more at the mines," Moses wrote boldly. "I could make the value of them this year in the state the mines are in . . . It would make a great alteration in our business –"[7] Inspired by Stephen's report of the money offered him for sheet lead, Moses opened a plant to produce it.[8]

Moses Austin's aggressive, near reckless, business posture veiled only to outsiders the helpless personal frustration he also felt. "Few events of my life," he wrote one associate, "has given me more unhappiness than the detention of my son Stephen with his Cargo in New Orleans," because it left Maria and the family stranded.[9]

Through the summer Maria waited and watched for Stephen, her apprehension for his safety growing in equal measure with her anticipation of his arrival each day that he did not come. The news of his sunken barge arrived early in August and relieved her worry on his account. But it left her a greater burden – the distress that her penniless exile would continue indefinitely. Distraught and in hopes that somehow a "ride & change of seean would be benificial to my health which had become very poor in Consequence of the Anxiety & Suspence my mind labourd under in regard to the fate of my dr. Stephen, together with the very Unpleasant Situation his not Comeing on in the spring had throne me into," she decided to borrow from her host and relative, Edward Sharp, the money she needed to travel to New Jersey to visit family. "Mr. Sharp made me a Tender of his purse Several times before I could reconsile myself to the Idea of borringing money," she confided to her husband, "but I got the better of this after I heard of Steph. Accident."[10] Actually Maria felt the need of the trip doubly, because to avoid spending money that summer she had denied herself a visit with her two children whom she had not seen in months.

The trip in no way masked from Maria the obvious and pressing fact that without the money Stephen was to bring, her stopgap of denial no longer would suffice. Emily's account at Miss Hall's School stood $100 in arrears. Maria needed to withdraw her daughter at once to avoid further expenses, but she had to have cash to do so. Again she turned to the faithful Henry Austin for help. He obliged, but rather than sending Emily to Philadelphia to join her mother, he put her with her aunt, Mrs. Elisha Lewis, Uncle Elijah's widow, in New Haven. There, he asserted, conscious of his own finite resources, "she could live free from expence of board."[11] Generously, Henry promised Maria that "as long as he has a dollar, I shall not want" and that he would "Advance what money I stand in need of for Absolute Expences." All he asked in return was frugality. Had he known Maria well at all, he would have known that she could not be otherwise. "I shall not ask for Another dollar if I can possibly do without it," she assured her husband yet one more time, "because I think it tis Imposeing on his [Henry's] Goodniss, & I flatter myself the next letter I get from you will point out some mode of paying your Nephew, as well as furnishing your famaly with the means of returning home this fall."[12] When her husband's letter finally did arrive, though, the bank notes he enclosed proved worthless—counterfeit.

Grasping for any potential relief, but perhaps motivated equally by familial indignation, Maria joined in a family suit to break her brother's will, which evidently cut his nearest kin out of his inheritance. A favorable verdict early in September sent Maria to Sussex, New Jersey, to dispose of a thirty-acre tract that came to her in the settlement and then, with her inheritance, the first money in months that she could call her own, on to Connecticut to visit her children.[13]

Maria reached Washington to be with little Brown on his ninth birthday. Brown ("James" as the Whittleseys called him) could have received no better present. He had seen his mother only once since she had left him in Washington as a seven-year-old boy. Brown wanted to talk of family.

Through his mother he sent warmest greetings to his father, and "Spoak with Affectionate warmth of all the servants in the famaly & in short of every one he ever [k]new." Maria beamed at the maturing she observed in her son, particularly when the Reverend Mr. Whittlesey said he "never saw a Child with a more Active mind." Reverend Whittlesey added that Brown "pursues everything he Undertakes with Avidity, is very Active & fond of play." To Maria's worry that Brown would miss important experiences by remaining in small, isolated Washington, his guardian countered that "a retired Situation . . . is by far the best till his mind becomes fixed on Study."[14]

More than the isolation of the community in which her son was growing up, Maria may have been worrying about the cost of Brown's residence with the Whittlesey family. She had been horrified to learn that the guardians had received not one dollar in reimbursement in more than a year. Maria immediately pledged one-third of her recent inheritance toward the account and called on Henry Austin again. But even this did not calm her mind. The Whittlesey family "has beene very good & kind to our Dr boy," she sobbed to Moses, "& it grieves me that it tis not in my power to pay . . . what is due."[15] In the end, overruling her concerns, she concluded to leave Brown with the Whittleseys.

All in all, the situation of the Austin family in the latter half of 1812 was little short of desperate. Only the prospect of good profits from sales of lead for the war effort gave immediate hope. But that very hope tied Moses to Mine a Breton and kept Stephen in New Orleans. Neither could leave to go after the stranded Maria, Brown, and Emily. In this plight, Moses' partner, James Bryan, saw his opportunity. He would go East and bring the Austin family home.

Moses seems to have been grateful. Maria rejoiced openly. On August 4, as she finished a letter to Moses, word came that someone had arrived to see her. Thinking it to be Bryan, she hurried into the parlor, her heart full with anticipation. There stood Henry Elliott. All he had brought was news of the mines. Good as it was, and "it Afforded me great pleasure to hear from all my friends & particularly my very Dr Husband, who he said Injoyd good Health, for which I am truly thankfull," his visit provided neither money nor a way home. Did Henry know anything of Bryan, she asked expectantly. No, "he saw nor heard nothing of Mr Bryan on his journey." The report devastated Maria. Leaping to the most disturbing thought she could think of, Maria moaned: "If any Misfortune has happend to him or the property, god only knows how I shall ever get home."[16] Bryan would not be stopped, though. He was driven by love. James Bryan intended to claim Emily for his wife.

Thirty-seven-years-old, twice Emily's eighteen years, Bryan knew his mind. He paid no heed to his brother, William, who warned him that "as to your going on for to git a wife I would think of that a while first.... She [Emily] Talks of gitting you. if She is for gitting I would...bee for Quitting, for a Wife is a thing easy got at any time." Apparently doubting that this argument would have much effect, William questioned the reputation of her family. "I think you might Marry in a family of full as much credit & honesty as Mosies family. I find that they have Made your Lead into shot at Herculaneum & entend sending it or has sent it off up cumberlin River into Tenesee to raise money for his own use." William might as well have saved his ink and paper. James had proposed marriage before she had left and during her absence had lost none of his affection for the slender and graceful young woman whose fair complexion complemented her dark hair and dark hazel eyes.[17]

Emily had been ready to accept her suitor's proposal when the journey East had been arranged. If the motive for the trip was to cool the relationship, it succeeded. After entering school and discovering more of the world than she had ever known in Louisiana, Emily "is sorry things was Carried so far. indeed she thinks very little about Matrimony at present," Maria wrote a few months after they had left.[18] Maria's relations and friends in the East delighted in that turn of events. They wanted Maria and her family to settle among them and knew full well, as Maria reported their words, that "Where fate fixes hur [Emily], theire we would wish to be also."[19] Maria understood, too, and concurred. "I must confess," she admitted to her husband, "I do not wish my daughter to settle in Louisianna." At the same time, however, she liked Bryan and would do nothing to hurt "so good & Amiable a man." She could not intentionally try to separate the two. She would let love dictate events.[20]

For his part, Moses could tell that the separation had broken no bonds between his daughter and Mr. Bryan. Consequently, he reminded Maria she must find out what she could about the man's family. "I shall attend particularly to that part of your letter which relates to our only Daughter," Maria replied obediently. "As yet I know but very little of Mr B's Connections. His father lives near Easttown, and his Uncle is an Eminent Merch. in the city [Philadelphia] & is said to be very Rich."[21]

Without question Uncle Guy Bryan, English educated, an astute businessman, heir to family property in England, and one of the wealthiest men of his time, was the Bryan best known to contemporaries. His father—James's grandfather—William Bryan II had brought the line from London to Bucks County, Pennsylvania, eighty years earlier. Behind him stretched a lineage that could be traced in unbroken succession through titled English forebears to Englebert, Seigneur de Brienne, in tenth-century Norman France. For most of Uncle Guy's contemporaries, however, the distance of relatives from him apparently constituted their chief interest in family connections.[22]

Whatever James knew of his genealogy, he knew Uncle Guy. Indeed, Uncle Guy likely had a hand in James's decision to go to Louisiana. The elder Bryan held a principal interest in one of the paramount supply stores of the region—the Bryan and Morrison establishment in Kaskaskia, where James worked upon his arrival in Upper Louisiana. By 1806 James had extended the operation to Mine a Breton, where he, like Moses in Richmond twenty-odd years earlier, operated the store. Not long afterward, he took charge of the Ste. Genevieve store as well. These two, he soon found, could not consume his abundant energy. Emulating Moses once again, Bryan opened his own mercantile business. Then finding a task in need of a businessman to do it, he established an enterprise hauling lead. He acquired both wagons to get the bars to the river and boats to move them to the retail markets. In 1808, if not earlier, he entered the lead business by superintending the mining operations of his associate William Morrison (of Bryan and Morrison) at Mine a Breton. But few make fortunes on the payroll of others. Bryan also explored the country for himself and, as did that handful of others of ability, means, and good fortune, found a rich territory in which he established his own mining area. In 1809, he opened Bryan's Mines along Hazel Run in present St. François County. The population of the little settlement soon numbered seventy miners, both free laborers working leases and slaves that Bryan, again like Austin, acquired for the purpose. The men took from the mines during their first year, 1809, some 600,000 pounds of lead, thirteen times the quantity obtained at Mine a Breton and the highest production of any mine that year.[23]

Between Bryan's residence in Mine a Breton and his business successes, it was inevitable that he and magnate Moses Austin would meet. In 1811, if not before, they joined financial interests when Moses offered Bryan a partnership in the Louisiana Lead Company and leased to him a sawmill on the Terre Bleue River, near Hazel Run, in which Moses had owned an interest for some years. By the time James Bryan sought Emily's hand, he had made himself a place in her father's circle.[24]

Bryan finally reached Philadelphia during the middle of October, 1812. Maria's spirits soared with relief at his safe arrival and with elation both at deliverance from her financial dependence on unselfish relatives and at having at last the certainty of returning home in a foreseeable future. Emily found even greater pleasure in his presence than did her mother. "I have every reason now to think she is Unchanged in hur Affection towards him," Maria phrased it to Moses.[25] No one doubted that Bryan reciprocated the sentiment. "He is all Attention to hur & myself," Maria told her husband. In preparation for meeting his family, Maria borrowed money from Bryan to buy appropriate clothes for her daughter. Emily "has had but few fashonable things, as she was at School all last winter—" Maria explained. Then the parade began. One after another "He has brought all his Connections that reside in the City to wait on us." On the day she wrote Moses about it, she and Emily had dined with James's mother and Uncle Guy. Maria liked them all, but especially his mother and sisters. For their part, Maria observed with pride, James's family "appear[s] to be very much Charmd with our Daughter."[26]

Maria, delighting in the association with the Bryans, enjoyed herself that fall more than in many months. Nevertheless her pleasure always was tempered by the unhappiness of her long absence from her husband. Moses felt the separation more even than she. Only a few months after his wife and children had left, the atmosphere of the Austin household had become so solemn that Stephen invited a friend to visit, observing that "A little company would be very acceptable at this time for I never saw this place half so dismal as it appears now – "[27] A year later, early in January, 1813, with Stephen having been gone eight of his ten months away from home, with Maria and the other children absent more than a year and a half, a lonely Moses moaned: "Little did I expect to be thus long deprived of the Company of my Dear family."[28]

In late March, 1813, after the worst of the winter weather had passed, Maria, Emily, and Bryan set out overland for home. Impatient to see her husband, Maria wrote Moses hoping he would meet them in Kentucky. Every day as they progressed through the state she looked in vain for him. He never came. Her three letters reporting their departure and route never reached Mine a Breton. Sometime in June, the travelers arrived home.[29] Jubilant to be reunited with her husband and oldest son, Maria never would make such a trip again.

The return of his family gave Moses his only cause for celebration that summer. Business, already bad, deteriorated further. Anyone could see it; everyone felt it. "You would be astonished to see the change in all Orders of Citizens in the Article of dress," Austin observed to Bryan. "Indian dressed Buckskin for Overhalls and frocks are now as universal as broadcloth used to be."[30] The change, all knew, resulted from the War of 1812. During the fall of that year, the bulk of the work force had been called to the ranks in anticipation of feared British-inspired Indian attacks. It was bad enough that their work did not get done and that products – like lead – were not prepared for market. Worse, their pay did not come promptly. The amount of money in circulation dropped dramatically. "I do not think any person about the Mines has Collected as much as to pay the expences of a Ride after the Debtors. that has been the case with me," Moses told Bryan, "and I know that its the same with Your Brother and William Bates." About the time that the men returned, the weather turned so cold and rainy that surface mining had to be all but abandoned. As if curtailed production did not upset the economy enough, "what makes the matter Still more distressing," Moses wrote, "*is*, that Lead when obtained will not command Money at more than 3/50 *Cents, or* −*375."* And, of course, every circumstance affected another situation. In this case, Moses noted, "the reduced price has driven most of the hands from the *mines*," which curtailed the business in Austin's store, his other primary enterprise. Demand remained strong, but with money in such short supply, how customers would pay their bills "is the question." He warned Bryan that "to *sell* any kind of goods on credit is absolute *ruin*." Everywhere he looked, Moses saw discouraging prospects. "Would to god I could give you something pleasing on the Subject of business," he lamented to Bryan. "Altho times was bad when you left this they are much more depressed at this moment—"[31]

Bryan knew it before Moses told him. His own business tottered on shaky footing. His brother, William, whom he had left in charge of his affairs, advised him to bring back no goods. They "answer a Damned poor purpose when you cannot git any thing for them. you may sell them & then...[for] three or four years [trust the buyers to whom credit was extended] & then if you want your pay they will say you are a Damned raskel they have paid you long ago."

Money was so tight and collections so poor that William could not scrape together enough to buy up lead selling for half its normal price. Neither could others. What they could do, however, was sue to recover debts. "Your friend Cracraft[?] has sued you & shaver without ever coming to ask for it," William told his brother. "There is some more talk of sueing & they may sue & be damned & I will sue as fast as them." In fact, William continued, "I have sued some of the People & intend to sue one & all. I then will know whether there is any thing to be got or not." Exasperated and frustrated by it all, though ready for the fight, William lashed out at the men in Louisiana. "I believe," he fumed, "if hell was raked from corner to corner with as big a rake as the Devil could hall he could not rake a damnder set together than there is in this Country." Then turning on his brother, he added bluntly, "I wish you to return as quick as you possibly can so that we may have all your mastakes rectified."[32]

Through it all, Moses apparently fared better than other mine owners. He alone had a deep shaft to work, and it provided a steady production. When the market improved temporarily, he became immoderately euphoric. "Lead is looking up," he reported to Bryan, "55 Dollares was offered at this place yesterday as I was told, by Kendel who is out after Lead. its our Interest to make all we can as Lead will be up."[33] In the anticipation, Moses longed for cash. "I am clearly of the Opinion that Ten thousand Dollars would Command Every Pound of Lead for sale this spring and Winter Would to god I could command that Sum a Speculation of moment could be made But I have not the means."[34] Clearly he did not, for a few months earlier, he had calculated that he owed $18,138 to factors and investors on the east coast.[35] Those in the mining business expected to shoulder heavy debts, but Moses' obligations were growing ominously large.

Often it happens that when a person feels down and unlikely to recover through traditional means, the individual will grasp at riskier ventures in the hope of reestablishing himself by one bold stroke. In January, 1813, Moses wrote Bryan that he had read a newspaper account of the invention, near Philadelphia, of a perpetual motion machine. Moses was skeptical, but if it were true, "The advantages to be derived from the use of such an invention in the Western Country passeth all the Ideas and imagination of man." Consequently, he begged Bryan to go like a pilgrim and, if he found such a machine, to obtain drawings.[36]

Austin's mind was too fertile, too active to stake his hopes on just one opportunity. In the same letter he commented also that he had been thinking about "an opening toward Mexico." Perhaps it was the article in the *Missouri Gazette* of November 14, 1812, reporting the progress of the revolution in Mexico, in particular the fall of San Antonio, that captured his attention. Perhaps his knowledge came from a former employee, Michael Quinn. On October 1, 1808, a Miguel Quinn wrote one Beulett, an attorney Austin later knew as a judge in St. Louis, respecting the market there. Quinn expected that business with a Mr. Hoistein, the French spelling of "Austin," at La Mina (the mine) would bring him north. Whatever gave Moses Austin the idea of trading with settlements in Spanish territory, early in January, 1813, the thought still percolated in his mind. "I have had Nothing to change a belief," he wrote Bryan, "that an adventure to that Country would be both safe and advantageous."[37]

What facts possibly could have led him to believe that establishing such a trade would be either safe or advantageous? If he was recalling the success of his own bold move to Spanish territory, he should have realized that the circumstances were far different then. Americans had been encouraged to come. The government of Mexico in 1812, however, unlike the government of Louisiana in 1796, had issued no invitation. If he was thinking, as some did, that the revolution had succeeded, he had read much too much into the November story and was badly mistaken. If he was thinking of the profit in establishing a commerce with the interior provinces of Mexico, he must have known that not one of the several expeditions dispatched overtly and covertly from St. Louis to Santa Fe during the past two decades had ever returned. The Spanish wanted no trade ties. Quinn's letter to Beulett corroborated that fact and described the risks and uncertainties he experienced trading in Mexico. If Quinn talked with Austin, his message could not have been rosy. Of course it was true that Pedro Vial, Austin's opponent in the land claims fight with the French at Mine a Breton, had come to Missouri from Santa Fe, and he could have excited an interest. But there is no reason to believe that he and Moses ever had an amiable conversation. Whatever stimulated Moses' original interest in a "Mexican adventure," he apparently dropped the idea for the time being. His back was not to the wall yet.

Clearly, though, Moses was in serious financial trouble. The war had not spurred the lead business of Mine a Breton as Moses had hoped. If he thought it still might, early in 1814 he learned otherwise. In answer to his inquiry, a correspondent in Charleston, South Carolina, reported a fine, strong demand for shot and sheet lead. "But even our present high rates would not pay carriage from Nashville," Adam Trinno advised him, "and during the war, we have no Safe water Conveyance from New Orleans –" Embarrassed himself by the situation, the South Carolinian apologized: "I regret that I cannot give better encouragement to industry – if any favorable change I will drop you a line on the Subject –"[38] Austin never heard from him again. Trinno's letter was just one more piece of the bad news that had been devastating business in Austin's country for a year and a half and which had created intense competition among those trying to survive.

Austin's relationship with John Rice Jones, which had been deteriorating for some years, collapsed in the midst of the struggle. It was the final act of a bitter parting, toward which they had been moving since the failure of the Louisiana Lead Company bill. Maria felt the tension, and turned caustic after reading a now-lost letter from her husband describing some act that Jones had committed. "I was as much shocked at the Villinny, deception and perfidy of those who I Considerd your friends as I was with the Account you gave of the Indians Approaching St. Louis," she wrote. "You must surely by this time be Sufficiently Acquainted with the Duplissity & falshood of mankind, as will hereafter make you suspious of every human being. This I know to a mind like yours is truly Distressing, but I think it will be more for your interrest to place Confidence in no one, but on the Contrary to view every man in the Country you are Compeld to reside in, as men who would take every Advantage." Knowing, though, how difficult it was for Moses not to confront those whom he believed held malice toward him, she added immediately: "I hope your prudence will point out the propriety of Confineing those Suspisions in your one [own] breast...."[39]

In the spring of 1813, the Renault claim fueled the growing rancor between the two men. Both held interests. Austin opposed Jones's demand for a one-quarter share in the claim, since Jones had contributed nothing to the capital. Austin already had sunk $2,600 into his one-eighth part. "With Jones I can say nothing more," Austin began. "I have recvd a most Billingsgate letter with denunciations against the Claim, and what he will do. he says 'it is in my power to prevent your realising those Golden dreams and *believe me the Inclination to do so* is not nor shall not be wanting.' " Austin could hold his rage no longer. "*The Soul of the man is spoken in this line*," he exploded. "*It is in* fact saying purchase me or I will act – the Villing!!!"[40] The atmosphere between them poisoned beyond recovery, the two came to a final and complete legal parting of the ways on February 24, 1814, by dissolving their last joint interest in the Mine a Breton.[41] They could not begin to agree on division of their two-tenths joint interest and turned the settlement over to three mediators.

In some measure, Austin's troubles, as those of all businessmen selling in distant markets, arose from the business methods and poor communications of the day. Matters that should have been settled readily often dragged on for years. In 1812 Moses still could not say whether the two boat-loads of pine staves he had sent to New Orleans in charge of his nephew Elias A. Elliott, who had committed suicide on the trip, had returned a profit. Accounts were simply too tangled.[42]

True, too, Moses made his situation no better by leaving some accounts unsettled. On August 15, 1812, John Francis Merieult, Austin's New Orleans agent of a decade earlier, called on Maria in Philadelphia and told her that he still had "what he supposed would be of Consequence" to Moses – the original papers of his grant of Mine a Breton from the Spanish government. Horrified and distressed that her husband had left such an important matter at loose ends, Maria implored Moses to attend to it. "Let me beg my Dr Husband," she wrote respectfully but firmly, "to Persivear in his Endeavours to settle up all old Accounts. You have loast a large fortune by placeing Confidence in those who have deceived you & I think you will never prosper till you are Clear of all old affairs & carry on businiss by yourself."[43]

Actually since at least 1807, Austin had been at odds with Merieult over the amount Austin owed and the charges claimed by the factor for lead sales in the years 1802-1805. Unable to reach agreement, Merieult in 1812 took Austin to court, where the parties agreed to put the matter to three referees. The arbiters concluded that the accounts stood basically as Merieult reported them and that, with interest, Austin owed his former agent $3,228.06. Austin objected to the interest award, and on points of law, succeeded in having the figure set aside. Nevertheless, a quantity of Austin's shot was seized and sold in the summer of 1814 to satisfy the judgment. Even then, two years would pass and a second judgment have to be issued against Austin before the account would be finally closed.[44]

While defending himself in one court against Merieult, Austin contended in another with Smith T over a debt of Joseph Decelle. Austin had guaranteed five of Decelle's notes, and after an obligation to Smith T matured without payment, Smith T filed suit against his debtor. During the trial, Moses happened to run into Smith T witness Thomas Dodge on the street in Ste. Genevieve. Moses spoke forthrightly. "If he [Dodge]

would not attend as a witness in the said case now pending in the General
Court of the Territory of Missouri," Dodge informed the court, "he the said
Moses would give this Deponent five hundred dollars." Moses denied the
charge. Four men, including one of Dodge's own witnesses, corroborated
Austin's story, and there the matter apparently died. But Smith T won his
suit and in 1814 hauled Austin and his fellow sureties into court to recover
the debt. Smith T won that case too. Decelle proved to be a bad risk for
the sureties. They ended up in court four more times because he could
not, or would not, cover his obligations.[45]

Countering Smith T, Austin brought an action of his own in a dispute
over title to a productive mine. On a night in 1811 or 1812, Austin, at home
in Durham Hall, talked with young attorney Daniel Roe about a rich lead
mine Austin believed to be covered by a claim of his, but which Smith T
possessed. Roe "was induced to remark to the said Austin that he believed
the trespassing might be put a Stop to, untill the title of said land could be
finally settled, whereupon the said Austin made certain propositions to
this deponent as an inducement for this deponent to undertake his cause."
Inexperienced in matters as large and volatile as Austin's, Roe requested
time to think about accepting the case. Austin consented. Roe then consulted with a colleague who agreed to help him for half the fee. The next
thing Roe knew, his colleague had taken the case entirely, claiming he had
made the arrangement through Austin's partner, John Rice Jones. Roe
then "found himselfe in a situation which would justify his taking a fee on
the other side of the question, or for Col. Smith the defd." Whether or not
on Roe's testimony, Austin lost the case. The judge refused to enjoin Smith
T from digging at the mines.[46]

Smith T chose Herculaneum to parry Austin's attack. As the financial
stringency of the country closed in on Austin's partner, Samuel Hammond, at the end of 1813, Hammond notified Austin that he must sell, and
quickly. Already Hammond had considered $3,000 for his interest, slightly
more than half what he thought his property worth, and rejected the offer
only on the grounds that it was not cash. Hammond notified Austin and
Bryan that they could have the lots for $3,000 cash. When Smith T heard
about it, he jumped at the opportunity. "Col. Hammonds has been offered
(3000) Three Thousand Dollars for Herculaneum by *Smith* and Von Phal,"
Stephen wrote his brother-in-law anxiously, "an also by Genl. Clark and
Genl. *Howard* in partnership to whom he will sell if you and Morrison do
not take it—"[47] Apparently Austin did not acquire Hammond's interest.
Even if his enemies did, Moses could enjoy some consolation in the confidence that the bidding showed in Herculaneum.

To Austin and Smith T, the court battles may have signaled a reinvigora-
tion of their long-standing, titanic feud, which in times past had forced
those throughout the Ste. Genevieve district, if not the larger Upper Loui-

siana region itself, to choose sides. But in 1813-1814 the struggle made only a small ripple in a much enlarged pond. Times had changed. The conflict had become just a tussle between two men and those close to them. No longer did their disputes rock the political stability of the region. Even they must have seen that their grip on political affairs had weakened. During the summer of 1812 President Madison signed into law the bill creating the Territory of Missouri. High on the agenda of the House of Representatives of the new Territory when it met in December was selection of eighteen names from which the President would pick nine for service on the Legislative Council. Both Moses Austin and John Smith T made the list from the Ste. Genevieve district. Neither received from the House the unanimous recommendation given ten other nominees, and neither was chosen for the service.[48]

Austin must have been disappointed. He had enjoyed his maneuverings behind the political scenes. Though economic woes absorbed most of his energy in 1812-1813, he evidently looked for ways to regain his lost influence. Soon he began work on what to all but his neighbors must have seemed a fantastic scheme – moving the territorial capitol to a site near his home, where, being able to visit with the political leaders, he could anticipate exercising some sway over affairs of the territory that concerned him.

In late June, 1813, Moses traveled to St. Louis on business, but scheduled his trip to permit himself to remain for the opening of the general assembly. The fate of a petition calling for formation of a county from, and including, the western townships of Ste. Genevieve County interested him particularly. On August 21, 1813, the House created Washington County, but drew boundaries unsatisfactory to residents along Grand River. A group led by Austin, who wanted Bryan's Mines encompassed by the new county, petitioned the legislature for an adjustment and in December, 1813, got their way.[49]

The next step in the process was selection of a permanent seat for the county government. The commissioners named to make the choice (Benjamin Elliott, a cousin-in-law of Moses, Martin Ruggles, who had come with Moses from Virginia, and Lionel Browne, nephew of Aaron Burr) came to the oldest and largest settlement within the new county, Mine a Breton, in February, 1814, to meet and make their choice. Moses offered them forty acres, Jones added ten, to locate the seat across the creek from Mine a Breton adjacent to Austin's property. They accepted the proposition and in June advertised the sale of lots in the new town of St. George.[50]

During the first three days of the sale, July 5-7, 1814, the commissioners for the town sold seventy-nine lots, which earned $5,080 to finance construction of the courthouse. The plans called for a beautiful stone and brick building, its central section soaring three stories into the sky, with graceful two-story wings flanking either side. Though the rooms were not massive—the center courtroom measured only thirty-feet square—the walls were, being two and a half-feet thick on the lower floor. The facade of the central tower boasted a "portico thirty feet long, projecting ten feet, supported by four brick columns, twenty four feet high." Porticos seventeen-feet high decorated the wings. These plans would produce a structure larger and more elaborate than the frontier county needed solely to provide for its own needs. As a territorial capitol, however, the building would do well.[51]

If the choice of location and the design of the courthouse gained general acceptance, the name of the new town did not. Within a month and a half of the notice of the lot sale, the name "St. George" had been abandoned. In its place they substituted a name that had been associated with the mines at least since 1811 when the community assembled for its traditional Fourth of July celebration and saluted their lead mines as "the Potosi of the United States."[52] "Potosi" it would be.

Having the county government at the old mine site brought new life to the community. Mine a Breton "has become a place of considerable busi-

Potosi, Missouri, 1819. Henry Schoolcraft used this view of Potosi in his contemporary book on the lead mines of Missouri. Durham Hall is the long building on the far side of Breton Creek on the left side of the picture. Commanding the hill in the center is the county courthouse Austin hoped would become the Territorial capitol of Missouri. Smoke rises from active lead furnaces and smelter houses. From Schoolcraft, *Lead Mines of Missouri.*

ness," Austin observed, "and contains about one hundred houses, some of which are valuable buildings." He could have added that the number of dwellings had more than doubled since 1807. "From its situation," he concluded with obvious satisfaction, Potosi "will become a large town. All the wealth and business of the mines will centre at this place."[53] Establishing the county government in Potosi brightened Austin's financial as well as political hopes.

Sadly, the immediate economic reality failed to measure up to the potential. Mine a Breton no longer yielded the quantities of ore it once had. Scores of workers digging steadily on Austin's property during his sixteen years there had left few surface areas unexplored and unworked. Compounding Austin's troubles, he could not count on a stable work force. As rich new discoveries occurred the always transient miners moved to the fresh diggings, leaving Austin by 1812 with a crew noticeably diminished from a decade earlier. The effect, his numbers showed, was pronounced. Production after 1808 totaled little better than half what it had been during the halcyon years of 1804-1808 and not much above the production of his first years. And these figures were only averages. The output of the war years clearly fell significantly below them.[54]

On top of the slumping production, the desperate wartime shortage of money continued to plague Austin and his associates. All lived on the brink of disaster and struggled just to keep one step ahead of their creditors. Stephen F. Austin had "not one Cent of money" in January, 1814, when his partner, James Bryan, left to take a load of their lead to New Orleans. "I am paying of[f] Mr. Roy and Seteling with him which takes all the money we have," Stephen reported, "and then not enough–" Bryan could afford to lose no time on the trip.[55]

Moses, also connected with Bryan, faced a similar situation toward the end of the year. The elder Austin had collected a settlement of about twenty pigs of lead. "If you can Obtain as many and Mr Ellis I suppose may have collected some," he wrote Bryan, "we may save our Credit."[56] Austin's salvation was short-lived, the vicious circle endless. Two months later in December, Moses drew on Elias Bates, the owner of a lead warehouse in Herculaneum, for all the lead he had on hand. Bates, who had nearly gone under twice already in the year, wrote Bryan immediately to "Tell [illeg.] to get lead to replace that I borrowed from Hammond to pay Macklott."[57]

James Bryan, on whom they all called, stood no better off than any of them. In 1813, within a year of borrowing $2,100 from Uncle Guy Bryan, he already had fallen behind in his payments. Uncle Guy probably found little consolation in the fact that James likely could have been more faithful to his obligation had most of the forty-eight men indebted to him been more faithful to theirs. "I cant Collect any [debts] of any consequence,"

James's brother, William, reported in the spring of 1813, "& what I do Collect I have to Sell for to Save your property I think I have things in such a fix now that perhaps I can save it but at one time I thought it would be sold in Spite of all I co[u]ld do." Looking over his brother's business and the economic conditions in the mine country, William continued: "Your Business lays in the hands of so many that are in need of all that is Collected that it is impossible for me to git any from them [and] when it is Collected...I am always duned & so much in want of Money that it is out of my power to do Business as I would do if I had wherewith to do with that I have added deturmination that I will never have anything to do with Business in the same way that yours is." Three weeks on the trail collecting debts had not yielded James's brother enough even to cover the taxes. William wanted out and told his brother so in no uncertain terms. "Lose no time in your Business & Return that I may git rid of the Botheration," he demanded, "for I am Bothered from every Quarter."[58] He was so bothered, in fact, that within a year William had begun drinking heavily and returned to Pennsylvania.[59]

A year later, with money no more plentiful than when William ran his business, James faced the added misfortune of a drought. It gripped his Hazel Run property so severely that his superintendent feared the water supply for the still might be lost completely. "It does not run thicker than a straw now," he wrote in September, 1814.[60]

Whatever the trial, James by then had won Emily and sealed his alliance with the Austin family. Observing their courtship in the summer of 1813, Maria wrote a cousin in Philadelphia that "this connection has beene for sometime in agitation," but she expected a wedding date near Christmas. However, when Stephen, an Ensign in the 2nd Regiment of the Missouri Territorial Militia, received orders to be ready to march against the Indians on September 1, the couple determined to wed before his departure—the day before. James could advance the date of his wedding but not of the house he was building for his wife at his mines on Hazel Run. Consequently, the bride and groom spent their first several months in Durham Hall.[61]

Maria reveled in having her growing family under her roof and eagerly looked forward to a grandchild in the summer of 1814. Emily's pregnancy progressed smoothly until a month before she was to deliver. As Maria recovered from "a sevear nervous complaint I had in my head which affected my eyes to such a degree I was neither able to read or write for several weeks," Emily came down "with the Measles of the Worse kind—her situation was truly Allarming...for ten days she was confined to her bed & but little hopes of ever rising from it—" Despite the odds, Emily gave birth to a premature, but "the most perfect mail Infant I ever saw." Then, nineteen-year-old Emily began to recover as the doctors had suggested she would. Joy filled the family for a few brief weeks until "to the astonishment of us all," Maria recalled sadly, the baby "was seized with this dangerous disease attended with the sore mouth, violent cough and fever– which terminated his short life when he was one month old–" Emily was devastated. Maria felt the loss at least as much as her daughter did. "Owing to Emily's illness, weakniss & Inability to take charge of it, the hole care" of the infant had fallen on her the same as if the baby had been her own.[62]

Not since 1804, when Moses almost died of an illness,[63] had his situation been so bleak and unhappy as it was in the early fall of 1814. He had lost his first grandchild. The debilitating old feud with Smith T had been rekindled without any real hope of satisfaction or financial improvement from the struggle. Business conditions that had been bad for more than two years had deteriorated at what must have seemed a yet more rapid rate, and none of Austin's schemes for pulling himself out of the financial debacle had, so far, shown any sign of working. Moses was staving off insistent creditors by drawing on credit with more patient ones. The cycle could not continue indefinitely. The fifty-two-year-old Austin surely knew it and may have thought again about leaving the mines. Though Maria likely argued against any move that would separate her from Emily and her family, even had she and Moses wanted to go, they must have recognized that they could not. Moses had sunk too deeply into the financial mire to be able to pull up stakes. He must find in Missouri a way to break the cycle.

CHAPTER X

M OSES AUSTIN had told the Spanish authorities nearly twenty years earlier in 1797; he had told the American leaders ten years before in 1804; and he had repeated it to Congress as recently as three years ago in 1811: the mining region in general and Mine a Breton in particular were rich beyond their imaginations. Properly worked, Mine a Breton alone could supply all the lead needed by the nation that held it. At the same time, its diggings could produce mineral enough for export. To Austin, these remarkable facts remained as patent in 1814 as they had been when he first reported them in his petition for a grant of the place. Consequently, the solution to his nagging financial distress was simple. He needed to produce more lead, which would yield more income, which, in turn, would end his trials. This conclusion typified Austin, whose nature consistently led him to be aggressive in times that, on the surface, appeared plainly suited to holding the line. But opportunity is defined, of course, by the way one looks at a problem.

The output of Moses' property had plummeted during the war, because the number of men in the pits had fallen dramatically. Austin could put his finger on two reasons for his loss of manpower: military duty that had drained men away and the lack of a circulating medium—money—with which to attract and keep those who remained to work. He could do nothing about the war. But neither could he sit idle, waiting helplessly for it to end and hoping forlornly for different times. One to take charge of his circumstances, Austin thought to remedy the labor shortage by putting slaves into the diggings. They were immune to both military service and to wage concerns. The money supply, he believed, could be increased if the Territory had a bank. Banks in those days issued their own currency. With the paper bank notes, mine owners could pay wages, laborers could pay outright for their purchases, and debtors could settle their accounts. The benefits of a bank for Austin, he probably perceived, could stretch far beyond simply putting cash in his pocket to hire hands.

To secure the slaves, Moses sent Stephen 250 miles east to Kentucky's third largest town of Russellville early in the fall of 1814 to arrange with Colonel Anthony Butler for twenty for himself and five for James Bryan. When in November a buyer from the East arrived at Mine a Breton desiring more lead than Austin had on hand, Moses erupted into euphoria. "If Ever there was a time that would Justify a high Price for Negroes," he told

Bryan, to whom he had referred the buyer, "It's at this moment Lead must be up the demand is great and *750* is given." Acting on his conclusion, Moses dispatched his overseer, John S. Brickey, to tell Stephen to more than double his order with Butler. "I am determin'd to take [slaves] at about 24 Thousand for *52* this will bring the Men at 600 Dollars Women at 500 Children from *200 275 and 300* In consiquence I have sent forward proper Securety for the Negroes."[1]

Why the Austins turned to the distant Butler for slaves is puzzling. Moses possibly had been referred to him by his friend in Russellville, J. Ficklin, or he may simply have known him for some years through a factor both used. Whatever circumstance brought young Austin and Butler face to face, the early negotiations between them went well. Moses' references had "made such a mention of the sufficiency of the security of myself and you [Bryan] and Stephen that little Doubt remains of obtaining the Negroes."[2] Yet the deal fell through. Perhaps Brickey's arrival with the request for more than double the number of slaves frightened Butler. Whatever the case, Stephen returned empty-handed. That suited neither party, however, and in February, 1815, "Stephen has written Colo Butler and accepted the Contract for Sixty Negroes for Ten Years with a little alteration by giving in Two old Negroes." The arrangement seemed quite satisfactory, since the Austins obtained the number of slaves they wanted. But how innocently trouble begins.[3]

What Moses should have realized before he pursued the business with Butler, but he appears to have downplayed, was that slaves came with a definite and relentless maintenance cost above their purchase. And it took precedence over other obligations. In December, 1814, Austin had to stock pork to provide for the 900-pound-per-month consumption of the slaves and household he already had. He bought the meat, but was unable at the same time to satisfy a demand against him for a mere $100. "I am in hopes you will make sales so as to get me 700 Dollars," he wrote Bryan, whom he had taken into his business on a par with his own son, "as I am in a little distress respecting the payment of the money prom[is]ed by Stephen."[4] Despite the ominous signs, however, Moses looked to the bright side. The slaves must make a difference. "This is doing well," he wrote at the beginning of 1815, "and if Continues will sett all things right again in a few month[s]—"[5]

A year later Austin's letters sounded a far different note. Nothing was right. Indeed, the grief, the desperation, the borrowing from one creditor to satisfy another had become more severe than ever. Send a load of lead to Elias Bates at his warehouse in Herculaneum, Moses begged his son-in-law in a typical letter, "or I shall be in real distress. Mr. Bates has made Use of all the Lead I have sent him Except the last *smelt*, and I have paid Captain Morgan 139 Dollars and to Stephen *150* Dollars to send to Kty

[Kentucky] which has so distressed me that I Shall I am fearfull suffur much unless I make up the money Immediately and to make things worse the furnace is so damaged [from heavy use most likely, since the intense, prolonged heat of a smelt turned the native stone to powder] she must be mended before I can make any more Lead."[6] Four months later when Stephen balanced the account, Moses owed Bates 13,713 pounds of lead, and Bates was "quite uneasy for fear that lead will not be in by the time he will be called on, as his Credit would suffer if he was called on and could not make up the lead."[7] Moses knew it. His credit was in the same fix. Unsettled accounts from as far in his past as Virginia hounded him through 1815 and 1816. Every session of court produced judgments against him, as creditors resorted to litigation to force settlements. Henry Austin gave up waiting for reimbursement of the money he had advanced to Maria and her children more than five years before and in April, 1816, won a substantial $2,000 award from his uncle.

Moses probably could not have paid Henry in any case, but the winter of 1815-1816 assured it. Extreme cold weather in January brought illness that "put Business back greatly." At one point Austin counted only six hands in the field digging. Production slumped again at a time when he could ill afford it. The worst of the matter, though, whether or not Moses realized it yet, was that his gamble, his bold expansion, had begun to backfire on him. Those slaves, even when they did not work, had to eat. The ongoing, fixed expense of feeding them magnified his burden. "All these things," he admitted in understatement after looking over his situation in 1816, "has press.d me greatly."[8]

Time pressed him, too. No longer did he have his own time in which to marshall resources to meet obligations. Overdue notes accumulated faster than he could satisfy them. Henry Austin, for one, waited two years after the judgment before receiving his settlement, and even then the payment came in the form of notes promising cash later. Relentless in the hands of Moses' creditors, time proved unkind to him also in the founding of the bank.

Moses had counted on the bank helping to create a condition in the Territory that would facilitate his financial revival. An admirer of Alexander Hamilton, father of the (First) Bank of the United States, Austin long had appreciated the control a well-run bank exercised over the economy. Indeed, more than twenty years earlier in 1791, the year the parent bank opened, he had called for locating a branch of Hamilton's institution in Richmond. It did not happen until long after Moses had left the city, and consequently he had never actually been associated with a bank when, in the summer of 1813, he joined Risdon H. Price, Rufus Easton, Sam Hammond, and other prominent St. Louis businessmen to create the Bank of St. Louis. This time the moment was ripe for quick action. In allowing the charter of the national bank to expire two years earlier, Congress had abandoned responsibility for providing banking services. Territorial and state legislatures raced into the vacuum, authorizing approximately 120 ventures in the succeeding three years. In Missouri, the new legislature joined the national tide by chartering the Bank of St. Louis, the first financial institution west of the Mississippi River, on August 21, 1813, the same day, as Austin watched with pleasure, that it created Washington County.[9]

Enthusiastic, the bank's organizers at once set about raising the capital for their institution by appointing commissioners to receive pledges to buy their stock at $100 per share. Austin opened the books at Mine a Breton. If the organizers expected others in the Territory to see the need of the bank as clearly as they did and for pledges to flow freely, they were sadly mistaken. The Territory's newspaper came out against them and published several stories describing both the evils of banking and the problems of paper currency. On this issue the *Missouri Gazette* reflected, rather than swayed, opinion. Most men in the Territory believed that paper bills, of no intrinsic value in themselves, could not possibly be as sound or safe as coins of gold and silver. Even had the newspaper favored the bank project, however, it could not have altered the basic fact that little surplus capital was available in the Territory for investment, in a bank or any other venture. With the primary labor force away in the military, economic activity in Missouri had slowed considerably. Compounding the situation, the federal government failed to pay its troops punctually. Most of the Missouri soldiers had to buy on credit and owed substantial sums, which, in turn, strangled the Territory's capitalists, like Austin, who owned stores. The bank's commissioners struggled against the odds for a month before they gave up.[10]

The campaign for subscriptions may have failed, but not the resolve of the organizers. They redrew the charter, obtained incorporation, and sought commitments until finally, on July 11, 1816, they could announce that the capital had been pledged. Two months later, the stockholders assembled to elect the board that would organize and oversee the bank's administration. In the balloting on September 2, Moses Austin, with 551 votes, earned the fifth seat on the thirteen-man board. Subsequently the board elected its most popular member, Austin's friend and partner, Sam Hammond, president of the institution. Two months passed while he assembled his staff and prepared the bank's quarters. Finally, on December 13, 1816, more than three years after the venture had been launched, the Bank of St. Louis opened its doors for business.[11]

In one respect, the delay in opening the bank worked to the institution's benefit. The economy of late 1816, quite unlike the depressed, stifled times in which the bank had been conceived, exuded expansion, speculation, and optimism. The War of 1812 had ended a year earlier. Men had returned to work on the farms, in the mines, and doing the other jobs that had to be done in a growing economy. Moreover, the end of the war let loose a tide of migration which swept into the Territory so vigorously that in the five years after the war the population more than doubled. By every measure, Missouri in 1816 was vibrant and growing.

In this atmosphere the government revived its interest in the lead mines on the public lands. In August, 1816, Josiah Meigs, Commissioner of the General Land Office, wrote Judge John B. C. Lucas, a former land commissioner in Missouri, asking him to prepare a report on the lead mines and salines of the Territory. Lucas called on Austin, still the one person with the greatest knowledge of the history, development, and current prospects of the mines. Austin not only agreed to prepare a report, he evidently wrote it and sent it off within a few days of Lucas's request. Meigs received it in Washington early in November, less than three months after he put his letter to Lucas in the slow and uncertain mails.[12]

The center of the lead mining district, Austin reported, had shifted little in the twelve years since his report of 1804. Washington County continued to be the hub of the lead region, Mine a Breton the hub of Washington County. The richness of the mines remained to Austin as clear and as incalculable as ever. Properly worked, the ground still held enough lead, he thought, to last an age. But he would place no dollar value on the land. "No miner," he wrote Meigs in a passage that summarized his points, "can tell the value of a mine beyond the length of his pick. Were the Government to say they would take $500 per acre for mineral land, few men would be Willing to give that sum, or a half of it; yet I have seen fifty feet of ground produce that amount in mineral in a month, with the labor of two or three miners."[13]

Having been asked his views on government policy, Austin, never shy or without an opinion, seized his opportunity to lecture the authorities again on the necessity of establishing a judicious program for leasing the federal lands for mining. To make the most of the public property, he argued from his experience at Mine a Breton, the government should encourage intensive shaft mining in place of wasteful surface digging. Further, it should take its rent in mineral, instead of cash, so that it, the same as any entrepreneur, could realize a profit from rising lead prices. Finally, the terms of the leases should be lengthened to encourage stability and longevity among those working the government land.

Austin's arguments were logical, cogent, succinct, and disregarded. No real change occurred during Moses' lifetime. His remained the only shaft mine. The government continued to collect its rents in cash. And the length of the lease period stayed so short that the turnover rate of lessees continued high. If Moses found the result of his labor frustrating, he never said so, probably because his own personal situation absorbed his attention.[14]

Reading the report, no one would have suspected that Mine a Breton was not providing Moses a sufficient income. Production figures appeared substantial. Austin included in the document his calculation that the mine yielded 360,000 pounds of lead annually from 1798 to 1804, and 800,000 pounds annually between 1804 and 1808, when an influx of population brought more miners into his diggings. Since 1808, on account of both the war and new discoveries of ore deposits, which siphoned off two-thirds of his hands, his production had fallen by nearly half to 400,000-500,000 pounds per year. The difference between his income at the turn of the century and in the middle of its second decade, however, was his overhead — the slaves and those persistent debts.

The gambit of bold expansion that always before in short order had pulled Moses out of a worsening situation was, in 1814, 1815, and 1816, working far slower, if at all. After two years without satisfying progress toward regaining his financial stability, Moses decided to take a completely new tack.

"There is strange revulitions taking place at Durham Hall," a disturbed Emily wrote her husband on November 6, 1816. Her father, evidently grown weary of the struggle, had told her that he intended to leave Durham Hall in the spring and move to Herculaneum. "I laught at him and tell him it is not so easy to move, but," she added, "he persists in it very posatively — "[15] Moses had made up his mind, indeed. He would quit the lead business.

A little more than a week after Moses astounded Emily with his news, he ratified papers turning over Mine a Breton, his lead smelting plant, and all the paraphernalia of mining that went with them. Unknown to Emily, the deal evidently had been in the making for some months. Early in the fall of 1816, when business was depressed, Stephen traveled to Kentucky to talk again with Anthony Butler. On October 26 they signed an agreement creating a partnership under the name of "Stephen F. Austin and Company" to mine lead on a large scale. Stephen's interest, it appears, would be the property and management, Butler's all or part of the work force. The deal struck, Stephen took the slaves, returned to Missouri, and completed the arrangement with his father. Barely two weeks past his twenty-third birthday, on November 18, 1816, Stephen recorded at the Washington County Courthouse his lease of all 5,000 arpents remaining of his father's Mine a Breton tract for the purpose of "farming, mining, Digging and raising lead ore and Smelting the Same." Father and son agreed that the convenant would run for five years from January 1, 1817, and that the payment to Moses would be 20% of all the lead produced.[16]

What impelled Moses Austin, after more than a quarter century in the lead business, to decide to leave it so abruptly? Perhaps it was his health. Moses through most of his life appears to have been no more sickly than the average person of his day, a remarkable fact considering that he administered a business which took him out of doors throughout the year. But once he passed his fiftieth birthday, illness seemed to come more frequently. Every year after 1811, some malady or other afflicted him. In mid-September, 1816, when he and Stephen were discussing the working of Mine a Breton before Stephen left for Kentucky, Moses reported himself "quite unwell and at this time can only Move from House to Office" across Breton Creek. This illness, he thought however, would prove to be more serious than previous ones. In declining an invitation to visit the Bryans, he lamented, "Would to God I could also Visit you at the Same time but I am I believe doomed to be always confined—"[17]

From the property leased to Stephen, Moses reserved only Durham Hall, his home for the past eighteen years. By 1816 the structure had evolved into an impressive, rambling place with several additions attached behind the original two-story house. Moses had weatherboarded and painted the exterior, plastered the interior walls, added fireplaces and installed glass in the windows. On the grounds, he had built stables, a "Kitching and double log house adjoining a Smokehouse and hen and pigeon house [and] the cabbins of the house servants." The approximately ten

Durham Hall, 1824. Austin changed the house considerably during his eighteen years there, adding in particular a porch in front and rooms behind. *Charles Alexandre Lesueur Drawings #42052, Museum d'Histoire Naturelle du Havre.*

acres of grounds he also held out consisted of a "back yard to the Barn and the Garden and orchard."[18] Yet, as comfortable as the place was, Moses had no intention of staying there long. A week before Christmas he invited Emily to bring her family and spend the observance in her old home, as "its likely its the last time Durham Hall will contain its Present Inhabitants."[19] He was about to begin, if he had not already begun, construction of a house on his property beside the square, overlooking the river in Herculaneum.[20]

With Stephen eager, energetic, and capable of taking over the work, it is not hard to understand why Moses decided to relinquish the lead mining business to him. But how Moses could leave Potosi so easily is less clear. True, some residents despised the community. "I draw an unfavorable inference as regards the state of literature & politeness," one writer commented to his storekeeper uncle in the town. "I would almost be willing to class...[the residents of Potosi] among semibarbarians in their festive enjoyment. I fondly wish you may see some more certain road to fortune & fame than this place could afford you."[21] If Moses shared that sentiment, which he certainly never indicated forthrightly, the citizens of Potosi and Mine a Breton did not hold it of him. They made him an officer of their July the Fourth celebration in 1816, put him on the board of the fledgling Potosi Academy in 1817, and after the first design of the courthouse proved too expensive to construct, made him a commissioner to redraw and build the structure. Seen through the eye of a businessman, the market of Potosi could not be uncomparable to that of Herculaneum, as Potosi held at least twice the population of Herculaneum on the river. And to at least one observer of both places, the settlement along Breton Creek presented the more attractive appearance. Traveler Henry R. Schoolcraft thought Potosi "built in a better style than the villages in the country generally." Indeed, he continued, it "has a neat and thriving appearance, and contains several handsome edifices."[22] Whatever Austin's reason for leaving, he would not be dissuaded.

For Stephen, the lease of Mine a Breton represented an opportunity, a challenge, and a trust. "I have taken possession of the Mines and the whole establishment here and Commenced business under the Stile of S. F. Austin and Co.," Stephen wrote his brother-in-law proudly on February 17, 1817. But could he make the property produce more efficiently and profitably than his father had? "My prospects at the Hill are not very promising," he recognized, partly because he could not escape beginning his career as a lead entrepreneur in the same hole in which his father already floundered. "The Money on your note in Bank which I used," he wrote Bryan, "I will repay as soon as the lead is made...." In addition, "write wheither you can make any arrangement to raise that Money. if not I must [raise it] by Some means or Execution will be out immediately – I am very much pushed at this time to make up the money for our Beef and Pork." The early troubles seemed to deepen his determination. The energy that drove him was love for his father, whom he respected and admired without reservation, and the desire to be worthy of the family's mantle that had fallen on his shoulders. The goal he set for himself was to erase all those nagging debts. "[I] am flattering myself with the pleasing hope of being able by the end of this year to free the Family from every embarrassment I shall literally bury myself this Spring and Summer in the Mines and if attention and industry will affect anything I shall do much." Stephen meant it. Without delay he began "sinking new Shafts— the furnace goes in this night and I expect to Make about 15000 pounds of Lead this Smelt which I will send immediately over to Hercum."[23]

Though Stephen would work unstintingly, he, like his father, needed the association of his kin. "When the family are gone," he told Bryan, "I hope Sister will not desert me, but will very often enliven the Hall with her Society when left here alone how I shall envy her the Company of little *Joel* his prattle would be music to me compared to the *dull* cheerless, chiling Silence which will pervade the Hall when deserted by all but a Solatary Batchelor!!!—"[24]

While loneliness was a liability of his new work, Stephen's strength of character in devotion to duty should have more than compensated for it. Like his father, but in a more gentle, personable way, Stephen had a presence and demeanor that commanded attention. Standing five feet eight or nine inches, he presented "a slender sinewy, graceful figure, of easy elastic movements, with small hands and feet, dark hair inclined to curl when damp, with large hazel eyes, [and] fair skin when not sun burned," recalled his nephew Moses Austin Bryan, who knew him well in later life. "His face was grave and thoughtful when not in the social circle, then it was animated and lit up by the gentle soul within; his voice was manly and soft, his colloquial powers fluent, persuasive and attractive, without being conscious of it himself; his magnetic power over others gave him the great influence he possessed . . . and his lofty practical intellect, his thorough forgetfulness of self."[25]

Since returning from the unsuccessful trip to New Orleans in 1812, Stephen had been working for and with his father, had served for more than three years as an officer in the Territorial Militia and had accumulated modest land holdings in Potosi and nearby Bellvue. More socially oriented than his father, on June 23, 1815, he had been initiated into the Louisiana Lodge No. 109 at Ste. Genevieve of the Ancient Free and Accepted Masons, the first lodge established west of the Mississippi River.[26] Two months later, still but twenty-one years old, he stood for and won election to one of Washington County's two seats in the Territorial Legislature of Missouri. Stephen handled politics well. He established himself, in the eyes of one observer at least, as one of the four "Chief rulers" of the House and was returned the next year.[27] Clearly by the time Austin took charge of Mine a Breton, he had made a name for himself.

Would Stephen seize every opportunity that came to him to improve his lead business? The question faced him eight days into his second term in the legislature. On December 10, 1816, Representative John McArthur from Ste. Genevieve, as custom prescribed, asked permission to introduce a measure. McArthur sought a resolution from the House praying Congress to place an additional duty on the importation into the United States of crude lead and to dedicate the revenue from the measure to the support of an academy at Potosi. Whether McArthur thought of it first, the idea of a protective tariff appealed to Stephen and Moses. The tariff once had given Moses Austin and Company the boost it needed to firmly establish the mining business in Virginia. Possibly a tariff could do the same for S. F. Austin and Company in Missouri.

On December 12, the day designated for McArthur to act, either he failed to introduce his memorial or else it was lost on first reading. We cannot know which, because the proceedings for that Thursday never were published. Whatever the case, Stephen had too much interest in the measure to let it die there. Seven days later Representative Austin of Potosi offered a measure virtually identical in its purpose. "Perhaps no Country in the world abounds with more numerous and productive Lead Mines than the United States," reads the memorial in the rambling prose Stephen used on formal occasions, "which if properly wrought it is believed would yeald a Sufficient Supply for home consumption, and afford a considerable Surplus for exportation thereby retaining in the Country the Capital which is at present sent abroad for that article and indeed have a tendency to convert the immence balance which is now against the United States and in favour of those Countries whence their supplies of Lead are drawn into a rapid accumulation of the internal wealth of the Country."[28] While Stephen composed the statement, the sentiment had belonged to Moses long before Stephen ever thought about such matters. Nevertheless, the truth of it, buttressed by arguments linking lead and the national defense, was strong and had swayed Congress once before.

Representative Evans saw no merit in the memorial and moved its rejection. Eight on the floor agreed with him, but his motion lost when twelve voted in the negative. A week later, on the day after Christmas, Stephen pushed the measure through third reading and cemented his victory two days later by obtaining concurrence in a resolution to communicate the memorial, along with other matters, to Congress.[29] The victory proved hollow for Stephen personally, though, because if Congress ever acted on the measure, the increase proved to be too little and too late to make a difference for him at Mine a Breton.

No tariff, however high, could make up for inferior quality lead, and for whatever reason, Stephen's product appears not to have measured up. "Some of the Bars have considerable dross," Elias Bates informed Stephen, acknowledging a shipment in August, 1817. "One allmost Broke in throwing it out of the waggon—"[30] Perhaps lower prices born of inferior grade product drove him to it, but before Stephen had been at the mines one year, he, like his father before him, had begun borrowing heavily. In December, 1817, he obtained some $2,000, part of it from the Bank of St. Louis. "I can safely recommend Mr Austin to be a Gentleman of respectability and worthy of Cr.," one reference wrote cheerfully in his behalf as Stephen prepared to travel to the east coast for supplies, "and hope the concern [the business to which the letter was written] will hold out such inducements as will be advisable for him to open an a/c, which no doubt will be exonerated in due season."[31] What no one knew was when "due season" would ever come.

Throughout the spring of 1817, Moses Austin appears to have traveled regularly between Durham Hall and Herculaneum, pushing the work on his house, which he hoped to move into in May. As with his others, it would be no ordinary house. Herculaneum's houses "were built of squared oak logs, and had bulky old-fashioned chimneys, built outside with a kind of castelated air, as they are seen in the old French and Dutch settlements

Herculaneum, Missouri, 1824. In Lesueur's sketch of Herculaneum, drawn three years after Moses Austin's death, Austin's house appears in the foreground, his shot tower commands the horizon on the cliff behind (north of) the settlement. *Charles Alexandre Lesueur Drawings #42070, Museum d'Histoire Naturelle du Havre.*

in Canada and along the vallies of the Hudson and Mohawk," the observant Henry Schoolcraft noted. "The arts of painting and guilding and cornices had not yet extended their empire" to the new waterfront village. Austin's home alone, he added, without giving further description, provided the only exception to the dull sameness.[32]

In June only flooring remained uncompleted, but when Austin finally occupied the place is uncertain. What was clear, he could not, while waiting on the house, delay establishing himself among the merchants of Herculaneum. He had opened a store by June, when he ordered from Bryan a load of boards he could use for shelves and countertop. "The late Storm has determined me not to trust my goods any longer in a log Cabbin than I can help and an Other Load of Plank will finish the Store."[33]

In July that store became the Herculaneum office for the *Pike*, the first steamboat to advertise that it called regularly at Herculaneum. True to an enterprising character in a new setting, Austin took on any business that gave him an advantage over his competitors.[34]

The regular visit of the *Pike* provided one more indication that Herculaneum was an important settlement and a location where a businessman, regardless of his historic ties to the community, likely could make money. The place had grown in ten years to a community of nearly forty houses, four stores, a post office, and a school. In his report to Meigs on the lead industry, Austin called Herculaneum "the great Depot for most of the lead that is made at the mines in Washington County," a fact corroborated by other observers and statistics published in the *Missouri Gazette*.[35]

Even by 1816, however, it had become more than simply a place of deposit and transhipment. Herculaneum also boasted lead manufacturing. Traveler Schoolcraft counted three shot towers when he visited in 1818. And in addition to its lead trade, Herculaneum "is surrounded on every side by fine farming land, and there are several excellent grist and saw mills in its vicinity," the town's proprietors advertised in the newspaper. "With those and many other advantages it is presumable that it must soon become a place of business and that it will increase in population, as fast as any other village in this territory. Several other manufactories of Lead are about to be established there, and in the neighborhood, and many discoveries of lead mineral have recently been made still nearer to this place, which promise well."[36]

Herculaneum's potential was definite, but its performance was a different matter. Business had been poor in the town for some time. Elias Bates had complained for more than a year, even telling Bryan once that with "no prospect of its being any better here—wish I was away from here."[37] But Bates stayed, and if Moses knew of his nephew's sentiment, he disregarded it. That was unfortunate, for in short order, by midsummer of 1817, Moses found himself in the same fix as Bates. Business ground to such a slow pace that he could make no sales, even where he found a demand. "I have sent you nothing of the Articles you have sent for," Moses responded fretfully to an order from his son-in-law, "because I have them not." He had no domestic cloth, saddles, bridles, or shoes in stock. "As to country linen its not to be obtained for Cash because it is not in the country I made every Exerti[on] in my power to get linen when in St Louis but could not the Domestics I expected, have Not arrived they are uncommonly difficult to obtain Coffee and sugar are Cash." Indeed, many goods "are Cash in hand and cannot be had without to purchase them with out money cannot be done."[38]

Once again, traditional pursuits had failed to answer his need. Moses looked for other means to make money and make it fast. Whatever he chose would have promise of greater reward than tending store, but also real risk of total failure. Still his way to salvage his fiscal well-being was to take a gamble. Two possibilities came to him. The first was a copper mining venture. In October, 1817, he signed a contract with Risdon H. Price, Stephen and Elias Rector, and Thompson Douglass, colleagues in the bank, to explore and mine the ore on their land in Monroe County, Illinois Territory, across the River from Herculaneum. It was a desperate, chancy arrangement. Should Austin find a mine alleged to be there, the owners would give him a share in the proceeds and an equal interest in the tract. But if he failed, the entire cost fell on him alone.[39] Nothing in the Austin Papers suggests that Moses consummated the contract. Any money he sunk in the deal, however, proved to be another empty expense he could ill afford.

The second gamble was to obtain major capital with which to reestablish himself. For the money he turned naturally to the Bank of St. Louis. Moses had supported the institution unreservedly, even insuring that his children held shares. "I do not wish any of my family should refuse To pay up such *shares* as they may hold," he told Emily in October, 1816, when he mentioned giving her five shares. Bryan, Moses hoped, would continue to hold at least ten of his own. "When the Bank is under way," Moses repeated, "it will be of great advantage to−al of−us−"[40] And so it was. The Austins, father and son, and James Bryan all borrowed sums in the early months.[41]

Not everyone saw the bank in such favorable light, however, as Moses well knew. During those three years searching for capital to launch the institution, a rift among the organizers festered to the point that several withdrew to form a rival bank. The same issue of the *Missouri Gazette* that announced the opening of the Bank of St. Louis reported also the formation of the Bank of Missouri.[42]

Moses and his colleagues remaining on the Board of the Bank of St. Louis recognized the serious challenge that the formation of a second bank posed to their enterprise. To better meet, if not stall, the competition, they decided to ask the legislature to make several revisions in their charter. With a leader of the legislature, Stephen F. Austin, being the son of a board member and a fellow stockholder, they evidently reasoned their chances of securing appropriate changes to be exceptionally good. They must have asked Moses to draft the paper detailing their wishes. This would explain the presence among the Austin Papers of a massive document in the elder Austin's hand outlining an appropriate structure for a territorial bank.

Moses wrote page upon page, alternately presenting his points matter-of-factly and advising his son on arguments to support them. Among the principal aims of the directors was a broadening of interest in their institution. They wanted to reduce the price of their stock so that more people could hold shares. "The greater number you have to support the Credit of your stock, and also the bank paper," he argued, the stronger the institution, "for no stock Holder will refuse the Notes of his own Bank –" To maintain the interest of the commercial and business communities leery of the potential of an inflated paper currency, "you may also urge the necessaty of a bank to bring back hard money which will be the consequence of a Territorial Bank." A "Territorial bank," as he stated it, was an institution structured like Hamilton's national bank, on the board of which would sit representatives of the legislature. Moses thought it vital to have the government interested in the institution and wanted the Territory "to hold as much stock as she can command money to Purchase," perhaps a quarter of the total. The boldest change proposed was to take for their bank the name of the rival bank. "The Name of the Territory annexed to the Charter," Austin scrawled, "will give Credit to the Notes and Value of the stock."

Moses, if not all the directors, must have sensed that some scheme for financing the Territory's interest in the bank would help to sell their changes. Consequently, Moses included in his paper for Stephen an elaborate plan for a lottery to raise, without taxes, the money for purchasing the government's shares of stock. The scheme would benefit the populace long after the lottery had been concluded, Moses quickly pointed out, because the earnings from the Territory's stock could be used to finance desperately needed internal improvements, in particular work on roads and bridges.[43]

If the directors found it easy to ask Stephen to carry their bill, Stephen found it difficult to do what they asked. Handling the bill would present him a serious conflict of interest. The very fact that he held stock in their institution, he recognized, compromised his strength in arguing in their behalf and against the rival bank. Nevertheless, he decided to offer the bill.

In mid-December, 1816, the rivalry of the two institutions came to a head in the House. Mustering all the eloquence at his command, Stephen took the floor to oppose chartering the Bank of Missouri. As his father had done on this critical matter, he wrote out his remarks, too. There was no margin of error for a misstated point. After explaining away his personal interest in the one bank, he attacked the other point by point. "One Bank is established in this T[erritory]," he said. "Let us make that one a Territorial one on the plan of the Ste B of K[entucky] and supp[res]s all others – I am opposed to this B[ank of Missouri] because the Country cannot support 2 B at this time and because there is not specie in . . .[the Territory] for their establishment." He knew from watching the operations of banks in other sections of the country that the result of competition in a market as small as Missouri must be chaos. "I am opposed to the establishment of another B because it will be rearing up in the heart of our Country two Rival Institutions who would view each other as adversaries plac'd in opposition by the Legislature to cut each others throughts as soon as possible by authorizing the establishment of another Bank[.] therefore at this time and under these circumstances," he warned his colleagues in the House, "you are sanctioning an imposition upon the People and fostering and encouraging a system of speculation whose operations if not seasonably checked will involve the Country in confusion, anarchy, and ruin."[44]

Stephen must have been persuasive. The Legislative Council voted four to three to postpone for two years any further consideration of the bill incorporating the Bank of Missouri. His own measure in behalf of the Bank of St. Louis, lacking the more controversial provisions in his father's document, and the proposal to establish a state lottery passed. But no act is final until the session is adjourned, and Stephen's complete victory proved to be short-lived. Within a week of the vote postponing consideration of the Bank of Missouri bill, the absent representative from Howard County arrived in St. Louis bent on overturning the vote and had changed the views of the head of the Legislative Council, who "*now thinks* (as I am told) that public good requires" creation of the second bank. To Stephen's astonishment and disgust, the Legislative Council reversed its earlier decision. He penned a blistering protest in behalf of himself and several members outraged at the "unpresidented unparliamentary and illegal manner" in which the bill had been resurrected and adopted. This time he swayed no minds. The action stood, and the rival Bank of Missouri became a reality.[45]

When the Bank of St. Louis began business in December, 1816, it met with gratifying popularity and a brisk demand for loans. In response, the institution issued, in a short period, a great amount of paper money. The economy of Missouri reacted with a heightened spirit of speculation and extravagance. Few seemed to notice that with less than half of its capital paid in, the bank easily could issue more notes than it could support safely.[46]

By February, 1817, all could see. "The Bank seemes to have Ruin this place," William Borown wrote Bryan on February 17. "At presant every on[e] Complayns how much it have Desapointed them."[47] The Bank of St. Louis received more criticism than it deserved. A decreasing number of immigrants bringing new cash into Missouri, aggravated by a shrinking money supply in the United States generally, contributed more heavily than did the bank's practices to tightening the economy of the Territory.[48]

In addition, by summer, the Bank of Missouri had opened its doors, and the competition that Moses and Stephen had feared not only materialized, but turned nasty. On July 5, 1817, Moses sent Bryan $100 in notes and apologized for drawing no more. "The situation of the Bank is such," he explained, "that Money cannot be had on your Note I have obtained a discount—but cannot draw money from the Bank." The cash he had, he had begged from John N. B. Smith, the Cashier. The Bank of Missouri, he told Bryan bitterly, had begun to make a run on the Bank of St. Louis by sending agents to buy Bank of St. Louis paper for redemption in specie. Naturally, "this has stopped all notes of Ours going out untill things become a little settled." For men juggling accounts as Austin was, the situation hurt. "*McDonald* must take Bank notes or he cannot be paid," Moses told Bryan flatly. Any more money could be obtained only at an unconscionable rate. "I would not have you to Draw Dollars from the Bank now not *for*, 50 pr C-t it would ruin us both in as much as every exertion is making by the Bank of Missouri to run us down and I *would* not obtain a Dollar but by the friendship of Mr Smith and If a hundred Dollars was to be called for and by you it would ruin our C-r in the Bank—"[49]

As if the run did not bring trouble enough, that fall the bank suffered two severe blows from which many contemporaries knew the institution would have a difficult time recovering. First, in mid November, the United States Treasury Department awarded to the Bank of Missouri, rather than to the Bank of St. Louis, the privilege of receiving deposits of public money from land sales. While the selection enhanced the reputation of the Bank of Missouri, it did not, on the face of it, question the integrity of the Bank of St. Louis. But that came soon afterward when President Hammond announced that the cashier, on his own initiative and without the knowledge or consent of any bank officer or director, had purchased a large sum of bills. Upon learning of the deed, the Board ordered that no more bills be bought. Cashier Smith ignored the directive "and arranged his plans when he went to Kentucky in October, 1817, so that on November 3rd he drew bills to an immense amount in favor of certain of his co-partners and sold them, and the bank did not get the proceeds, even though the bills were signed by him alone, not countersigned by the president as required by the charter."[50]

If it could not recover the money, the bank had lost nearly $60,000. The institution limped along for a few months, during which time the directors divided into two factions over the question of retaining the offending cashier. They "drew the whole town in as partizens," observed one director.[51]

On February 11, 1818, the two sides met for the showdown, and when a majority voted to replace John Smith with T. W. Smith, three directors resigned. Several unhappy stockholders took charge of the bank facility, ousted the directors, and locked the doors. One of the three resigned directors charged in the *Missouri Gazette* that Hammond, Austin, and T. W. Smith, their new cashier, had directed the coup. First, he argued, they opposed dismissing John Smith. Then, by prior arrangement, they pushed through the appointment of T. W. Smith, who had resided in the country only a few months and not recently. His election, the disaffected director continued, more than any other matter, caused the breach on the board.[52]

Moses never recorded his role in the confrontation, but after the meeting, he left the board, too. A sympathetic observer thought the damage from the unsavory event would be minimal. "The Bank in consequence has been shut for some days," Director Robert Simpson declared, "but will open on tuesday next— it is purfectly solvent and will be able to withstand the shock such circumstances generally produce in Banking institution. and I have no doubt will eventually be benefited by it."[53]

Moses must have shared his former colleague's confidence. The day after the bank reopened, on March 11, 1818, he took out a loan of $15,000. No scrap of paper hints at how he planned to spend the money. Perhaps he thought to sink it into his lead mining business, which Stephen so far had had no better success than he at making a paying enterprise. As collateral for the loan, Moses put up his sprawling, comfortable Durham Hall, all its outbuildings, and 640 acres of his Mine a Breton tract, property whose title the United States had recognized only seven months earlier when federal authorities had surveyed and entered it on the township plats.[54]

Moses once again had executed a bold stroke in a bid to recover his financial stability. But this time, by putting the centerpiece of his estate and a major portion of his still-rich diggings on the line, he had taken a greater chance than ever he had before.

Perhaps he had borrowed so much for so long that he saw no difference between this and all those other times. Certainly he appears never to have changed his lifestyle as his financial horizon dimmed. Early in 1818, as through all the previous good times and bad, he continued to live well. Receipts among the Austin Papers show that year in and year out he provided his household the "best coffee," white Havana sugar, "fine shoes," and various good liquors.[55]

Moses Austin's stability and continuity through all the years rested, too, on his family. The circle was close knit. When James Bryan married Emily, he became one of Moses' children as completely as if he had been born an Austin. Moses called him "son" and relied on him as fully as he did on Stephen. The senior Austin doted over his first living grandchild, Emily's second baby, William Joel Bryan. Joel's father kept the letter the toddler's mother wrote in November, 1816, after taking the eleven-month-old child to Durham Hall. "Our darling Boy walks very well and is a very good Child as yet," she told her husband, "but I am afraid his Gra[n]d - Parents will spoile him."[56]

The next year, 1817, Moses saw his fourteen-year-old youngest son for the first time apparently since the boy left with his mother in the summer of 1811 at the age of seven. During the six-year absence, Moses, as was his want, had carried on with the boy a correspondence similar to that which he had had with Stephen and Emily before him. "I thank Pa for the advise he gave me," Brown wrote on one occasion, "and I hope that I shall profit by it." Clearly he already had profited by his stay with the Whittlesey family in Connecticut, for his letter shows a polished address superior to that of either Stephen or Emily at the same age.[57]

Maria, one would suspect, worried Moses more than any of the others. Her health, like his, began to fail. In part her condition resulted from falls. In 1816, after one, her bruises proved to be "much worse then was at first expected and," Moses told Emily, "I am doubtfull will confine her for some time her face is better but every other part of her body—is *bad* and gives her much pain."[58]

If not the injuries from this fall, then an illness of equal magnitude that afflicted her at about the same time caused her New Jersey cousin, Edward Sharp, to exclaim in March, 1817, his pleasure that "your life has been so wonderfully saved."[59] By that time the rheumatism, about which she had been complaining for some years, had crippled her right arm so severely she no longer could write.[60]

Despite it all, in June, 1818, Moses' hopes soared as they had not for four years. "Lead is looking up," he wrote Bryan. "Mr Bates Sold 45 thousand at *5 Dollars* and Shott *at 750.*" Perhaps at last prices had risen and would hold at the higher levels long enough to permit him to restore his ragged finances and take care of his family. "I shall make you all the Lead I can - Command and as Mr Cox will not want his Lead for some time I hope we may make out."[61]

Moses, always the optimist, truly had every reason to hope. But hope had to be grounded in a sound knowledge of, and balance between, the sources of his difficulties and his opportunities. Imperceptible to him, that loan from the Bank of St. Louis had shifted the balance. Whether or not he and Bryan would make out, now depended more on the stability of the institution to which he had mortgaged the foundation of his income than upon the market for the lead he mined.

CHAPTER XI

HOW DID Moses Austin intend to redeem his collapsing finances? He must have had definite plans. To obtain the $15,000 loan from the Bank of St. Louis in March, 1818, he had taken the extraordinary risk of mortgaging Durham Hall, the centerpiece of his principal asset, the Mine a Breton property. Yet he put none of the money into strengthening either the mines or his other staple business, the store in Herculaneum. In July, not four months after he took the loan, his son Stephen fumed in exasperation that Moses' business lay "all in confusion—" Moses knew it, too. After offering to guarantee a note of his son-in-law, James Bryan, he admitted that his credit "would Not answer." Most likely, the elder Austin used the money to settle obligations, especially those pressed upon him by court judgments. Used in that way, the money could only add to Austin's financial burden, not relieve it.

Feeling his back to the wall, Austin concluded to take the ultimate step. On June 5, 1818, less than three months after he obtained the loan, Moses announced abruptly in the *Missouri Gazette* that he was offering both the Mine a Breton tract and the Herculaneum store for sale. Austin evidently had given up on his prospects in Missouri and, as he had done when business at the Virginia mines had gone sour, looked to a place new and distant to recoup his fortune. "I *am* greatly dissatisfied and wish to Change my situation," he wrote not long afterward. "Would to god my business was closed I would leave the country in a week—"[1]

Moses first set his sights on "the North," likely Pennsylvania near his wife's relatives or Connecticut near his. If a move of such magnitude hinged upon the closing of his businesses in Missouri, he would have deluded himself to believe that he could leave soon. The economy of Missouri in 1818 ran on credit and debt, fed primarily by speculation in land and by inflation caused by money easily available from the unregulated state banks. So many, as Austin, had borrowed so much, they could repay their debts only if the speculation and inflation sped on. In Missouri, that depended on the continuing flow of immigrants ready to pay the higher prices, on the willingness of sellers to continue to accept promises to pay, and on the stability of the banks.[2] If the new settlers ever stopped coming, if creditors ever turned to collecting debts more than to creating them, the consequences would be disastrous.

Austin saw one early sign of trouble—a reluctance to sell on credit. "Not a pound can be had either of coffe or Sugar with out Cash in hand," he observed to Bryan in June, 1818. Austin managed nevertheless to trade shot for the goods, but warned his son-in-law, "When you receive what I shall receive for you, Keep it I cannot say when I can lett you have any more."[3]

Perhaps Austin did not recognize the sign for what it was. Looking back, Maria thought he simply disregarded it, believing either that the end would not come soon or that, when it did, he could ride out any hard times. Good observer that she was, Maria was right as far as she remembered. But she had forgotten the uncharacteristic weakening of resolve that momentarily seized her husband late in the summer of 1818. "If I can obtain a purchaser will sell all my proprety in this country," Moses declared firmly in September, after his property had been on the market for three months. "I am Determined to sell as soon as I can." Yet when offered the tidy sum of $50,000 for the mine tract, he refused it contemptuously.[4]

Perhaps Moses really did not want to sell and leave. He sent no other notice of sale to the paper during the rest of 1818. But a shrewd business-person has to know when to sell, even if the proposition is not all one would like and even if it hurts to part with the property. Since the mines apparently were not producing the income Austin needed, simply holding them helped him only if a more lucrative offer could be anticipated, an eventuality that should have seemed unlikely in an economy noticeably deteriorating to a cash and carry basis. Still, the optimist in the aging Austin evidently led him to hold out and pass up a real opportunity to settle the financial woes that had been both plaguing him and growing steadily worse for years.

Within a month, the wisdom of Austin's decision appeared to have been substantiated. Bank President Sam Hammond wrote Austin exuberantly in October, 1818, that St. Louis merchants with whom he had talked thought the time ripe for resurrecting the Bank of St. Louis, which had suspended operations once again not long after Moses had obtained his loan. The Board of Directors boldly asked, through Representative Stephen F. Austin, that the Legislature conduct an investigation "into the causes of the embarrassments and present state of that institution," confident of the basic soundness of their enterprise.[5] Though Moses left the Board in December before the bank reopened and could no longer influence the administration of the institution, the directors maintained a clear line to him by electing Stephen to fill his father's place.

Moses' spirits should have risen still further the next month when Jefferson County was created and Herculaneum made the county seat. He pledged a sum toward construction of the courthouse. More than that, he seized his opportunity. "This town . . . will soon become a place of first consequence," he prophesied to the world in February, 1819, in a typical boomer style of advertisement for town lots. "Persons wishing to possess themselves of Lots, had better now come forward and embrace the present opportunity to purchase."[6] Whatever his success at Herculaneum, in Potosi in March he realized $1,500 from six pieces of property sold out of his Mine a Breton estate.[7]

Even with the good news and the sales, Moses surely knew that his finances still tottered precariously. Stephen knew it. "When the day arrives that the whole family are out of Debt," he promised his brother-in-law at the end of 1818, "I mean to *celibrate it* as my *wedding* day—which never will come untill then."[8] Intensely loyal to his father, Stephen indeed meant what he said. He went to his grave eighteen years later one of the great figures of American history but still a bachelor.

Far more than on the money he could realize from the sale of small pieces of real estate in Herculaneum or Potosi, Moses Austin's future depended upon events in St. Louis. The troubled Bank of St. Louis re-opened its doors early in March of 1819. In a strong positive bid to consolidate its position, the bank began at once liquidating its debts by redeeming its paper currency (issued, as was the style of the day, in the form of prom-issory notes) and by paying off claims. To finance the move, the directors called in the money the bank had out on loan. They also obtained a judg-ment against Cashier John Smith's co-partners for $56,000, nearly the full value of that one crippling, overdue, illegally made loan.[9] The bank never received a penny of the amount, however, and the burden of stabilizing the institution fell on others.

News of the sudden call rocked the Austins. Where could Moses raise $15,000, plus interest, so fast? He hurried to St. Louis to talk with bank offi-cials. Stephen, a director since December, sent Cashier William M. O'Hara a scalding letter. "My Father and family have been amongst the firmest sup-porters the Bank ever had," he began. But that was not the only reason his father's loan should be excepted from the unexpected call. "If the money my Father owes was *all paid* in at once, would it remain in the vaults? or would it be lent out again?—it certainly would be loaned out—" Stephen asserted, see-ing no advantage to the bank in the second loan over the first. Indeed, if his father "can make them *safe* (which he has already done [by pledging against the note, in addition to his original collateral of Durham Hall, his considerable holding of bank stock]) why not let the loan stand, or must *he* be ruined to satisfy some others who wish to borrow money?" Flushed with anger, Stephen blistered the bank with his answer. "If the Directors are governed by *that* principle they need not calculate to have Friends long of any kind." Indeed, if the bank "is to become an instrument of oppression to ruin men without necessity—" he vowed, "I shall wash *my* hands of it, and endeavor to give it the *Character* and *Standing*...which it will *then* merit."[10]

Neither Moses' meeting nor Stephen's letter caused the bank to drop, or even stall, its demand for the retirement of the elder Austin's loan. Enraged, but in full recognition that they could not parry the onslaught of the institution Moses had helped to found, father and son retreated to the hospitable surroundings of Durham Hall to plot their course. Since Stephen had proven no more effective than his father at coaxing profits from their traditionally most lucrative asset, Mine a Breton, they must have concluded at the outset that they had to find some new enterprise. Moses had an idea. "He proposed to me," Stephen recorded for his brother years later, "the idea of forming a colony in Texas.... The project was discussed by us...for several days, and adopted."[11]

Stephen's matter-of-fact tone likely reflected the character of their discussion. Moses' proposal was no desperate plan of a broken man. On the contrary, it combined both the bold stroke that Moses always sought when he needed to revive, reinvigorate, or redirect his business and the practical possibility of achievement that turned most of his ideas from dream to reality.

Few men were better qualified by experience to lead a colony into Spanish territory than Moses Austin. He knew, first, what was involved in recruiting for a colony, because he had done it in securing miners for Austinville. He knew, second, what it took to move a colony from one country to another, as he had done that, too, in 1798 in leading his followers from Virginia to Spanish Louisiana. He knew, third, what to expect in dealing with Spanish officials, having worked with functionaries and officers up to the highest levels on the confirmation of his grant and on concerns of his Mine a Breton settlement prior to acquisition of Louisiana by the United States. So convinced was he of his ability, he had, only a few months earlier, told Henry Schoolcraft the fanciful story of his entry into St. Louis in January, 1797, in which he manipulated the local Spanish officials into giving him the attention he wanted.[12] Finally, he knew what was required in founding and establishing a settlement on a firm foundation, since he had accomplished the work three times already at Austinville in Virginia, at Mine a Breton in Spanish Louisiana, and at Herculaneum in Missouri.

To Austin's calculating mind, moreover, the time was right. Of course, American leaders had spoken for years of Texas as territory that by rights should be liberated by Americans from the tyranny of European monarchy. Representative Stephen F. Austin knew the words. During the traditional July the Fourth celebration of oratory, cannon fire, and feasting at Potosi in 1818, he spoke them in delivering the honored principal address of the day.

> *The same spirit that unsheathed the sword of Washington,*
> and sacrificed servitude and slavery in the flames of the Revolution," he told the crowd, "will also flash across the Gulph of

Mexico, and over the western wilderness that separates independent America from the enslaved colonies of Spain, and
darting the beams of intelligence into the [illeg.] souls of their
inhabitants, awake them from the stupor of slaves, to the
energy of freemen, from the degradation of vassals to the dignity of sovereigns. Already is this great work commenced,
already are the banners of freedom unfurled in the south—
Despotism totters, liberty expands her pinions, and in a few
years more will rescue spanish America from the dominion of
tyranny.[13]

The difference between July 4, 1818, or any previous time, and April of
1819 was a treaty. The news had reached Moses only within a matter of
weeks that at the end of February, 1819, after years of border disputes, the
United States and Spain had concluded the Adams-Onis Treaty defining,
among other matters, the western extent of the Louisiana Purchase. In
exchange for uncontested title to both East and West Florida, Washington
abandoned any and all claim to Texas. Land west of the Sabine River and
the 98th meridian, and south of the Red River, by the agreement became
once again, as it had not been for nineteen years, undisputed Spanish
domain. That single fact made Moses' plan possible. The treaty settled for
Americans which government had the right to issue land titles. "Grants
from the Spanish authorities," Stephen recalled his father's conclusion,
"would therefore be valid."[14]

Their plan agreed to, each partner had work to do. Moses would ascertain the best means of laying the project before the Spanish government.
Stephen would go to Arkansas to see about developing a base that could
be used in an overland migration to supply provisions and offer a resting
place until a location could be established in Texas. Memory of the difficult flatboat trip down the Ohio River in 1798 evidently made Moses reluc-
tant to plan for moving any group the thousand-plus miles to Texas by
water.[15]

Stephen looked forward to his job. He already had the location staked
out. And, as Moses well knew, his son had been trying to get away from
the mines for more than a year to visit it. The place lay on Long Prairie on
the northeast side of the Red River, below the mouth of the Little River, in
far southwestern Arkansas. A fine site it was, too, "the first large prairie
on Red river, from the mouth up," wrote a visitor early in 1819. "It bluffs to
the river, runs back fifteen or twenty miles, and is surrounded by a heavily
timbered country."[16] Moreover, it lay only about ten miles from the Texas
boundary.

Stephen must have acquired the property late in 1817 through one of the
followers of the Reverend William Stevenson. "Long a successful
preacher of the Methodists, and now one of their most worthy presiding

Elders,"[17] Stevenson the year before had led a group of respected Washington County farmers to settle in the remote location. He had selected a wonderfully rich spot on which cotton flourished. Moreover, he located just above the infamous Great Raft, a logjam ninety-miles long, where his community was positioned to command the business of flatboats operating above the obstruction.[18] The settlement took root.

Early in 1818, Stephen asked Bryan, then in Arkansas, to inspect and report on the place. Bryan would have to give a strongly unfavorable appraisal to discourage Stephen. The younger Austin had caught speculation fever. After he learned in December, 1817, that "Orders have lately come on the Surveyors office here to prepare the Red River Country for Market as soon as possible" and he saw New Madrid certificates, which entitled the holder to claim 640 acres of public land in Arkansas west of New Madrid and north of the Arkansas River, rise to the astonishing value of $12 per acre, he "determined to Sell all your [Bryan's] Flour here and buy a Madrid claim with the money, which I will locate on My improvement in the Long Prairie—" Stephen urged his brother-in-law "to return as quick as possible with all the money you [can] and buy Madrid Claims [with which to] Secure some land there before it is too late."[19] By March, 1818, the worth of Stephen's Red River property had, in his mind, inflated practically beyond imagination. "I value my improvement in the Long Praire at 100$ pr. acre for it will yeald an interest on the money (calculating the land at 100$ pr. acre) of at least 25 pr. cent and pay the expence of working it besides."[20]

However exaggerated his appraisal, Stephen evidently understood quite well that the more settled the community, the more secure the foundation for his valuation. "A small Store will do very well there," he advised Bryan, urging him to supply stock.[21] Moses concurred. He called his son and son-in-law to join him in Herculaneum on July 25 "to make some *arrangements* for the fall business," in which he planned to take an interest himself.[22] Stephen would be responsible for the store, and by fall he had arrangements nearly complete. In his euphoria over prospects at Long Prairie, Stephen, as his father had done so often before him, based his promises on his expectations. "I will account to you for all articles you may furnish at the highest rates," he wrote Bryan, qualifying his promise: "as soon as I am able to do so—"[23] On this occasion Stephen enjoyed the good fortune once characteristic of his father. The mercantile operation blossomed. Extensive accounts among the Austin Papers suggest that a mercantile network intertwining the dry goods interests of Stephen and his brother-in-law spread to perhaps as many as seven locations in Arkansas and Louisiana, with the Long Prairie store chief among them.[24]

With arrangements completed for the store, Stephen early in 1819 returned to land speculation. In these dealings he probably operated on his own. His father already had tried and quit the business. In the dark early months of 1816, when Moses was borrowing lead from one account to pay another and through it all sinking farther into debt, he seized upon New Madrid claims for a remedy. These certificates had been issued by the federal government the year before to inhabitants of the town of New Madrid on the Mississippi River who had lost their property in the devastating earthquake of 1812. No one should have been surprised that a lively trade developed in the certificates. Nevertheless, Moses proceeded cautiously before chancing the speculation. Then, after holding claims for only three months, he concluded that the market had failed him, and in June, rather than pay for the claims he had obtained, Moses tried instead to return one, if not all of the certificates to the friend from whom he had acquired them.[25]

His father's experience did not dampen Stephen's enthusiasm. On the contrary, the continuing market in the claims may have bolstered his resolve. Whatever the case, in January and February, 1819, he promised more than 8,000 precious dollars to acquire interests in five claims. Stephen bought no more only because his father's need for money circumscribed the capital available to him. But he increased his resources by joining forces with two partners with whom he shared undivided interests. The two would acquire the claims; Stephen would locate them.

Eager to begin his work, Stephen tidied up his business affairs in Missouri. This in itself was no mean task. "Every cent I owe in the Country must be paid before I can start—" he told bank cashier and partner O'Hara. But with his father working to settle Stephen's principal remaining obligation, more than $4,000 due the bank, Stephen looked forward to the pleasing prospect his father could not enjoy that "when I start I shall be able to go nearly *quite free*."[26]

In Arkansas Stephen spread their holdings so that the partners held interests in two areas. One site lay along the Ouachita River near the mouth of the Caddo River. Perhaps young Austin learned of the area from one of Stevenson's followers, since the minister had settled there for a time, or maybe the fact that Bryan was working salines in the area influenced his choice. The second location Stephen chose lay at the Little Rocks, a prominent outcropping on the south bank of the Arkansas River at the crossing of the St. Louis to Louisiana road.[27] Stephen did well. "The locations we have made are considered by every one to be the best that could have been made in the country and will certainly yeild a handsome profit the moment they can be brought into market," he boasted to O'Hara in June, 1819, after inspecting the sites.[28]

Though then at the height of anticipation in the speculation, Stephen abruptly quit the business. He told O'Hara, in the same letter, that he had turned over his interests in the two locations to Bryan. Bryan had agreed to assume a $1,400 note O'Hara held against Stephen and had given Stephen his farming interest at Long Prairie. Stephen evidently intended to devote himself to improving the Long Prairie property in anticipation of the Texas venture.[29]

Stephen's enterprises—both agricultural and mercantile—at Long Prairie prospered during the course of the next several months. The fact was not lost on his former partners. Bryan, O'Hara, and a third colleague seized the opportunity to strengthen their own interests, and, probably not coincidentally, to further establish and promote the idea of a movement to Texas through Long Prairie. The last issue of the *Missouri Gazette* for 1819 carried news from them dated October 20 announcing establishment of the town of Fulton on Long Prairie at "the point at which the main road leading from Missouri and many of the northern and eastern states to the extremely fertile province of Texas will cross said river."[30]

Seemingly on the brink of achievement again Stephen, a second time, suddenly entertained plans to quit. Two weeks before his former partners sent off the advertisement extolling their settlement on Long Prairie, Stephen wrote a friend along the Mississippi inquiring into the possibility of moving to that bottom land. He had lost interest in Long Prairie, he told his correspondent, in part because the Red River had disappointed him as an artery of commerce. More basically, he blamed the unhealthy Arkansas country where illness had dogged him almost since his arrival.

Perhaps his poor physical condition explains Stephen's unusually unsettled temperament in 1819. Twice he laid promising plans. Twice he did, or prepared to, walk away from them. More curious yet, not a month after he wrote so seriously of leaving Arkansas, and before his correspondent on the Mississippi River could have replied, Stephen F. Austin, on his twenty-sixth birthday, did another about-face and announced his candidacy for the seat in Congress accorded the newly created Arkansas Territory. Was he serious in his bid? He would have to run as a write-in candidate, since the deadline had passed to get his name on the printed ballot. And he had virtually no time to campaign, because the voting would take place in less than two weeks. Whether he truly wanted the congressional seat, Austin received such strong support throughout southern Arkansas, where he had worked and traveled, that he ran second in a field of six and missed election by only 58 out of 1,272 votes. Stephen clearly could win friends and build a following. All he needed was to find his mission.[31]

No matter how well preparations progressed for the Austins' Texas scheme, the work contributed not one dollar toward settling the demand the bank held against Moses. By May of 1819, the senior Austin stood no closer to paying off his note than he had been in March, or even the year before. He had received no offers on his Mine a Breton property since he had scoffed at $50,000 the previous September. Admitting the unlikelihood of finding a buyer in Missouri at his price, Moses concluded that he must look elsewhere. The man to help him do it, he realized, had been living under his roof since early the previous August.[32]

Henry Rowe Schoolcraft of New York had come to Missouri in the summer of 1818 to gather data for his first and very successful book, *A View of the Lead Mines of Missouri.* When the twenty-five-year-old traveler reached Herculaneum on July 23, 1818, and told the purpose of his visit, he was introduced to Moses Austin. The two discussed Schoolcraft's proposed work for two or three days, during which Austin, as was his way, struck a cordial relationship with the visitor. He "warmly approved my plan of exploring the mines, and offered every facility in his power to further it,"[33] Schoolcraft recalled, including a room in Durham Hall to gather and study his specimens.

The young scientist accepted gladly. He worked on local samples for two months before trekking for three in the back country of Missouri and Arkansas, after which he settled again at Durham Hall until May of 1819 preparing his manuscript. Deeply appreciative of Austin's unselfish help, Schoolcraft recorded in more than one of his books how the aging mine entrepreneur's hospitality "impressed me with sentiments of respect for his public, and regard of his private character, which I should do great injustice to my feelings, if I did not commemorate in this public manner."[34] What better man to solicit for help in selling the Mine a Breton tract? No one, save Austin himself, knew the property more completely.

If Moses approached Schoolcraft on the matter before the young man left, not until afterward, on June 8, 1819, did he formalize the arrangement by mailing a power of attorney to his friend. In the cover letter, Austin offered a commission of 5 percent and said he would take $50,000 for the entire property sold in one transaction, or $58,200 if sold in up to eight parcels. Moses valued the "Home Estate" at $15,000 and wanted it sold first, "in as much as the buildings are fast going to ruin." But, however the place was disposed of, "my situation demands Six Thousand Dollars, by October." That was the essential fact, for "unless I sell so as to command that sum by that time I must be disgraced and my property sold for what it will command."[35]

Despite that chilling prospect, and still confident that he could get his price, Moses asked Schoolcraft to obtain for him wallpaper, a box of house glass, gilded frames in which to hang his Austin family arms and various mirrors, and a dozen chairs and five settees "deep and guilt and fashionable." Spare no cost, Austin commanded, as these would be used by him personally.[36]

Three days later, on June 11, Moses wrote again, but a very different letter. After thinking about matters for seventy-two hours, he had changed his mind. No longer was simply closing with the bank and settling comfortably in Herculaneum sufficient. "My objects," he stated unequivocally, "is to leave the territory." Consequently, "all the property at the Mines I would sell at a reduced price rather then keep it." Indeed, he concluded, "I am so much disposed to close my business that I have a wish you should make sales of Durham Hall at any rate and If you cannot obtain the price I have *named* see how much you can get and lett me know. If within a Jump of my expectations I shall take it."[37]

Austin did want to leave Missouri. More than that, however, he wanted to avoid the humiliation of losing his property to those he once counted as friends, but who proved to value his property more highly than his friendship. Hardly had his previous letters begun their long, slow journey to New York than Moses took up his pen again on June 20, addressing Schoolcraft twice, in separate cities, to increase the chance that what Austin had to say would reach his agent at the earliest possible moment. The letters reflected a new and desperate tone.

> For god sake sell If you can and lett me have power to Draw for 5 or 6 thousand Dollars If you can do no better. If this is not done I shall be in the power of my Enemies. my Debts are about 5750 Dollars I have sold in goods and Land 27 Thousand Dollars 10000 of which I have Deposited in stock to discharge my bank Debt the balance is now 1/3 Due but I cannot collect a 100 Dollars nor can I meet my pressing Demand and under such circumstances my Enemies calculate to ruin me. I give you this Information as an excuse for my pressing request for you to make Sale of my Estate. . . . I am so determined to leave this Territory that I must press you to sell.[38]

Impatient, fearful, and hopeful all at once, Moses suggested new tactics. If Schoolcraft could find no buyers through his individual contacts, try auctioning the place. "Money I must have, be the case and the sacrifice what It may therefore you will take this as your authority to make sale of as much as will command me 12 Thousand Dollars."

Yet he still clutched the hope of a quick sale. He wanted to hope. With an eye evidently on buying into a land deal in Arkansas, Moses called on Schoolcraft in the name of friendship to "try with out Delay to help me to Draw for 3000 Dollars immediately."[39] But Austin must have realized how futile his request was. No business conducted over the distance between New York and Missouri could be concluded even quickly, much less immediately.

This was the last letter to Schoolcraft in which Moses wrote of anything but desperation and sale. He must have suspected that it would be. "A few days has made a change in things," he added before closing. "The Bank of St. Louis I am Doubtfull will be under the Necessity of Winding Up there business under such circumstances I shall suffer most distructively I have

*14000 Do*llars in Bank stock and If the Bank are oblg'd to wind up – I am Doubtfull I shall loose 5000 *Dollars* under such circumstances I must sell at least for 10 or 12 thousand Dollars at some price."[40]

Moses was right about the bank. Since March, it had redeemed $14,000 in bills and liquidated $12,000 of its debt. But $26,000 was not enough to save it. Word of its closing came on July 12, 1819, in a long public notice signed by its new president, Risdon H. Price.

> The directors of the Bank of St. Louis, finding that the operations of the Bank cannot be continued either with profit to the stockholders or advantage to the community have determined to suspend the business of the bank; a general meeting of the stockholders has therefore been called, to take into consideration the propriety of continuing or closing finally its concerns; and in the meantime, to save the creditors of the bank from losses, or unnecessary delay in the liquidation of their demands, the directors have made specific assignments of the effects of the Bank, appropriating them so as to discharge the debts due by the Bank, as promptly as possible.... If losses are to be sustained the stockholders only will be the sufferers, and they having an opportunity to inspect the course of operations pursued by the Bank minutely, can satisfy themselves as to the necessity of the present course....[41]

Austin was right, too, that the closing would press him yet more severely. On July 18, a week following the announcement of the bank's failure, the officers assigned the assets of the business to trustees Price, Hammond, and Simpson, who, in turn, listed at the top of their collectables: "The proceeds of a Sail instituted against Moses Austin, or the claims on which said Sail is founded."[42] The trustees, representing stockholders expecting to lose no less than 30 percent on their investment, needed especially to collect the larger sums.

Moses calculated once more the amount he stood to lose on his bank stock, and he dropped his asking price again. He notified Schoolcraft to reduce the figure by one-fourth to $9 per acre. Financial disaster loomed as the certain alternative to no sale. It was that simple. "Nothing can equal the change in times since you have left us," Austin observed. "I am clearly of opinion that 3/4 of the men in business will be ruined and unless I can dispose of some of my property I must be also ruined. I cannot obtain money by sales in this country and I had better make a sacrifise by the sale of so much of my estate as will raise the money I want and take better care of the Balance."[43]

Every day that passed, the full extent of Austin's desperate situation became more plain. As bad as the failure of the Bank of St. Louis was, "I am Clearly of Opinion," he wrote on July 26, six days after learning of the bank's collapse, "that property could not be turned into Cash at any price at this moment. the suspension of payments at the NashVille Bank and the discredit of all the Ohio paper also North Carolina has put a stop to all business *and* nothing is now spoken of but ruin and Distress." Austin was vulnerable at the worst possible time. "With such a View of things you may Judge my feelings when I tell you that I *must raise* six thousand Dollars by Octbr. next if it takes all the property I have." He dropped his asking price by another quarter to $6 per acre. "You will think me *mad*," he continued almost apologetically. "So I am for to be in the hands of Enemies that will ruin me If they can and no way to Exchange my property into Mony to discharge *myself* except through my Enemies is sufficient to make any man *mad* and almost lay hands on himself." Moses felt so desperate that he cut the price another 50 cents an acre before closing his letter.[44]

The weekly mail run from Herculaneum had not taken the pouch containing Moses' two letters of July 26 when he wrote again, on July 28, lowering his price to $4, only one-third what it had been a month and a half earlier. "You will therefore take into consideration my Situation and make sale for at some rate in the name of every thing that is good, greate and friendly," he pleaded with Schoolcraft. "Make sale of my property think of my family and think of those that have treated you kindly in a strange country and for god Sake do the best you can.... god grant I may here from you soon."[45]

After nearly two months of writing letters every few days but receiving no reply—two months without knowing whether Schoolcraft had prospects, or was making any effort at all in his behalf, without knowing even whether his letters reached their destination—Moses was becoming frantic. This time, unlike all the other occasions when he had faced an imminent due date on a debt, he could not borrow to make the payment. Though he likely would have been willing to continue the pattern of creating a new long-term obligation to satisfy the immediate demand, there was simply no source from which to raise the money. His debt was too great, money too tight. "Nothing can equal the General Distress for money—" he told his son Brown.[46] Neither profits from his store nor occasional land sales could meet his need. Nothing he himself could do could stop the impending catastrophe.

Austin's salvation lay in Schoolcraft's hands alone. "If I had recd condemnation and to be executed on the 20 day of October," he wrote in anguish to the New Yorker, "I could not under go greater torments."[47] Worry consumed him. Sleep eluded him. He could only sit at his writing desk drafting letter upon letter dropping his price in hopes that thereby he could snare whatever prospective buyer Schoolcraft might find. He apologized for sending so many letters, but not for wanting to hear something.

"When I take my pen to write you I am absolutely Doubtfull you will be disgusted at the receipt of so many letters and not look at them, but my feelings are such that I cannot lett a mail pass with out saying some thing on paper...pray write me some thing that will give me some hopes."[48] The waiting to hear was the worst of it. But he would wait for a long time still. On July 30, when Moses wrote this, his eleventh letter of the past seven weeks, Schoolcraft had yet to receive even the second one.[49]

When not writing, Moses thought about the men eager to get their hands on his property, and he swelled with rage. "Could you see the exultation of some of my Enemies and the calculations on the sacrifise of my property," he told Schoolcraft, "you would then Excuse me for the extreme Distress of mind. For the love of God and your Distress friend *sell* at some price to help me with seven thousand Dollars—"[50] The thought of his creditors waiting like scavengers for his financial downfall stirred him to new action, and he obtained two separate ten-day delays on the call for his payment, pushing the due date into November. In addition, he sold a tract to Bryan and his old friend since Virginia, Martin Ruggles, to protect it from confiscation should he lose everything else.

If Schoolcraft could find no Americans interested in his mine property, try selling to Englishmen, Moses advised. Austin had heard they were pouring into New York looking for western lands in which to invest. He would turn over the entire property on July 30 for $40,000; on August 13 for $35,000; on August 21 for $30,000.[51]

Only the condition of his precious Maria turned Moses' mind from worry over his financial situation. That August, a succession of personal blows devastated her. The trials began when her close friend, a Mrs. Evans, died. Preceded in death three weeks by her husband, she left their son in the Austins' care. "What will be don with him I cannot tell [.] your Mother cannot take care of him," Moses explained to his son, Brown. "Her Health is such that its as much as she can do to take care of hirself." On top of that, another of Maria's friends, who evidently had been lodging for quite some while in the Austin household in Herculaneum, "removed her trunk last week to *Wilkens* and your Dear Mother is left with out any female friend." The worst of it to Moses' mind, though, was that "this change has been brought about in consequence of the most unfounded abuse [concerning his debt?] and those that have been instrumental in bringing the business about are now to receive the benefit of there Damanable conduct."[52]

On September 16, the mail finally brought some relief when Moses at last received letters from Schoolcraft in answer to the sixteen he by then had dispatched. They set him at ease only by confirming that Schoolcraft was trying to sell the mine estate. Moses acknowledged them and almost anticlimactically asked for help once again. But he must have realized that no begging, pleading, advising, or suggesting from him could make a difference any more. There was no longer time enough for a letter to reach Schoolcraft, be acted on, and the news returned to Austin before the bank foreclosed. Austin's letter of September 17 was the last he addressed to his agent.[53] That only confirmed the resignation all could see when he gave his proxy and apparently did not attend the bank stockholders' meeting held to decide whether to close the institution for good.

Who would not have become despondent in the face of unrelenting pressure to settle old debts large and small? Many, if not most, creditors sued in the courts. Some had been patient a long while. The Reverend Whittlesey from Connecticut joined the litigants in 1819 in his bid to recover what he had invested in Brown. No doubt to Austin's dismay, but not surprise, the courts regularly awarded judgments in favor of the plaintiffs. When, that fall, he could not meet three awards totaling $2,100, the creditors foreclosed. On October 6, 1819, the sheriff of Jefferson County seized various of Austin's properties, including his large two-story home and outbuildings in Herculaneum, as well as seventy-five lots, one containing a good cabin. Moses survived this attack when his son-in-law bought the property at the sheriff's sale.[54]

Bryan had saved his father-in-law, but Moses knew he could not call on Emily's husband indiscriminately. James Bryan had troubles of his own. A year earlier his business had nearly collapsed while he was in Arkansas on such an extended trip that Moses had added a room to his home in Herculaneum specifically for Emily and her children. At one point, creditors threatened to attach cargo already loaded on his boats about to sail for New Orleans. Emily saved the shipment by having enough of it unloaded and sold to settle the debts. She realized that her husband might be unhappy with that turn of events, "but nothing else can be done." She knew on the one hand "that it is your wish that every one should be pay'd," and on the other that she could collect none of the debts due him to use in liquidating the calls on him. "Ah!" she scolded, "if you had taken the advice of your wife, and shown less indulgence, you would not been put to all this difficulty." Matters were no better at Hazel Run. "I cannot conceive how you have arrange your business out their," she wrote in disgust, "for if any of them are called on to settle or arrange business; the Answer is they have know power to do it; this is what Gillit told in Herculanium."[55]

Through 1819, Bryan, like Austin, struggled against unfavorable court judgments totaling several thousand dollars. Moreover, he found it difficult to manage closely interests in Missouri and in Arkansas at the same time, especially the salines and land speculation on the Caddo River. He had returned from Arkansas just in time to save his father-in-law's property but, evidently, too late to save his own. Uncle Guy Bryan had given up waiting patiently for repayment of the money he had loaned his nephew in 1812, had sued and won. On October 11, 1819, the sheriff sold about 2,500 acres in several tracts, including the Hazel Run homeplace itself, to satisfy the $3,495 judgment.[56]

Moses could not buy it. He could not even meet pledges he had made. In that unhappy October, the officers of Jefferson County filed suit to force Austin to honor his promise of a sum toward construction of the courthouse, but the sheriff somehow failed to serve the papers. Not until January, 1820, did he approach Moses. When the law officer arrived at Austin's home on the Tenth and demanded entry, the scene resembled the events of Independence Day, 1806, when Colonel John Smith 'T' mustered the militia to demand possession of Austin's cannon. If the sheriff thought that Austin's financial tribulations had quenched his contentious spirit, he soon learned otherwise. From outside, the sheriff told Austin of his two options: "either to acknowledge he had legally Served said writ on me some time between the 15 and last of Nov. and I was also required to agree that I made this acknowledgment fully and with out restraint, [or] on my refusal he swore he would force his way into my house by Brakeing Down my door with an ax which he had then uplifted ready to execute his denounciation." Austin, blood boiling, refused to sign, took position, and vowed to kill the next person to come through the door.

Before the situation got truly out of hand, cooler heads prevailed. Someone persuaded Moses "to accept of the lesser evil to avoid the greater." He signed. But after the sheriff left, Austin wrote a scathing denunciation of the sheriff's actions, which he published and distributed to the citizens of Jefferson County. "When our rights are invaded it is of no Consequence to the Citizen or subject whether it comes by the hand of an Emperor King or Demon in office under a Republic," he declared. "They are alike distructive of all security to person and property."[57]

Austin, too, had debts to collect, and doubtless filed suits of his own. Those obligated to him were, of course, no better able to pay than he. That same January, when one debtor could not repay money Moses had loaned him to purchase a still, the man deeded the property to Austin and promised to work off the balance by laying brick for two years. The difference between Austin and his creditors was that Austin's creditors wanted his property, not an arrangement.[58]

Somehow Austin managed to stall the bank into the year 1820. Perhaps the hope that Schoolcraft would succeed in making a sale held the bank in check. Though Schoolcraft did try to sell Mine a Breton and did remain interested in Austin's fate, there is no record that Austin ever heard from him again after mid September of 1819. Had he admitted just how slow the mail was, Austin could have expected nothing more. Most of his letters apparently reached Schoolcraft after the deadline Austin had given

Schoolcraft for the sheriff's seizure. The New Yorker had little reason to keep trying to effect a sale.

Early in February, 1820, when he apparently realized that Schoolcraft had failed to find any buyers, Austin calculated realistically the full extent of his loss in the bank failure. "My estate is greatly injured and I shall not save over *15000 dollars*," he informed his son, Brown, who was stranded without money at school in Kentucky. "After all is settled I loose *26,000 Dollars* by the bank of St. Louis its that business that has so much injured me."[59]

Moses could never stop fighting for sums that large. But the period of time in which to fashion deals had been reduced from weeks to days. The bank's attorney, Rufus Pettibone, notified Moses early that month that he had a plan. Austin's hopes soared. When Pettibone arrived from St. Louis, he offered a deal whereby Moses would lose Mine a Breton and most of the lots he still held in Potosi and Herculaneum, but would retain his home place in Herculaneum and "a few thousand dollars to live on." Moses wilted. "The sacrifice is beyond anything I could have contemplated," he informed Bryan. The bank gave Austin five days to consider the proposition and decide, as Moses termed it, "my fate hereafter." Austin did not want to make the decision alone and called on Bryan to counsel with him. "I am unwilling to do anything that Will give you dessattisfaction," but "I pray You to come immediately or it may be to late to do anything."[60]

The three did work out an arrangement in which Austin signed over the Mine a Breton property to Rufus and Levi Pettibone and Bryan. It was only a stopgap that merely shifted the burden of paying off the bank to Bryan and the Pettibones equally. Bank officials, led apparently by O'Hara, were not about to let that happen. When Rufus Pettibone reported to the Cashier that Austin had conveyed to him his 103 shares of bank stock to liquidate the debt, O'Hara, "who pretended to examine the books for that purpose," replied that Austin overstated his holdings by 19 shares. Then O'Hara suggested that if Pettibone would not try to enjoin the bank, which was suing Austin for the amount of the stock, the bank would secure Pettibone for the figure he had committed to pay Austin.[61]

Disappointed by O'Hara's counterproposal, but believing Bryan unable to meet his obligations, Pettibone accepted, and the papers were drawn up for execution on Saturday, March 11, 1820. Austin, Pettibone said, approved the agreement. Likely Austin only acquiesced. But it was a moot point, because approve it or not, the result was the same for him. On March 11 the sheriff arrested and imprisoned Moses Austin for his debts. Austin wrote a statement for the newspaper, which, if he remembered his condemnation of his brother, Stephen, for his financial indiscretions, must have been the most painful few lines he ever wrote.

My Creditors are hereby notified, that on Saturday the 25th

inst. between the hours of ten in the forenoon and three of the
clock in the afternoon. . . , I shall make application to James
Rankin and David Bryan, Esqrs. two Justices of the peace, in
and for the county of Jefferson, at my dwelling house in the
town of Herculaneum. . . to be permitted to take the benefit of
the several laws of this territory concerning insolvent debtors,
and to be released from my imprisonment, when and where
you may attend if you think proper.[62]

In pushing relentlessly for repayment of Moses Austin's $25,000 note,
the Bank officers, more than any others, had driven Austin to final financial collapse. Nevertheless, they continued to profess their desire to help
him. "I think you may rest satisfied that the ultimate advantages shall not
be withheld from Mr Austin's family," Cashier O'Hara wrote Bryan. "I will
pledge my influence to secure them in that way."[63] Austin clung to a wisp
of hope. Before his statement appeared in print on March 22, he wrote
Bryan to "make hast and come to this place that you may go immediately
to St Louis or the Mine A Burton estate will be lost and all my house hold
goods sold at the Mines."[64] Moses' old friend, William Ficklin, unable to do
anything but watch, saw the situation more clearly. "All of Mr. Austin's
land in this country will be sold by the sheriff next week, if Mr. Pettibone
don't raise the money to pay the judgments," he told Schoolcraft. "If
he does, Pettibone gets the land." Either way, Austin lost his property.
On March 21, the entire Mine a Breton tract was sold, evidently to
Pettibone.[65]

What remained for Moses Austin in Missouri? He had done everything
he knew to do, mentally and physically, to settle his obligations and save
the property on which his financial integrity rested, and he had failed. "I
found nothing I could do would bring back my property again," he later
wrote Brown. "And to remain in a Country where I had enjoyed *welth* in a
state of *poverty* I could Not submit to."[66] Austin prepared to leave for
Arkansas to confer with Stephen, "and determine what I then shall do."[67]

APPROACHING HIS fifty-ninth birthday, Moses Austin ought to have been, as others, slowing the pace of life and looking toward the end of his working days. He should have earned it by his long and productive career in lead mining and smelting. With his lead enterprise shattered, however, and his principal estate in the hands of creditors, he could not do like others. Austin had to choose between either settling for a life of very modest means, haunted by the memories of his former affluence, or dedicating his energies to recovering the financial comfort he once had enjoyed. For a man to whom the rewards of wealth – public respect, luxuries, and the satisfaction of providing munificently for his family – ranked high in importance, he had, in fact, no choice. He had to find a way to amass a new fortune.

Neither the tried-and-true dry goods business, in which he had been engaged for thirty-eight years, nor any other occupation he could pursue in Missouri held out the promise of profits sufficiently quick and lucrative to attract Austin. The most certain and rapid avenue to wealth that he could see lay in opening a new career in a new country, that is, in becoming a colonizer in Spanish Texas. To be honest, however, Moses had no way of knowing how good his vision was. All he knew for sure was that he had the experience and the energy to carry out the work he proposed. But would the Spanish government grant him permission to introduce a colony of Anglo Americans? The answer to that question lay at the end of a journey of a thousand miles, much of the route only a trail blazed through the wilderness, the rigors of the trip enough to test the endurance of the most seasoned traveler.

If the challenge of the trip or the likelihood of Spanish disapproval worried Moses, he did not show it. On the contrary, on May 12, 1820, Austin burned the bridges behind him. He sold his Herculaneum shot tower to his nephew, Elias Bates, and quit the lead business forever. For a final $2,000, he ended a thirty-one-year career during which he had charted the way for raising the lead industry quantum steps above the crude state in which he had found it. The times afforded no leisure for reflection, however, for Austin had a trip to make.[1]

Moses Austin had been looking forward to the journey for a year, ever since he and Stephen had formulated their plans. In his anticipation, the elder Austin made no particular secret of the scheme. He told Schoolcraft

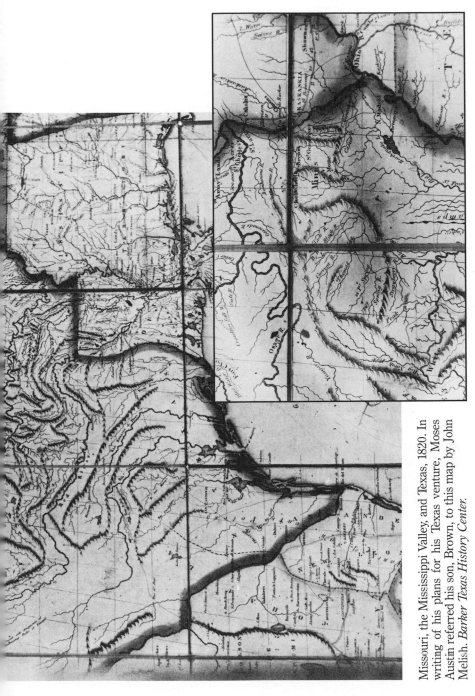

Missouri, the Mississippi Valley, and Texas, 1820. In writing of his plans for his Texas venture, Moses Austin referred his son, Brown, to this map by John Melish. *Barker Texas History Center.*

about it before the scientist left in May, 1819. And he mentioned it in several communications to his agent that summer. These were the only optimisitic passages in Moses' otherwise heartrending letters to Schoolcraft.

Why should Moses guard his plans? Others likely would beat him to Texas. "Stephen F. Austin says tell Mr Schoolcraft that two grand expeditions are now underway for the spanish country," Moses reported on Independence Day of 1819. "300 families are making ready to take possession of that part of Red River with in the *spanish lines which* comes with in 10 miles of his plantation an Other is now making up to take possession of *St Antone* under the command of a General Long."[2]

The Austins—father and son—followed the progress of James Long's expedition with more than casual interest. Rallying southwesterners unwilling to accept those provisions of the Adams-Onis Treaty that relinquished the claim of the United States to Texas, Long left Natchez, Mississippi, in June, proceeded up the Red River, and quickly captured Nacogdoches, the seat of Spanish government in eastern Texas. After issuing a brave declaration of independence, Long left for Galveston Island to treat with corsair Jean Lafitte. For Austin, the news got better. "I have heard from my son Stephen," Moses wrote in mid-August, who "states that the expedition to Texas is going on with Great energy and thinks St *Antone* will be in the hands of the Americans in all October next. the army and the General Long has advanced into the province of *Texas* and rais'd the Republican Standard and Hundreds are Daly Crossing the *Sabino*— I understand that the first object will be to establish a provisional government and give *640 acres* of land to each *Soldier* and Officer in the same proportion that unite themselves with the army. many men of property and reputation have already *join'd* both Spanish and Americans not a Royal *Standard* is now rais'd short of St *Antone.*"

Moses himself was ready to follow the crowd streaming into Texas. "For God sake sell my estate," he begged Schoolcraft, "and If you think of coming on or wish to visit that country I will go with you."[3] Austin was being polite. He meant to go at as early a moment as he could, whether or not Schoolcraft went. "When I have paid the present demands," he told his friend on September 17, "I shall be *free* with the balance of my estate, and as I intend to hold myself free from any engagement, I shall as soon as my business is Closed in this Country visit St Antonia, which place I have but little doubt is now in the hands of the Americans."[4]

Fortunately Austin did not begin his journey to Texas at the time he wrote that last letter to Schoolcraft. The invaders, far from holding San Antonio, had been driven from Nacogdoches shortly after taking it. News of Long's defeat, which Moses received probably in November, appears to have changed his plans in only one respect. Apparently it prompted him to seek a record, which he could present to officials in Texas, documenting his earlier connection with the Spanish empire. Austin sent to Washington on January 16, 1820, for a copy of the passport the Spanish ambassador had issued him in 1797. After it finally arrived, likely in early May, Moses was ready to leave.[5]

Austin evidently decided on his route to Texas too late to inform his son and son-in-law in Arkansas. Stephen clearly had no idea when, where, or even whether to expect Moses. Uncharacteristically, he seemed not to care. Normally intensely loyal to his father, Stephen had become so depressed that he made virtually no effort to accommodate his father's wish, expressed earlier, to meet with Bryan and him in Arkansas.

"If my Father should come to Little Rock," he wrote Bryan early in June as the elder Austin made his way south, "you may tell him that I wish to go to the Mouth of White River to live if I can take any thing there to begin with and if that cannot be done I shall go down the Mississippi and seek employ."[6] Stephen's enthusiasm for Arkansas and for the Texas venture apparently had dissipated as he discovered that the Long Prairie site was not the healthy, invigorating place he and his father sought as a stop where their colonists could rest and recuperate. His lagging zeal then foundered in concern over the financial agony of his family. "If my Father saves enough to support him and you get through your difficulties so as to support Emily in the stile she aught to live," he had told Bryan earlier, "I shall be satisfied. as for myself I believe I am nearly indifferent what becomes of me, or whether I live or die, unless I am to be of use to my Family by living, and then I should be as anxious to live as any one."[7]

Stephen's gloomy despair probably would have disappointed, and might have disgusted, his father. Moses never had given in to adversity and certainly had not hung his head. No beaten man would be making the journey he had undertaken. Possibly, Stephen's message never reached his father, though, since the young man's prospects and outlook changed abruptly about the time that Moses may have arrived in Little Rock. On July 10, Governor James Miller swore in young Austin, intimate with the law of the Territory from his work in the Missouri Legislature, as Judge of the First Judicial Circuit of Arkansas. The position assured Stephen what he then apparently wanted most—a steady income large enough for him both to live on and to assist his family.[8]

Euphoria must have been short-lived, as Moses could not have been in Little Rock long before he contracted the ague and fever that swept the settlement that summer. Though fatal to no one, the illness nevertheless proved so debilitating that one sufferer recalled it clearly more than half a century later. Daniel Witter, who also remembered Moses' visit, reminisced that when he, Witter, first observed victims of the affliction, he "could hardly understand how any one could shake with cold in such excessively hot weather, and was rather disposed to think it a sort of mental delusion. But he soon had his skepticism shook out of him."[9]

Moses recovered, but remained in Little Rock for several months. Perhaps a lengthy convalesence confined him. More likely, however, the high stakes contest for control of the Little Rock site distracted his thoughts of Texas. Two factions—one led by his son, the other by William Russell of St. Louis—vied for possession. Both believed the location, which the Austins called "Little Rock" and Russell named "Arkopolis," soon would be selected the site of the permanent capital of the Territory. All knew that, as rapidly as Arkansas was gaining population, selection would mean tidy profits for the group that controlled the land.

The Austin faction rested its claim on entries made under New Madrid certificates; Russell asserted right by preemption. Tradition holds that the Austin group occupied the Little Rock site first and that Moses Austin had a small house built in the fall of 1819. "This rude structure, partly constructed of cypress slabs set up on end," wrote Little Rock historian Dallas Herndon, "is said to have been the first house" of the settlement.[10] No surviving records substantiate the tradition. In fact, they suggest the contrary. In the latter half of 1819, when the cabin was built, Austin was absorbed in his struggle to save his financial integrity. Moreover, when Amos Wheeler, Jr., an associate of Stephen's partner O'Hara, arrived at Little Rock in mid-November, 1819, to take possession for the Austin group and to lay off the town, which he tried unsuccessfully to name "Wheelersville" for himself, he acknowledged the existence of another interest. "A compromise was attempted, but Twenty five thousand dollars was asked of me," he fumed indignantly to his father, "to which I objected." After satisfying himself that his associates held good title to three-fourths of the area, Wheeler began at once solidifying his hold on the property by erecting several buildings.[11]

Stephen, who had filed the claim for the site, anticipated trouble. "As there is some little probability that this business may bring about a personal dispute between Russell and myself," he informed O'Hara at the end of 1819, "I wish to have a clear understanding with you relative to one point, on which Russell I expect will place great stress. He will try to shew that I knew there was a preemption right at the place when we made the location." All that Stephen had seen were the remains of an entry. "As well as I recollect the facts were these— when I made out the memorandum for this location I informed you that there was a small improvement which, I had been informed, was abandoned and which was not settled in time for a preemption right, and *that I did not know there was a preemption right here when the locations was made—*" That existing building led the wise Stephen to seek legal counsel on the validity of a preemption claim south of the

Arkansas River. Whatever opinion he received did not persuade him to stop Wheeler's construction.[12]

Russell tolerated the Austin claim until the end of April. Then, using the most public forum available to him, the *Arkansas Gazette*, he sent an open letter to Austin, Bryan, O'Hara "and all others concerned or interested in any sort or pretence of claim to any part. . . of the lands joining the southwardly margin of the Arkansas river, at and near a place called Little Rocks." After asserting his "prior and better right and claim" to the land, he thundered: "I will not pay for any improvements made or caused to be made by you or any other persons upon any part of the said lands." Moreover, "I will claim damages for the trespasses committed by you and others thereon."[13]

Stephen growled in return, but only in a private letter to Bryan. "Were it not for this man Russell," he wrote in unbounded, bitter contempt, "our unfortunate family might yet be enabled to secure a small, but decent competence for if his opposition was removed I believe there would be no difficulty in getting the seat of government removed to the L. Rock, which might be the means of saving a worthy and respectable family from total ruin and want whereas he gains nothing by his opposition, *but the pleasure* of gratifying his enmity and passions which I *once* thought were rarely to be met with in the human brest, but I have *now* learnt to be surprised at nothing I see in man, unless it is when I find him honest—"[14]

If Russell thought that his bluster would cause his rivals to abandon the contest, he was sorely disappointed. Wheeler appears to have kept on building.[15] Undaunted himself, Russell filed suit to vindicate his claim. In August, to his horror, the court ruled against him. "Mortified and Chagrined at his dissapointment," reported Elias Austin Elliott, Moses' nephew who ran the store that the Austin faction kept in Little Rock, Russell "yet shows all the venom of a rattle snake in June."[16]

The battle shifted that fall to the chamber of the Territorial legislature sitting in regular session. Representative William Stevenson of Hempstead County, the minister who had led the colony of Washington County farmers into southwestern Arkansas four years earlier, joined by the representative of Pulaski County (in which Little Rock lay), moved on October 11 for removal of the temporary seat of government to Little Rock effective June 1, 1821, and for acceptance of the offer of the Austin group to donate lots for the use of the Territory. Both measures carried and were signed. The lawmakers would go no farther, however, and rejected the subsequent Stevenson bill calling on Wheeler and his associates to construct, on land not in dispute, a building for the legislature.[17]

With the government coming to Little Rock, Russell on November 11, 1820, took out space in the newspaper again. "WAR!" he called the contest between the competing claims and rejected the validity of locating New

Madrid certificates at Little Rock. His strong words seemed to take effect. Within a week or two, perhaps only a day or two, of the attack, Stephen abandoned Arkansas. Those who knew young Austin knew that Russell could take no credit, however. The legislature on October 25, in restructuring the court system of the Territory, had abolished the bench on which Stephen sat. Once again the young man had no steady income, and apparently no hope of having any, as the Panic of 1819 had crippled the economy. His cousin Elias Elliott in Little Rock could give him no encouragement. He wrote Bryan on October 29, 1820, that "Money is not to be got here and I shall have to commence Suits generally— of late I have made but little sales, as I find it will not do to trust the best men here—as they cannot raise Cash—"[18]

Their prospects in Arkansas suddenly withered, Stephen and Moses huddled in Little Rock to decide their future course. Moses had his mind fixed on resuming his journey to Texas. He had been talking about it through the summer, probably seeking a traveling companion. His storekeeper nephew Elias joked about joining him, but recoiled in horror when the talk turned serious. "I cannot contrive where you got the information of my going to the Spanish Country," Elias wrote Bryan. "I have not had an Idea of it and never spoke of it except to Mr Austin in a Jesting way."[19] Stephen likely did not want to go either. The Austin family, in his view, needed cash. A job in New Orleans, a location that had been in his thoughts since June, attracted him more than the uncertain trip to Texas. The city, he recalled nine years later, probably influenced by subsequent history, offered another advantage, too. There he could "make some preparatory arrangements. . . facilitating the transportation of families, farming supplies, &c. and getting ready to proceed to Havana in the event of its being necessary to have recourse to the government in Spain" for permission to settle a colony in Texas.[20] After they agreed to go their separate ways, it remained only to provide Moses with the traveling companion he should have. Stephen gave him his slave, Richmond, and a gray horse.[21]

Moses made his way south to Natchitoches, Louisiana, then west to Hugh McGuffin's cabin, half-way between Natchitoches and the Sabine River. At McGuffin's, Austin met Jacob Kirkham and Jacob Forsythe, both also on their way to Texas, Kirkham chasing run-away slaves, so he said, Forsythe to ask permission to settle in the province. Banding together for the trip, the three left McGuffin's on November 27 on the 400-mile trek to San Antonio de Bexar, the capital of Texas. For almost four weeks they rode, the bulk of the journey through a wilderness so empty that the only geographical features Austin noted were the eight major rivers they crossed.

The travelers reached their destination two days before Christmas and proceeded directly to the office of the governor to report their business.

When Moses began speaking of bringing a colony of Americans to Texas, Governor Antonio Martínez flatly refused to listen and ordered him away. In leaving the civil administration building, Moses chanced to run into the Baron de Bastrop, whom he had met only once in his life, years earlier when the two, while traveling, happened to stop at the same tavern. As they renewed their acquaintance, Austin, of course, explained the purpose of his trip. Moses' goal so caught Bastrop's interest that the popular, respected Baron decided to speak to the governor on Austin's behalf. As a result, Austin received permission to remain in San Antonio long enough to develop his proposal.[22]

Could this fantastic story of the Austin-Bastrop meeting, an encounter that changed the course of history, possibly be true? Bastrop's biographer believes not. He could determine neither the time nor the place where the two had originally met. He searched for a hint of a meeting in Kentucky or Tennessee during the winter of 1796-1797, when Moses crossed the country to inspect the lead mines of Upper Louisiana and Bastrop traveled the area seeking recruits for his Arkansas colony. The closest scrutiny of Moses' thorough journal of his trip reveals no encounter with anyone even remotely resembling Bastrop. Biographer Charles Bacarisse doubts, too, that their meeting in San Antonio could have been pure coincidence. The two men just had to have been in correspondence, and about what else than trade possibilities within the Spanish territories? On the basis of three letters – the first written seven years before Moses left for Texas, the second containing no more than the Baird surname, and the third indicating that the Austins knew James Baird, Sr., whom the Spanish clapped in prison for trying to open trade with Santa Fe – on this evidence he concludes that Austin came to Texas to develop a trade route from the Gulf coast to Santa Fe.[23]

Little Rock historian Dallas T. Herndon, working strictly on logic, questions the story on the ground that the drama of an event often grows as a tale is told. Chances are especially good, he contends, that this story was improved because, even if Stephen, the only person to make the story public, reported it faithfully, he had gotten it secondhand. As Stephen never saw his father again after they parted at Little Rock, he had to have heard the story from his mother, his cousin Elias Bates, or someone else who talked with Moses. Herndon could have added that Moses himself was not above improving a good tale.[24]

Neither author suggests why Moses, or his kinsfolk, would fabricate or enlarge the story. It portrays Austin only as the beneficiary of good fortune, not as the hero, as he painted himself in the tale he embellished for Schoolcraft of his entry into St. Louis. Bacarisse's documentation is hardly sufficient to support his imaginative hypothesis, much less to dispute the contemporary word of Moses' own son. Moreover, since Moses habitually consulted with his son and son-in-law in forming business plans and decisions, the elder Austin would have acted most uncharacteristically in concealing from them the exciting and unusual idea of, not to mention a long correspondence regarding, opening a trade to the Spanish territories of Texas and New Mexico. Stephen, if he knew the Bastrop story to be false, would have acted even more uncharacteristically by telling it anyway.

Discarding the theories of skeptics does not, however, corroborate the story. Since Bastrop's version of the incident was never recorded, the only way to substantiate Moses' words is to find, if it occurred, the occasion when the two men took lodging in the same establishment. In his search for the event, biographer Bacarisse overlooked the one other trip that Moses made from the lead mines before 1805, the year that Bastrop left the United States for good. Records show that in May, 1801, business drew both Austin and Bastrop to New Orleans, a city of only 10,000 clustered in the area known today as the "French Quarter." Moreover, the authentication of documents took each man to the office of notary Pedro Pedesclaux within three weeks to the day of the other. On top of that, Austin had arrived in the city by May 15, barely a week after Bastrop visited Pedesclaux. Bastrop, who turned up next, and not immediately, in Arkansas, need not have left New Orleans shortly after notarizing his documents in order to accomplish his journey north in good time.[25] The likelihood that the two met in travelers' lodging, just as Stephen reported, while on business in New Orleans in May, 1801, is more plausible than any argument so far advanced refuting the story of their chance meeting in San Antonio.

If the encounter between Austin and Bastrop in the United States took nineteen and a half years to pay dividends, their meeting in San Antonio proved immediately fortuitous for Austin. From his initial interview with the governor, Moses could have believed only that the Spanish would never grant him, or any American, permission to establish a colony in Texas. Moses should have expected nothing more. The Spanish consistently had striven to seal their eastern border against their neighbors, first the French, then the Americans. Americans were especially unwelcome, because so many, James Long the most recent, came intent on taking the province by force. Policymakers in Spain and Mexico in recent years had actively sought to block the American advance by establishing settlements to populate the country with those loyal to the king. The *Missouri Gazette* in the fall of 1819 reported a plan to sell Texas to Swiss investors, and the editor waxed hot over this Spanish attempt to thwart American manifest destiny.[26] Spanish exclusion of Americans was no recent policy of Governor Martínez's.

As Bastrop listened to Austin and considered whether to speak to his friend the governor on Austin's behalf, he doubtless pondered Martínez's likely reaction to Austin's proposal to bring 300 families to settle in Texas. The idea, Bastrop probably suspected, should appeal to Martínez personally. It was common knowledge that the governor had worked since he arrived in Texas in 1817 to develop the agriculture and economy of his jurisdiction. If Bastrop's suspicions were true, then Martínez's hostility toward Austin probably reflected only the long-standing official Spanish policy. The Baron may not have known that Martínez had direct orders to admit no Americans into Texas, and that the strained relations between the governor and his superior, Commandant of the Eastern Interior Provinces, Joaquin de Arredondo, gave Martínez strong reason to enforce the directive to the letter. Austin had an advantage, however, since the 1797 passport that he carried demonstrated his acceptance by Spanish officialdom. Whatever Bastrop's reasoning, his intuition evidently told him that Austin's proposal coincided with Martínez's interests.

Bastrop's hunch was well-founded. When he took Austin back to talk with Governor Martínez on the 23rd, Martínez granted Austin permission to stay in San Antonio. And when the two returned to the governor's office the day after Christmas, Martínez accepted Austin's proposal enthusiastically and, describing Austin as "a man of some honesty and formality," recommended it to Arredondo. Austin's plan for bringing 300 industrious, acceptable Americans to Texas to improve the land, serve as a buffer against the uncontrolled American invasion, and establish firmly the Spanish hold on the territory, continued Martínez, "is, in my opinion, the only one which is bound to provide for the increase and prosperity in his settlement and even others in this Province."[27]

Receiving the governor's endorsement, Moses had accomplished his work in San Antonio. His proposal had been accepted at the first level and was on its way to higher authority. Along with that he had, as was his way, forged a strong friendship with the governor. "The Governor was pleased to say," he told Bastrop, "that if I returned I might depend on his friendship." Probably assuming that Bastrop would mention his sentiment to the governor, Moses added that "On my part I assure you that I shall make use of every Exertion in my power to promote the interest of the Government that gives me protection."[28]

In the company of Jacob Kirkham and Richmond again, Austin rode out of Bexar on December 29, 1820, less than a week after he had arrived. About fifty miles into the journey, where the road crossed the San Marcos River, Kirkham told Austin that five Spaniards who were to have left San Antonio with them would, instead, meet them at the Colorado River, thirty miles ahead. The men would bring a herd of mules that Kirkham would buy and drive to the United States. If the men had not arrived at the rendezvous point, Kirkham said, he had promised to wait for them.

Moses sensed trouble. He "objected to have anything to do with them or detain for them unless they brought with them a pasport." Traffic in horses and mules, he told Kirkham bluntly, violated direct orders of the governor. Kirkham responded that he had given no encouragement to the men other than agreeing to purchase whatever stock they brought. Unpacified, Austin must have continued to press his objection until Kirkham admitted that he was taking delivery of stolen government property. Moreover, Kirkham added, Austin might as well cooperate, because word was circulating in San Antonio that he, Austin, was a party to the illicit scheme. Before Austin and Kirkham left San Antonio, Kirkham and his conspirators "had stated to some of there friends that he Kirkham was to detain at the *River Colorado* with the Other American and Conduct them [the stolen animals] with in the *United States*."[29]

This information stunned Moses. The implication that he was trading in stolen animals jeopardized his colonization project. He had no intention of cooperating with Kirkham and wanted to contact the governor as soon as he could. Kirkham obviously could not let Austin return to the capital to spread the alarm and gave him no choice but to continue traveling with him and his stock. The two kept what must have been an uneasy peace until they reached the Trinity River. After dark one night, Kirkham took all the horses, pack mules, and provisions, and disappeared into the wilderness, leaving Moses and Richmond stranded. The two decided not to move in the dark and bedded down to await dawn. Sometime before daylight the stillness of the night erupted when a panther pounced upon Moses. Since Austin lay under, not inside, the buffalo skin that covered him, the animal failed to get a good hold. Moses scrambled from under the robe making the loudest, fiercest, most terrible noise he could, and the startled cat fled into the woods.[30]

Though Moses survived this experience without injury, he and Richmond faced a desperate situation. They were afoot in wet, raw winter weather, with no clothing except what they had on. Worse, they had no food and no means of obtaining any. Stories conflict. One says that Kirkham took their firearms, another that the guns were useless because Austin's gunpowder was too damp to ignite. Either way, the men could take none of the abundant game around them in the woods. For eight days they pushed themselves on, rafting swollen rivers and living on roots and berries. Both took colds and fever that developed into pneumonia – "flux," as contemporaries called it.[31]

Maria Austin, who had disapproved of Moses' journey, and who apparently had not heard from him in months, became so apprehensive for her husband in December that she sent his nephew, Elias Bates, after him to find out whether Moses had gone to Texas. One of the Austin family told Mirabeau Lamar years later that Bates made his way to McGuffin's cabin, where he stopped for a night. Before sunup the next day, "A stranger came...and called for assistance, a mere skeleton on the verge of death by starvation." Bates did not recognize the shrunken figure that entered the house until the man spoke. "The voice...[was that] of his uncle of whom he was in search. It was Moses Austin—"[32]

Without doubt the shadow of a man that came through McGuffin's door was Austin, but the man who saw him and told the story was not Elias Bates. By the time Moses reached McGuffin's cabin in mid-January, 1821, Bates already had left for New Orleans. On January 20, Stephen wrote his mother from the city that "Elias Bates arrived here this day in a Steam Boat from Alexandria; he went as far as the Sabine and heard that Father had arrived at St Antonio and was to be back at Natchitoches by the 15th of February; he was well."[33]

How wrong Stephen's information was. After Moses reached McGuffin's, he collapsed and was put to bed. Though weak from his ordeal, Austin nevertheless tended to his business. He wrote Governor Martínez, Bastrop, and Felix Trudeau, the Spanish agent in Natchitoches, relating the Kirkham story so as to clear himself of suspicion of complicity and to warn his friends about the man.[34]

If Moses doubted that Governor Martínez would accept his explanation, or that the Spanish authorities would grant his petition, he kept it to himself. Outwardly, he looked forward to his future in Texas. Austin reported to Bastrop the potentially important news he learned on the Sabine that the United States government had set aside land for the Choctaw Indians, and Americans who had pushed into far southwestern Arkansas would have to vacate the dedicated domain by May. The timing could not be better for Austin. "They might be very available," he calculated, "if they could [be] allowed to settle in the Province of Texas."

Anyone knew, who had been on the frontier as long as Austin, that when Americans moved, many went where they pleased without first asking permission. Probably to demonstrate his attention to the government from which he hoped to gain favor, Austin cautioned, if Bastrop wanted to tell Martínez, that "The Government ought to be on its guard against them; they may prove to be dangerous." Bastrop did, indeed, forward the warning.[35]

Where opportunities continued to open regarding Texas, the only news from Missouri was bad. Elias Bates had left word for his uncle "that the total failure of the Bank of St Louis has involved me in a loss of (30 000) thirty thousand Dollars investments I had made in said Bank," Austin told Bastrop. That sobering report dictated Austin's course. If Moses had intended to remain on the frontier seeking recruits, he would have to return instead to Missouri to "settle and save the balance of my property."[36]

While word of the financial debacle focused Austin's thoughts again on his troubles in Missouri, it simultaneously stirred his anticipation of his Texas adventure. He resolved–"life and Health admitting"–to return shortly to make his home and begin his new life. But to establish himself and his colony in the way that he wanted, he needed Bastrop's aid. No port, or even town, existed on the Texas coast. And under Spanish law, towns did not spring up as they did in the United States wherever an entrepreneur chose. On the contrary, they were institutions regulated by the government in almost every particular, including location. Austin wanted to plant a town at the mouth of the Colorado River where he could ship his belongings, begin his farming, and receive colonists coming by sea. He asked Bastrop to secure permission for him to lay out a *pueblo*, or at least to establish the predicate for Moses to request the authorization when he returned and could talk to the governor personally.

He would tell the governor–at least he wrote Bastrop so that Bastrop could tell him–that the proposed settlement, for which Austin later suggested the name "Austina," would prosper beyond anything the Spanish had ever seen in Texas. "People of the first class," he predicted, "would immediately Resort to this Establishment with property that would secure their fidelity to the King and Constitution of Spain." Their industry in one short year would create a town so dynamic that the effects would reach to the capital and, he thought, "make a Change in the State and condition of Saint Antonio beyond any thing you can now believe."[37]

Austin's letter still radiates his excitement for and anticipation of his proposed Texas venture. It takes no keen observer to see the same eagerness also in the schedule he set for himself. He told Bastrop that he planned to return to Missouri, settle his affairs, gather supplies and colonists, and make his way back to Texas to establish his home, all in only four months, by May. That itinerary would have been ambitious for a healthy man. But Moses was not well. Since reaching McGuffin's, he had been unable to get up from his bed, much less travel. When Bates arrived from New Orleans seeking his uncle, he found him in such a decrepit state that Elias evidently did not recognize his relative until the old man spoke. For three weeks, perhaps longer, Moses lay immobilized, some said near death.

As soon as Austin could muster the strength to travel, about mid-February, he, with Bates, left for Missouri. Richmond had not recovered sufficiently to make the trip, and Moses found a place where the slave would receive medical attention but could satisfy the bill with his labor. Though Austin apparently would not admit it, he was in no better condition to travel than Richmond. Before he and his nephew had gone twenty miles–before they reached Natchitoches–Austin felt strong pains in his chest. Likely resulting from coughing up the gray mucus of pneumonia, the agony became so severe that he had to interrupt the trip and resort to bed rest again. When the two men resumed their journey, they traveled by the easiest means they could, by boat down the Red and up the Mississippi rivers.[38] Austin finally reached Herculaneum on March 23, 1821, apparently looking thin, gaunt, and drawn. He was, to his wife's anxious eyes, "but a shadow of his former self." All indications are that Austin collapsed into bed once more.

Though spent physically and in desperate need of rest and recuperation, Moses could not relax. Emotionally he soared at the peak of excitement. His petition had been approved. "For these sufferings," he wrote exuberantly to his son James Brown on March 28, five days after arriving home, "I have been fully paid by obtaining a grant for myself and family of land and also for 300 families— I shall settle on the Colorado within (2) miles of the sea and three days sale from the Mississippia—Where I shall lay of[f] a town under the protection of the Spanish Government. . . .[The location is] a spot of country desirable to behold—overflowing with Wealth and *Health* in this situation I shall soon reinstate myself in property. I have already offers to fill up the families which will bring me about 18,000 dollars." Moses finally had in hand the key to a new life in which he could recover his wealth. "God bless you my son and," he added, his eyes fixed on a future beyond his present infirmity, "look up for happy Days."[39]

Brown's may have been the first letter Moses wrote after hearing the news. Austin could have learned of his good fortune only hours, perhaps a day or two, earlier when Erasmo Seguin caught up with him. Governor Martínez's personal emissary, Seguin had been following Austin's path since February 26 to tell him not only that his request to introduce a colony of Anglo Americans into Texas had been approved, the first request ever granted for American immigration, but also that Bastrop had succeeded in obtaining permission for Austin to open a port, the first authorized on the Texas coast.[40] Moses Austin, miraculously it must have seemed, had been awarded the two concessions he had sought.

Seguin could have told Austin, too, that the Spanish government had acted on his petition in record time. Governor Martínez had written his endorsement on December 26, 1820, and sent the petition to Governor General Arredondo in Monterrey. Arredondo could not have had it more than a day or two before he added his endorsement on January 16 and communicated it to the Provincial Deputation. The legislative body must have given its consent the following morning, because before the sun set on January 17, Arredondo, basking in "the most flattering hopes. . .that the said province will receive an important augmentation, in agriculture, industry, and arts, by the new emigrants," had dispatched word of the favorable action to Governor Martínez. The Texas executive received Arredondo's message early in February, barely six weeks after he had dispatched the petition from San Antonio.[41]

The haste reflected a radical change in Spanish policy, of which Austin had been totally unaware when he rode into San Antonio on December 23, and of which he became the first recipient. Only months before, in March, 1820, liberal forces in Spain had seized control of the government, ended the king's absolutist rule, and reinstated the liberal Constitution of 1812. As part of its early reforms, the national legislature relaxed land laws in the New World specifically to develop the American territories. In September, the lawmakers took the unprecedented step of opening Spanish possessions to foreigners simply upon condition that they respect the constitution, laws, and customs of the country, profess the Roman Catholic faith, present evidence of industry and good character, and have a trade or profession.[42] Word of this sweeping reversal of the centuries-old exclusionist policy, on its way down through the governmental hierarchy, met Austin's petition in Monterrey on its way up.

However much of the background on the approval of Austin's petition Seguin told him, the envoy's news "surpast his [Austin's] most sanguine expectations," Maria wrote her cousin, Edward Sharp, five months later.[43] It was news that excited, inspired, and compelled action.

Two tasks stood between Austin and his departure for Texas: settling his affairs with the Bank of St. Louis and making preparations to plant a colony in a wilderness. Reckoning with the bank, to liquidate his obligations in Missouri, came first. During his absence, the bank, "not satisfied to close the mortgage alone[, but also] to secure the debt[,] proceded on Austin's notes[,] obtained a Judgement[,] issued execution and sold the *whole* of the Mine a Burton Tract," wrote James Scott, the attorney most intimately familiar with the case.[44] The sale made news as far away as Nashville and Louisville, at least the editor of the *Missouri Gazette*, in the October 3 edition, asked papers in those cities to pick up the story for their readers. "Besides its value for agricultural purposes which is equal to that of any Land in the state," the bank advertised, the 4,000-acre Mine a Breton tract "contains an inestimable quantity of Lead Ore, . . . a number of fine streams of water, suitable for mill seats," and "the flourishing village of Potosi, a considerable part of which will be sold with the tract." Bank President Risdon H. Price, whose association with Austin in various business capacities dated back at least seven years to the founding of the bank, acquired the property at the sale on December 11 with the pitifully low bid of $7,000. Price moved into Durham Hall in the spring of 1821, probably before Moses returned to Missouri.[45]

News of the sale angered Austin. "His confidence had been abused and he deceived," he believed, "by those in whose hands he had placed his property."[46] Mine a Breton would have fetched at least $12,000, nearly double what Price paid, "had it not been Stated Publickly that it Was purchased for my binefit." Moses decided that the only way to settle the matter was for him to go to St. Louis and talk face-to-face with officials of the bank "to bring my bisness to a close with said Bank—and to ask such Credits as I consider myself Justly intitled to."[47]

Maria begged him to be in no hurry about the dealings, instead to rest and give his body time to recuperate. But Moses refused. "Such was his anxiety to arrange all his business in this quarter," she cried later, "I could not prevail on him to attend to his health and take those medicines necessary to restore it." As soon as he could mount a horse, he rode away.[48]

The meeting in St. Louis did not go well. In assessing the collateral on his loan, Austin and the bank officers could reconcile no closer than $4,000 their respective valuations of his bank stock, no closer than $5,000 their appraisals of Mine a Breton. All told, bank officials, "calculating that I would never return," credited him for only $17,000, less than two-thirds of his appraisal. "This I will not take," he stormed to Bryan. Moreover, "I find there conduct has been so unauthorised that I can sett a side the sale of the mine a Burton estate and obtain a Credit for the full amount of my stock unless they make a compromise with me."

Where the prospect of recovering his Mine a Breton tract would, in other times, probably have pleased Austin, in April, 1821, it did not. He needed the cash. "I am in a most unpleasant situation," Moses confided to his son-in-law, "with out a Dollar to get a shirt washed." Maria lacked "common necessaries she is out of flour and meat." As painful as this was, the prospect of being saddled with administration of the property bothered him more. It would interfere with his real goal of leaving for Texas.[49]

The week that Moses expected to be in St. Louis turned into three. Neither side budged. When he learned that a stockholders' meeting would be held soon, he pressed Bryan to attend. "See if something cannot be don to take the Books and papers from the present holders," he urged on April 21, "and stop more money going into the hands of those that *now* hold command."[50]

The dispute did not go unnoticed outside the bank. Later that Saturday, after Moses had finished his letter to Bryan, "one generous and disinterested man, even a lawyer, steped forward and vollanteered his services to your persecuted Father," Maria, bitter over the bank's treatment of her husband, wrote Stephen later. This man, whom she never identified, branded the sale of Mine a Breton illegal and offered, for no compensation unless he succeeded, to recover the property for Austin. Moses accepted. The now-anonymous lawyer argued the case so forcefully that before the Board adjourned that Saturday, he "brought them to a compromise and your Father after the greatest perplexity and delay, at length obtained a full receipt from the Directors."[51]

Triumphant and relieved, Moses explained to Bryan the next day that his account had been adjusted such that he owed the Bank $280, not $9,000. "After much difficulty and an ungodly sacrefice I shall clear myself and family from Debt," he wrote with great distress at the cost but obvious satisfaction at the result. "All my other business is nearly closed and after collecting every Cent against me in this town it amounts only to about (550) Dollars which sweeps my Debt the Judgment of [Anthony] Butlers excepted." More pleasing, the settlement had been achieved without his having to give up everything he owned. At least for the time being, Austin hung onto his home and the other property he still held in Herculaneum.[52]

The way had been cleared for Moses to concentrate on his Texas project, but the struggle in St. Louis had taken its toll. When Moses reached Herculaneum again, early in May, he was, as Maria had seen him at the end of March, "spent and exhuasted with fatigue." More than in March, however, emotion, desire, and anticipation drove him fatally on. In his excitement, he refused to admit what his wife saw clearly. Never having recovered from the pneumonia he had contracted four months earlier in January, the fifty-nine-year-old Moses was steadily draining his health by allowing his body no opportunity to recover. "I felt greatly allarmed," she cried, "and did all I could to prevail on him to take advice and postpone his Journey a few days." He had business in Potosi that he must tend to before he could leave for Texas, he replied. There was no time for rest. "You know his determined and persevering disposi[t]ion," Maria reminded Stephen sadly. "He had fixed the 25 of May for leaving this country and he had not a moment to loose." Four days after returning to Herculaneum, and after giving a power of attorney on May 9 for the collection of $1,831 in debts due him, Austin left again.[53]

Austin had to go, he may have felt, because he had become the catalyst for many who wanted to move to Texas. Word of his concession had spread widely throughout Arkansas and Missouri in the two months since Seguin had arrived in the United States. The editor of the St. Louis *Enquirer* expressed the sentiment of his readers when he trumpeted in the May 19 edition that "the most important fact respecting Texas which has come to our knowledge is, that a concession of the immediate country at the mouth of the great river Colorado has actually been made to a gentleman of the West, by the Spanish authorities, on condition that he will cultivate the lands and bring with him a certain number of families." On the strength of such reports alone, people began making plans to follow Austin. "It is understood," the writer added, "that a portion of the Arkansas emigration will embark in this enterprise."[54]

Of that there was no doubt. Several residents of Pecan Point on the Red River some miles west of Long Prairie "had heard of this enterprise of Austin's," a contemporary wrote, "and they are now making preparations to join the colony."[55] Along the Sabine River, the Reverend Joseph Bays waited with about two dozen families he had brought from Missouri in 1820.[56]

Austin must have been pleased by the strong interest in his project, but he knew that he was not yet ready to receive the immigrants. He needed to prepare his site, which meant clearing land and planting his first crop — corn, he thought — erecting a house for his headquarters, and, most important of all, building a stockade and blockhouse from which to defend his domain, which he believed to extend over some 200,000 acres. "I well know your dear Father Anticipated trouble from the Savages and he intended to erect a fort," Maria recalled. "I have often heard him Say that the first worck that was don Should be the building of a kind of fort where he and his Compannions would be Safe in case of an attack from the hostile Indians—"[57]

Austin calculated that with about thirty men he could complete the clearing, planting, and building in about six months — by the first of the year, if his schedule held firm and he could, as he planned, leave for Texas at the end of May. By the time he departed Herculaneum for Potosi, where he intended to recruit, he already had six of the thirty hands under contract. They had signed with him in St. Louis on April 22, the same happy day that he settled with the Bank. More pleasant still, each agreed to give six months' labor, the contract specified, in exchange for 640 acres of land.[58]

While Moses devoted all his energy to setting up the Texas project, Stephen evidently shrugged off both his father's work and the growing interest in the Texas immigration. To the younger Austin, a salaried job that placed money in his hands steadily, however slowly, offered the certainty and security he seemed to value most. Consequently, his path from Little Rock had led to New Orleans, where "with the hope of getting employ; I offered to hire myself out as clerk, as an overseer, or anything else," he admitted to his mother. "But business is too dull here to get into business. There are hundreds of young men who are glad to work for their board." Stephen needed more return than simply his board if he was to help his mother and sister.

At the end of November, before he could have spent many days in his search, Stephen had, he recognized at once, the "good fortune to get acquainted with Joseph H. Hawkins Esqr. (formerly of Lexington Kentucky) who gave me employ in an office." A lawyer and former member of both the Kentucky legislature and the United States Congress, the thirty-four-year-old Hawkins was no average attorney. Neither was his offer to Stephen Austin. Beyond the standard room and board, plus instruction in the law, this generous man allowed Austin money for clothes and agreed to advance cash for him to buy groceries for his family in Missouri. More remarkable even than that, Hawkins expected no repayment until the young man had begun earning a living at the bar, at least eighteen months hence. "An offer so generous and from a man who two months ago was a stranger to me," Stephen wrote, "has almost made me change my opinion of the human race."

Stephen accepted Hawkins's proposition and shortly borrowed "money enough to purchase a few groceries for you [his mother] and sister, which I have shipped on board the Velocipede Capt. Beckwith." Sending $10 in a separate letter, Stephen apologized that "this is all I can do now– when I earn some more I will send another supply and will try to keep you and Bryan's family supplied with sugar and Coffee at least." He hoped in the long run, however, to provide more than momentary necessities. His ultimate goal, the same as his father's, was to earn the family's independence. "If I am left alone a few years," he told his mother, "I may get up and pay all [the Missouri debts] off."[59]

The only problem was that he would earn nothing during the eighteen months he would be studying law. He still needed a paying job. Consequently, exhibiting a drive reminiscent of his father, the young man found an editorial position with the *Louisiana Advertiser*, the salary from which could supplement, if not replace, the money Hawkins was willing to advance for the Austin family.[60]

However much Stephen might want to devote himself to his studies and his newspaper work, Moses could not complete his arrangements for Texas without him. The elder Austin knew, though, from letters which have not survived, that his son needed encouragement about the Texas project. "I hope and pray you will Discharge your Doubts, as to the Enterprise," he exhorted his son on May 22 from Herculaneum in a particularly upbeat letter. "Raise your Spirits times are changing a new chance presents itself nothing is now wanting but Concert and firmness." Moreover, opportunities abounded. In addition to the colonization project, Moses had seen that San Antonio offered a good market for a quick return on bacon and flour. "Be on the look out and exert yourself with all your power," he urged, to find a supply they could take to Texas.

And on the topic of money, which Moses still lacked, "If any means can be commanded[,] use your utmost to have everything brought into motion and a vessell ready that no Delay take place[.] everything," he concluded, "Depends On expedition." Moses urged Stephen's prompt attention all the more, perhaps, because he himself once again had been "Detained to make a finish of my business Which I hope will take place in a day or two."

Finally, what Moses needed the most immediately from his employed son, he wrote, was temporary jobs for three new contract hands. Stephen learned of this request when the men appeared at his door, his father's letter in hand.[61]

As Moses completed his preparations with minimal resources, he had to find some additional ones with which to bring his son Brown home. "You may justly think that your Father has cast you from his protection and forgotten that he has such a *son* living," Moses admitted at the end of March, 1821, to the young man, who, following in his older brother's footsteps, was attending Transylvania University in Kentucky. "Could I have releaved your situation I would have don so month[s] past."[62]

Brown, indeed, may have wondered. During the two years he had been at Transylvania, he had received from his father little but good words about taking advantage of his opportunity for an education. "Lett me pray you to remember that now is the time to obtain your improvements," Moses had instructed his son in a typical passage. "A Day now lost is of the utmost consequence to you and can never be *recalled* an educatione is of more consequence than money. lett it be therefore your first care."[63] But both knew that money was essential to making the most of an educational opportunity.

Moses sincerely had attempted to send what he could, but $5 here and $10 there could not meet the need. The only alternative Austin had seen, which would relieve him of responsibility for Brown's support, was a commission for the young man in the military. In the spring of 1820, as the elder Austin approached bankruptcy, he tried through Horace Holley – the President of Transylvania, the husband of his niece, Mary Austin, and a constituent of powerful Congressman Henry Clay – to get the young man mustered into the Navy. As the matter proceeded, a despondent Moses apologized to his son in February, 1820, for the situation he was in. "I am sorry my son to say that my situation will not allow me to do for you what I could wish but when I am clear of all my difficulties I can then say what I can do for you in the mean time I shall forward to you Money – to pay your bills and Cloth you as your station in life requires." However unpleasant any circumstances became, Moses always tried to look to the future, and so he instructed his children to do also. "Keep up your spirits and hope for the best and make the exertions that is with in your power," he counseled Brown, "and I have not a Doubt but all will turn out as you wish."[64]

News of the approval of Austin's plans in Texas, coupled with the failure of the effort to have Brown commissioned, caused Moses to exert new energy in his son's behalf. At the end of March, 1821, Moses sent a note from Stephen for $150 to settle Brown's obligations. When the note fell at least $50 short of paying all of the bills, the father somehow found a man willing to advance the difference. "Return him thanks for his uncommon Kindness," Austin advised his son, "for without his friendship I do not know how I should have made up the money."[65]

With Brown at last freed, Moses counseled him to return to Missouri as rapidly as he could. The father wanted the young man to accompany him to Texas and then to enter college at Monterrey in Mexico. The opportunity to meet people and learn Spanish, Moses assured Brown, "will be of more Consiquence to you than you can now conceive of."[66] We can only wonder how seventeen-year-old Brown, who already had spent nearly half of his life away at school, received the suggestion.

Late in May, with Brown on his way home, hopefully, and the three new contract hands proceeding to New Orleans, Moses himself prepared to travel to Potosi. Maria again entreated him not to leave. He was no healthier than he had been when he returned from Texas at the end of March. And since then, in his excitement over his colonization opportunity, he had driven himself, if anything, harder than usual. Still he would not heed his wife's plea.

The thirty-five-mile ride to his old home, which Moses had made easily many times before, this time exhausted him. At the end of his journey, Austin made his way directly to the home of Dr. McGrady, collapsed, and lay in bed several days, unable to attend to any business.[67]

As soon as he felt strong enough to concentrate on business, Austin settled his affairs, engaged some young men as hands, and rode with them for Bellvue, about ten miles from Potosi. He arrived as rundown as he had been when he had reached Potosi. He spent two days in bed in Bellvue before resuming his ride to Emily's home on Hazel Run. This trip consumed every ounce of energy Austin had left. He arrived so weak on June 2, he could not dismount by himself. He had to be helped off the horse.

Moses insisted that, contrary to appearances, his condition was not as critical as his family believed. To prove it, after resting the night he began settling his accounts with Bryan and made plans to leave for Herculaneum two days later, on Tuesday, June 5. Maria in Herculaneum waited and watched anxiously for her husband's return that Tuesday. Instead, an express rider brought her the message that Moses lay gravely ill at Hazel Run. Maria asked Dr. John M. Bernhisel, a young, freshly trained, and highly recommended doctor from Philadelphia, to accompany her and left at once for her son-in-law's place.

As soon as she saw her husband, Maria knew that "the disease was gaining fast on his sistom." Dr. Bernhisel agreed. He called Moses' disorder "dangerous, it being a Violent attack of Inflamation on the brest and lungs, attended with a high fever." The doctor did what he knew to do. To bring the body fluids into balance, he blistered and bled Austin copiously for twenty-four hours. At the conclusion of the treatment, he saw improvement, he said, and announced that Moses was so far "out of danger," he, Dr. Bernhisel, would return to Herculaneum. Maria wanted desperately to believe the physician and "flatterd myself he [Moses] was much better—" For the next two days she remained by her husband's bed administering his medicine every hour as directed. Moses improved further. "We all thought him on the mend," she told Stephen, until Thursday night, when his fever rose dramatically. At four o'clock on Friday morning, June 8, Maria "discovered the St Antony fire was all over his face and he had

great difficulty in breathing we sent instantly for Dr B." Through the succeeding hours Maria maintained her anxious vigil. Sometime that day she
wrote Stephen of her worry. "Oh my son I greatly fear it [his two-day
improvement] was only a delusion, so apt are [we] to flatter ourselves with
that which will contribute to our happyness his fever has returned this day
with great violence. he breathes with much difficulty and seems in great
distress boath in body and mind—in short my son I feel much allarmed
about him."

The relapse proved far more serious than Maria at first recognized. It
broke her husband's spirit. At last he acknowledged the seriousness of his
condition. And the more clear it became to Moses that he would not be
leaving for Texas, the more distressed he became. "Your Father had completed all his business in this quarter much more to his satisfaction than he
ever expected to do," she told Stephen in her letter of June 8. Moreover,
his arrangements for the Texas adventure had taken shape much to his
satisfaction. "Everyone has the highest opinion of his plans and many only
waiting till thay know he has made the Establishment when they mean to
follow him. several young men has already gown [gone] and many now
waiting to start with him." The acceptable settlement of his business
affairs, the success of his preparations, and the people waiting on him—the
satisfaction and the anticipation—"all those things," Maria observed, "dis-
tracts his mind and increases his disordor."

The time had come for Moses, on the brink of what he hoped would be
his greatest work, to relinquish it to others.

> He called me to his bed side, [Maria wrote on June 8, the day
> it happened.] I asked him if he did not wish [Dr.] McGrady sent
> for after a considerable exertion to speak he drew me down to
> him and with much distress an difficulty of speech, told me it
> was two late, that he was going—that he shold not live 24
> hours. he beged me to tell you to take his place tell dear
> Stephen that it is his dieing fathers last request to prosecute
> the enterprise he had Commenced, that he had set his heart
> two much on it but for some wise purpose, god had prevented
> his travelling the rode he had planed out. he had opened and
> prepared the way for you and your brothers and that he felt a
> conviction you would be successful and independant in a few
> years...and if god in his wisdom thought best to disappoint
> him in the accomplishment of his wishes and plans formed for
> the benefit of his family, he prayed him to extend his goodness
> to you and enable you to go on with the business in the same
> way he would have done had not sickness and oh dreadful to
> think of perhaps death, prevented him from accomplishing—

Two days later, on Sunday, June 10, 1821, Moses Austin died.

EPILOGUE

MOSES AUSTIN'S death caused his wife, Maria, more than normal anguish. An unusual and oppressive heat wave, in which Eastern Missouri sweltered in early June of 1821, aggravated the state of inflammation of Moses Austin's remains so greatly that the family had to bury the body quickly. They put it in a simple coffin of rough pine boards and laid it to rest in the burial ground on the Bryan property only a short distance from the Hazel Run cottage in which Austin had died.

More than just her husband's body, Maria saw his dream of the Texas project and of recovering his fortune interred with him. "Oh my Son," she cried to Brown in Kentucky, "how it greaves my heart when I reflect on the hardships Suffrings and fatigue he had to go through to effect this great object and now to know that all his fond and flattering expectation of realizeing future welth and indipendence are now buried in the Silent tomb—"[1]

In her grief, Maria had read in the letter of Joseph H. Hawkins, Stephen's mentor and patron, only the condolences. But the other message Hawkins conveyed would have excited Moses more than any news since the approval of his Texas proposition. Stephen, who before his father's death "had set his heart on facilitating the views of his father in his contemplated settlement in Texas," had succeeded in convincing Hawkins to back the colonization venture. "Believing the enterprise laudable, and perhaps promising some reward to those who would toil in its prosecution," the wealthy New Orleans attorney informed her, "I agreed to meet the proposition of his Father, and take a joint interest in the grant and settlement...I had expected his father here as soon as his health would permit, and was prepared to further his views by every friendly effort in my power—...I have advanced Stephen all the funds he desired...and have promised to furnish more as he requires them—"[2] Moses Austin, through his once-doubting son, had, at the moment of his death, been given the financial underpinning needed to lay his Texas project on a firm foundation.

Before the end of the year, Maria appreciated the import of Hawkins's commitment. In December, she "truly rejoiced to find your [Stephen's] prospects in Texas are So much more flattering than I had any Idea of." More important to her, she understood that because of it "you will have it in your power to fulfill the last request of your dear deceased father."[3]

Stephen did just that. He accomplished the settlement of Texas so well that he is revered as "The Father of Texas" and is remembered by having the capital city of the State named for him.

Maria worried, as she had every reason to, about her own financial situation. Moses' debts pressed his estate relentlessly. In July, the United States Post Office gave up waiting for payment of monies due from the Mine a Breton post office, which Austin had served for years as postmaster, and ordered the district attorney to file suit. Worse, after James Bryan completed his inventory of the estate, he found liabilities exceeding assets by $15,000. But the cruelest circumstance to Maria was that several family members, to whom Moses had been considerate, chose to dispute their obligations.[4]

She might have been depressed, too, by Bryan's less than adequate administration of the estate. Her son-in-law, however, as she knew, had troubles of his own. Financially insecure since the Panic of 1819, he had begun arranging his own affairs, apparently to protect his family in the event that he followed his father-in-law into bankruptcy. For thirteen months after Moses died, Bryan maintained his solvency. But on July 16, 1822, after an illness of ten days, he died of "the Fever that swept many of your old, and intimate Friends to an earlly Grave —" Emily reported to her older brother. "Their were more sudden Death's . . . than ever was known in Missouria before." Bryan's estate should have been well positioned to provide for his survivors, Emily explained to Stephen, since "to secure something for his Children, and to be inabled to pay every just Debt, he put his property out of his hands." As his father-in-law had done, "he confided in those that he considered his Friends —" And as had been the case with Moses' affairs, Bryan's survivors, too, found none of his associates "that thinks them-selves sufficiently interested in the welfare of the Family, to step forward to see that justice is done to the orphens."[5]

The loss of Emily's husband reduced her, her widowed mother, and her four young children, the last one born only two days before her father caught his fatal fever, to living "like Hermits; by our own industrey & economy we have indeavoured to live tolerable comfortable," Emily told Stephen, "but when I say that, I say all —"[6] Maria may have made bonnets as she had done earlier for sale in the store in Little Rock. Her daughter taught school and took in boarders to make ends meet.

The women's situation made the loss of Durham Hall rankle all the more. It was the place, Emily reminisced to Stephen, "where the happyest period of our lives were spent, enjoying peace, plenty, and a contented mind." By contrast, she reported in disapproval, it "has passed into the hands of *Strangers*, and become the resort of the Fashionable & Gay."[7] Maria, and Emily especially, clung to a hope of recovering their old home-place, if not all the Mine a Breton land, which they firmly believed had been stripped from Moses by greedy one-time friends in the bank. "I have been told that if you were hear to examin all the Papers," Emily urged Stephen, "that you would find that the Deed Given by the Sherif to Ross was not of any account. many pretend to say that the property might be recoverd by the Heirs of Moses Austin...thier has been a great deal of the rascality of the St. Louis bank business come to light especially considering that unfortunate business of Fathers."[8] Attorney James Scott evidently agreed, as he offered at his own expense to pursue recovery of the Mine a Breton estate. In return he asked a one-half interest in whatever he recovered.[9]

For all her bitterness, Emily apparently did not want to enter the fight. She pursued the matter no further until after her marriage in September, 1824, to James F. Perry of the Potosi Perrys. Perry in 1826 solicited attorney Scott's opinion on the likely success of a suit for recovery. Scott, recently involved in litigation over Risdon Price's title to Durham Hall, discouraged the idea. Austin's title from the Spanish government never had been perfected, he reported, and even if it had been, Moses appeared to have lost it. If the bank had not acquired title directly by the foreclosure proceeding, then Austin, in his eagerness in April, 1821, to release himself from his obligation to the Bank, had relinquished his claim to ownership when, in the settlement, he had condoned the results of the foreclosure.

Durham Hall, 1870s. The house, a shambles of its former proud appearance, burned to the ground in 1876. This, the only photograph ever taken of the building, was made not long before the house was lost. *Mine a Breton Historical Society, Potosi, Missouri.*

Moreover, if the heirs recovered an interest in the property, Scott believed they would assume also the debt owed the bank. For that reason, the attorney advised against a suit.[10] The Austin descendants had taken no steps by 1836, when John Deane, then owner of Durham Hall, went to court to perfect his title. In the absence of objections from the Perrys, who by that time had moved to Texas, Deane succeeded.

There the issue lay for twenty-eight years, until the United States Congress on February 14, 1874, two years before a run-down Durham Hall burned to the ground, passed a measure recognizing Moses Austin's Spanish title and relinquishing any claim the United States might have by virtue of the failure of the Board of Land Commissioners to confirm the title to Austin. Far from promoting the interests of the Austin family, however, the bill had been offered by Missouri representatives responding to constituents upset by a recent opinion of the Commissioner of the General Land Office that title to the land still resided in the United States. The Austin descendants nonetheless seized their opportunity, took the issue to court, and pursued it for nine years until the United States Supreme Court on January 5, 1888, upheld the 1836 Deane decision.[11]

Within a few months of her husband's death, when it appeared that the Hazel Run property might be sold, Maria complained to Stephen that "the Idea of leaving the body of my dear Husband on the land of Strangers, in an open field, is truly distressing to my feelings I have thought if it was possible for my dear Son to come to this Country next fall, the body could be taken up and placed in another Coffin. . . it will be Some sattisfaction to us [Maria and Emily], to remove your dear parent from a Country where he had been so crually persicuted."[12]

Stephen never came home, Bryan died, and by the summer of 1823, though Maria's desire may have remained, her will did not. "Mother often says that she will never see *Texas or you* but expects to lay her bones by the Side of Father–" Emily told her older brother two years after their father had died. "I indeavour to laugh her out of the idea, but it appears to be fixed on her mind. she has become quite religious, and spends much of her time in studying her Bible– that, and her little Grandson– *James Guy*. . .appears to give her more pleasure than any thing else in this world."[13] On January 8, 1824, Maria died at Hazel Run and was buried beside her husband.[14]

Not many years after her death, the property was sold. By 1830, the cemetery had "been turn'd out into a common, & I am told," Emily reported to Stephen in disgust, "that the Railing, that I had put round the graves is pulled down." Conscious of her mother's original desire, Emily vowed that she would never "leave this Country, sattissfyed with-out their bodies are taken up. I think it is my *duty* to have it done." She wanted the remains to be "deposited in som[e] publick burying-ground, & a Monument of *brick* built over them, with an inscription placed in it, to show my *Children* (if I should leave this Country) where the *remains* of their grand Parents are deposited, (in case that they should ever revisit Missouri)."[15]

Stephen agreed. He suggested the cemetery in Ste. Genevieve, since all burial grounds in Potosi lay on private land. But when William Milam, then owner of Durham Hall, in 1831 donated to Potosi a plot for a cemetery, Emily and her husband concluded to move the remains there to lie on land once a part of the grounds of Durham Hall. The Perrys worked fast if they completed the move before they themselves left Missouri for Texas in June of that same year.[16]

However that may be, the removal attracted first local, then statewide attention. "When the coffin was taken up it was found to be rotten, but, to the utter astonishment of all present," John S. Brickey recalled for Wetmore's *Missouri Gazetteer*, "the body of the deceased was in a state of perfect soundness, except the nose and some of the fingers; all the features (except as above) remaining perfect and entire, and having every appearance of petrifaction. Though no one present did any thing more to the body than press it with their hands, several who saw it have affirmed that 'it was as hard as wood, if not stone!' I merely mention the fact, as being out of the ordinary course of nature...The body appeared of a dark or black colour...There are several persons now living here who were eyewitnesses to the fact above related."[17]

The petrifaction story begged investigation by idle snoopers. A St. Louis newspaper reported in 1889 that, indeed, "the grave in the Presbyterian Cemetery was opened [apparently not long after Austin had been reinterred] by parties who were curious to learn if it was true, and the coffin found open, as if the vandals had been interrupted in their work. The body, however, was not disturbed, and the grave has not been molested again to this date."[18]

By the end of the century, the grave could be recognized easily, as a wild cherry tree with two trunks, each eighteen inches in diameter, issued from it and had broken the handsome brick wall Emily had wanted erected over the remains. In the spring of 1895, the half-century-old tree had to be taken down to protect the site. A concrete and stone vault fitted with a marker bearing the simple, but inaccurate inscription: "Moses Austin, 1761-1820," replaced the brick wall (and is there yet in 1986). A local milling company bought the fine wood and shaped most of it into walking canes. The substantial stump of the tree, nearly three feet in diameter where the roots began to spread out, was sawed, hewn, and dressed into a comfortable seat. The artifact became so well known that in 1904, "one of Washington County's contributions to the Missouri forestry exhibit at the World's Fair will be the stump of the famous wild cherry tree which grew on the grave of Moses Austin." Missourians thought it would attract the

Moses Austin's grave, 1890s. This picture was made not long before the cherry tree was cut down in 1895 and the grave repaired. Dudley G. Wooten, ed., *A Comprehensive History of Texas.*

particular attention of Texans on account of its historical associations.[19]

Whatever notice it attracted in 1904 had faded by 1911, when a request from the treasurer of Washington County to the Texas legislature for money to maintain the grave caused a reporter from Austin to remark on how few Texans knew the location of Moses Austin's final resting place. Predictably, the legislature ignored the request. Matters took a different turn in 1930, when a Missouri newspaper reported that talk among some Texans had turned from stumps and money to Austin's remains themselves. Texas had established a State Cemetery in the 1850s and early in the twentieth century begun moving the remains of prominent Texas figures to it. The remains of Stephen F. Austin already had been given reburial in the most prominent location in the sixteen-acre domain.[20]

To celebrate the centennial of the Texas Revolution of 1836, Texans looked for ways to honor their historical figures, Moses Austin chief among them. "It is a pity that the great state of Texas in this Centennial year," Texana collector Alexander Deinst told the annual meeting of the Texas Agricultural Workers' Association on January 8, 1937, "could put hundreds of statues and memorials and spend millions, worthily, and yet not one little stone, one-foot square, no monument, no marker, no city, no county, nothing has ever been done by the great state of Texas, in memory of this wonderful man with his transcendent vision of the colonizing of Texas, carried to fruition by his son Stephen F. Austin. All honor to Stephen F. Austin, whom the State of Texas has honored in every way, but Moses Austin, as the originator and founder of the idea, is certainly also entitled to receive recognition for his services, and his remains should be brought from the uncared grave in Missouri and placed in our State Cemetery."[21]

Louis Wiltz Kemp, a member of the Texas Historical and Landmark Commission and the person dedicated above all others to the work of gathering the remains of Texas's heroes and heroines into the State Cemetery, concurred. As 1937 ended, he arranged with Thurlow B. Weed, a prominent Austin mortician, for the removal to the State Cemetery of some two dozen remains.[22]

By April, 1938, Weed had completed more than 15 removals, some from outside Texas. Having encountered no difficulties with any of them, he anticipated none when he left for Missouri.[23] Weed drove directly to the capital to obtain from the State Health Department a permit for the removal, but, after presenting his credentials and letters of approval from Texas descendants, he learned that such permits were issued by county authorities. In Potosi the next day, April 21, Weed went first to the city cemetery, located the keeper, and told him of his mission. The man not only expressed no reservation, he even suggested the undertaker get help to clear away the brush and weeds and to assist in the digging. Weed hired three men, as he wanted to complete the work on April 21, San Jacinto Day, the anniversary of the battle that won the independence of Texas. With picks and shovels the hands cleared the ground and began tearing away the side of the stone and concrete vault.

The activity in the normally quiet cemetery naturally attracted attention. A crowd gathered. One newspaper account reported that when the onlookers learned that the remains were being exhumed for reinterment in Austin, Texas, a committee was quickly dispatched to Mayor William L. Edmunds and City Marshal C. J. Richeson to get them to put a stop to the work. Several citizens of Potosi considered the grave, however much neglected, a local historical shrine. Only the previous February, the Civic League of Potosi had begun collecting a fund to purchase a bronze tablet to mark the grave with appropriate biographical information. The Mayor went to the cemetery with Richeson, demanded to see Weed's permit, and, learning that he had none, ordered the work stopped.[24]

Weed recalled the events differently. He said 25 years later that, with the work underway, he went to the office of Dr. George F. Cresswell, Washington County Registrar of Vital Statistics and a prominent local physician, to obtain the necessary permit. Dr. Cresswell, without knowledge of events at the cemetery, objected to Weed's plan and, the doctor recalled, "then

Moses Austin's grave, 1979. *Photograph by the author.*

and there told Weed that he had no right to remove Austin's remains and that he would not have a permit to do so." After warning Weed to halt the digging and ordering him to return the next morning, Dr. Cresswell said he informed Mayor Edmunds of Weed's mission.[25]

Weed and his wife checked into a local hotel to await the morrow. Officials of Potosi, by contrast, became increasingly agitated the more they thought about the brazen action of the Texan. "Who do those people think they are," Mayor Edmunds asked the world through a statement to United Press, "to send a man up here to try to get the body of Austin? Why, that grave is one of the landmarks of this community. Austin founded this town. He opened the first lead mine here. I'll fight the whole state and everyone in town will back me up."[26]

Weed discovered just how upset local officials had become when, as he and his wife finished eating dinner, Mayor Edmunds and another man came to their table and asked him to step outside to talk. "Two or three other men were outside in a car," Weed recalled. "I thought they might shoot me since I thought they had a belligerent attitude." Weed quoted the Mayor as saying, "Why in the--hell are you trying to steal that body?" At the unfounded accusation, the undertaker lost his own temper, "and things were said that should not have been said." Edmunds threatened to throw Weed in jail, but decided not to because Weed was an old man. The Mayor said he told Weed "that he had better put the grave back into the condition that he had found it and then leave town." Weed shot back that he would not leave town "until a council meeting was held to pass a resolution against the removal of the remains and furnish him a copy to show the Texas authorities."[27]

Mayor Edmunds convened a special Council session the next morning, April 22. Weed explained his mission and told the Council "that he was not trying to create hard feelings, but was trying to prevent unnecessary delay and trying to facilitate matters."[28] Unmoved, the Council passed one order halting the removal without an order by a state court and another requiring restoration of the grave to its former condition.[29]

The Weeds left Potosi as quickly as they could and returned to Austin, arriving on Saturday, April 23. That same day, the undertaker presented the Council resolutions to officials of the State Board of Control, for whom he worked under the contract, who concluded to pursue the matter no further. Frustrated, Lou Kemp gave the press his gratuitous opinion that the poor condition in which the grave had been kept "reflected somewhat on Texas." Mayor Edmunds shot back indignantly that the tomb "was in excellent condition until their workmen tore out the side of the vault Thursday"[30] and added that "inasmuch as the family of Austin saw fit to bury him in Potosi, I see no reason why his tomb should be disturbed now."[31]

The incident attracted wide notice, interest, and comment on both sides. One Missouri historian thought Weed "might have been acting, almost, under orders from old Moses himself. Austin had a way of treating Missourians, when first he came to this country, with similar disrespect for their rights or feelings." A Texan suggested Missourians "give Moses Austin a break and send him down to join Stephen F." An irate Missourian, claiming to know Moses' preference, threw down the gauntlet in response. "Potosi replied in the finest Missouri tradition," the person wrote. "Her answer was NO. An unequivocal, unmistakable No. If it must be war, so be it. Death might be the price. Even so, the pioneer who founded Potosi, charted Potosi, breathed into its dust the breath of life, set its feet upon the path it has fatefully followed—Potosi's sire and patron saint would ride down the gales to obliteration with Potosi."[32]

Within days after Weed left town, the citizens of Potosi, at their mayor's call, took the constructive steps of cleaning up the cemetery and organizing a Moses Austin Memorial Society to provide a suitable memorial.[33]

Texas Lieutenant Governor Walter F. Woodul, chair of the Texas Historical and Landmark Commission, and unhappy with the decision of the Board of Control to let matters be, on May 7 called on Governor James V. Allred to take action to secure Austin's remains. Governor Allred first should contact the office of the Governor of Missouri, but, if the request for removal were refused, the press release threatened, court action would follow. The Texans soon learned that litigation offered their only avenue to obtain Austin's remains. The Attorney General of Missouri had ruled in the meantime that the Governor lacked jurisdiction in the matter.[34]

Governor Allred took a less belligerent tack and at the end of the month sent Texas Secretary of State, Edward Clark, to Potosi as his personal representative to try to quiet the situation. "One of my primary reasons for being here," Clark told the citizens of Potosi, "is that Gov. Allred directed me to offer the apologies of the State of Texas for the event that occurred when an undertaker from Austin came here some time ago and began work toward removing the remains of Moses Austin without first having secured a permit from the local registrar . . . [or] permission of the local city government. The State of Texas has made provision to build a magnificent memorial in the State Cemetery at Austin in memory of Moses Austin if we were permitted to rebury him there." In addition, Clark carried an offer of $1,000 to erect a suitable marker at the gravesite if the citizens of Potosi would allow Texas to transfer the remains to its State Cemetery. The Potosi authorities rejected the offer out of hand.[35]

Spurned in the effort to remove Austin's remains, Texas proceeded with plans for erecting an appropriate memorial in San Antonio. Miss Waldine Tauch won the design competition with her plan to depict Austin "at his most important moment in history: standing with outstretched hand holding the rolled document which gave him the right to settle Anglo Americans in Texas." The statue, located on Main Plaza across from the Spanish Governor's Palace, was unveiled on May 15, 1939.[36]

After the Moses Austin Memorial Society failed in 1938 to raise money sufficient to erect a suitable marker at Austin's grave, and the Missouri Legislature in 1941 contributed no more than the sanction of a state commission to direct the project, little was heard of the effort until the Potosi Lions Club took a hand. Early in January, 1949, John W. Smith, club secretary, addressed the Texas Historical Society proposing to let Austin's bones go to Texas. "All we want is just a modest city hall—say about $50,000," he explained. "We'd heard that Texas would give almost anything for Moses Austin's bones."[37] Receiving no reply, Smith on January 28 wrote again, this time to Governor Beauford Jester. The second letter drew considerable attention. Missourian L. L. Richardson wondered whether Austin's bones really ever had been moved from Hazel Run, and concluded that in any case "A man worth $50,000 after being dead 128 years is something of a treasure-trove to investigate."[38] Mayor Edmunds and Charles van Ravensway, director of the Missouri Historical Society, found no humor in the proposition, and the Mayor announced flatly that the Lions Club had no jurisdiction over the bones. Governor Jester put an end to the overture simply by ignoring it, encouraged this time by Lou Kemp, who nevertheless remembered the failure to move Austin's bones in 1938 as one of the few defeats he suffered in his years working to honor prominent figures of Texas history.[39] The Lions Club succeeded in raising only ire, but no money. Austin's grave continued to bear its incorrect inscription.

Since then, the story of the events of 1938 has resurfaced periodically in both humorous and serious veins, depending upon the bent of the writer. And it has grown, having become styled "The Battle of Potosi," whose cast of characters has swelled to include a shotgun-wielding city marshal on the one side and some Texas Rangers on the other. One Texas historian, obviously angered at the rancor caused by continuing resurrection of the unpleasant memories, contacted the participants for their reminiscences, then wrote a long article for publication in 1963 detailing the events and showing that nothing like a battle ever occurred. But it has not stopped the publication from time to time of rumors that Texas is poised to come for the bones.[40]

Maria was prophetic to worry that her husband's grave might be lost if his remains were left on the Hazel Run property. In 1979 the old Bryan burial ground, even with its dozens of graves, the most recent interment dating from the 1940s, lay obscured so far back in the woods

Old Bryan Cemetery at Hazel Run. Though Moses Austin was buried on family land, his widow and later his daughter wanted the remains removed to a public cemetery. The body was taken to Potosi in 1831. By 1979 the cemetery had fallen into such decay that only one (dating from the 1940s) of the more than 100 burials could be identified. *Photograph by the author.*

that the cartographers who compiled the area topographical map for the United States Geological Survey failed to find and include the cemetery. Fortunately her children were able to honor her wishes by having the remains of their parents moved to Potosi. Sadly, however, their own goal of erecting a suitable marker over their father's grave has yet to be realized.

Would that Moses' appearance were as certain as our knowledge of the location of his remains. No likeness of him, beyond the verbal descriptions of his short stature, corpulence, beautiful teeth, and charming smile was known to exist until an elderly woman wrote his grandson, Guy M. Bryan, sometime during the 1890s that she possessed a portrait. The work had been commissioned years before, the lady claimed, by her husband, a steamboat captain who hauled lead for Bryan's grandfather. Austin, she added, spared time enough for only two sittings during one passage on the boat. Bryan consulted with both Bryan and Perry descendants. None had ever heard of a portrait. Consequently, "feeling that on account of the lapse of years, the family could not assert the authenticity of the canvas,"[41] Bryan declined to purchase the painting.

Only a few years later, in 1904, a portrait reputed to be of Austin turned up on display at the Louisiana Purchase Exposition in St. Louis, doubtless the same fair at which the stump of the cherry tree from Austin's grave also was on view. If genuine, the portrait represented a major historical find, and following the fair, representatives of the Missouri Historical Society approached owner James T. DeShields, Texas historian and collector, about acquiring the work. DeShields needed the money. But when pressed for proof of authenticity, "he was evasive . . . He wrote instead that he had once had an affidavit but couldn't find it, and referred vaguely to having purchased the portrait years before from . . . [Texana collector and publisher] H. P. N. Gammel of Austin."[42]

Despite the weak certification, the Society bought and displayed the portrait, but its validity has been in contention ever since. Austin family historian Laura Bryan Parker in 1918 disowned the painting when she wrote that the work never had belonged to any member of the family. But some years later, Hally Bryan Perry studied the portrait and "apparantly with great exacting detail convinced herself of its genuineness." She herself "looked enough like Moses Austin's picture," several members of the family recalled her saying, "as to make the family resemblance apparant."[43]

No one produced firm evidence regarding the portrait's legitimacy until someone questioned whether the black cravat and coat in which the figure is dressed represented a style popular only after Austin's death. Society officials investigated, agreed, and removed the portrait from public view.[44] But if the handsome man in the portrait is not Moses Austin, who

Moses Austin. The authenticity of this portrait rests on the word of Texana collector James T. DeShields, from whom the Missouri Historical Soceity acquired the painting early in this century. DeShields delivered no substantive data to support his claim. Those who believe the portrait to be Austin point both to the striking similarity in facial features between Austin family members and the figure in the portrait, and to the resemblance of the figure to written descriptions of Austin. After art critics argued that the clothing in which the subject is depicted represents a fashion in vogue after Moses Austin's death, Society officials came to doubt the authenticity and removed the portrait from public view. *Missouri Historical Society.*

is he? Until the identity of the face in the picture is conclusively settled, this portrait, identified for decades as Moses Austin, will continue for many to picture the founder of the American lead industry and the man who obtained initial permission to settle Anglo Americans in Spanish Texas.

Even if we never describe Moses Austin's appearance conclusively, the significance of his contribution to the development of the American nation cannot be disputed. Austin founded the lead industry in the United States. So seminal was his work that the historian of the industry, Walter Renton Ingalls, named the second of four epochs in its history the "Austin Period." This epoch, according to Ingalls, spanned Austin's years in Missouri. Where the first epoch was characterized by inconsequential efforts to mine and smelt lead, the Austin Period is recognized by the introduction of "bolder methods of mining and improved methods of smelting, which were of considerable importance in his day and taught the miners of Missouri how to operate."[45] Those improved methods were the ones Austin had first introduced into Virginia through the miners he had recruited from Britain. Where Virginia production fell dramatically after Moses left, even though many of the British miners remained at the Austinville diggings, in Missouri the efficient methods, under his entrepreneurial direction, brought production to a level that satisfied the American market during Austin's lifetime and for decades thereafter.

A contribution as great as Austin's, made in such a short span of history—basically the eighteen years from 1798 to 1816—could not help but be felt far beyond the relatively small area in which he, the catalyst, personally worked. For Missouri, the impact could be measured economically in the revenue Austin earned. The former dean of Missouri historians, Floyd Shoemaker, concluded that Austin "probably added more to the wealth of Missouri than anyone else at that time, with the possible exception of some of the larger St. Louis fur dealers."[46]

For the lead industry, the depth of Austin's contribution is evident by the simple fact that it long outlasted him. The methods that Austin introduced and used remained the technical foundation of the industry as it expanded geographically for forty years after his death. The third epoch in the history of the lead industry, identified by Ingalls as the years from Austin's death to the introduction of heavy mechanical equipment, which revolutionized both the mining and smelting of lead after the Civil War, saw production, from mines in Missouri and Wisconsin in particular, increase until America supplied its own and much of the world's needs.[47]

Austin would not have been surprised. He had declared to the Spanish in his request for the grant of Mine a Breton that the mines could meet the needs of both the colonies and Spain. To American authorities following the Louisiana Purchase he repeated the assertion by forecasting that the mines could supply all of the American and considerable of the world demand.

Indeed, Austin's vision was so clear that even contemporaries could see and profit by it. Only five years after Austin's death, Lieutenant Martin Thomas, the officer responsible for the government lead mines in the western country, acknowledged, in a communication forwarded to the United States Senate, his debt to Austin. "I have quoted freely from the late Mr. Austin's report to Mr. Meigs on the subject of the lead mines," the officer wrote, "because I found his statements generally correct, and some of his predictions fulfilled to the very letter...."[48]

The technology that Austin introduced and spread was neither secret nor highly complex. Any person of enterprise and vision could have accomplished what Austin did. But Austin alone united the talents, knowledge, and entrepreneurial dedication to create the lead industry of the United States.

Moses Austin played an equally significant role in American History in pushing westward and in taming the American frontier. He opened the lead mines region of Missouri, if not the lead mines area of Virginia, to settlement. He planted at Potosi the first permanent non-Indian settlement in Missouri west of, and back from, the bank of the Mississippi River. Austin's work is easy to see, because he left a chain of towns in his wake: Austinville at the mines in Virginia, and Potosi at the mines and Herculaneum on the Mississippi River in Missouri, all still active communities. He may have helped guide the early development of Little Rock and likely encouraged the founding of Fulton, both communities in Arkansas. No student of the Austin genealogy could be surprised at Moses' pioneering. Most of his forebears possessed a similar drive, and all, beginning with Richard Austin who brought the line to America, died in communities west of the ones in which they were born.

Obtaining initial permission to introduce a colony of Anglo Americans into Spanish Texas is, of course, the accomplishment for which Austin is most widely remembered. His enterprise led to the second largest territorial acquisition of the adjacent United States. Moreover, the tale of the trip to Texas and of his deathbed call to his oldest son to take over the work rank among the most dramatic stories of the westward movement.

Contemporary observers recognized that Moses' Texas success equalled, if not exceeded in importance for the country, the work he had done in developing the mining industry. Sometimes those who know a person firsthand see most clearly, and can sum up best, the essence of the individual. So it happened for Austin. From his pioneering spirit to his cultivated taste, from his town building to his colony planning, from Virginia to Missouri to Texas, Moses Austin truly was, as the editors of newspapers in Missouri and Arkansas described him to their readers without fear of contradiction, "a gentleman of the West."

NOTES

CHAPTER I

The notes contain shortened references. Full information can be obtained from the Bibliography, pages 273-289.

1   The story of Austin's one and only visit to San Antonio was recorded in two slightly different versions by his son, Stephen F. Austin. One appears in the history of Anglo Texas that Stephen wrote for his colonists in 1829 (see David B. Gracy II, *Establishing Austin's Colony: The First Book Printed in Texas, With the Laws, Orders and Contracts of Colonization*, 2). The other, fuller, version, which he wrote for his younger brother, appears in Dudley G. Wooten, *A Comprehensive History of Texas, 1685 to 1897*, vol. 2, pp. 442-443.

2   He did not go to the building presently known as the "Governor's Palace." In 1820, it was the residence of the commander of the military establishment. Charles Ramsdell, *San Antonio: A Historical and Pictorial Guide*, 104, 108.

3   Declaration of Moses Austin in Eugene C. Barker, ed., *The Austin Papers*, vol. 2, pt. 1, pp. 370-371; Charles Bacarisse, "The Baron de Bastrop: Life and Times of Philip Hendrik Nering Bogel, 1759 to 1827," pp. 233-240.

4   Martínez to Commandant General, January 4, 1821, Nacogdoches Archives; Moses Austin's Application for Colonization Permit, [December 26, 1820], in Barker, ed., *Austin Papers*, vol. 2, pt. 1, pp. 371-372, Ambrosio Maria de Aldasoro to Antonio Martínez, January 17, 1821, in *ibid.*, 372-373.

5   Edith Austin Moore and William Allen Day, comps., *The Descendants of Richard Austin of Charlestown, Massachusetts, 1638*, pp. 7, 9-10; John Camden Hotten, ed., *The Original Lists of Persons of Quality; Emigrants; Religious Exiles; Political Rebels; Serving Men Sold For a Term of Years; Apprentices; Children Stolen; Maidens Pressed; And Others Who Went From Great Britain to the American Plantations, 1600-1700*, pp. 298-299.

6   "Crossing the Atlantic in 1638: Passengers Aboard the Ship Bevis," *The Second Boat*, 1 (May, 1980), 13; David B. Gracy II, "George Washington Littlefield: A Biography in Business," 4.

7   George Macaulay Trevelyan, *England Under The Stuarts*, 144.

8   *Ibid.*, 52.

9   "Crossing the Atlantic in 1638," *The Second Boat*, 1 (May, 1980), 13; Moore and Day, *Richard Austin*, 9-10; Gracy, "Littlefield," 4; Trevelyan, *Stuarts*, 144.

10 Moore and Day, *Richard Austin*, 9-10; Eugene K. Austin, "The Austin Family in America, 1638-1908," pp. 125, 135.

11 Moore and Day, *Richard Austin*, 9-11; Paul R. Austin, *Austins to Wisconsin*, 2-3, 8; Myrtle M. Jillson to Mrs. John Beretta, May 23, 1967, Beretta Papers.

12 Rowley church record, quoted in Jillson to Beretta, May 23, 1967, Beretta Papers.

13 James Hammond Trumbull, ed., *Memorial History of Hartford County, Connecticut, 1633-1844*, vol. 1, p, 385.

14   Robert Hayden Alcorn, *The Biography of a Town: Suffield, Connecticut, 1670-1970*, pp. 5-12; Trumbull, *Memorial History of Hartford County*, vol. 1, pp. 385-386; H. S. Sheldon, *Documentary History of Suffield, 1670-1749*, p. 7, map; John Warner Barber, *Connecticut Historical Collections*, 108.

15   Sheldon, *Documentary History of Suffield*, 98.

16   *Ibid.*; Trumbull, *Memorial History of Hartford County*, vol. 1, pp. 386-388, 405; Jillson to Beretta, May 23, 1967, Beretta Papers; Alcorn, *Biography of a Town*, 12.

17   Laura Bryan Parker, "Facts Concerning Moses Austin, His Family, and Forebears," 4-7; Alcorn, *Biography of a Town*, 24.

18   The records do not make clear whether this house belonged to Anthony Austin, Sr., or to his namesake son, but the evidence suggests the former. Anthony, Sr., the town clarke, kept the official records in his house. This Anthony Austin House burned, and the effects of a fire are evident in the town records of 1704 (Mr. and Mrs. Gregor Lang to DBGII, interview, October 22, 1978; Notebooks in Delphina Clark Papers).

19   Mr. and Mrs. Lang to DBGII, October 22, 1978; Alcorn, *Biography of a Town*, 28; Parker, "Facts," 2, 7; Austin, *Austins to Wisconsin*, 11-13.

20   Parker, "Facts," 7. Years later, the meeting house was moved to a location over Anthony Austin's grave. His stone stands in the burying ground adjacent to the building.

21   Edna Perry Deckler, comp., "Austin-Perry Memorandum," *Stirpes*, 9 (March, 1969), 39; Sheldon, *Documentary History of Suffield*, 21.

22   Moore and Day, *Richard Austin*, 14-18; Parker, "Facts," 7; Trumbull, *Memorial History of Hartford County*, vol. 1, pp. 396, 398; Charles S. Bissell, *Antique Furniture in Suffield, Connecticut, 1670-1956*, pp. 14, 23; Austin, *Austins to Wisconsin*, 8-9.

23   Trumbull, *Memorial History of Hartford County*, vol. 1, pp. 405-406; Alcorn, *Biography of a Town*, 72; Moore and Day, *Richard Austin*, 14-18, 24-27; Richard L. Bushman, *From Puritan to Yankee*, 53; Lois Kimbell Mathews Rosenberry, *Migrations from Connecticut Prior to 1800*, p. 7-11; Albert E. Van Dusen, "The Trade of Revolutionary Connecticut," 24.

24   William Chauncey Fowler, *History of Durham, Connecticut; From the First Grant of Land in 1662 to 1866*, pp. 3-21, 103-105, 106, 153-156, 172, 226; Milton H. Whited, *Durham's Heritage: Men and Homes of Early Durham*, 37ff; Barber, *Connecticut Historical Collections*, 522; R. Baldwin, *A Map of the Colonies of Connecticut and Rhode Island*.

25   Meeting, December 11, 1744, Durham Town Records; Fairchild to Austin, April 14, 1743, Deed, Grantees, Durham Town Records, vol. 5, p. 446.

26   Elizabeth Mansfield to DBGII, interview, October 23, 1978; John Frederick Kelly, *Early Domestic Architecture of Connecticut*, 5-23.

27   Elias Austin, Inventory of Estate, File 1777, No. 118, Middletown Probate District, Estate Papers, RG 4, Records of the Probate Courts, Connecticut State Archives; Milton H. Whited, "Elias Austin, 1718-1776"; Van Dusen, "The Trade of Revolutionary Connecticut," 65; Sarah Jones to Stephen Austin, Elijah and Archibald Austin, Moses Austin, Martha and Moses Bates, Gloriana Eliot, Deed, July 8, 1782, Grantees, Durham Town Records, vol. 9, p. 235.

28   Moore and Day, *Richard Austin*, 27-28; Fowler, *History of Durham*, 286, 288, 290, 293, 295, 306, 308, 311.

29   Mildred Mathewson Scranton, Old Houses of Connecticut: Historical and Technical Information in Regard to the Elias Austin House, Durham, Middle-

sex County, Connecticut Society of Colonial Dames of America; Whited, *Durham's Heritage*, 71.

30 Trumbull, *Memorial History of Hartford County*, vol. 1, p. 302.

31 Whited, *Durham's Heritage*, 95-96.

32 Samuel Stow quoted in Bushman, *From Puritan to Yankee*, 135.

33 Austin, Inventory of Estate; "An Account of the Number of Inhabitants, in the Colony of Connecticut, January 1, 1774," in *The Wyllys Papers: Correspondence and Documents Chiefly of Descendants of Gov. George Wyllys of Connecticut, 1590-1796*, vol. 21, pps. 486-492; *Connecticut and Parts Adjacent* (map); Scranton, Old Houses of Connecticut: Historical and Technical Information in Regard to the Elias Austin House; Whited, *Durham's Heritage*, 14, 95-96; Trumbull, *Memorial History of Hartford County*, vol., p. 302; Bushman, *From Puritan to Yankee*, 110-111, 132-133; Fowler, *History of Durham*, 21, 30, 226; Van Dusen, "The Trade of Revolutionary Connecticut," 63; Linda Susan Luchowski, "Sunshine Soldiers: New Haven and the American Revolution," 301.

34 Meeting, December 13, 1763, Durham Town Records. Also Meetings of December 2, 1746, December 13, 1748, December 11, 1750, December 12, 1752, December 13, 1757, December 11, 1759, December 2, 1764, and December 10, 1771.

35 Fowler, *History of Durham*, 44.

36 Bushman, *From Puritan to Yankee*, 19-20, 12.

37 Fowler, *History of Durham*, 302-303, 102-103; Meeting, December 14, 1773, Durham Town Records.

38 *Connecticut Courant* (Hartford), June 30, 1772; Moore and Day, *Richard Austin*, 27ff; Fowler, *History of Durham*, 299ff.

CHAPTER II

1 *Connecticut Courant* (Hartford), November 19, 26, December 10, 1771, October 22, 1772; Albert E. Van Dusen, "The Trade of Revolutionary Connecticut," 142.

2 Van Dusen, "The Trade of Revolutionary Connecticut," 116.

3 *Connecticut Courant* (Hartford), January 18, 1774.

4 Richard L. Bushman, *From Puritan to Yankee: Character and the Social Order in Connecticut, 1690-1765*, p. 287; Richard J. Purcell, *Connecticut in Transition: 1775-1818*, p. 9.

5 William Chauncey Fowler, *History of Durham, Connecticut: From the First Grant of Land in 1662 to 1866*, pp. 306, 308, 311, 321, 332; Edith Austin Moore and William Allen Day, comps., *The Descendants of Richard Austin of Charlestown, Massachusetts, 1638*, pp. 55-56; Linda Susan Luchowski, "Sunshine Soldiers: New Haven and the American Revolution," 14, 16, 18, 103; Van Dusen, "The Trade of Revolutionary Connecticut," 20.

6 Elias Austin Will, October 12, 1776, File 1777, No. 118, Estate Papers, Middletown Probate District, Records of the Probate Courts, RG 4, Connecticut State Archives; Milton H. Whited, "Elias Austin, 1718-1776," n. p.; Sarah Jones to Stephen Austin, Elijah and Archibald Austin, Moses Austin, Martha and Moses Bates, Gloriana Eliot, Deed, July 8, 1782, Grantees, vol. 9, p. 235, Durham Town Records.

7 Sarah Jones to Stephen Austin, Elijah and Archibald Austin, Moses Austin,

Martha and Moses Bates, Gloriana Eliot, Deed, July 8, 1782, Grantees, vol. 9, p. 235, Durham Town Records.

8   Moses Austin to Stephen Austin, Private Account, December 20, 1801, Stephen Austin to James Austin, July 9, 1800, Austin Papers; *Connecticut Courant* (Hartford), December 24, 1782; Van Dusen, *Middletown*, 23, 30; Martin, *Merchants and Trade*, 102-107, 140-157.

9   Fowler, *Durham*, 291, 302-303, 321, 323, 325; Samuel Bates's tombstone, Durham Cemetery; Inscriptions, p. 6, Durham Town Collection; Sarah Jones to Stephen Austin, Elijah and Archibald Austin, Moses Austin, Martha and Moses Bates, Gloriana Eliot, Deed, July 8, 1782, Grantees, vol. 9, p. 235, Durham Town Records; Moore and Day, *Richard Austin*, 61.

10 James G. Percival, "Report," *The Mattabesset Silver Lead Mining Co.: Reports of James G. Percival, et al., with the By-laws of the Company*, 11-14; Van Dusen, *Middletown*, 19-21; *History of Middlesex County, Connecticut, With Biographical Sketches of Its Prominent Men*, 76; Edna Perry Deckler, comp., "Austin-Perry Memorandum," *Stirpes*, 7 (December, 1967), 151; James Alexander Gardner, *Lead King: Moses Austin*, 17.

11 Van Dusen, *Middletown*, 22-24, 34-35.

12 *Connecticut Courant* (Hartford), August 18, 1777, and various issues 1777-1781; Van Dusen, "The Trade of Revolutionary Connecticut," 246-252, 256; Albert E. Van Dusen, *Connecticut*, 163.

13 John Warner Barber, *Connecticut Historical Collections*, 48; Margaret E. Martin, *Merchants and Trade of the Connecticut River Valley, 1750-1820*, pp. 74-88; Van Dusen, "The Trade of Revolutionary Connecticut," 257.

14 Chester McArthur Destler, "Barnabas Deane and Barnabas Deane & Company," *Connecticut Historical Society Bulletin*, 35 (January, 1970), 13, 16-17; Chester McArthur Destler, "Barnabas Deane and Barnabas Deane & Company," 20, 29; Stephen Austin to Wadsworth, October 16, 18, 1780, August 9, 24, 1782, May 5, 1791, Wadsworth Papers; [Stephen Austin], Examination of Bankrupt, January 31, 1804, Case 204, Bankruptcy Records, U.S. District Court for the Eastern District of Pennsylvania, RG 21, Records of District Courts, Federal Archives and Records Center, Philadelphia. (This document will be cited hereafter as: "SA, Examination of Bankrupt.")

15 Carl Bridenbaugh and Jessica Bridenbaugh, *Rebels and Gentlemen: Philadelphia in the Age of Franklin*, 26-27; George Winthrop Geib, "A History of Philadelphia, 1776-1789," p. 170; Rezin Fenton Duvall, "Philadelphia's Maritime Commerce with the British Empire, 1783-1789," pp. 101, 354.

16 Jedidiah Morse, *The American Universal Geography: Or a View of the Present State of All the Empires, Kingdoms, States and Republicks in the Known World, and of the United States of America in Particular*, vol. 1, p. 329; Sam Bass Warner, Jr., *The Private City: Philadelphia in Three Periods of Its Growth*, 3-9; Bridenbaugh and Bridenbaugh, *Rebels and Gentlemen*, 4-7; Geib, "History of Philadelphia," 15, 39, 167-168; Duvall, "Philadelphia's Maritime Commerce," 36-38; *Southwark, Moyamensing, Weccacoe, Passyunk, Dock Ward for Two Hundred and Seventy Years*, 21; Ellis Paxon Oberholtzer, *Philadelphia: A History of the City and Its People, A Record of 225 Years*, vol. 1, p. 34; John Russell Young, *Memorial History of the City of Philadelphia From Its First Settlement to the Year 1895*, vol. 1, pp. 371, 373.

17 William Henry Egle, ed., *Pennsylvania Archives*, 3rd Series, vol. 16, p. 778; SA, Examination of Bankrupt; Duvall, "Philadelphia's Maritime Commerce," 350, 353; Robert A. East, *Business Enterprise in the American Revolution Era*, 239.

18   Geib, "History of Philadelphia," 167-168, 174; Oberholtzer, *Philadelphia*, 314; *Macpherson's Directory for the City and Suburbs of Philadelphia*, n.p.; Warner, *Private City*, 6-7.
19   Genealogical Notes, in Eugene C. Barker, ed., *The Austin Papers*, vol. 2, pt. 1, p. 1; Stephen Austin to Moses Austin, February 23, 1801, Moses Austin to Stephen Austin, Private Account, February 20, 1801, Austin Papers; Egle, *Pennsylvania Archives*, 3rd Series, vol. 16, p. 778; Isaac Weld, Jr., *Travels Through the States of North America and the Provinces of Upper and Lower Canada During the Years 1795, 1796, and 1797*, p. 54; Barber, *Connecticut Historical Collections*, 48; Van Dusen, "The Trade of Revolutionary Connecticut," 249-252; *Southwark, Moyamensing, Weccacoe, Passyunk, Dock Ward for Two Hundred and Seventy Years*, 19.
20   [Joseph Poultney], "A Letter of Joseph Poultney," *Pennsylvania Magazine of History and Biography*, 52 (1928), 95.
21   East, *Business Enterprise in the American Revolution Era*, 257.
22   Fuller to John Donaldson, November 17, 1784, Benjamin Fuller Papers.
23   Fuller to Francis West, November 17, 1784, Fuller Papers; East, *Business Enterprise in the American Revolution Era*, 246; Duvall, "Philadelphia's Maritime Commerce," 131, 382-383.
24   Genealogical Notes in Barker, *Austin Papers*, vol. 2, pt. 1, p. 1, Stephen Austin, Account, n. d., in *ibid.*, 63.
25   Moses Austin to Mary Brown, January 25, 1785, Austin Papers.
26   Agreement, February 28, 1676, Indenture, October 13, 1682, Austin Papers; *Pennsylvania Journal* (Philadelphia), September 12, 1771; Family Bible, Line of Mary Mitchell, Genealogy of Haley Bryan Perry, Haley Bryan Perry Papers.
27   Henry Simpson, *The Lives of Eminent Philadelphians, Now Deceased*, 381-382.
28   Duvall, "Philadelphia's Maritime Commerce," 46; Charles Henry Hart, "Colonel John Nixon," *Pennsylvania Magazine of History and Biography*, 1 (1877), 200; Estate of Isaac Sharp Esq deceased to Benjamin Fuller, February 16, 1769, Fuller to Samuel Sharp, August 13, 1785, Fuller to Judith Sober, April 8, 1788, Fuller Papers.
29   Benjamin Fuller to John Mitchell, June 25, 1785, Fuller to John Hathorn and Edward Dunlop, June 30, 1785, Fuller Papers; *Macpherson's Directory*, n. p.
30   Abia Brown to Maria Brown, July 15, 1780, in Harriet Smither, ed., *The Papers of Mirabeau Buonaparte Lamar*, vol. 5, p. 5.
31   Benjamin Fuller to John Mitchell, June 25, 1785, Fuller Papers; [Laura Bryan Parker, ed.], "A Letter from Mary (Mrs. Moses) Austin," *Quarterly* of the Texas State Historical Association, 10 (1907), 343.
32   Benjamin Fuller to John Mitchell, September 30, 1785, Fuller Papers; Genealogical Notes, in Barker, *Austin Papers*, vol. 2, pt. 1, p. 1. Maria was a common nickname for women named "Mary." Moses' Richmond contemporary and later great jurist, John Marshall, used it for his wife (Albert J. Beveridge, *The Life of John Marshall*, vol. 1, pp. 159, 165).

CHAPTER III

1   Virginius Dabney, *Richmond: The Story of a City*, 34.
2   Samuel Mordecai, *Richmond in By-Gone Days: Being Reminiscences of an Old Citizen*, 45-46; Albert J. Beveridge, *The Life of John Marshall*, vol. 1, p. 171;

Benjamin Latrobe, *Plan of Part of the City of Richmond*; Jedidiah Morse, *The American Universal Geography: Or a View of the Present State of All the Empires, Kingdoms, States and Republicks in the Known World, and of the United States of America in Particular*, vol. 1, p. 382.

3   "An Old Virginia Correspondence," *Atlantic Monthly*, 84 (1899), 537; Dabney, *Richmond*, 31; Henry Howe, *Historical Collections of Virginia*, 308; W. Asbury Christian, *Richmond: Her Past and Present*, 22-23.

4   Christian, *Richmond*, 15, 19-21, 27; Mordecai, *Richmond*, 40-41; Dabney, *Richmond*, 33; Louise Ellyson, *Richmond on the James*, n. p.; Marylou Rhodes, *Landmarks of Richmond: Places to Know and See in the Nation's Most Historic City*, 117-118; John P. Little, *History of Richmond*, 65.

5   Modecai, *Richmond*, 63; Thomas Rutherford, "Narrative of Thomas Rutherford, 1786-1852," 24; Beveridge, *Life of Marshall*, vol. 1, p. 166; Little, *History of Richmond*, 89; Isaac Weld, Jr., *Travels Through the States of North America and the Provinces of Upper and Lower Canada During the Years 1795, 1796, and 1797*, pp. 190-191.

6   Christian, *Richmond*, 21; Beveridge, *Life of Marshall*, vol. 1, p. 200; "An Old Virginia Correspondence," *Atlantic Monthly*, 84, p. 537; Howe, *Virginia*, 308; *Virginia Gazette and General Advertiser* (Richmond), September 28, 1791.

7   Harry M. Ward and Harold E. Greer, Jr., *Richmond During the Revolution*, 132-133; Mordecai, *Richmond*, 25-30, 210; George T. Starnes, *Sixty Years of Branch Banking in Virginia*, 16.

8   Thomas Rutherford to Hawsley and Rutherford, December 26, 1785, Thomas Rutherford Letter Book; Dabney, *Richmond*, 47.

9   Rutherford to Hawsley and Rutherford, February 21, 1786, Rutherford Letter Book.

10 Rutherford to Hawsley and Rutherford, December 6, 1786, Rutherford Letter Book.

11 Austin to Westcott, June 28, 1787, Thomas W. Streeter Collection.

12 Rutherford to Hawsley and Rutherford, December 6, 1786, Rutherford Letter Book.

13 Austin to Westcott, June 28, 1787, Streeter Collection; [Richmond City, Virginia,] Hustings Order Books #1 and #2; Benjamin Fuller to Moses Austin, September 22, 1785, Fuller Papers; Petition and Remonstrance from the Merchants of the City of Richmond, October 30, 1787, Petitions; Rutherford, "Narrative," 33.

14 Austin to Westcott, June 28, 1787, Streeter Collection; Genealogical Notes in Eugene C. Barker, ed., *The Austin Papers*, vol. 2, pt. 1, p. 1.

15 Richmond Personal Property Tax List, 1781-1792; Richmond Taxable Property, 1787; Fuller to Austin, January 31, 1787, Fuller Papers; Christian, *Richmond*, 30; Dabney, *Richmond*, 34.

16 Mordecai, *Richmond*, 199; Henrico County, Virginia, Deed Book 2, pp. 628-629; Rhodes, *Landmarks of Richmond*, 118; Weld, *Travels*, 190-191.

17 Maria to Moses Austin, August 24, 1789, in Barker, *Austin Papers*, vol 2, pt. 1, pp. 7-9.

18 Austin to Wadsworth, January 20, 1788, Wadsworth Papers.

19 Robert A. East, *Business Enterprise in the American Revolution Era*, 249; John C. Miller, *The Federalist Era, 1789-1801*, pp. 1-4.

20 Austin to Wadsworth, January 20, 1788, Wadsworth Papers.

21 SA, Examination of Bankrupt; Austin to Wadsworth, March 28, April 27, May 12, June 25, July 20, 1788, January 17, 1790, Wadsworth Papers; Fuller to Moses Austin, January 8, 1788, Fuller Papers.

22 Stephen Austin to Wadsworth, January 20, 1788, July 4, 1789, Wadsworth Papers; SA, Examination of Bankrupt.

23 William Cullen Bryant, ed., *Picturesque America; or, The Land We Live In*, vol. 1, pp. 339, 341.

24 Joseph Martin, *A New and Comprehensive Gazetteer of Virginia and the District of Columbia*, 466, 467; Morse, *American Universal Geography*, Map.

25 Lyman Chalkley, "Before the Gates of the Wilderness Road: The Settlement of Southwestern Virginia," *Virginia Magazine of Biography and History*, 30 (1922), 183-184, 188; Ray Allen Billington, *Westward Expansion: A History of the American Frontier*, 147-148, 161, 163.

26 SA, Examination of Bankrupt; Moses and Stephen Austin to Governor, May 22, 1789, Executive Papers.

27 Thomas Jefferson, *Notes on Virginia*, 26.

28 L.W. Currier, *Zinc and Lead Region of Southwestern Virginia*, 75; William Kohler, "The Lead Mines," 1; Wythe Lead and Zinc Mine Company, Abstract of Title; "Austinville Mine Completes Two Centuries," *Commonwealth*, vol. 23, no. 12 (December, 1956), 54; Arthur Hecht, "Lead Production in Virginia During the Seventeenth and Eighteenth Centuries," *West Virginia History*, 25 (April, 1964), 174; Mary B. Kegley, "The First Settlers," *Wythe County Historical Review*, 1 (July, 1971), 17; Frederick B. Kegley, "Shot Tower at Jackson's Ferry," *Journal of the Roanoke Historical Society*, vol. 3, no. 1 (Summer, 1966), 2; Frederick B. Kegley, "A Sentinel of the Southwest: The Old Shot Tower at Jackson's Ferry on New River," 3.

29 Campbell County, Virginia, Bicentennial Commission, Historical Committee, comp., *Lest It Be Forgotten: A Scrapbook of Campbell County, Virginia*, 124-127; Rosa Faulkner Yancey, *Lynchburg and Its Neighbors*, 8; Philip Lightfoot Scruggs, *Lynchburg, Virginia*, 3-5; H. H. Gwathmey, *Historical Register of Virginians in the Revolution*, 489; Dorothy T. Potter and Clifton W. Potter, Jr., *Lynchburg: "The Most Interesting Spot,"* 26-27; "Lynch Law," *William and Mary Quarterly*, ser. 1, vol. 13 (1905), 203-205; Crockett to Preston, April 7, 1779, in "The Preston Papers Relating to Western Virginia," *Virginia Magazine of History and Biography*, 26 (1918), 371-372; Agnes Graham Sanders Riley, "James Newell, 1749-1823," The Historical Society of Washington County, Virginia, *Publications*, ser. 2, no. 8 (July, 1970), 26; Hecht, "Lead Production in Virginia During the Seventeenth and Eighteenth Centuries," *West Virginia History*, vol. 25, p. 177.

30 War Office to Governor of Virginia, June 6, 1782, in William P. Palmer and Sherwin McRae, eds., *Calendar of Virginia State Papers*, vol. 3, p. 188, Charles Dick to Colonel George Muter, September 5, 1780, in *ibid.*, vol. 1, p. 372, David Ross to Governor, March 27, 1781, in *ibid.*, vol. 1, p. 602; Julian P. Boyd, ed., *The Papers of Thomas Jefferson*, vol. 17, p. 24.

31 Colonel William Preston to Governor Jefferson, April 13, 1781, in Palmer and McRae, *Calendar of Virginia State Papers*, vol. 2, p. 36, Captain John Peyton to Colonel Thos. Meriwether, February 20, 1785, in *ibid.*, vol. 4, p. 11, Attorney General's Opinion, July 17, 1785, in *ibid.*, vol. 4, p. 42, William Hay to Governor, June 10, 1782, in *ibid.*, vol. 3, pp. 189-190; Kegley, "A Sentinel of the Southwest," n. p.; Jefferson, *Notes on Virginia*, 27.

32 Jefferson, *Notes on Virginia*, 26-27; Arthur Harrison Cole, ed., *Industrial and Commercial Correspondence of Alexander Hamilton Anticipating His Report on Manufactures*, 95.

33 Kohler, "The Lead Mines," 1; Captain John Peyton to Colonel Thos Meriwether, February 20, 1785, in Palmer and McRae, *Calendar of Virginia State*

Papers, vol. 4, p. 11; Hecht, "Lead Production in Virginia During the Seventeenth and Eighteenth Centuries," *West Virginia History*, vol. 25, pp. 174-175; Jefferson, *Notes on Virginia*, 27; Blair Niles, *The James: From Iron Gate to the Sea*, 206-209.

34 SA, Examination of Bankrupt; Moses and Stephen Austin to Governor, May 22, 1789, Executive Papers.

35 Moses and Stephen Austin to Governor, May 22, 1789, Executive Papers.

36 Moses Austin and Company to Wadsworth, October 12, 1789, Stephen Austin to Wadsworth, November 29, 1789, Wadsworth Papers.

37 Helen Jordan, "Selections From the Military Correspondence of Colonel Henry Bouquet, 1756-1764," *Pennsylvania Magazine of History and Biography*, 33 (1909), 225-226; Stephen Austin to Wadsworth, November 29, 1789, Moses Austin and Company to Wadsworth, February 4, 1790, Wadsworth Papers.

38 Austin to Wadsworth, January 17, 1790, November 29, 1789, Wadsworth Papers.

39 Austin to Wadsworth, January 24, 1790, Wadsworth Papers.

40 J. H. P., "The Wythe Lead Mines," n. p.; Wythe Lead and Zinc Company, Abstract of Title.

41 *The Virginia State Capitol, Richmond, Virginia*, n. p.

42 *Ibid.*; Colonel William Davis to Governor, February 16, 1789, in Palmer and McRae, *Calendar of Virginia State Papers*, vol. 4, p. 563, Report of Committee as to Removal into New Capitol, June 9, 1789, in *ibid.*, vol. 4, p. 643, Hay to Governor, June 11, 1790, in *ibid.*, vol. 5, pp. 150-151.

43 *The Virginia State Capitol*, n. p.; Report of the Committee to Whom was Referred the Letter of the Directors of the Public Buildings With Their Accounts, &c., Through Mr. Edward Carrington, and Agreed to by the House, December 14, 1789, in Palmer and McRae, *Calendar of Virginia State Papers*, vol. 5, pp. 77-78; Mordecai, *Richmond*, 58.

44 Report of the Committee to Whom was Referred the Letter of the Directors of the Public Buildings With Their Accounts, &c., Through Mr. Edward Carrington, and Agreed to by the House, December 14, 1789, in Palmer and McRae, *Calendar of Virginia State Papers*, vol. 5, p. 78.

45 Hay to Governor, January 6, 1790, Executive Papers; Journal of Council, January 30, 1788, in Palmer and McRae, *Calendar of Virginia State Papers*, vol. 4, p. 207.

46 Moses Austin and Company to Wadsworth, February 4, 1790, Stephen Austin to Wadsworth, January 24, 1790, Wadsworth Papers; Burr, Bill, February 22, 1795, Austin Papers.

47 Austin to Wadsworth, January 17, 1790, Wadsworth Papers; Victor S. Clark, *History of Manufactures in the United States*, vol. I, p. 288; F. W. Tausig, *The Tariff History of the United States*, 10-15.

48 Stephen and Moses Austin to Governor Randolph, n. d., Executive Papers.

49 Governor Randolph to Thomas Jefferson, July 10, 1790, in Boyd, *Papers of Thomas Jefferson*, vol. 17, pp. 23, 24.

50 Arthur Campbell, R. Sayers, Wm. Migomry to Beverley Randolph and Council of State, June 23, 1790, enclosure in Stephen and Moses Austin to Governor Randolph, n. d., Executive Papers. Editors Palmer and McRae in *Calendar of Virginia State Papers*, vol. 5, p. 186, assigned the date of July 13 to the Austins' letter. That date could not be accurate, since Randolph wrote Jefferson on July 10 after receiving the Austins' letter with the enclosed report.

51 *Tariff Acts Passed By the Congress of the United States From 1789 to 1909*, p.

18; Jefferson to John Harve, July 25, 1790, in Boyd, *Papers of Jefferson*, vol. 17, p. 270, Notes to Beverley Randolph to Jefferson, July 10, 1790, in *ibid.*, vol. 17, p. 24; Act of Congress, December 6, 1790, in Palmer and McRae, *Calendar of Virginia State Papers*, vol. 5, p. 267.

52 Cole, *Correspondence of Hamilton*, 304; Miller, *Federalist Era*, 64-65.

53 *Journal of the House of Delegates of the Commonwealth of Virginia*, December 24, 1790, p. 156.

54 Hay to Governor, June 15, 1790, Executive Papers.

55 *Journal of the House of Delegates of the Commonwealth of Virginia*, December 24, 1790, p. 156.

56 *Ibid.*

57 Hay to Austin, January 4, 1791, in Palmer and McRae, *Calendar of Virginia State Papers*, vol. 5, pp. 241-242; Minutes of Directors' Meetings, Capitol Accounts, January 19, 1791, Executive Papers.

58 *Virginia Gazette and General Advertiser* (Richmond), September 8, 1790, June 22-July 6, August 17, 1791.

59 Merchants and Inhabitants of the City of Richmond to General Assembly, November 26, 1787, Petitions; "Bank of the United States," *Virginia Magazine of History and Biography*, 8 (January, 1907), 294; Miller, *Federalist Era*, 55-62; Starnes, *Sixty Years of Branch Banking in Virginia*, 18-21, 24; James O. Wettereau, "Branches of the First Bank of the United States," *Journal of Economic History*, 2 (December, 1942), 76.

60 *Virginia Gazette and General Advertiser* (Richmond), January 5, 1791.

61 *Ibid.*, September 14, 1791.

62 *Ibid.*, August 31, 1791.

63 Cole, *Correspondence of Hamilton*, 93, 95.

64 Wythe Lead & Zinc Mine Company, Abstract of Title; Stephen Austin, Moses Austin, Saml. Paine, Charles Lynch, John Field, Bond, February 25, 1792, in Bankruptcy Records.

65 *Virginia Gazette and General Advertiser* (Richmond), December 14, 1791, February 1, 1792.

66 SA, Examination of Bankrupt.

67 Stephen and Moses Austin, Agreement, January 18, 1792, Austin Papers.

68 Moses Austin and Company to John Marshall, William Nelson and William Hay, Bond, February 25, 1792, William Hay to Sir, May 9, 1804, Bankruptcy Records.

69 Moses Austin & Company to John Marshall, William Nelson, and William Hay, February 25, 1792, SA, Examination of Bankrupt; Christian, *Richmond*, 44; Mordecai, *Richmond*, 44; Stephen Austin and Moses Austin, Agreement, February 26, 1792, Austin Papers.

70 SA, Examination of Bankrupt.

CHAPTER IV

1 Crockett to Governor, September 5, 1790, in William P. Palmer and Sherwin McRae, eds., *Calendar of Virginia State Papers*, vol. 5, p. 205.

2 *Virginia Gazette and General Advertiser* (Richmond), December 21, 1791, January 11, 1792. The Austins still may have had all the hands they wanted. In an accounting in April, 1797, the firm listed 20 slaves, at least 14 of whom were males (Schedule of Property, April 26, 1797, Austin Papers).

3 Alexander Hamilton, "Report on Manufactures," in Arthur Harrison Cole,

ed., *Industrial and Commercial Correspondence of Alexander Hamilton Antici-pating His Report on Manufactures*, 288.

4   SA, Examination of Bankrupt.

5   *Virginia Gazette and General Advertiser* (Richmond), December 21, 1791, Jan-uary 11, 1792.

6   SA, Examination of Bankrupt.

7   P. Dick to ____, Note, November 26, 1794, Etting-Gratz Crogan Papers; Wil-liam Walter Hening, *The Statutes at Large; Being a Collection of All the Laws of Virginia From the First Session of the Legislature in the Year 1619*, vol. 1, p. 158.

8   Joseph and Rhodney Anthony to Moses Austin and Company, Deed, Novem-ber 11, 1792, Campbell County, Virginia, Deed Book 5, pp. 152-153; Moses Austin and Company to Charles Austin, Deed, May 10, 1800, *ibid.*, 606-608; Agnes Graham Sanders Riley, "James Newell, 1749-1823," The Historical Society of Washington County, Virginia, *Publications*, ser. 2, no. 8 (July, 1970), 23; Samuel Mordecai, *Richmond in By-Gone Days: Being Reminiscences of an Old Citizen*, 53; *Virginia Gazette and General Advertiser* (Richmond), August 31, 1791; Virginius Dabney, *Richmond: The Story of a City*, 37.

9   *Gazette of the United States* (Philadelphia), August 15, 1792.

10 SA, Examination of Bankrupt.

11 *Ibid.*; Moses Austin and Stephen Austin to Thomas Ruston, Indenture, November 2, 1792, Wythe County, Virginia, Deed Book 1, pp. 147-148; Ruston to Moses Austin, June 1, 1794, in Eugene C. Barker, ed., *The Austin Papers*, vol. 2, pt. 1, p. 11.

12 SA, Examination of Bankrupt; William Kohler, "The Lead Mines," 3.

13 Beverley Randolph to Thomas Jefferson, July 10, 1790, in Julian P. Boyd, ed., *The Papers of Thomas Jefferson*, vol. 17, pp. 23-24, Thomas Jefferson to John Harvie, Jr., July 25, 1790, in *ibid.*, 270; Various Accounts, Austin Papers; Harry Toulmin (Marion Tinling and Godfrey Davies, eds.), *The Western Coun-try in 1793, Reports on Kentucky and Virginia*, 102.

14 Samuel Coleman to Governor, July 11, 1794, in Palmer and McRae, *Calendar of Virginia State Papers*, vol. 7, p. 212.

15 Dabney Minor to Lieutenant Governor, August 7, 1794, in *ibid.*, 249-250.

16 Directors to Governor, June 14, 1792, Executive Papers.

17 Hay to Moses Austin & Co., June 12, 1792, in Directors to Governor, June 14, 1792, Executive Papers.

18 Directors to Governor, June 14, 1792, Executive Papers.

19 *Journal of the House of Delegates of the Commonwealth of Virginia*, December 14, 1792, pp. 187-188; Hening, *Statues at Large*, vol. 13, pp. 540-541.

20 Coleman to Governor, July 10, 1794, in Palmer and McRae, *Calendar of Vir-ginia State Papers*, vol. 7, p. 211.

21 Coleman to Governor, July 11, 1794, in *ibid.*, vol. 7, p. 212.

22 *Journal of the House of Delegates of the Commonwealth of Virginia*, December 13, 1794, pp. 89, 88.

23 William Fourchee to Governor, December 12, 1797, in Palmer and McRae, *Calendar of Virginia State Papers*, vol. 8, p. 455, Fourchee to Governor, Octo-ber 23, 1798, in *ibid.*, 521-522; Governor to Directors, March 11, 1797, Execu-tive Letter Book, Executive Papers.

24 Statement of Stephen Austin, n. d., in Barker, *Austin Papers*, vol. 2, pt. 1, p. 63, Ruston to Moses Austin, June 1, 1794, in *ibid.*, 10-11; Ruston to Moses Austin, June 6, 1794, Austin Papers.

25 Stephen Austin to Brother, February 23, 1801, Austin Papers; Statement of

Stephen Austin, in Barker, *Austin Papers*, vol. 2, pt. 1, p. 63. Stephen in 1800 claimed the Manning Merrill debt stood at $700 (Stephen Austin to James Austin, July 9, 1800, Austin Papers).

26 Blanchard to Moses Austin, May 17, 1795, in Barker, *Austin Papers*, vol. 2, pt. 1, p. 22.

27 Austin to Wadsworth, June 25, 1795, Wadsworth Papers.

28 Stephen Austin to Moses Austin, March 23, 1801, Austin Papers.

29 SA, Examination of Bankrupt.

30 Blanchard to Moses Austin, March 17, 1795, in Barker, *Austin Papers*, vol. 2, pt. 1, p. 22; Stephen Austin to Michael Gratz, August 14, 1795, in Byars, *B. and M. Gratz*, 248-249.

31 Stephen Austin to Moses Austin, February 23, 1801, Austin Papers; Stephen Austin to Michael Gratz, August 14, 1795, in Byars, *B. and M. Gratz*, 248-249.

32 Account of Robert Gamble, February 18, 1795, Austin Papers.

33 Blanchard to Moses Austin, May 17, 1795, in Barker, *Austin Papers*, vol. 2, pt. 1, p. 22.

34 Samuel Coleman to Council, February 25, 1790, in Palmer and McRae, *Calendar of Virginia State Papers*, vol. 5, p. 119, A. Lewis to Governor, March 11, 1793, in *ibid.*, vol. 6, p. 304, Moses Austin to James Wood, December 12, 1795, in *ibid.*, vol. 8, p. 324, Samuel Paine to Governor, March 28, 1806, in *ibid.*, vol. 9, pp. 474-475; Governor to James McGavock, May 24, December 10, 1794, Governor to Stephen and Moses Austin, May 24, 1794, Governor to Stephen and Moses Austin & Co., December 10, 1794, Executive Letter Book, Executive Papers.

35 Wythe County Deed Book 1, pp. 184-185, 195, 303, Book 2, pp. 12, 44, 413-414; Wythe Lead and Zinc Mine Company, Abstract of Title; Partnership Agreement, April 20, 1796, in Barker, *Austin Papers*, vol. 2, pt. 1, pp. 28-29; Mordecai, *Richmond*, 199; R. Gamble to John Preston, April 7, 1796, Preston Papers; *Virginia Gazette and General Advertiser* (Richmond), June 1, 15, 1796.

36 Fuller to Moses Austin, March 16, 1786, Fuller Papers.

37 George Edward Pankey, *John Pankey of Manakin Town, Virginia, and His Descendants*, 116-117; Frances Earle Lutz, *Chesterfield—An Old Virginia County*, 136-137.

38 List of Militia, Wythe County, 1796, Executive Papers; Wythe County Court, Order Book, 1795-1805, p. 84; W. Tate to Governor, May 28, 1795, in Palmer and McRae, *Calendar of Virginia State Papers*, vol. 8, p. 250; James Newell, Certification of Moses Austin as Captain of Militia, July 4, 1796, Wythe County Deed Book 1, p. 390.

CHAPTER V

1 George P. Garrison, ed., "A Memorandum of M. Austin's Journey from the Lead Mines in the County of Wythe in the State of Virginia to the Lead Mines in the Province of Louisiana West of the Mississippi, 1796-1797," *American Historical Review*, 5 (1900), 523-524.

2 Dudley G. Wooten, ed., *A Comprehensive History of Texas, 1685 to 1897*, vol. 1, p. 440.

3 Jedidiah Morse, *The American Universal Geography: Or a View of the Present State of All the Empires, Kingdoms, States and Republicks in the Known World, and of the United States of America in Particular*, vol. 1, 757; Henry Rowe Schoolcraft, *Travels in the Central Portions of the Mississippi Valley*,

240; Account with Baker & Conejas, 1794, Observations on Account, June, 1802, Austin Papers.

4   Pierre Charles de Hault Delassus Deluzieres, *An Official Account of the Situation, Soil, Produce, &c. of that part of Louisiana, Which lies between the Mouth of the Missouri and New Madrid, or L'Anse a la Graise, and on the West Side of the Mississippi, Together with an Abstract of the Spanish Government, &c.*, 3.

5   Moses Austin, Memoire, January 26, 1797, translation in James A. Gardner, "The Life of Moses Austin," 774.

6   Austin to John Preston, November 7, 1796, Preston Papers; Garrison, "Memorandum of M. Austin's Journey," *American Historical Review*, vol. 5, p. 526.

7   Garrison, "A Memorandum of M. Austin's Journey," *American Historical Review*, vol. 5, pp. 523-524.

8   *Ibid.*, 525-526.

9   *Ibid.*, 527.

10 *Ibid.*, 529.

11 *Ibid.*, 531.

12 *Ibid.*, 531.

13 *Ibid.*, 532.

14 *Ibid.*

15 *Ibid.*, 533, 532.

16 Schoolcraft, *Travels in the Central Portions of the Mississippi Valley*, 242-243.

17 *Ibid.*, 242.

18 Garrison, "A Memorandum of M. Austin's Journey," *American Historical Review*, vol. 5, pp. 535, 534; Louis Houck, *A History of Missouri From the Earliest Explorations and Settlements Until the Admission of the State into the Union*, vol. 3, p. 60.

19 Garrison, "A Memorandum of M. Austin's Journey," *American Historical Review*, vol. 5, p. 535; Houck, *History of Missouri*, vol. 1, p. 58n., vol. 2, p. 48; Moses Austin to Lieutenant Governor DeLassus, February 5, 1800, in Eugene C. Barker, ed., *The Austin Papers*, vol. 2, pt. 1, pp. 49-50.

20 Edwin C. McReynolds, *Missouri: A History of the Crossroads State*, 25; Schoolcraft, *Travels*, 242; Houck, *History of Missouri*, vol. 1, p. 349; Gregory M. Franzwa, *The Story of Old Ste. Genevieve*, 41-54.

21 Floyd Calvin Shoemaker, "Judge John Rice Jones: The Living Chronicle of Passing Times," 3, 5-7; Gayle Talbot, "John Rice Jones," *Southwestern Historical Quarterly*, 35 (October, 1931), 146; Floyd Calvin Shoemaker, "Fathers of the State," *Missouri Historical Review*, 10 (October, 1915), 5-6.

22 Moses Austin, *A Summary Description of the Lead Mines in Upper Louisiana: Also, An Estimate of Their Produce, For Three Years Past*, 17-18.

23 Henry Rowe Schoolcraft, *Journal of a Tour into the Interior of Missouri and Arkansaw, from Potosi, or Mine a Burton, in Missouri Territory, in a South-West Direction, toward the Rocky Mountains; Performed in the Years 1818 and 1819*, p. 3; Henry Rowe Schoolcraft, *Scenes and Adventures in the Semi-Alpine Region of the Ozark Mountains of Missouri and Arkansas*, 145; Henry Rowe Schoolcraft, *A View of the Lead Mines of Missouri: Including Some Observations on the Mineralogy, Geology, Geography, Antiquities, Soil, Climate, Population, and Productions of Missouri and Arkansaw, and Other Sections of the Western Country*, 52.

24 Welton Lyle Willms, "Lead Mining in Missouri, 1700-1811," pp. 45-51; Walter B. Stevens, *Centennial History of Missouri (The Center State); One Hundred Years in the Union, 1820-1921*, vol. 2, p. 403; Christian Schultz, *Travels on an Inland Voyage Through the States of New York, Pennsylvania, Virginia, Ohio,*

Kentucky and Tennessee and Through the Territories of Indiana, Louisiana, Mississippi and New Orleans Performed in the Years 1807 and 1808, including a Tour of nearly 6000 Miles, vol. 2, pp. 49-50.

25 Austin, *Summary Description of the Lead Mines*, 4.

26 *Ibid.*, 17-18; Moses Austin, "Observation on Lead Mines," in *American State Papers, Public Lands*, vol. 3, p. 708.

27 Garrison, "A Memorandum of M. Austin's Journey," *American Historical Review*, vol. 5, p. 540.

28 Austin, *Summary Description of the Lead Mines*, 8; Garrison, "A Memorandum of M. Austin's Journey," *American Historical Review*, vol. 5, p. 540.

29 Austin, *Summary Description of the Lead Mines*, 9-10; Schoolcraft, *View of the Lead Mines of Missouri*, 94-97.

30 Garrison, "A Memorandum of M. Austin Journey," *American Historical Review*, vol. 5, p. 540.

31 Austin, Memoire, in Gardner, "Life of Moses Austin," 772-774; Garrison, "A Memorandum of M. Austin's Journey," *American Historical Review*, vol. 5, p. 540.

32 Austin, Memoire, in Gardner, "Life of Moses Austin," 772.

33 Willms, "Lead Mining in Missouri," 43-53; Houck, *History of Missouri*, vol. 1, pp. 360, 367-378; Austin, *Summary Description of the Lead Mines*, 10; Moses Austin to Kendall and Bates, [December, 1797], Austin Papers.

34 Austin, Memoire, in Gardner, "Life of Moses Austin," 773.

35 Houck, *History of Missouri*, vol. 2, p. 225; Eugene Morrow Violette, "Early Settlements in Missouri," *Missouri Historical Review*, 1 (October, 1906), 46; John C. Miller, *The Federalist Era, 1789-1801*, pp. 186-192.

36 Willms, "Lead Mining in Missouri," 55; Houck, *History of Missouri*, vol. 1, pp. 363-364; Moses Austin to Lieutenant Governor DeLassus, February 5, 1800, in Barker, *Austin Papers*, vol. 2, pt. 1, p. 50.

37 Partnership Agreement, January 26, 1797, in Barker, *Austin Papers*, vol. 2, pt. 1, p. 29.

38 *Ibid.*, 29-31; Austin to Jones, Deed, June 24, 1807, Washington County, Missouri, Deed Book #47, pp. 242-244. Austin told a somewhat different story a decade and a half later when he and Jones squared off in court (See "The Answer of Moses Austin to the Bill of Complaint of John Rice Jones, July 27, 1813, in John Rice Jones vs. Moses Austin, 1812-1813," cited in James Alexander Gardner, *Lead King: Moses Austin*, 44-47. [This document has disappeared since Gardner saw it, and Gardner's excerpts are the only remaining evidence of it.]).

39 François Valle to Austin, [January 28, 1797], in Barker, *Austin Papers*, vol. 2, pt. 1, p. 31; Houck, *History of Missouri*, vol. 1, pp. 217-218.

40 Garrison, "A Memorandum of M. Austin's Journey," *American Historical Review*, vol. 5, p. 541; Jonas Viles, "Population and Extent of Settlement in Missouri before 1804," *Missouri Historical Review*, 5 (July, 1911), 202; Houck, *History of Missouri*, vol. 1, 362-365.

41 "The Answer of Moses Austin," in Gardner, *Lead King*, 51-52.

42 Garrison, "A Memorandum of M. Austin's Journey," *American Historical Review*, vol. 5, p. 542.

43 Stephen Austin to James Austin, June 24, 1797, in Barker, *Austin Papers*, vol. 2, pt. 1, p. 36.

44 Stephen Austin to James Austin, June 29, 1797, in Barker, *Austin Papers*, vol. 2, pt. 1, p. 36-37, Moses and Stephen Austin: Dissolving Partnership, June 15, 1797, in *ibid.*, 35-36; Notice, June 15, 1797, Stephen Austin to Mary Ruston,

June 15, 1797, Joseph Shaw, Receipts, July 18, 19, 1797, Austins to Ruston, Account, January 1, 1797, Austin Papers; Thomas Ruston, Certificates of Discharge, July 7, 1801, February 26, 1802, Book A, p. 148, Bankruptcy Records.

45   SA, Examination of Bankrupt.

46   Genealogical Notes, in Barker, *Austin Papers*, vol. 2, pt. 1, p. 2; Moses and Stephen Austin: Dissolving Partnership, June 15, 1797, in *ibid.*, 35-36.

47   Agreement, June 20, 1797, Moses Austin, Private Account with Stephen Austin, 1782-1797, Austin Papers; Maria and Moses Austin to Stephen Austin, Deed, July 1, 1797, Wythe County, Virginia, Deed Book 2, pp. 147-149.

48   *Tariff Acts Passed By the Congress of the United States From 1789 to 1909*, p. 44; SA, Examination of Bankrupt; Arthur P. Whitaker, "Reed & Forde: Merchant Adventurers of Philadelphia," *Pennsylvania Magazine of History and Biography*, 41 (July, 1937), 257.

49   "The Answer of Moses Austin," in Gardner, *Lead King*, 56-58; Houck, *History of Missouri*, vol. 1, pp. 370-371; Stephen Austin to Moses Austin, June 29, 1797, in Barker, *Austin Papers*, vol. 2, pt. 1, pp. 36-37, Passport, in *ibid.*, 37-38, Moses Austin to Kendall and Bates, [December ____, 1797], in *ibid.*, 38-39, Genealogical Notes, in *ibid.*, 2; Schedule of property left, May, 1798, Austin Papers; Moses Austin to James Newell, Sale of Ferry, May 28, 1798, Wythe County Deed Book 2, pp. 254-255, Moses and Maria Austin to James Austin, Deed, May 25, 1798, in *ibid.*, 264-265, Moses and Maria Austin to Thomas Jackson, Deed, May 26, 1798, in *ibid.*, 288-289.

50   Genealogical Notes, in Barker, *Austin Papers*, vol. 2, pt. 1, p. 2, Note on Passport, in *ibid.*, 38; William Chauncey Fowler, *History of Durham, Connecticut: From the First Grant of Land in 1662 to 1866*, p. 210; Moses Austin to Carlos DeLassus, August 13, 1799, Legajo 216-B, Papeles de Cuba.

Chapter VI

1   *American State Papers, Public Lands*, vol. 3, p. 682; Moses Austin to Kendall and Bates, [December ____, 1797], in Eugene C. Barker, ed., *The Austin Papers*, vol. 2, pt. 1, pp. 38-39.

2   Austin to Kendall and Bates, [December ____, 1797], in Barker, *Austin Papers*, vol. 2, pt. 1, p. 38.

3   *Ibid.*; *American State Papers, Public Lands*, vol. 3, p. 682; Map of Mine a Breton, August, 1799, Mapas y Planos #198, Austin to Carlos DeLassus, August 13, 1799, Legajo 216-B, Papeles de Cuba; Moses Austin, *A Summary Description of the Lead Mines in Upper Louisiana: Also, An Estimate of Their Produce, For Three Years Past*, 8; Henry Rowe Schoolcraft, *A View of the Lead Mines of Missouri: Including Some Observations on the Mineralogy, Geology, Geography, Antiquities, Soil, Climate, Population, and Productions of Missouri and Arkansaw, and Other Sections of the Western Country*, 19.

4   Austin, *Summary Description of the Lead Mines*, 21; *American State Papers, Public Lands*, vol. 3, p. 682; Map of Mine a Breton, August, 1799, Mapas y Planos #198, Papeles de Cuba; Charles Alexandre Lesueur, Mine a Breton, Drawing #42052; Durham Hall, 1871, Photograph, Missouri Historical Society; Gregory M. Franzwa, *The Story of Old Ste. Genevieve*, 26.

5   Richmond City, Virginia, Personal Property Tax List, 1787; *Virginia Gazette and General Advertiser* (Richmond), August 31, 1791, March 7, 1792.

6   Stoddard, *Sketches of Louisiana*, p. 327

7 *Ibid.*, 321-328; Franzwa, *Old Ste. Genevieve*, 31-34, 46-48, 51-52; Lucille Basler, *Ste. Genevieve: Mother of the West, 1725*, p. 25; Louis Houck, *A History of Missouri From the Earliest Explorations and Settlements Until the Admission of the State into the Union*, vol. 1, p. 360.

8 Austin to Kendall and Bates, [December ____, 1797], in Barker, *Austin Papers*, vol. 2, pt. 1, p. 39.

9 Noel M. Loomis and Abraham P. Nasatir, *Pedro Vial and the Roads to Santa Fe*, 414-415; Elizabeth A. H. John, *Storms Brewed in Other Men's Worlds: The Confrontation of Indians, Spanish, and French in the Southwest, 1540-1795*, pp. 657, 731-757; J. B. Valle, et al., Deed of Gift, September 27, 1798, Mines Envelope; Francis Lund vs. Pierre Vial, Folder 380, Roll 24, Ste. Genevieve Archives; Welton Lyle Willms, "Lead Mining in Missouri, 1700-1811," p. 62.

10 "The Answer of Moses Austin to the Bill of Complaint of John Rice Jones, July 27, 1813, in John Rice Jones vs. Moses Austin, 1812-1813," cited in James Alexander Gardner, *Lead King: Moses Austin*, 63.

11 *Ibid.*, 64, 63.

12 *Ibid.*, 64.

13 Willms, "Lead Mining in Missouri," 60.

14 Moses Austin to Lieutenant Governor DeLassus, February 5, 1800, in Barker, *Austin Papers*, vol. 2, pt. 1, 50-51.

15 Austin to DeLassus, August 13, 1799, Legajo 216-B, Papeles de Cuba.

16 François Valle to Carlos DeLassus, August 19, 1799, Legajo 216-B, Papeles de Cuba.

17 DeLassus to Austin, May 14, 1799, Austin Papers; *American State Papers, Public Lands*, vol. 3, p. 699; *Report from the Commissioner of the General Land Office, December 10, 1835*, 24th Cong., 1st Sess., Senate Document #16, in *Missouri Land Claims*, 266-267; Houck, *History of Missouri*, vol. 2, p. 228.

18 Austin to Carlos DeLassus, August 13, 1799, Legajo 216-B, Papeles de Cuba.

19 "The Answer of Moses Austin," in Gardner, *Lead King*, 63; Moses Austin to Lieutenant Governor DeLassus, February 5, 1800, in Barker, *Austin Papers*, vol. 2, pt. 1, p. 51.

20 Houck, *History of Missouri*, vol. 2, pt. 1, p. 327; Moses Austin to Lieutenant Governor DeLassus, February 5, 1800, in Barker, *Austin Papers*, vol. 2, pt. 1, p. 51; *American State Papers, Public Lands*, vol. 3, pp. 671, 683.

21 "The Answer of Moses Austin," in Gardner, *Lead King*, 67-68.

22 Maria and Moses Austin to William Shannon, Deed, March 1, 1811, Ste. Genevieve County, Missouri, Deed Book B, page 138; Lucille Basler, *A Tour of Old Ste. Genevieve*, n. p.; Franzwa, *Old Ste. Genevieve*, 52; Austin to Valle, April 1, 1801, Legajo 218, Papeles de Cuba.

23 Valle to Lieutenant Governor DeLassus, August 19, 1799, Legajo 216-B, Papeles de Cuba.

24 DeLassus, Order, August 19, 1799, Captain François Valle Collection.

25 "The Answer of Moses Austin," in Gardner, *Lead King*, 69; Pierre DeLassus to Austin, July 28, 1799, Austin Papers.

26 "The Answer of Moses Austin," in Gardner, *Lead King*, 69; Houck, *History of Missouri*, vol. 1, pp. 331-333, vol. 2, pp. 62, 135; Moses Austin to Lieutenant Governor DeLassus, February 5, 1800, in Barker, *Austin Papers*, vol. 2, pt. 1, p. 53; Pierre DeLassus to Austin, July 28, 1799, Austin Papers.

27 Houck, *History of Missouri*, vol. 2, pp. 223-224; Valle to Soulard, April 5, 1800, Legajo 217-B, Papeles de Cuba.

28 Antoine Soulard to Austin, May 1, 1800, in Barker, *Austin Papers*, vol. 2, pt. 1,

p. 54; Soulard to Wilkinson, June 30, 1806, in Clarence Edwin Carter, comp. and ed., *The Territorial Papers of the United States*, vol. 13, pp. 523, 526, 530; Houck, *History of Missouri*, vol. 2, p. 58.

29   Valle to Beauvais, April 5, 1800, Legajo 217-B, Valle to Carlos DeLassus, May 30, 1800, Legajo 217, Papeles de Cuba; Map of Mine a Breton, Mapas y Planos #198, Survey of Austin's Property, May, 1800, Mapas y Planos #260; Austin, *Summary Description of the Lead Mines*, 7; Valle to [?], June 18, 1800, Austin Papers.

30   Antoine Soulard to Austin, June 30, 1800, in Barker, *Austin Papers*, vol. 2, pt. 1, p. 55; Valle to Austin, June 28, 1800, Legajo 217-B, Papeles de Cuba.

31   Moses Austin to Stephen Austin, February 23, 1801, Austin Papers.

32   Moses Austin, "Observation on Lead Mines," in *American State Papers, Public Lands*, vol. 3, p. 711; Schoolcraft, *View of the Lead Mines*, 19.

33   Austin, "Observation on Lead Mines," in *American State Papers, Public Lands*, vol. 3, pp. 707-708, 710; Schoolcraft, *View of the Lead Mines*, 19; Henry Rowe Schoolcraft, *Travels in the Central Portions of the Mississippi Valley*, 243.

34   Timothy Flint, *History and Geography of the Mississippi Valley*, vol. 1, p. 302; Christian Schultz, *Travels on an Inland Voyage Through the States of New York, Pennsylvania, Virginia, Ohio, Kentucky and Tennessee and Through the Territories of Indiana, Louisiana, Mississippi and New Orleans Performed in the Years 1807 and 1808, including a Tour of nearly 6000 Miles*, vol. 2, p. 50.

35   Memo. Notice to Mineral Diggers on M. Austin's Land, n. d., Austin Papers.

36   Schoolcraft, *View of the Lead Mines*, 97-106; Austin, *Summary Description of the Lead Mines*, 9; [Wyman J. Jones], *A History of the St. Joseph Lead Company From Its Organization in 1864 to January 1, 1892*, 10-11; Arthur Raistrick and Bernard Jennings, *A History of Lead Mining in the Pennines*, 121-127, 135-139; William H. Pulsifer, *Notes for a History of Lead and an Inquiry into the Development of the Manufacture of White Lead and Lead Oxides*, 100.

37   Austin, *Summary Description of the Lead Mines*, 9-10; Moses Austin to John Bowyer, Receipt, June 24, 1799, Austin Collection; Austin to DeLassus, May 14, 1799, Austin Papers.

38   Austin, *Summary Description of the Lead Mines*, 10, 19-20; Willms, "Lead Mining in Missouri," 43, 52-56; Note Sur La Louisiane, [1798], #95, Memoir Sur la Louisiane, [n.d.], #1, Correspondence Politique, Louisiane et Florides, 1792 a 1803, Etas Unis: Supplement 7, Archives of the Ministry of Foreign Affairs. Some of the increase, to be sure, resulted from the opening of new mines (Willms, "Lead Mining in Missouri," 66-67). Elias Bates testified that Austin manufactured 100,000-200,000 pounds of lead annually during this period (*American State Papers, Public Lands*, vol. 3, p. 683).

39   Moses to Henry Austin, April 28, 1808, Austin Papers.

40   Charles to Moses Austin, June 18, 1798, in Barker, *Austin Papers*, vol. 2, pt. 1, pp. 39-40.

41   Stephen to James Austin, December 28, 1798, Austin Papers; Stephen Austin to James Austin, January 24, 1899, in Barker, *Austin Papers*, vol. 2, pt. 1, p. 46.

42   Stephen to James Austin, March 8, 1799, July 9, 1800, Austin Papers.

43   Stephen Austin to Moses Austin, February 23, 1801, Austin Papers; Stephen Austin to Charles Austin, Deed, May 10, 1800, Wythe County Deed Book, vol. 3, pp. 40-41.

44   Stephen Austin to James Austin, July 9, March 8, October 22, 1799, Austin Papers.

45 James Austin to Moses Austin, April 6, Stephen Austin to Moses Austin, September 14, 1800, Austin Papers.

46 James Austin to Moses Austin, April 6, 1800, Austin Papers.

47 Stephen Austin to James Austin, July 9, 1800, Austin Papers.

48 James Austin to Moses Austin, April 6, 1800, Austin Papers.

49 Stephen Austin to Moses Austin, September 14, 1800, Austin Papers; Charles Austin to Moses Austin, December 8, 1800, in Barker, *Austin Papers*, vol. 2, pt. 1, pp. 57-59; Decree, January 9, 1806, Middletown, Connecticut, Land Records, vol. 39, pp. 60-63; SA, Examination of Bankrupt.

50 Stephen Austin, Statement, in Barker, *Austin Papers*, vol. 2, pt. 1, p. 63.

51 Stephen Austin to Moses Austin, February 23, 1801, Austin Papers.

52 Stephen Austin to James Austin, July 9, 1800, Austin Papers.

53 Stephen Austin to Moses Austin, September 14, 1800, February 23, 1801, Austin Papers.

54 Stephen Austin to Moses Austin, February 23, 1800, Moses Austin & Company to Stephen Austin, Account, February 20, 1801, Austin Papers; Charles Austin to Moses Austin, December 8, 1800, in Barker, *Austin Papers*, vol. 2, pt. 1, pp. 57-59.

55 James Austin to Moses Austin, October 15, 1801, Austin Papers.

56 Stephen Austin to Moses Austin, February 23, July 25, 1801, Austin Papers.

57 Stephen Austin to Moses Austin, February 23, 1801, Austin Papers.

58 Stephen Austin to Moses Austin, July 25, 1801, Austin Papers.

59 James Austin to Moses Austin, March 22, 1802, October 25, November 15, 1801, Austin Papers.

60 Decree, June 8, 1802, Judgment, Marshall v. Paine, September 10, 1803, Bankruptcy Records.

61 Wythe County, Virginia, Land Tax Books, 1793-1813; Wythe Lead and Zinc Mine Company, Abstract of Title; James Alexander Gardner, "The Life of Moses Austin," 314-315.

62 Soulard to Moses Austin, February 17, 1801, in Barker, *Austin Papers*, vol. 2, pt. 1, p. 66.

63 Soulard to Austin, October 19, 1800, *ibid.*, 56-57.

64 Journal of a Voyage Down the Mississippi, *ibid.*, 69-74; Harry Toulmin (Marion Tinling and Godfrey Davies, eds.), *The Western Country in 1793, Reports on Kentucky and Virginia*, 116-117.

65 Stephen Austin to Moses Austin, February 23, 1801, Austin Papers.

66 Stephen Austin to Moses Austin, February 23, 1801, December 23, 1801, Memo of Account, May 15, 1801, Merieult to Austin, Account, May 14, 1802, Maria Austin to Moses Austin, August 16, 1812, Austin Papers; [New Orleans] Records and Deliberations of the Cabildo, Book 3, p. 188; Lead Shipments in Barker, *Austin Papers*, vol. 2, pt. 1, p. 55, Way Bills in *ibid.*, 75-76; Merieult to Austin, Account, June 2, 1801, Merieult vs. Austin.

67 *American State Papers, Public Lands*, vol. 3, p. 683; Pedro Pedesclaux, Acts, vol. 39, pp., 369-370; Memorandum of Account, May 15, 1801, Austin Papers.

68 [Soulard Testimony], Undated, Austin Papers.

69 A French measure of 196 feet, 6 inches (Franzwa, *Old Ste. Genevieve*, 30).

70 Price List, February 19, 1799, in Barker, *Austin Papers*, vol. 2, pt. 1, p. 47, Price List, 1799-1802, *ibid.*, 64-65, John Stuart to Moses Austin, December 5, 1801, *ibid.*, 80; Findlay to Austin, Account, April 12, 1802, Austin to [Bates], [April, 1802], Austin Papers; Austin to Merieult, June 18, 1802, January 25, May 2, 1803, Account "A," Merieult vs. Austin; Austin to Findlay, Statement, October 7, 1801, and various accounts in James Bryan Papers.

71   Dudley G. Wooten, ed., *A Comprehensive History of Texas, 1685 to 1897*, vol.
      1, p. 441.
72   Valle to DeLassus, May 16, 1802, [Valle] to Nicolas Lachance, July 26, 1801,
      Valle to [DeLassus], August 20, 1801, Legajo 218, J. Baptiste and François
      LeClaire to Carlos DeLassus, August 20, 1801, Legajo 217-B, Papeles de
      Cuba; Genealogical Notes, in Barker, *Austin Papers*, vol. 2, pt. 1, p. 2; Willms,
      "Lead Mining in Missouri," 58; Franzwa, *Old Ste. Genevieve*, 59-60; Houck,
      History of Missouri, vol. 1, p. 371.
73   Austin to Unidentified, June 6, 1806, John B. C. Lucas Collection.
74   *Ibid.*; Pierre de Lassus de Luzierre to Moses Austin, July 31, 1802, in Barker,
      Austin Papers, vol. 2, pt. 1, pp. 82-83.
75   Houck, *History of Missouri*, vol. 2, pp. 334, 355-363; Valle to Carlos DeLassus,
      June 5, 1803, Legajo 218, Papeles de Cuba.
76   Austin to Merieult, January 25, 1803, Merieult vs. Austin.
77   Antoine Soulard to Governor Wilkinson, June 30, 1806, in Carter, *Territorial
      Papers*, vol. 13, p. 523; *American State Papers, Public Lands*, vol. 3, p. 683;
      Houck, *History of Missouri*, vol. 2, pp. 219-220, 228; Austin to [Bates], [April,
      1802], Austin Papers.
78   Austin to James Richardson, August 2, 1803, in Barker, *Austin Papers*, vol. 2,
      pt. 1, p. 85; Austin to Soulard, August 4, 1803, *ibid.*, 85-87; Houck, *History of
      Missouri*, vol. 2, p. 285.
79   Austin to Soulard, January 20, 1804, in Barker, *Austin Papers*, vol. 2, pt. 1, p.
      91, Soulard to Austin, February 17, 1801, *ibid.*, 67-68; Soulard to Austin, Feb-
      ruary 12, 1803, Austin Papers; Soulard to Governor Wilkinson, in Carter, *Ter-
      ritorial Papers*, vol. 13, pp. 522-524; Houck, *History of Missouri*, vol. 2, p. 226.
80   Austin to Soulard, January 20, 1804, in Barker, *Austin Papers*, vol. 2, pt. 1, pp.
      91-92.
81   Austin to Soulard, August 4, 1803, in Barker, *Austin Papers*, vol. 2, pt. 1, p. 86.
82   Houck, *History of Missouri*, vol. 2, pp. 364-364; Valle to DeLassus, February
      14, 1804, Legajo 218, Papeles de Cuba; *Farmer's Journal and Philadelphia
      Advertiser*, April 18, 1806, quoted in Soulard to Wilkinson, June 30, 1806, in
      Carter, *Territorial Papers*, vol. 13, pp. 528-529.
83   Houck, *History of Missouri*, vol. 2, p. 366.
84   Austin to Elliott, August 18, 1803, in Barker, *Austin Papers*, vol. 2, pt. 1, pp.
      87-88.

CHAPTER VII

1   Stoddard to the President, June 16, 1804, in Thomas Jefferson, *Message from
      the President of the United States to Both Houses of Congress, 8th November,
      1804*, n. p.
2   Louis Houck, *A History of Missouri From the Earliest Explorations and Settle-
      ments Until the Admission of the State into the Union*, vol. 2, pp. 355-370;
      Moses Austin, *A Summary Description of the Lead Mines in Upper Louisiana:
      Also, An Estimate of Their Produce, For Three Years Past*, 7-22.
3   Austin, *Summary Description of the Lead Mines*, n. p.
4   *Ibid.*, 19.
5   Jefferson, *Message from the President*, 5.
6   Simeon Baldwin to David Daggett, November 19, 1804, quoted in William E.
      Foley, "Territorial Politics in Frontier Missouri, 1804-1820," p. 56.
7   Welton Lyle Willms, "Lead Mining in Missouri, 1700-1811," pp. 77-79.

8 Houck, *History of Missouri*, vol. 2, p. 383; Foley, "Territorial Politics," 53.

9 Floyd Calvin Shoemaker, *Missouri's Struggle for Statehood, 1804-1821*, pp. 17-19; Houck, *History of Missouri*, vol. 2, pp. 375, 377, 385, 393; Foley, "Territorial Politics," 39-42.

10 Foley, "Territorial Politics," 59-60; Willms, "Lead Mining in Missouri," 77-79.

11 Willms, "Lead Mining in Missouri," 70-72.

12 Henry Rowe Schoolcraft, *A View of the Lead Mines of Missouri: Including Some Observations on the Mineralogy, Geology, Geography, Antiquities, Soil, Climate, Population, and Productions of Missouri and Arkansaw, and Other Sections of the Western Country*, 114.

13 Christian Schultz, *Travels on an Inland Voyage Through the States of New York, Pennsylvania, Virginia, Ohio, Kentucky and Tennessee and Through the Territories of Indiana, Louisiana, Mississippi and New Orleans Performed in the Years 1807 and 1808, including a Tour of nearly 6000 Miles*, vol. 2, pp. 52-53; Houck, *History of Missouri*, vol. 3, pp. 56, 73-74; Willms, "Lead Mining in Missouri," 86.

14 Quoted in Foley, "Territorial Politics," 65.

15 Thomas Perkins Abernethy, *The South in the New Nation*, 46, 67-68, 201-206, 214, 266; James Ripley Jacobs, *Tarnished Warrior: Major-General James Wilkinson*, 227; Houck, *History of Missouri*, vol. 2, pp. 375, 400, 406; Israel Dodge, Purported Deposition, [November 24, 1805], in Clarence Edwin Carter, comp. and ed., *The Territorial Papers of the United States*, vol. 13, p. 293; John Rice Jones to Austin, February 10, 1808, Austin Papers.

16 James Wilkinson to Seth Hunt, in Carter, *Territorial Papers*, vol. 13, p. 213.

17 Hunt to Wilkinson, June 30, 1805, in Carter, *Territorial Papers*, vol. 13, p. 208, Hunt to Smith T, June 30, 1805, in *ibid.*, 209, Hunt to Wilkinson, July 2, 1805, in *ibid.*, 209, Wilkinson to Smith T, July 5, 1805, in *ibid.*, 210, Smith T to Wilkinson, July 8, 1805, in *ibid.*, 210-211; Foley, "Territorial Politics," 50-52.

18 Robert Sidney Douglass, *History of Southeast Missouri*, vol. 1, p. 60; Frederick Bates to William Hull, June 17, 1807, in Thomas Maitland Marshall, ed., *The Life and Papers of Frederick Bates*, vol. 1, p. 145. Valle Higginbotham, Smith T's descendant and sympathetic biographer, asserts that, rather than the ten to fifteen men Smith T is "said to have killed," the names of only three can be found (Higginbotham, *John Smith T: Missouri Pioneer*, 51).

19 Willms, "Lead Mining in Missouri," 86.

20 Higginbotham, *John Smith T*, 1-53; John F. Darby, *Personal Recollections of Many Prominent People Whom I Have Known, and of Events — Especially Those Relating to the History of St. Louis — During the First Half of the Present Century*, 84-86; Valle Higginbotham, "John Smith T," De Soto (Missouri) *Press*, January ?, 1964; Foley, "Territorial Politics," 69; Willms, "Lead Mining in Missouri," 82-83.

21 Wilkinson to Smith T, July 5, 1805, in Carter, *Territorial Papers*, vol. 13, p. 210.

22 Smith T to Wilkinson, July 8, 1805, in Carter, *Territorial Papers*, vol., 13, p. 211, Hunt to Wilkinson, July 2, 1805, in *ibid.*, 209, Wilkinson to Smith T, July 5, 1808, in *ibid.*, 210, Wilkinson to Secretary of War, September 21, 1805, in *ibid.*, 222.

23 Austin to Easton, August 14, 1805, Rufus Easton Papers.

24 Austin to Wilkinson, July 22, 1805, in Eugene C. Barker, ed., *The Austin Papers*, vol. 2, pt. 1, p. 97

25 Austin to Easton, August 15, 1805, Easton Papers.

26 Easton to Austin, July 29, 1805, Easton Papers.

27   Amos Stoddard to Mother, June 16, 1804, Amos Stoddard Papers; Eugene
     Morrow Violette, "Early Settlements in Missouri," *Missouri Historical Review*,
     1 (October, 1906), 52.
28   Austin to Smith T, July 22, 1805, Austin Papers.
29   Inhabitants of Ste. Genevieve District to Governor Wilkinson, [June 26, 1805],
     in Carter, *Territorial Papers*, vol. 13, pp. 142, 141-144.
30   Austin to Wilkinson, July 22, 1805, in Barker, *Austin Papers*, vol. 2, pt. 1, p.
     98.
31   *Ibid.*, 97.
32   Easton to Austin, July 29, 1805, Easton Papers; Clarence E. Carter, "The
     Burr-Wilkinson Intrigue in St. Louis," *Bulletin of the Missouri Historical Soci-
     ety*, 10 (July, 1954), 453.
33   Easton to Austin, July 29, 1805, Easton Papers.
34   Austin to Easton, August 14, 1805, Easton Papers.
35   *Ibid.*
36   Wilkinson to Secretary of State, September 21, 1805, in Carter, *Territorial
     Papers*, vol. 13, pp. 219-220.
37   Secretary Browne to the President, in *ibid.*, 545.
38   Will C. Carr to Austin, August 12, 1806 [1805], in Barker, *Austin Papers*, vol.
     2, pt. 1, p. 113; Willms, "Lead Mining in Missouri," 87; Marshall, *Frederick
     Bates*, vol. 1, p. 126n; Houck, *History of Missouri*, vol. 2, p. 383.
39   Austin to Easton, August 14, 1805, Easton Papers.
40   *Ibid.*
41   Austin to Easton, October 9, 1805, Easton Papers.
42   Dodge to Governor Wilkinson, November 20, 1805, in Carter, *Territorial
     Papers*, vol. 13, pp. 292, Dodge, Purported Deposition, [November 24, 1805],
     in *ibid.*, 292-293.
43   Austin to Easton, October 9, 1805, Easton Papers.
44   Carter, "The Burr-Wilkinson Intrigue," *Bulletin of the Missouri Historical
     Society*, vol. 10, p. 452.
45   *Ibid.*, p. 458, Abernethy, *The South in the New Nation*, 265-272.
46   Carter, "The Burr-Wilkinson Intrigue," *Bulletin of the Missouri Historical
     Society*, vol. 10, pp. 452-453; Marshall, *Frederick Bates*, vol. 1, pp. 25-27.
47   Carter, "Burr-Wilkinson Intrigue," *Bulletin of the Missouri Historical Society*,
     vol. 10, pp. 449-450, 453-455; Abernethy, *The South in the New Nation*, 266;
     Israel Dodge, Purported Deposition, [November 24, 1805], in Carter, *Territo-
     rial Papers*, vol. 13, pp. 292-293; Houck, *History of Missouri*, vol. 2, p. 405.
48   Secretary Browne to the President, July 14, 1806, in Carter, *Territorial Papers*,
     vol. 13, p. 545; Carter, "Burr-Wilkinson Intrigue," *Bulletin of the Missouri His-
     torical Society*, vol. 10, p. 452; Frederick Bates to William Hull, June 17, 1807,
     in Marshall, *Frederick Bates*, vol. 1, p. 145.
49   William C. Carr to the Attorney General, November 13, 1805, in Carter, *Terri-
     torial Papers*, vol. 13, pp. 273, 270, Israel Dodge, Purported Deposition,
     [November 24, 1805], in *ibid.*, 293.
50   Carter, "Burr-Wilkinson Intrigue," *Bulletin of the Missouri Historical Society*,
     vol. 10, p. 456.
51   Easton to the President, January 17, 1805, in Carter, *Territorial Papers*, vol.
     13, pp. 85-86.
52   Carr to Secretary of the Treasury, November 14, 1805, in Carter, *Territorial
     Papers*, vol. 13, pp. 274-275.
53   Harry R. Burke, "Moses Austin and the Lead For Aaron Burr," Harry Burke
     Papers.

54   Carr to Secretary of the Treasury, November 14, 1805, in Carter, *Territorial Papers*, vol. 13, pp. 274-275; Moses Austin, "Observation on Lead Mines," in *American State Papers, Public Lands*, vol. 3, pp. 707-712.
55   James Austin to Moses Austin, March 22, 1802, Austin Papers.
56   Schultz, *Travels on an Inland Voyage*, vol. 2, pp. 51-52.
57   Thomas Westcott to [Moses Austin ?], January 21, 1806, Deadwich and Tatum to Austin, March 25, 1804, Austin Papers.
58   Austin to James Maxwell, May 4, 1806, Maxwell to Austin, May 18, 1806, Austin Papers.
59   Missouri Territory vs. James Scott, Notes, Lucas Collection.
60   Austin to Dear Sir, July 6, 1806, Lucas Collection.
61   Austin to Henry, July 4, 1806, in Barker, *Austin Papers*, vol. 2, pt. 1, p. 109.
62   *Ibid.,* 109-110.
63   Austin to Dear Sir, July 6, 1806, Lucas Collection.
64   *Ibid.*
65   Notice, [1806?], in Barker, *Austin Papers*, vol. 2, pt. 1, p. 123; Willms, "Lead Mining in Missouri," 87.
66   John Smith T vs. Moses Austin, Notes, Lucas Collection.
67   Austin vs. Smith T, September 1806 (folder 520), Reuben Smith vs. Moses Austin, September, 1806 (folder 527), Smith T vs. Austin, June, 1807, and Reuben Smith vs. Austin, March, 1807 (folder 542), all in Ste. Genevieve Archives; Smith T vs. Austin, 1807, Records of the General Court, Supreme Court of Missouri.
68   Actually, Austin and Smith T had met to discuss the charges and found they could agree on nothing.
69   Austin to Smith, August 7, 1806, in Barker, *Austin Papers*, vol. 2, pt. 1, pp. 111-112.
70   Green Dewit vs. James Smith, Notes, U.S. vs. James Keith & others, Notes, Lucas Collection.
71   *American State Papers, Public Lands*, vol. 3, p. 633; "The Answer of Moses Austin," cited in James Alexander Gardner, *Lead King: Moses Austin*, 70; Schultz, *Travels on an Inland Voyage*, vol. 2, p. 48.
72   Stephen F. Austin to the Cherokees, April 24, 1826, in Barker, *Austin Papers*, vol. 2, pt. 2, p. 1308; Valle to De Celle Duclos, March 1, 1803, Legajo 218, Papeles de Cuba.
73   Moses Austin to Stephen F. Austin, December 16, 1804, in Barker, *Austin Papers*, vol. 2, pt. 1, p. 93.
74   Austin to Daniel Phelps, June 10, 1804, in Barker, *Austin Papers*, vol. 2, pt. 1, pp. 92-93, Moses Austin to Stephen F. Austin, December 16, 1804, in *ibid.*, 93-94, Genealogical Notes, in *ibid.*, 2; Edith Austin Moore and William Allen Day, comps., *The Descendants of Richard Austin of Charleston, Massachusetts, 1638*, p. 51.
75   John Warner Barber, *Connecticut Historical Collections*, 301; Florence S. Mary Crofut, *Guide to the History and the Historic Sites of Connecticut*, vol. 2, pp. 492-493; Norris Galpin Osborn, *History of Connecticut*, vol. 5, pp. 190-192; A. P. Willard to Mattie Austin Hatcher, February 24, 1930, Clipping File.
76   Genealogical Notes, in Barker, *Austin Papers*, vol. 2, pt. 1, p. 2.
77   *Ibid.*; Mrs. Howard W. Woodruff, "Original Baptismal Register, 1759-1811: The Church of Ste. Genevieve," *Missouri Miscellany*, 9 (March, 1980), 32; Houck, *History of Missouri*, vol. 2, p. 215.
78   Foley, "Territorial Politics," 92-94; Jacobs, *Tarnished Warrior*, 229.
79   Carter, "The Burr-Wilkinson Intrigue," *Bulletin of the Missouri Historical*

Society, vol. 10, pp. 458-460; Abernethy, *The South in the New Nation*, 280-292; Milton Lomask, *Aaron Burr: The Conspiracy and Years of Exile, 1805-1836*, pp. 150-197; Darby, *Personal Recollections*, 88; Richard M. Clokey, *William H. Ashley*, 16.

80   Darby, *Personal Recollections*, 88-89.

81   Foley, "Territorial Politics," 100.

82   Acting Governor Bates to the President, May 6, 1807, in Carter, *Territorial Papers*, vol. 14, pp. 120-121; Marshall, *Frederick Bates*, vol. 1, 25-27, Bates to John Smith T, May 1, 1807, in *ibid.*, 109-110; Foley, "Territorial Politics," 100-101.

CHAPTER VIII

1   Thomas Maitland Marshall, ed., *The Life and Papers of Frederick Bates*, vol. 1, pp. 3-18.

2   Frederick Bates to Frederick Woodson, May 1, 1807, in *ibid.*, 111-114.

3   Bates to James Madison, September 25, 1807, in *ibid.*, 194-195.

4   Bates to William Hull, June 17, 1807, in *ibid.*, 146; Bates to Moses Austin, September 12, 1807, in Eugene C. Barker, ed., *The Austin Papers*, vol. 2, pt. 1, pp. 137-138.

5   Phelps to Austin, July 22, 1807, in Barker, *Austin Papers*, vol. 2, pt. 1, pp. 130-131; Bates to Madison, September 25, 1807, in Marshall, *Frederick Bates*, vol. 1, p. 194.

6   Frederick Bates to Richard Bates, December 17, 1807, in Marshall, *Frederick Bates*, vol. 1, 238.

7   *Ibid.*, 242.

8   Ficklin to Austin, February 18, 1808, Austin Papers.

9   Bates to Madison, September 25, 1807, in Marshall, *Frederick Bates*, vol. 1, pp. 194-195.

10   Carr to Austin, June 28, 1806, in Barker, *Austin Papers*, vol. 2, pt. 1, pp. 105-106; Welton Lyle Willms, "Lead Mining in Missouri, 1700-1811," p. 84.

11   Notice, [1806?], in Barker, *Austin Papers*, vol. 2, pt. 1, p. 123; Louis Houck, *A History of Missouri From the Earliest Explorations and Settlements Until the Admission of the State into the Union*, vol. 3, pp. 38-40; Exhibit J, Item 138, Entry J16, vol. 44, Record of Testimony in Private Land Claims, Private Land Claims in Missouri, Division D, RG 49, Records of the Bureau of Land Management, General Land Office.

12   Bates to Albert Gallatin, September 8, 1807, in Marshall, *Frederick Bates*, vol. 1, p. 181, Austin to Bates, [March 27], 1808, in *ibid.*, 318; Moses Austin, *A Summary Description of the Lead Mines in Upper Louisiana: Also, An Estimate of Their Produce, For Three Years Past*, 12.

13   Frederick Bates to Elisha Baker, Moses Austin, Darius Shaw and Joseph Whittlesey, May 30, 1807, in Barker, *Austin Papers*, vol. 2, pt. 1, pp. 126-127.

14   Bates to Richard Bates, May 31, 1807, in Marshall, *Frederick Bates*, vol. 1, p. 137.

15   Hunt to Bates, February 7, 1808 (two letters), in Marshall, *Frederick Bates*, vol. 1, pp. 275-277, Bates to Hunt, February 7, 1808, in *ibid.*, 277-278; Houck, *History of Missouri*, vol. 2, pp. 228-229; Henry Rowe Schoolcraft, *A View of the Lead Mines of Missouri: Including Some Observations on the Mineralogy, Geology, Geography, Antiquities, Soil, Climate, Population, and Productions of Missouri and Arkansaw, and Other Sections of the Western Country*, 14-17, 75.

16 Bates to Gallatin, February 9, 1808, in Marshall, *Frederick Bates*, vol. 1, p. 280.

17 Deposition of Richard Horn, February 16, in *ibid.*, 286, 285.

18 Bates to Gallatin, February 9, 1808, in *ibid.*, 280.

19 Austin to Bates, [March] 27, 1808, in *ibid.*, 317.

20 Moses Austin to Emily Austin, June 20, 1812, in Barker, *Austin Papers*, vol. 2, pt. 1, p. 210. Italics mine.

21 Austin to Wingfield Bullock, July 16, 1808, Austin Papers.

22 Austin to Elias Hains, July 25, 1808, Austin Papers.

23 Moses Austin to Henry Austin, July 25, 1808, Moses Austin to Charles Carr, July 20, 1808, Moses Austin to Charles Elliott, June 20, 1808, Henry Austin to Moses Austin, July 7, 18, 1808, Austin Papers; [?] to Dear Sir, July 24, 1806, Receipt, January 2, 1807, John [illeg.] to Bryan, Promissory Note, July 19, 1808, James Bryan Papers.

24 Austin to Elliott, June 20, 1808, Austin Papers.

25 Moses Austin to Charles Carr, July 20, 1808, Austin Papers.

26 Moses Austin to Henry Austin, July 25, 1808, Austin Papers.

27 Moses Austin to Henry Austin, April 13, 1808, in Barker, *Austin Papers*, vol. 2, pt. 1, p. 147, Henry Austin to Moses Austin, in *ibid.*, 147-148, Seth Hunt to Austin, July 20, 1808, in *ibid.*, 149, Austin to Hunt, in *ibid.*, 150-151, Austin to Hunt, [May 3, 1808], in *ibid.*, 154, Hunt to Austin, in *ibid.*, 162-163; Moses to Henry Austin, April 13, 1808, Austin Papers.

28 Austin to Hunt, September 19, 1808, Austin Papers.

29 Bates to Gallatin, February 9, 1808, in Marshall, *Frederick Bates*, vol. 1, pp. 281-282; Memorandum of Agreement, in Barker, *Austin Papers*, vol. 2, pt. 1, pp. 123-124; Kendal and Magt to Austin, Deed, January 9, 1809, General Book C-1, p. 91, Office of the Recorder of Deeds of St. Louis; Stella M. Drumm, "Samuel Hammond," *Missouri Historical Society Collections*, 4 (1923), 402-422; Clarence Edwin Carter, comp. and ed., *The Territorial Papers of the United States*, vol. 13, p. 194; Willms, "Lead Mining in Missouri," 80-82.

30 G. W. Featherstonhaugh, *Excursion Through the Slave States, From Washington on the Potomac to the Frontier of Mexico; With Sketches of Popular Manners and Geological Notices*, 73.

31 Austin and Wife, and Hammond and Wife to Trustees for Herculaneum Town, June 8, 1818, Deed Book G-1, pp. 298-301, Office of the Recorder of Deeds; Bates to Gallatin, December 25, 1808, in Marshall, *Frederick Bates*, vol. 1, p. 273, vol. 2, p. 53. Between 1811 and 1813, they put in a public square – called Union Square – south of Austin's property.

32 Austin to Hunt, [May 3, 1809], Barker, *Austin Papers*, vol. 2, pt. 1, p. 153. Not two years after he and Hammond laid out Herculaneum, Moses decided to dispose of his property in rival Ste. Genevieve to concentrate his interests at his mines and in his town. Austin had owned a place in the old French settlement since he had paid Amable Partnais dit Mason $200 in 1798 for a lot and cabin to provide a home for his family before they moved to Durham Hall. In succeeding years, Austin enlarged the house and its dependencies substantially. In particular, he put in a cellar for storing lead. Still, Moses rented the house more than he lived in it. Two unhappy experiences renting the place to cousins in 1809 and 1810, the very years in which Herculaneum proved the economy of its location in cutting his freighting costs, must have confirmed Moses' resolve to sell. The $2,000 purchase price he received in March, 1811, which likely represented a handsome profit, could only have confirmed his decision. (Maria and Moses Austin to William Shannon, March 1, 1811, Ste. Genevieve, County, Missouri, Deed Book B, p. 138; Austin to Valle, April 1,

1801, Legajo 218, Papeles de Cuba; Carr to Austin, June 28, 1806, in Barker, *Austin Papers*, vol. 2, pt. 1, p. 106, Austin to Phelps, Lease, December 26, 1809, in *ibid.*, 163; An Exhibit of the Expense of building Store House, Accounts, Austin to Phelps, January 5, 1810, Credits to the House in Village, 1801-1811, Austin Papers; Gregory M. Franzwa, *The Story of Old Ste. Genevieve*, 52; Lucille Basler, *A Tour of Old Ste. Genevieve*, n. p.; Houck, *History of Missouri*, vol. 3, p. 194.)

33   Willms, "Lead Mining in Missouri," 103; Floyd Calvin Shoemaker, "Herculaneum Shot Tower," *Missouri Historical Review*, 20 (July, 1926), 215; *Missouri Gazette* (St. Louis), January 11, November 16, 1809, March 8, 1810.

34   Edith Austin Moore and William Allen Day, comps., *The Descendants of Richard Austin of Charlestown, Massachusetts, 1638*, pp. 37, 56, 119; Rebecca Smith Lee, *Mary Austin Holley: A Biography*, 12-15, 57, 61; Moses Austin to Stephen F. Austin, December 16, 1804, in Barker, *Austin Papers*, vol. 2, pt. 1, pp. 94-95, H. Austin to J. Bryant [Bryan?], [July, 1806], in *ibid.*, 110, Austin to John Francis Merieult, June 20, 1807, in *ibid.*, 127-128, Horace Austin to Moses Austin, August 20, 1807, in *ibid.*, 134-135; George Edward Pankey, *John Pankey of Manakin Town, Virginia, and His Descendants*, 116-118; "The Dr. Aaron Elliott House (1805)," courtesy Mrs. Garighity, Ste. Genevieve, Missouri; Basler, *A Tour of Old Ste. Genevieve*, n. p.; Houck, *History of Missouri*, vol. 3, p. 193.

35   Moses Austin to Henry Austin, April 13, 1808, Stephen Austin to Henry Austin, in Henry Austin to Moses Austin, July 18, 1808, Austin Papers.

36   Moses Austin to Henry Austin, April 28, 1808, Austin Papers.

37   Henry Austin to Moses Austin, July 7, 18, 1808, Austin Papers.

38   Austin to Hart, Barton, and Hart, May 3, 1809, in Barker, *Austin Papers*, vol. 2, pt. 1, pp. 155, 154.

39   Hunt to Austin, n.d., Austin Papers; Austin to Bond, May 3, 1809, in *ibid.*, 155.

40   Protest, January 27, December 29, 1809, Hart, Bartlet and Cox, Account, February 24, 1810, Austin Papers; J. Leander Bishop, *A History of American Manufactures from 1608 to 1860*, vol. 2, p. 155; William H. Pulsifer, *Notes for a History of Lead and an Inquiry into the Development of the Manufacture of White Lead and Lead Oxides*, 319; Harry M. Tinkcom, "Sir Augustus in Pennsylvania: The Travels and Observations of Sir Augustus J. Foster in Early Nineteenth-Century Pennsylvania," *Pennsylvania Magazine of History and Biography*, 75 (1957), 397.

41   Account and Receipt, January 10, 1810, James Austin and Moses Austin, Agreement, February 23, 1810, Hart, Bartlet and Cox, Account, April 30, 1810, Austin Papers; Lead Production, in Barker, *Austin Papers*, 166-167, Memorandum of Moses Austin's Estate [ca. 1810], in *ibid.*, 350, Financial Statement, June 9, 1810, in *ibid.*, 173.

42   Austin to Hunt, [May 3, 1809], in Barker, *Austin Papers*, vol. 2, pt. 1, p. 154; Austin to Isaac Tomlinson & Co., Account, June 13, Austin to Smiths Taylor and Co., June 22, 1810, Invoice, July 12, 1810, various accounts, August 6-11, 1810, Austin Papers.

43   Jones to Austin, July 12, 1811, Account, 1809-1810, Fees and cost in Renauts Claim, n. d., Austin Papers; Bates to Gallatin, October 17, 1811, in Marshall, *Frederick Bates*, vol. 2, p. 203.

44   *Missouri Gazette* (St. Louis), February 7, 14, 21, 28, 1811.

45   Bates to Gallatin, June 20, 1811, in Marshall, *Frederick Bates*, vol. 2, p. 181.

46   Bates to Gallatin, October 17, 1811, in *ibid.*, 204.

47 Smith T to Bates, December 24, 1811, in *ibid.*, 212.
48 Petition to Congress by Moses Austin and John Rice Jones, January 21, 1811, in Carter, *Territorial Papers*, vol. 14, pp. 433-435.
49 *American State Papers, Finance*, vol. 4, p. 429; Bishop, *A History of American Manufactures*, 155.
50 Henry Austin to Moses Austin, July 30, 1811, Austin Papers.
51 William Morrison to Bryan, November 7, 1806, August 1, 1808, April 3, 1809, May 30, [1809], Madam Russ to James Bryan, Bill, June 11, 1808, N. Pusey to Bryan, April 29, 1809, William Spradling to Bryan and Morrison, undated, Bryan to John Butler, 1809-1810, James Bryan to Bryan and Morrison, undated, Elijah Butler to Bryan, November 7, 1811, Jesse Cooper to Bryan, April 12, 1810, John N. Corwell to Bryan, August 10, 1810, Abraham Baker to Bryan, September 19, 1809, William Bates to Bryan, promissory note, September 27, 1810, William Morrison to Pusey, ____ 26, 1809, Robert Morrison to Bryan, October 8, 1809, Bryan Papers; Schedule of stock and payment on shares, n. d., Austin Papers; Richard H. Collins, *History of Kentucky*, vol. 2, p. 488.
52 *Missouri Gazette* (St. Louis), August 8, 1811.
53 Maria Austin to Moses Austin, February 23, 1812, Austin Papers.
54 Henry Austin to Moses Austin, July 30, 1811, Austin Papers; Austin to Jones, Deed, June 24, 1807, St. Louis, Missouri, Deed Book F-1, p. 392; [?] to Dear Sir, July 24, 1806, Receipt, January 2, 1807, Bryan Papers.
55 Maria Austin to Moses Austin, March 29, 1812, Austin Papers.
56 Maria Austin to Moses Austin, April 6, 1812, Austin Papers.
57 Maria Austin to Moses Austin, April 25, 1812, Austin Papers; Carter, *Territorial Papers*, vol. 14, p. 436n; Petition of Moses Austin, January 21, 1811, 11th Congress, and Original Bill to Incorporate the Louisiana Lead Company, 12th Congress, RG 46, Records of US Senate; *Missouri Gazette* (St. Louis), May 16, 1812.
58 Moses Austin to Emily Austin, June 20, 1812, in Barker, *Austin Papers*, vol. 2, pt. 1, p. 211.
59 *Ibid.*; Genealogical Notes in Barker, *Austin Papers,* vol. 2, pt. 1, p. 2.
60 E. Lewis to Moses Austin, May 26, 1811, in *ibid.*, 190-191; List of Licenses to Trade with Indians, October 26, 1810, in Marshall, *Frederick Bates*, vol. 2, p. 201.
61 Maria Austin to Moses Austin, July 29, 1811, Austin Papers.
62 Maria Austin to Moses Austin, September 8, July 29, August 16, 1811, Austin Papers.
63 Maria Austin to Moses Austin, August 26, 1811, Austin Papers.
64 *Ibid.*
65 Maria Austin to Moses Austin, November 29, 1811, Austin Papers.
66 Maria Austin to Moses Austin, September 21, 1811, Austin Papers; Moses Austin Bryan to Beauregard Bryan, September 25, 1889, Declaration of Texas Independence Signers Collection.
67 Maria Austin to Moses Austin, November 12, 1811, Austin Papers.
68 Moses Austin to Emily Austin, June 20, 1812, in Barker, *Austin Papers*, vol. 2, pt. 1, p. 210.
69 *Ibid.*
70 Maria Austin to Moses Austin, November 29, 1811, Austin Papers.
71 Maria Austin to Moses Austin, July 29, 1811, Austin Papers.
72 Maria Austin to Moses Austin, November 29, 1811, Austin Papers.
73 *Ibid.*

74   Emily Austin to Moses Austin, December ___, 1811, Austin Papers.
75   Maria Austin to Moses Austin, March 16, 1812, Austin Papers.
76   Maria Austin to Moses Austin, April 25, March 16, 1812, Austin Papers.
77   Certificate of Scholarship and Conduct, January 7, 1808, in Barker, *Austin Papers*, vol. 2, pt. 1, p. 144.
78   Horace Austin to Moses Austin, August 20, 1807, in *ibid.*, 135, Austin to Hart, Barton & Hart, July 18, 1809, *ibid.*, 159, Certificate, *ibid.*, 171, Isaac L. Baker to Stephen F. Austin, July 1, 1810, *ibid.*, 174, Receipts in *ibid.*, 182-183, 185, 194-195; Ernest Trice Thompson, *Presbyterians in the South, 1607-1861*, pp. 264-266; Maria Austin to Moses Austin, August 26, 1811, June 7, 1812, Austin to Phelps, January 5, 1810, Moses Austin to Stephen F. Austin, Memorandum and Instructions, April 28, 1812, Austin Papers.
79   Moses Austin to Stephen F. Austin, April 28, 1812, in Barker, *Austin Papers*, vol. 2, pt. 1, pp. 202-204.
80   Maria Austin to Moses Austin, May 15, 1812, Austin Papers.
81   Maria Austin to Moses Austin, April 25, 1812, Austin Papers.
82   Austin to Bryan, June 20, 1812, Austin Papers.
83   Maria Austin to Moses Austin, June 7, 1812, Austin Papers.
84   Maria Austin to Moses Austin, June 21, 1812, in Barker, *Austin Papers*, vol. 2, pt. 1, pp. 211-212.

Chapter IX

1   Maria Austin to Moses Austin, August 4, 1812, Austin Papers.
2   Maria Austin to Moses Austin, September 14, 1812, Austin Papers.
3   Maria Austin to Moses Austin, August 4, 1812, Austin Papers.
4   *Ibid.*
5   Stephen Austin to Moses Austin, July 12, 1812, in Eugene C. Barker, ed., *The Austin Papers*, vol. 2, pt. 1, p. 216, Moses Austin to James Bryan, October 19, 1812, in *ibid.*, 218; William Bryan to James Bryan, August 24, 1812, James Bryan Papers.
6   Moses Austin to James Bryan, October 19, 1812, in Barker, *Austin Papers*, vol. 2, pt. 1, p. 218, 219; Austin to Bryan, July 15, 1812, Austin Papers.
7   Moses Austin to Stephen Austin, September 26, 1812, in Barker, *Austin Papers*, vol. 2, pt. 1, p. 217.
8   Moses Austin to James Bryan, October 19, 1812, in *ibid.*, 218, Moses Austin to Charles Staples, Bill, in *ibid.*, 215; Austin to Bryan, July 15, 1812, Austin Papers.
9   Moses Austin to James Bryan, December 4, 1812, in Barker, *Austin Papers*, vol. 2, pt. 1, p. 220.
10   Maria Austin to Moses Austin, October 25, August 4, 16, September 14, 1812, Austin Papers.
11   Maria Austin to Moses Austin, August 4, 1812, Austin Papers.
12   Maria Austin to Moses Austin, August 4, 16, October 25, 1812, Austin Papers.
13   Maria Austin to Moses Austin, August 16, September 14, 1812, Austin Papers.
14   Maria Austin to Moses Austin, October 25, 1812, Austin Papers.
15   Maria Austin to Moses Austin, September 31, 1812, Austin Papers.
16   Maria Austin to Moses Austin, August 4, 1812, Austin Papers; Moses Austin to Bryan, October 19, 1812, in Barker, *Austin Papers*, vol. 2, pt. 1, p. 219.
17   William Bryan to James Bryan, August 24, 1812, Pusey to Bryan, May 20,

1810, Bryan Papers; Moses Austin Bryan to Beauregard Bryan, September 25, 1889, Declaration of Texas Independence Signers Collection.

18 Maria Austin to Moses Austin, November 12, 1811, Austin Papers.

19 Maria Austin to Moses Austin, May 15, 1812, Austin Papers.

20 Maria Austin to Moses Austin, March 16, June 7, 1812, Austin Papers.

21 Maria Austin to Moses Austin, August 16, 1812, Austin to Bryan, June 20, 1812, Austin Papers.

22 Carter Royston Bryan, comp., "De Brienne-Bryan," n. p.

23 William Morrison to Bryan, November 7, 1806, August 1, 1808, April 3, 1809, May 30, [1809], Madam Russ to Bryan, Bill, June 11, 1808, N. Pusey to Bryan, April 29, 1809, William Spradling to Bryan and Morrison, undated, Bryan to John Butler, 1810(?), James Bryan to Bryan and Morrison, undated, Elijah Butler to Bryan, November 7, 1811, Jesse Cooper to Bryan, April 12, 1810, John N. Corwell to Bryan, August 10, 1810, Abraham Baker to Bryan, September 19, 1809, William Bates, promissory note, September 27, 1810, William Morrison to Pusey, ____ 26, 1809, Robert Morrison to Bryan, October 8, 1809, Bryan Papers; Henri Brackenridge, "Sketches of the Territory of Louisiana," in *Missouri Gazette* (St. Louis), June 27, 1811.

24 Austin and Bryan, Agreement, January 8, 1811, Austin to Montgomery, Agreement, January 8, 1811, Austin Papers; Austin, "Observation on Lead Mines," *American State Papers, Public Lands*, vol. 3, p. 708.

25 Maria Austin to Moses Austin, October 25, August 16, 1812, Austin Papers.

26 Maria Austin to Moses Austin, November 16, 1812, Austin Papers.

27 Stephen F. Austin to James Bryan, October 8, 1811, in Barker, *Austin Papers*, vol. 2, pt. 1, p. 195.

28 Moses Austin to Bryan, January 4, 1813, in *ibid.*, 224.

29 James Bryan to William Bryan, March 8, 1813, Henry Elliott to James Bryan, Receipt, April 3, 1813, Bryan Papers; Mary Austin to Rebecca Leaming, September 2, 1813, Austin-Leaming Letters; Moses Austin to Bryan, June 25, 1813, Austin Papers.

30 Austin to Bryan, January 4, 1813, in Barker, *Austin Papers*, vol. 2, pt. 1, pp. 222-223.

31 Moses Austin to James Bryan, December 4, 1812, in *ibid.*, 221, 220; William E. Foley, "Territorial Politics in Frontier Missouri, 1804-1820," pp. 142-144.

32 William Bryan to James Bryan, August 24, 1812, Bryan Papers.

33 Moses Austin to Bryan, December 31, 1813, Austin Papers.

34 Austin to Bryan, January 4, 1813, in Barker, *Austin Papers*, vol. 2, pt. 1, p. 222.

35 Exhibit No. 13, [June 1, 1812?], Austin Papers.

36 Moses Austin to Bryan, January 4, 1813, in Barker, *Austin Papers*, vol. 2, pt. 1, p. 223.

37 *Ibid.*; Catalog of Men in the Company's Employ, 1799-1810, Austin Papers; Mattie Austin Hatcher, *The Opening of Texas to Foreign Settlement, 1801-1821*, pp. 142-143.

38 Adam Trinno to Moses Austin, February 10, 1814, Stephen F. Austin to Bryan, January 13, 1814, in Barker, *Austin Papers*, vol. 2, pt. 1, pp. 237, 236.

39 Maria Austin to Moses Austin, October 25, 1812, Austin Papers.

40 Austin to John Scott, May 28, 1813, in Barker, *Austin Papers*, vol. 2, pt. 1, pp. 224, 225.

41 Unidentified statement, Austin Papers; *History of Franklin, Jefferson, Washington, Crawford and Gasconade Counties, Missouri*, 494.

42 Memorandum in Barker, *Austin Papers*, vol. 2, pt. 1, p. 222.

43   Maria Austin to Moses Austin, August 16, 1812, Austin Papers.

44   Papers in case of John Francis Merieult vs. Moses Austin; Stephen F. Austin
     to Moses Austin, April 10, 1816, Statement, 1815, Austin Papers; Francis
     Mereiut vs. Moses Austin, Washington County, Missouri, Circuit Court Index,
     1814-1821, p. 69.

45   Documents in case number unknown, John Smith T vs. Austin & Elliott, #22,
     James Rosberry and John Swan vs. Austin and the Elliotts, #21, Robert Sto-
     thard vs. Austin and the Elliotts, #20, Thomas Blakeley vs. Austin and the
     Elliotts, #19, Jacob Blaisdel vs. Austin and the Elliotts, #18, Records of the
     Superior Court, Box 18, Supreme Court of Missouri Case Files.

46   Richard S. Thomas vs. Moses Austin, #6, Records of the Superior Court, Box
     19, Supreme Court of Missouri Case Files.

47   Stephen F. Austin to Bryan, December 30, 1813, in Barker, *Austin Papers*, vol.
     2, pt. 1, p. 234, Hammond to Austin, December 29, 1813, in *ibid.*, 223.

48   Foley, "Territorial Politics," 149-159, 162-164; Moses Austin to Bryan, January
     4, 1813, in Barker, *Austin Papers*, vol. 2, pt. 1, p. 224; *Missouri Gazette* (St.
     Louis), December 26, 1812, March 13, 1813.

49   Austin to Bryan, June 25, 1813, Austin Papers; Petition, undated, in Barker,
     Austin Papers, vol. 2, pt. 1, p. 235; *Laws of a Public and General Nature of the
     District of Louisiana, of the Territory of Louisiana, of the Territory of Missouri
     and of the State of Missouri, Up to the Year 1824*, pp. 283-290; *History of
     Franklin, Jefferson, Washington, Crawford and Gasconade Counties*, 480-481.

50   Austin to Benjamin Elliott, Martin Ruggles, Lionel Browne, Deed, July 22,
     1814, Washington County, Missouri, Deed Book A, 47-48, Moses and Maria
     Austin to Stephen F. Austin, Deed, June 4, 1814, *ibid.*, 24-25; *Missouri Gazette*
     (St. Louis), July 4, 1814; *History of Franklin, Jefferson, Washington, Crawford
     and Gasconade Counties*, 482-483.

51   *Missouri Gazette* (St. Louis), August 13, 1814; *History of Franklin, Jefferson,
     Washington, Crawford and Gasconade Counties*, 484-485.

52   See above, page 131.

53   Austin, "Observation on Lead Mines," *American State Papers, Public Lands*,
     vol. 3, p. 709; *History of Franklin, Jefferson, Washington, Crawford and Gas-
     conade Counties*, 480; Louis Houck, *A History of Missouri From the Earliest
     Explorations and Settlements Until the Admission of the State into the Union*,
     vol. 3, pp. 182-183.

54   Austin, "Observation on Lead Mines," *American State Papers, Public Lands*,
     vol. 3, p. 708-711.

55   Stephen F. Austin to Bryan, January 19, January ____, 1814, Austin Papers.

56   Moses Austin to Bryan, September 7, 1814[?], Austin Papers.

57   Elias Bates to Bryan, December 6, 1814, Bryan Papers.

58   William Bryan to James Bryan, March 8, 1813, Guy Bryan to James Bryan,
     April 21, 1813, Estate of James Bryan to Guy Bryan, n. d., Bill, List of Notes,
     January, 1813, Bryan Papers.

59   Charles Avery to James Bryan, September 8, 1814, William Bennett to James
     Bryan, October 11, 1813, Bryan Papers.

60   George McGahan to Bryan, September ?, 1814, Bryan Papers.

61   Mary Austin to Rebecca Leaming, September 2, 1813, March 10, 1814,
     Austin-Leaming Letters.

62   Mary Austin to Rebecca Leaming, August 28, [1814], Austin-Leaming Letters.

63   Moses Austin to Stephen F. Austin, December 16, 1804, in Barker, *Austin
     Papers*, vol. 2, pt. 1, p. 94.

CHAPTER X

1   Austin to Bryan, November 25, 1814, in Eugene C. Barker, ed., *The Austin Papers*, vol. 2, pt. 1, p. 243, Austin to Bryan, September 2, 1814, *ibid.*, 241; Richard H. Collins, *History of Kentucky*, vol. 2, pp. 480, 487.

2   Austin to Bryan, September 2, 1814, in Barker, *Austin Papers*, vol. 2, pt. 1, p. 241.

3   Moses Austin to Bryan, October 18, December 7, 18, 1814, February ?, 1815, Austin Papers; Instructions [1812?], Anthony Butler Papers; Jona. Taylor and Company, Receipt, March 1, 1810, in Barker, *Austin Papers*, vol. 2, pt. 1, p. 170, Stephen Austin to Moses Austin, March 25, 1815, *ibid.*, 251.

4   Austin to Bryan, December 17, 12, 1814, Austin Papers.

5   Austin to Children, January 22, 1815, Austin Papers.

6   Austin to Bryan, January 31, 1816, in Barker, *Austin Papers*, vol. 2, pt. 1, p. 255.

7   Stephen F. Austin to Moses Austin, April 10, 1816, Austin Papers.

8   Austin to Bryan, January 31, 1816, in Barker, *Austin Papers*, vol. 2, pt. 1, p. 255; Austin to Bryan, January 22, 1816, *ibid.*, 254; Receipts, James Bryan Papers; Statement, 1815, Austin Papers; Statement, December 18, 1815, Receipt, November 4, 1817, Moses Austin to Charles Lucas, December 21, 1815, John B. C. Lucas Collection; Henry Austin vs. Moses Austin, Washington County, Missouri, Circuit Court Index, 1814-1821, pp. 88, 111.

9   *Missouri Gazette* (St. Louis), August 8, 1811; "Bank of the United States," *Virginia Magazine of History and Biography*, 8 (January, 1907), 291-295; George T. Starnes, *Sixty Years of Branch Banking in Virginia*, 18-20; James O. Wettereau, "Branches of the First Bank of the United States," *Journal of Economic History*, 2 (December, 1942), 76; Bray Hammond, *Banks and Politics in America: From the Revolution to the Civil War*, 86; Robert Lawhead Kirkpatrick, "History of St. Louis, 1804-1816," pp. 14, 114; Louis Houck, *A History of Missouri From the Earliest Explorations and Settlements Until the Admission of the State into the Union*, vol. 3, p. 191; John F. Darby, *Personal Recollections of Many Prominent People Whom I Have Known, and of Events—Especially Those Relating to the History of St. Louis—During the First Half of the Present Century*, 5; John Ray Cable, *The Bank of the State of Missouri*, 47.

10 Breckinridge Jones, "One Hundred Years of Banking in Missouri, 1820-1920," *Missouri Historical Review*, 15 (January, 1921), 346-349, 357-358; Hammond, *Banks and Politics in America*, 282.

11 Jones, "One Hundred Years of Banking in Missouri," 352-354; Cable, *Bank of the State of Missouri*, 48, 52; *Missouri Gazette* (St. Louis), January 4, July 13, September 7, 21, December 14, 1816.

12 Josiah Meigs to Judge Lucas, August 9, 1816, Lucas Collection; Josiah Meigs to Moses Austin, November 4, 1816, in Clarence Edwin Carter, comp. and ed., *The Territorial Papers of the United States*, vol. 15, pp. 200-201; Rufus Easton to Moses Austin, November 18, 1814, in Barker, *Austin Papers*, vol. 2, pt. 1, p. 242.

13 Moses Austin, "Observation on Lead Mines," *American State Papers, Public Lands*, vol. 3, p. 709.

14 *Ibid.*, 709-710; Martin Thomas to George Bomford, January, 1828, *ibid.*, vol. 4, p. 558; George Bullitt and T. Quarles to G. Graham, January 31, 1824, *ibid.*, vol. 3, p. 667.

15 Emily Bryan to James Bryan, November 6, 1816, James Franklin Perry
    Papers.
16 Moses Austin to Stephen F. Austin, Deed, November 18, 1816, Washington
    County, Missouri, Deed Book A, 107-111; Moses Austin to Bryan, September
    16, October ?, 1816, Austin Papers.
17 Austin to Bryan, September 16, 1816, ?, 21, 1812, January 14, 30, 1816, Austin
    Papers; Austin to Bryan, September 3, 1813, in Barker, *Austin Papers*, vol. 2,
    pt. 1, p. 228; Bryan to George McGahan, May 15, 1813, Bryan Papers.
18 Moses Austin to Stephen F. Austin and Anthony Butler, Deed, November 18,
    1816, Washington County, Missouri, Deed Book A, 107-111; An Exhibit of
    Mills and Buildings at Mine A Burton, 1799-1809, Austin Papers; "The
    Answer of Moses Austin to the Bill of Complaint of John Rice Jones, July 27,
    1813," cited in James Alexander Gardner, *Lead King: Moses Austin*, 70.
19 Moses Austin to Dear Children, December 18, 1816, Perry Transcripts, Austin
    Papers.
20 Price List, n. d., in Barker, *Austin Papers*, vol. 2, pt. 1, pp. 262-265; Moses
    Austin to Bryan, November 9, 1816, Austin Papers.
21 John Baldwin to James F. Perry, February 4, 1817, Perry Papers.
22 Henry Rowe Schoolcraft, *A View of the Lead Mines of Missouri: Including
    Some Observations on the Mineralogy, Geology, Geography, Antiquities, Soil,
    Climate, Population, and Productions of Missouri and Arkansaw, and Other
    Sections of the Western Country*, 48, 46; *Missouri Gazette* (St. Louis), July 27,
    August 10, 1816; Moses Austin to James Bryan, October 16, 1816[?], Austin
    Papers; *History of Franklin, Jefferson, Washington, Crawford and Gasconade
    Counties, Missouri*, 484-485, 525; Receipt, July 6, 1816, Bryan Papers; Potosi
    Academy Lottery ticket book, in Barker, *Austin Papers*, vol. 2, pt. 1, p. 304;
    Houck, *History of Missouri*, vol. 3, p. 69; George W. Showalter, *Potosi, Mis-
    souri: A Bicentennial Scrapbook, 1763-1963*, n. p.
23 Austin to Bryan, February 17, 1817, in Barker, *Austin Papers*, vol. 2, pt. 1, p.
    300.
24 *Ibid.*
25 Moses Austin Bryan to Beauregard Bryan, September 25, 1889, Declaration
    of Texas Independence Signers Collection.
26 Thomas Maitland Marshall, ed., *The Life and Papers of Frederick Bates*, vol.
    2, pp. 268, 280; Stephen F. Austin, Appointment, January 24, 1815; Moses and
    Maria Austin to Stephen F. Austin, Deed, June 7, 1814, Washington County,
    Missouri, Deed Book A, 24-25, Moses Bates to Stephen F. Austin, Deed,
    March 30, 1815, *ibid.*, 79-80; Militia Report, n. d., in Barker, *Austin Papers*,
    vol. 2, pt. 1, pp. 240-241; Fines assessed by a Battalion Court, Daniel Dunklin
    Papers; William R. Denslow, *10,000 Famous Freemasons*, 39.
27 M. McGirk to Charles Lucas, December 22, 1816, Lucas Collection; *Missouri
    Gazette* (St. Louis), December 7, 1816.
28 Memorial to Congress, n. d., in Barker, *Austin Papers*, vol. 2, pt. 1, pp. 290-
    291.
29 *Missouri Gazette* (St. Louis), August 9, 1815, December 2, 1816, January 11,
    18, 1817.
30 E. Bates to S. F. Austin & Co., August 2, 1817, in Barker, *Austin Papers*, vol. 2,
    pt. 1, p. 318.
31 Robert Pogue to Heerl & Pogue, December 9, 1817, *ibid.*, 326; Promissory
    Notes, October 14, November 19, 1817, Austin Papers.
32 Henry Rowe Schoolcraft, *The American Indians: Their History, Condition
    and Prospects, From Original Notes and Manuscripts*, 30.

33 Austin to Bryan, June 22, 1817, *Austin Papers.*
34 *Missouri Gazette* (St. Louis), July 25, 1817; Stephen F. Austin to Bryan, February 17, 1817, Moses Austin to Bryan, June 30, 1817, in Barker, *Austin Papers,* vol. 2, pt. 1, pp. 300, 316; Moses Austin to Bryan, September 29, 1818, Austin Papers.
35 Austin, "Observation on Lead Mines," *American State Papers, Public Lands,* vol. 3, p. 709; Schoolcraft, *A View of the Lead Mines of Missouri,* 46; Stephen Austin to Moses Austin, March 25, 1815, in Barker, *Austin Papers,* vol. 2, pt. 1, p. 251; Samuel Hammond, Moses Austin, and Paul and John Kingston, Indenture, May 24, 1811, Deed Records of St. Louis County, Book C-1, p. 568, Moses and Mary Austin, Samuel and Eliza Hammond to John W. Honey, Indenture, July 29, 1813, *ibid.,* Book D, 288-289; *Missouri Gazette* (St. Louis), June 19, 1818.
36 *Missouri Gazette* (St. Louis), September 23, 1815.
37 Bates to Bryan, April 5, 1815, Bryan Papers.
38 Austin to Bryan, July 21, 1817, in Barker, *Austin Papers,* vol. 2, pt. 1, p. 317; Elias Bates to Bryan, April 5, October 14, 1815, November 4, 1816, Bryan Papers.
39 Contract, October 9, 1817, in Barker, *Austin Papers,* vol. 2, pt. 1, pp. 321-322.
40 Moses Austin to Emily Bryan, October 12, 1816, in *ibid.,* 260.
41 Moses Austin to Bryan, January 17, 1817, *ibid.,* 299, Stephen F. Austin to Bryan, February 17, 1817, *ibid.,* 299-300.
42 *Missouri Gazette* (St. Louis), December 14, 1816; Jones, "One Hundred Years of Banking in Missouri," 366-370.
43 Memorandum, n. d., in Barker, *Austin Papers,* vol. 2, pt. 1, pp. 265-271; *Missouri Gazette* (St. Louis), December 14, 1816, January 11, 1817.
44 Reflections Respecting the Bank Question 1816-1817, in Barker, *Austin Papers,* vol. 2, pt. 1, p. 272-281.
45 Statement [in Stephen's hand], n. d., *ibid.,* 283-285; A Bill concerning the finances of this Territory and to create a permanent Bank Fund for Territorial purposes, [January, 1817?], *ibid.,* 281-283; William Russell to Charles Lucas, December 29, 1816, Lucas Collection; *Missouri Gazette* (St. Louis), January 27, 1816.
46 Jones, "One Hundred Years of Banking in Missouri," 360-361; Cable, *Bank of the State of Missouri,* 52; Hammond, *Banks and Politics in America,* 39; M. McGirk to Charles Lucas, December 22, 1816, Lucas Collection.
47 William Borown to James Bryan, February 12, 1817, Bryan Papers.
48 Timothy Flint, *Recollections of the Last Ten Years in the Valley of the Mississippi,* 154, 155; Jones, "One Hundred Years of Banking in Missouri," 348-349.
49 Austin to Bryan, July 5, 1817, in Barker, *Austin Papers,* vol. 2, pt. 1, pp. 316-317.
50 Jones, "One Hundred Years of Banking in Missouri," 360-361, 374-376; Cable, *Bank of the State of Missouri,* 52; Hammond, *Banks and Politics in America,* 39.
51 Robert Simpson to John B. C. Lucas, March 8, 1818, Lucas Collection.
52 *Missouri Gazette* (St. Louis), March 18, 1818; Jones, "One Hundred Years of Banking in Missouri," 361-364; Cable, *Bank of the State of Missouri,* 54-55.
53 Robert Simpson to John B. C. Lucas, March 8, 1818, Lucas Collection.
54 Moses Austin to Bank of St. Louis, [Deed of Trust], March 11, 1818, Washington County, Missouri, Deed Book A, 234-236; Moses Austin Survey #430, Missouri Record of Land Titles, vol. A, 100-102; Record of Testimony in Private Land Claims in Missouri, vol. 44, #J16.

55   Samuel Perry and Company to Stephen F. Austin, Bill, 1816-1817, in Barker, *Austin Papers*, vol. 2, pt. 1, pp. 300-303.
56   Emily Bryan to James Bryan, November 6, 1816, Austin Papers.
57   James E. B. Austin to Moses Austin, September 24, 1816, Austin Papers.
58   Moses Austin to Emily Bryan, August 14, 1816, James B. Austin to Moses Austin, September 24, 1816, Moses Austin to Bryan, February ?, 1815, Austin Papers.
59   Edward Sharp to Maria Austin, March 12, 1817, Moses Austin to Bryan, July 5, 1817, Austin Papers.
60   Stephen F. Austin to Bryan, February 17, 1817, in Barker, Austin Papers, vol. 2, pt. 1, p. 300.
61   Moses Austin to Bryan, June 22, 1818, Austin Papers.

CHAPTER XI

1   Austin to James Bryan, September 13, 1818, in Eugene C. Barker, ed., *The Austin Papers*, vol. 2, pt. 1, p. 333; Stephen F. Austin to Bryan, July 3, 1818, *ibid.*, 330-331; Moses Austin to James Bryan, July 28, 1818, Mary Austin to Mrs. Grace Sharp, n. d., Austin Papers; *Missouri Gazette* (St. Louis), June 12, 1818; [Laura Bryan Parker, ed.], "A Letter from Mary (Mrs. Moses) Austin," *Quarterly* of the Texas State Historical Association, 10 (1907), 345.
2   Floyd Calvin Shoemaker, *Missouri and Missourians: Land of Contrasts and People of Achievements*, vol. 1, p. 252.
3   Austin to Bryan, June 22, 1818, Austin Papers.
4   Mary Austin to Mrs. Grace Sharp, n. d., Austin Papers; Moses Austin to James Bryan, September 13, 1818, in Barker, *Austin Papers*, vol. 2, pt. 1, p. 333.
5   Samuel Hammond to Austin, October, 1818, Austin Papers; *Missouri Gazette* (St. Louis), November 27, December 18, 1818.
6   *Missouri Gazette* (St. Louis), January 8, 1819; Broadside, February 26, 1819, in Barker, *Austin Papers*, vol. 2, pt. 1, pp. 336-337; J. Findley and Timothy Williams to Moses Austin, Receipt, January 10, 1819, James Bryan Papers.
7   Moses and Mary Austin to Israel McGready, Deed, March 1, 1819, Washington County, Missouri, Deed Book A, 342-344, Moses and Mary Austin to Joseph McCormack, Deed, March 14, 1819, *ibid.*, 344-345, Moses and Mary Austin to Israel McGready, Deed, March 18, 1819, *ibid.*, 352-354, Moses and Mary Austin to John C. Brickey, Deed, March 18, 1819, *ibid.*, 358, Moses and Mary Austin to S. Rhoads Fisher, Deed, March 18, 1819, *ibid.*, 369-370, Moses and Mary Austin to John Brickey, March 22, 1819, *ibid.*, 372-373.
8   Stephen F. Austin to James Bryan, December 31, 1818, in Barker, *Austin Papers*, vol. 2, pt. 1, p. 335.
9   *Missouri Gazette* (St. Louis), July 14, 1819.
10   Austin to O'Hara, April 5, 1819, in Barker, *Austin Papers*, vol. 2, pt. 1, p. 341.
11   Dudley G. Wooten, ed., *A Comprehensive History of Texas, 1685 to 1897*, vol. 1, p. 442.
12   See above, p. 59.
13   *Missouri Gazette* (St. Louis), July 24, 1818.
14   Wooten, *Comprehensive History of Texas*, vol. 1, p. 442; Mattie Austin Hatcher, *The Opening of Texas to Foreign Settlement, 1801-1821*, pp. 276-277.
15   David B. Gracy II, ed., *Establishing Austin's Colony: The First Book Printed in Texas, With the Laws, Orders and Contracts of Colonization*, 2.

16 W. B. Dewees, *Letters From An Early Settler of Texas*, 14; Moses Austin to Henry R. Schoolcraft, July 4, 1819, Henry Rowe Schoolcraft Papers.

17 *Arkansas Gazette* (Little Rock), February 2, 1821.

18 *Ibid.*; Memorandum for Bryan and J. F. Colerba, undated, Austin Papers; Dallas T. Herndon, *The Centennial History of Arkansas*, vol. 1, p. 761; Dewees, *Letters From An Early Settler of Texas*, 12; Walter N. Vernon, *William Stevenson: Riding Preacher*, 30-42.

19 Austin to Bryan, January 3, 1818, in Barker, *Austin Papers*, vol. 2, pt. 1, p. 327.

20 Austin to Bryan, July 3, 1818, in Barker, *Austin Papers*, vol. 2, pt. 1, pp. 330.

21 *Ibid.*, 331.

22 Austin to Bryan, July 17, August 13, 1818, Austin Papers.

23 Austin to Bryan, November 2, 1818, in Barker, *Austin Papers*, vol. 2, pt. 1, p. 333-334.

24 Memorandum of Account, March 29, 1819, *ibid.*, 338-339; Accounts, October 23, 1818-January 20, 1819, Austin Papers; List of Amounts, Undated, James Bryan Papers.

25 Austin to Charles Lucas, June 16, 1816, John B. C. Lucas Collection.

26 Austin to O'Hara, April 7, 1819, in Barker, *Austin Papers*, vol. 2, pt. 1, p. 342.

27 Memorandum Concerning Land Speculations, Various Dates, *ibid.*, 337, Stephen F. Austin to O'Hara, April 7, 1819, *ibid.*, 339; Eloy Dejarbois, New Madrid Certificate, February 24, 1819, William M. O'Hara and Wife to Stephen F. Austin, March 5, 1819, John E. Knight Papers.

28 Austin to O'Hara, June 16, 1819, in Barker, *Austin Papers*, vol. 2, pt. 1, p. 344.

29 *Ibid.*, 344-345, Memorandum of Debts, Undated, *ibid.*, 350; James Bryan, Agreement, June 16, 1819, Memorandum of S. F. Austins Notes paid by J. Bryan, Undated, J. Bryan to S. F. Austin, June 19, 1819, Austin Papers; William O'Hara and James Bryan, Partition, August 16, 1820, Pulaski County, Arkansas, Deed Book A, pp. 274-289.

30 *Missouri Gazette* (St. Louis), December 29, 1819; James Bryan and Robert Andrews to Moses Madden, Agreement, November 20, 1819, Bryan Papers; Memorandum, January 1, 1820, in Barker, *Austin Papers*, vol. 2, pt. 1, p. 351-352, Bill, [January 27, 1820], *ibid.*, 353, Richard Thurmond to Stephen F. Austin, February 15, 1820, *ibid.*, 356.

31 Stephen F. Austin to Major Jacob Pettit, October 5, 1819, Natchez Trace Collection; Robert L. and Pauline H. Jones, "Stephen F. Austin in Arkansas," *Arkansas Historical Quarterly*, 25 (Winter, 1966), 342-344; Manuscript History of Arkansas, Robert W. Trimble Collection.

32 Henry Rowe Schoolcraft, *Travels in the Central Portions of the Mississippi Valley*, 247n.

33 Henry Rowe Schoolcraft, *Scenes and Adventures in the Semi-Alpine Region of the Ozark Mountains of Missouri and Arkansas*, 38; Henry Rowe Schoolcraft, *The American Indians: Their History, Condition and Prospects, From Original Notes and Manuscripts*, 29.

34 Schoolcraft, *Travels in the Central Portions of the Mississippi Valley*, 247; Schoolcraft, *The American Indians*, 34, 39.

35 Austin to Schoolcraft, June 8, 20, 1819, Austin to Schoolcraft, Power of Attorney, June 9, 1819, Schoolcraft Papers.

36 Austin to Schoolcraft, June 8, 1819, Schoolcraft Papers.

37 Austin to Schoolcraft, June 11, 1819, Schoolcraft Papers.

38 Austin to Schoolcraft, June 20, 1819, Schoolcraft Papers.

39 Austin to Schoolcraft (two letters), June 20, 1819, Schoolcraft Papers.

40   Austin to Schoolcraft, June 20, 1819, Schoolcraft Papers.
41   *Missouri Gazette* (St. Louis), July 14, 1819.
42   Paper relating to the effects of the Bank of St. Louis, July 19, 1819[?], T. C. Link Papers; Breckinridge Jones, "One Hundred Years of Banking in Missouri, 1820-1920," *Missouri Historical Review*, 15 (January, 1921), 365; John Ray Cable, *The Bank of the State of Missouri*, 55.
43   Austin to Schoolcraft, July 20, 26, 1819, Schoolcraft Papers.
44   Austin to Schoolcraft, July 26, 1819, Schoolcraft Papers.
45   Austin to Schoolcraft, July 28, 1819, Schoolcraft Papers.
46   Moses Austin to James E. B. Austin, August 12, 1819, in Barker, *Austin Papers*, vol. 2, pt. 1, p. 347.
47   Austin to Schoolcraft, August 5, 1819, Schoolcraft Papers.
48   Austin to Schoolcraft, August 12, 1819, Schoolcraft Papers.
49   Austin to Schoolcraft, July 28, 30, 1819, and undated fragment, Schoolcraft Papers.
50   Austin to Schoolcraft, August 18, July 30, August 5, 13, 1819, Schoolcraft Papers; Jno Perry and M. Ruggles vs. Risdon H. Price, Defendants brief, n. d., Hamilton R. Gamble Papers.
51   Austin to Schoolcraft, July 30, August 5, 13, 1819, Schoolcraft Papers.
52   Moses Austin to James E. B. Austin, August 12, 1819, in Barker, *Austin Papers*, vol. 2, pt. 1, p. 346.
53   Austin to Schoolcraft, September 17, 1819, Schoolcraft Papers.
54   Various cases listed in Jefferson County, Missouri, Circuit Court Record Book, 3-10, 19-20, 26, 31-32, 36-37, 70, 73, 75-77, 86, 103; Orders of the Jefferson County Court, May 5, July 13, 1819, Record of Sheriff's Sale, Jefferson County, March 3, 1820, Bryan Papers; Shoemaker, *Missouri and Missourians*, vol. 1, pp. 309-310; Notice of Sheriff's Sale, Jefferson County, Missouri, Deed Book A, 184-185, Sheriff to James Bryan, Deed, November 23, 1819, *ibid.*, 362-364; F. White, Receipt, November 9, 1819, Austin Papers; John G. Gamble vs. Austin, #21, Box 23, and #40, Box 18, Supreme Court of Missouri Case Files.
55   Emily Bryan to James Bryan, November 25, 1818, S. F. Austin to Bryan, December 5, 1818, Austin Papers.
56   Notice of Sheriffs Sale, October 11, 1819, Bryan Papers; Bank of St. Louis vs. James Bryan, Summary of Case, 1818-1819, Bryan Papers; James Cummins to James Bryan, July 15, 1819, in Barker, *Austin Papers*, vol. 2, pt. 1, p. 345-346; Stephen F. Austin to Bryan, June 2, 1820, James Austin to James Bryan, October 5, 1819, Moses Austin to James E. B. Austin, October 31, 1819, Austin Papers.
57   To the Citizens of the County of Jefferson, January 10, 1820, in Barker, *Austin Papers*, vol. 2, pt. 1, pp. 352, 353.
58   Thomas Brock to Austin, [Deed of Trust], January 27, 1820, Austin Papers.
59   Austin to James E. B. Austin, February 8, 1820, in Barker, *Austin Papers*, vol. 2, pt. 1, p. 355; Shoemaker, *Missouri and Missourians*, vol. 1, p. 493.
60   Austin to Bryan, February 4, 1820, Austin Papers.
61   Rufus Pettibone and James Bryan, Memorandum, February 17, 1820, Austin Papers; Moses and Mary Austin to James Bryan, Rufus and Levi Pettibone, Deed, February 15, 1820, Washington County, Missouri, Deed Book A, 454-455; William J. Bryan et al. vs. Ferdinand B. Kennett et al., *Transcript of Record*, 66-74, 78-79, 84-85, 132-133.
62   *Missouri Gazette* (St. Louis), March 22, 1820.
63   O'Hara to Bryan, March 23, 1820, Austin Papers.

64 Moses Austin to Son, March 15, 1820, Austin Papers.
65 William Ficklin to Schoolcraft, March 16, 1820, Schoolcraft Papers; Bryan et al. vs. Kennett et al., *Transcript of Record*, 33-37.
66 Moses Austin to James E. B. Austin, April 8, 1821, in Barker, *Austin Papers*, vol. 2, pt. 1, p. 385.
67 Moses Austin to James Austin, February 8, 1820, *ibid.*, 355.

CHAPTER XII

1 Genealogical Notes, in Eugene C. Barker, ed., *The Austin Papers*, vol. 2, pt. 1, p. 3; [Laura Bryan Parker], "A Letter from Mary (Mrs. Moses) Austin," *Quarterly* of the Texas State Historical Association, 10 (1907), 345; Moses and Maria Austin to Elias Bates, Deed, May 12, 1820, Jefferson County, Missouri, Deed Book A, 602-604.
2 Austin to Schoolcraft, July 4, June 11, 20, 1819, Schoolcraft to Thomas Ritchie, May 15, 1848, Henry Rowe Schoolcraft Papers; *Missouri Gazette* (St. Louis), October 17, 10, November 3, 10, December 1.
3 Austin to Schoolcraft, August 19, 1819, Schoolcraft Papers.
4 Austin to Schoolcraft, September 17, 1819, undated fragment, Schoolcraft Papers.
5 J. Meigs to Moses Austin, March 9, 1820, in Barker, *Austin Papers*, vol. 2, pt. 1, p. 356.
6 Austin to Bryan, June 2, 1820, in Barker, *Austin Papers*, vol. 2, pt. 1, p. 364.
7 Austin to Bryan, April 30, 1820, in *ibid.*, 359; Robert L. and Pauline H. Jones, "Stephen F. Austin in Arkansas," *Arkansas Historical Quarterly*, 25 (Winter, 1966), 344, 346; David B. Gracy II, ed., *Establishing Austin's Colony: The First Book Printed in Texas, With the Laws, Orders and Contracts of Colonization*, 1-2.
8 Executive Register for the Arkansas Territory, 1819-1836, in Clarence Edwin Carter, comp. and ed., *The Territorial Papers of the United States*, vol. 19, p. 789; James Miller to Stephen F. Austin, Commission, July 10, 1820, in Barker, *Austin Papers*, vol. 2, pt. 1, pp. 365-366. The Executive Register shows that the appointment had been made on February 10, but the oath not administered for five months.
9 Margaret Ross, ed., "From First, the Little Rock Site Favored; Old Settler Speaks of His Fellow Pioneers," *Arkansas Gazette* (Little Rock), January 11, 1959; Elias A. Elliott to Sir, July 28, 1820, Austin Papers.
10 Dallas T. Herndon, *The Centennial History of Arkansas*, vol. 1, p. 832; F. M. H., "Biography of Dr. Matthew Cunningham," *The Arkansas Pioneers*, vol. 1, no. 1 (September, 1912), 8.
11 Wheeler to Father, November 11, December 30, 1819, Margaret Smith Ross Collection; *Arkansas Gazette* (Little Rock), May 20, 1820; Moses Austin to Schoolcraft, September 17, 1819, Schoolcraft Papers.
12 Stephen F. Austin to William M. O'Hara, December 31, 1819, Darby Papers; Witter quoted in Margaret Smith Ross, "From First, the Little Rock Site Favored; Old Settler Speaks of His Fellow Pioneers," *Arkansas Gazette* (Little Rock), January 11, 1959.
13 *Arkansas Gazette* (Little Rock), May 20, 1820.
14 Stephen F. Austin to James Bryan, April 30, 1820, in Barker, *Austin Papers*, vol. 2, pt. 1, p. 359.
15 Louis Houck, *A History of Missouri From the Earliest Explorations and Settle-*

ments Until the Admission of the State into the Union, vol. 3, p. 53; Wheeler to Father, May 21, 1820, Ross Collection; Carter, *Territorial Papers of the United States*, vol. 19, p. 380n.

16   E. A. Elliott to James Bryan, August 28, 1820, Elias A. Elliott to Sir, July 28, 1820, Austin Papers; Ross, "From First, the Little Rock Site Favored," *Arkansas Gazette* (Little Rock), January 11, 1959; Memorandum and Price List, in Barker, *Austin Papers*, vol. 2, pt. 1, pp. 361-363.

17   *Arkansas Gazette* (Little Rock), October 14, 21, 28, 1820.

18   Elliott to James Bryan, October 29, 1820, Austin Papers.

19   *Ibid.*

20   Gracy, *Establishing Austin's Colony*, 2.

21   Moses Austin, Memorandum and Itinerary, in Barker, *Austin Papers*, vol. 2, pt. 1, p. 368, Stephen F. Austin to Maria Austin, [January 20, 1821], *ibid.*, 373, 374; Jones and Jones, "Stephen F. Austin in Arkansas," *Arkansas Historical Quarterly*, vol. 25, p. 350; *Arkansas Gazette* (Little Rock), November 11, 1820; Gracy, *Establishing Austin's Colony*, 3.

22   Memorandum and Itinerary, in Barker, *Austin Papers*, vol. 2, pt. 1, p. 368, Examination of Moses Austin, *ibid.*, 370; Examination of Jacob Kirkham and Jacob Forsai, Nacogdoches Archives; *Arkansas Gazette* (Little Rock), June 23, 1821.

23   Charles A. Bacarisse, "The Baron de Bastrop: Life and Times of Philip Hendrik Nering Bogel, 1759 to 1827," pp. 134-135; Charles A. Bacarisse, "Baron de Bastrop," *Southwestern Historical Quarterly*, 58 (January, 1955), 325-326; Dudley G. Wooten, ed., *A Comprehensive History of Texas, 1685 to 1897*, vol. 1, p. 442; Charles A. Bacarisse, "Why Moses Austin Came to Texas," *Southwestern Social Science Quarterly*, 40 (June, 1959), 16-23.

24   Dallas T. Herndon, *Why Little Rock Was Born*, 59-61.

25   Pedro Pedesclaux, Acts, 1801, vol. 38-39, New Orleans Notary Archives; Moses Austin vs. Pasqual Detchemendy, Document #1801052701, Judicial Records of the Spanish Cabildo; Bacarisse, "The Baron de Bastrop," 86. See above, pp. 89-90.

26   Mattie Austin Hatcher, *The Opening of Texas to Foreign Settlement, 1801-1821*, pp. 252-276.

27   Antonio Martínez to Joaquin de Arredondo, [December 26, 1820], Malcolm McLean, comp. and ed., *Papers Concerning Robertson's Colony in Texas*, vol. 1, pp. 301-302; Austin's Petition to Introduce 300 Families into Texas, December 26, 1820, in Hatcher, *Opening of Texas to Foreign Settlement*, 354.

28   Austin to Bastrop, January 26, 1821, in Barker *Austin Papers*, vol. 2, pt. 1, p. 380.

29   Moses Austin to Antonio Martínez, January 26, 1821, Moses Austin to Felix Trudeau, *ibid.*, 377-378, 381-382.

30   Statement, *ibid.*, 377; Gracy, *Establishing Austin's Colony*, 3.

31   Genealogical Notes, in Barker, *Austin Papers*, vol. 2, pt. 1, p. 3; Wooten, *Comprehensive History of Texas*, vol. 1, 443.

32   Notes on Moses Austin, Document #2407, Mirabeau Buonaparte Lamar Papers.

33   Austin to Mother, [January 20, 1821], in Barker, *Austin Papers*, vol. 2, pt. 1, p. 373.

34   Moses Austin to Antonio Martínez, January 26, 1821, *ibid.*, 377-378, Moses Austin to Felix Trudeau, February 3, 1821, *ibid.*, 381-382, Austin to Bastrop, January 26, 1821, *ibid.*, 379-380; Wooten, *Comprehensive History of Texas*, vol. 1, p. 443.

35 Austin to Bastrop, January 16, 1821, quoted in Bastrop to Martínez, [about February 1, 1821], in Barker, *Austin Papers*, vol. 2, pt. 1, p. 381; *Arkansas Gazette* (Little Rock), February 27, 1821; St. Louis *Enquirer*, May 19, 1821, quoted in *ibid.*, June 23, 1821.

36 Austin to Bastrop, January 26, 1821, in Barker, *Austin Papers*, vol. 2, pt. 1, p. 381.

37 Austin to Bastrop, January 26, 1821, *ibid.*, 379, Moses Austin to James E.B. Austin, April 8, 1821, *ibid.*, 387.

38 Gracy, *Establishing Austin's Colony*, 2; Wooten, *Comprehensive History of Texas*, vol. 1, p. 443; Moses Austin and Douglass Forsythe, Agreement and Receipts, January 22, 1821, in Barker, *Austin Papers*, vol. 2, pt. 1, p. 375.

39 Moses Austin to James E. B. Austin, March 28, 1821, *ibid.*, 384-385.

40 Bastrop to Austin, March 2, 1821, *ibid.*, 384, Governor Martínez to Felix Trudeau, February 26, 1821, *ibid.*, 383-384.

41 Arredondo to Martínez, January 17, 1821, quoted in Martínez to Austin, February 8, 1821, in Gracy, *Establishing Austin's Colony*, 33.

42 Hatcher, *Opening of Texas to Foreign Settlement*, 278-281, 283-285, 291-292; Carlos E. Castañeda, *Our Catholic Heritage in Texas, 1519-1936*, vol. 4: *The Transition Period: The Fight for Freedom, 1810-1836*, pp. 186-187; Bacarisse, "The Baron de Bastrop," 131.

43 [Parker], "A Letter from Mary (Mrs. Moses) Austin," *Quarterly* of the Texas State Historical Association, vol. 10, p. 345.

44 Scott quoted in James F. Perry to S. F. and J. B. Austin, November 5, 1826, in Barker, *Austin Papers*, vol. 2, pt. 2, p. 1491.

45 *Missouri Gazette* (St. Louis), October 3, November 23, 1820; Jno Perry and M. Ruggles vs. Risdon H. Price, Defendants brief, n.d., Hamilton R. Gamble Papers.

46 [Parker], "A Letter from Mary (Mrs. Moses) Austin," *Quarterly* of the Texas State Historical Association, vol. 10, p. 345.

47 Austin to President and Directors, undated, Austin Papers.

48 Maria Austin to Stephen F. Austin, August 25, 1821, in Barker, *Austin Papers*, vol. 2, pt. 1, p. 408.

49 Austin to Bryan, April 21, 22, 1821, *ibid.*, 387-389.

50 Austin to Bryan, April 21, 1821, *ibid.*, 387, 388, Moses Austin to J. E. B. Austin, March 28, 1821, *ibid.*, 385.

51 Maria Austin to Stephen F. Austin, August 25, 1821, *ibid.*, 408.

52 Austin to Bryan, April 22, 1821, *ibid.*, 388; Jno Perry and M. Ruggles vs. Risdon H. Price, Defendants brief, n.d., Gamble Papers; William J. Bryan et al., *vs.* Ferdinand B. Kennett et al., *Transcript of Record*, Supreme Court of the United States, October Term, 1883, No. 137, p. 116.

53 Maria Austin to Stephen F. Austin, August 25, 1821, in Barker, *Austin Papers*, vol. 2, pt. 1, p. 409; Moses Austin to John Metcalfe, Power of Attorney, May 9, 1821, *ibid.*, 390-392.

54 St. Louis *Enquirer*, May 19, 1821, quoted in *Arkansas Gazette* (Little Rock), June 23, 1821.

55 W. B. Dewees, *Letters From An Early Settler of Texas*, 23.

56 Walter Louis Tubbs, "Elder Joseph L. Bays, A Pioneer Texas Baptist Preacher," 3-7.

57 Maria Austin to Stephen Austin, April 26, 1822, in Barker, *Austin Papers*, vol. 2, pt. 1, p. 500.

58 Agreement, April 22, 1821, *ibid.*, 389-390, Moses Austin to James E.B. Austin, March 28, April 8, 1821, *ibid.*, 385-386.

59   Stephen F. Austin to Maria Austin, [January 20, 1821], *ibid.*, 373, 374; William
     B. Victor, *Life and Events*, 122, 128.
60   Stephen F. Austin to Maria Austin, [January 20, 1821], in Barker, *Austin
     Papers*, vol. 2, pt. 1, 374; Wooten, *Comprehensive History of Texas*, vol. 1, p.
     445; A. J. Morrison, "Joseph H. Hawkins," *Tyler's Quarterly Historical and
     Genealogical Magazine*, 3 (1922), 20-22.
61   Moses Austin to Stephen F. Austin, May 22, 1821, in Barker, *Austin Papers*,
     vol. 2, pt. 1, p. 393.
62   Moses Austin to James E. B. Austin, March 28, 1821, *ibid.*, 385.
63   Moses Austin to James E. B. Austin, August 12, 1819, *ibid.*, 347.
64   Moses Austin to James E. B. Austin, February 8, 1820, *ibid.*, 354, Moses Aus-
     tin to James E. B. Austin, February 2, 1820, *ibid.*, 353, Moses Austin to James
     E. B. Austin, February 23, 1820, *ibid.*, 355.
65   Moses Austin to James E. B. Austin, April 8, 1821, *ibid.*, 386.
66   *Ibid.*, 386, Moses Austin to James E. B. Austin, March 28, 1821, *ibid.*, 385,
     Moses Austin to Bryan, April 22, 1821, *ibid.*, 388-389; [Parker], "A Letter
     from Mary (Mrs. Moses) Austin," *Quarterly* of the Texas State Historical
     Association, vol. 10, p. 346.
67   This account is formed from two letters Maria wrote Stephen, the first on
     June 8, two days before Moses' death, the other on August 25, 1821, two and a
     half months later. See: *Austin Papers*, 394-395, 408-410. See also Death Certif-
     icate, June 16, 1821, *ibid.*, 395-396, James E. Brown Austin to Brother, Janu-
     ary 29, 1822, *ibid.*, 471; John M. Bernhisel to Jas Bryan, Receipt, November
     29, 1821, Austin Papers; *Missouri Gazette* (St. Louis), June 19, 1821; Wooten,
     Comprehensive History of Texas, vol. 1, pp. 443-444.

EPILOGUE

1   Maria Austin to James E. B. Austin, August 3, 1821, in Eugene C. Barker, ed.,
     The Austin Papers, vol. 2, pt. 1, p. 405.
2   Hawkins to Maria Austin, June 27, 1821, *ibid.*, 397-398, Agreement between
     Austin and Hawkins, November 14, 1821, *ibid.*, 428.
3   Maria to Stephen F. Austin, December 15, 1821, in Barker, *Austin Papers*, vol.
     2, pt. 1, 450; William B. Victor, *Life and Events*, 129-130.
4   AB Jr. to Robert Wash, July 26, 1821, in Clarence Edwin Carter, comp. and
     ed., *The Territorial Papers of the United States*, vol. 15, p. 740; Thomas Oliver,
     Certification of James Bryan as Executor, June 15, 1821, Austin Papers;
     James Bryan to Stephen F. Austin, January 15, 1822, in Barker, *Austin
     Papers*, vol. 2, pt. 1, 465, Maria Austin to Stephen F. Austin, January 19, 1822,
     ibid., 468-469.
5   Emily Bryan to Stephen Austin, July 1, September 28, 1823, Maria to
     Stephen Austin, October 5, 1823, E. A. Elliott to James Bryan, August 28,
     1820, Austin Papers; William J. Bryan *vs.* Ferdinand B. Kennett, *Transcript of
     Record*, Supreme Court of the United States, October Term, 1883, No. 137, p.
     17; Stephen F. Austin to James Bryan, June 2, 1820, in Barker, *Austin Papers*,
     vol. 2, pt. 1, pp. 363-364; Judgments, Court of Common Pleas, Hempstead
     County, Arkansas. Bryan died and was buried in Herculaneum.
6   Emily Bryan to Stephen Austin, September 28, 1823, April 30, 1824, Austin
     Papers.
7   Emily Bryan to Stephen Austin, July 1, 1823, Austin Papers.
8   Emily Bryan to Stephen Austin, April 30, 1824, Austin Papers.

9   Emily Bryan to Stephen Austin, September 28, 1823, Austin Papers.

10 James F. Perry to Stephen F. and James B. Austin, November 5, 1826, in Barker, *Austin Papers*, vol. 2, pt. 2, p. 1491; Emily to Stephen Austin, January 9, 1825, March 20, year unknown, Austin Papers; Bryan et al. vs. Kennett et al., *Transcript of Record*, 17.

11 "William J. Bryan et al., *vs.* Ferdinand B. Kennett et al.," *U.S. Reports 113*, October Term, 1884, pp. 102-103, 127, 179-199; Bryan et al., *vs.* Kennett et al., *Transcript of Record*, 1-153.

12 Maria Austin to Stephen F. Austin, January 19, 1822, in Barker, *Austin Papers*, vol. 2, pt. 1, pp. 469-470.

13 Emily Bryan to Stephen Austin, July 1, 1823, Austin Papers.

14 Emily Bryan to Stephen Austin, December 30, 1823, April 30, 1824, Austin Papers; Genealogical Notes in Barker, *Austin Papers*, vol. 2, pt. 1, p. 6.

15 Emily Bryan to Stephen Austin, March 20, year unknown, Austin Papers.

16 *History of Franklin, Jefferson, Washington, Crawford and Gasconade Counties, Missouri*, 519.

17 Alphonso Wetmore, comp., *Gazetteer of the State of Missouri*, 235.

18 St. Louis *Daily Globe-Democrat*, March 24, 1889.

19 *History of Franklin, Jefferson, Washington and Gasconade Counties*, 521; Unidentified clipping, Mr. and Mrs. John W. Beretta Papers; Potosi *Journal*, April 30, 1895, April 20, May 4, 1904. One of the canes is on display in the Museum of the Daughters of the Republic of Texas in the Old Land Office Building on the capitol grounds in Austin.

20 Kansas City *Times*, February 5, 1930, quoted in "Texas Would Honor Moses Austin," *Missouri Historical Review*, 24 (1930), 470; Walter Prescott Webb and H. Bailey Carroll, eds., *The Handbook of Texas*, vol. 2, pp. 661-662.

21 Alexander Deinst, "Moses Austin and His Son Stephen F. Austin," Alexander Deinst Papers.

22 Ernest C. Shearer, "Moses Austin: Let Him Rest in Peace," *Sul Ross State College Bulletin*, vol. 43, no. 3 (September, 1963), 110-111.

23 *Ibid.*, 111.

24 *Ibid.*, 111-112; Undated clippings, George Showalter Collection; St. Louis *Globe-Democrat*, April 22, 1938, St. Louis *Post-Dispatch*, April 21, 22, 1938; Potosi *Independent-Journal*, April 28, 1938; Adella B. Moore to Mary Towle, May 28, 1939, Jo Burford Papers. Shearer's dates all appear to be in error according to newspaper accounts of April 21, to which he lacked access.

25 Shearer, "Moses Austin," *Sul Ross State College Bulletin*, vol. 43, no. 3, p. 112.

26 Undated clipping, Showalter Collection.

27 Shearer, "Moses Austin," *Sul Ross State College Bulletin*, vol. 43, no. 3, p. 112.

28 *Ibid.*, 113.

29 St. Louis *Post-Dispatch*, April 21, 1938.

30 St. Louis *Post-Dispatch*, April 24, 1938; Shearer, "Moses Austin," *Sul Ross State College Bulletin*, vol. 43, no. 3, p. 113.

31 Potosi *Independent-Journal*, April 28, 1938.

32 Harry R. Burke, "'Texas' Attempt to Obtain Moses Austin's Body Parallels Mining Pioneer's Own Tactics," St. Louis *Globe-Democrat*, May 6, 1938; Undated clippings, Showalter Collection.

33 Shearer, "Moses Austin," *Sul Ross State College Bulletin*, vol. 43, no. 3, p. 114; St. Louis *Post-Dispatch*, April 27, 1938; Undated clippings, Showalter Collection.

34 Potosi *Independent-Journal*, May 12, 1938.

35 *Ibid.*, June 2, 1938; Edward Clark to DBGII, Interview, March 31, 1979.

36   Alice Hutson, *From Chalk to Bronze: A Biography of Waldine Tauch*, 91-104; San Antonio *Express*, July 10, 1938, May 16, 1939. This building is not the one in which Austin met Martínez (see above, p. 233, n. 2).

37   Shearer, "Moses Austin," *Sul Ross State College Bulletin*, vol. 43, no. 3, p. 116.

38   Undated clipping, Beretta Papers.

39   Kansas City *Star*, January 30, 1949; Potosi *Independent-Journal*, February 3, 1949; Kemp to Jester, February 15, 1949, Beauford Jester Papers; Shearer, "Moses Austin," *Sul Ross State College Bulletin*, vol. 43, no. 3, pp. 116-119; "Texas Collection," *Southwestern Historical Quarterly*, 42 (July, 1953), 125.

40   Potosi *Independent-Journal*, January 16, 1962, August 8, 1968; Shearer, "Moses Austin," *Sul Ross State College Bulletin*, vol. 43, no. 3, pp. 107-120.

41   Edna Perry Deckler, comp., "Austin-Perry Memorandum," *Stirpes*, 8 (March, 1968), 22.

42   "Directors Notebook," *The Bulletin* of the Missouri Historical Society, 18 (April, 1962), 274; Webb and Carroll, eds., *Handbook of Texas*, vol. 1, p. 669.

43   Travis B. Bryan, Jr., to Garland Adair, November 17, 1958, Hally Bryan Perry to Mrs. N.H. Beauregard, October 21, 1923, Beretta Papers.

44   "Director's Notebook," *The Bulletin* of the Missouri Historical Society, vol. 18, p. 274.

45   Walter Renton Ingalls, *Lead and Zinc in the United States: Comprising An Economic History of the Mining and Smelting of the Metals and the Conditions Which Have Affected the Development of the Industries*, 214-215.

46   Floyd Calvin Shoemaker, *Missouri and Missourians: Land of Contrasts and People of Achievements*, vol. 1, p. 139.

47   Ingalls, *Lead and Zinc in the United States*, 62, 214-215, 124.

48   *American State Papers, Public Lands*, vol. 4, p. 559; Ingalls, *Lead and Zinc in the United States*, 105. This is Austin's "Observation on Lead Mines" report of 1816 on the condition of the Missouri mines (see above, pp. 161-162.)

BIBLIOGRAPHY

PRIMARY SOURCES

Archival Groups and Manuscript Collections

Austin, Elias. Will and Inventory of Estate. File 1777, No. 118, Middletown Probate District, Estate Papers, RG 4, Records of the Probate Courts, Connecticut State Archives, Hartford.

Austin,, Moses. Documents, 1787, 1812. Beinecke Rare Book and Manuscripts Library, Yale University, New Haven, Connecticut. A letter and account illuminate two periods in Austin's life.

Austin, Stephen F. Appointment. Texas State Archives, Austin.

Austin-Leaming Letters. Eugene C. Barker Texas History Center, University of Texas at Austin. This correspondence between Maria Austin and cousins in Philadelphia illuminate Moses Austin's last years.

Austin Collection. San Jacinto Museum of History, Deer Park, Texas. Receipts from the Missouri mines, family bible, and artifacts.

Austin Papers. Eugene C. Barker Texas History Center, University of Texas at Austin. These business and personal papers of Moses Austin and Stephen F. Austin form the basis for any study of Moses Austin's life.

Austinville, Virginia, History. Southern Historical Collection, Chapel Hill, North Carolina. This collection contains a manuscript history of Austinville.

Bankruptcy Records, United States District Court for the Eastern District of Pennsylvania, RG 21, Records of District Courts. Federal Archives and Records Center, Philadelphia. The records of Stephen Austin's bankruptcy proceeding constitute Case #204 (Microfilm publication M-993, Roll 24). Cited as "SA, Examination of Bankrupt."

Beretta, Mr. and Mrs. John W. Papers. In possession of Mr. and Mrs. Beretta, San Antonio, Texas. The Berettas accumulated and compiled these letters and clippings in the course of their research on Moses Austin.

Bexar Archives. Eugene C. Barker Texas History Center, University of Texas at Austin. These records of the Spanish government in Texas contain documents pertaining to Moses Austin's visit to San Antonio.

Bissell, Daniel G. Papers. Missouri Historical Society, St. Louis. Letters among the Bissell Papers discuss the Bank of St. Louis.

Bogy Papers. Missouri Historical Society, St. Louis. Legal documents among these files bear on Austin's commerical lead smelting.
   Austin deposited silhouettes of Moses and Maria Austin.

Bryan, James. Papers. Eugene C. Barker Texas History Center, University of Texas at Austin. These business and personal papers of Moses Austin's son-in-law illuminate his personal life and especially his business career after 1812.

Buford, Jo. Papers. Copies in possession of Frank Magre, Herculaneum, Missouri. Ms. Buford accumulated various documents concerning the history of eastern Missouri and the Bryan burial ground.

Burke, Harry R. Papers. Missouri Historical Society, St. Louis. Burke prepared a research paper on the Burr Conspiracy.

Butler, Anthony. Papers. Eugene C. Barker Texas History Center, University of Texas at Austin. A few items concern Butler's interest in Mine a Breton.

Campbell County, Virginia. Deed Book No. 5. Virginia State Archives, Richmond. This record documents Austin's real estate transactions in Lynchburg.

Carr, William C. Papers. Missouri Historical Society, St. Louis. These papers of Moses Austin's attorney and friend document business and legal affairs of Austin.

Chauncey Family. Papers. Manuscripts and Archives, Sterling Memorial Library, Yale University, New Haven, Connecticut. These papers document life in Durham, Connecticut, and particularly a transaction of Elias Austin.

Clark, Delphina. Papers. Kent Memorial Library, Suffield, Connecticut. This local historian compiled extensive information on the history of Suffield.

Clipping File. Eugene C. Barker Texas History Center, University of Texas at Austin. Included is a letter from A.P. Willard to Mattie Austin Hatcher, February 24, 1930, concerning Stephen F. Austin and Bacon Academy.

Correspondence Politique, Louisiane et Florides, 1792 a 1803, Etas Unis: Supplement 7. Archives of the Ministry of Foreign Affairs, Paris. This series of records contains documents describing the Mississippi Valley, and mentioning Mine a Breton, prior to the Louisiana Purchase.

Darby Papers. Missouri Historical Society, St. Louis. Included are Stephen F. Austin letters relating to his Arkansas venture.

Declaration of Texas Independence Signers Collection. Eugene C. Barker Texas History Center, University of Texas at Austin. The letter of Moses Austin Bryan to Beauregard Bryan, September 25, 1889, describes both Emily Austin Bryan and Stephen F. Austin.

Dienst, Alexander. "Moses Austin and His Son, Stephen F. Austin." Manuscript of a talk, January 8, 1937. Alexander Dienst Papers, Eugene C. Barker Texas History Center, University of Texas at Austin.

Dunklin, Daniel. Papers. Joint Collection: Western Historical Manuscript Collection and State Historical Society of Missouri Manuscripts, University of Missouri, Columbia. The Papers contain documentation on militia musters in which Stephen F. Austin participated.

Durham Town Collection. Connecticut Historical Society, Harford. Includes a list of inscriptions from gravestones in the old Durham cemetery.

Durham Town Records. Grantees. Durham Town Recorder's Office, Durham, Connecticut. These books record the Austin real estate holdings in Durham.

_____. List of Ratable Estates, 1745. Original in possession of Mrs. Francis, courtesy Mr. Milton Whited, Meriden, Connecticut. Tax list.

_____. Meetings. Durham Town Recorder's Office, Durham, Connecticut. Minutes of town meetings.

Easton, Rufus. Papers. Missouri Historical Society, St. Louis. These papers of an Austin associate illuminate transactions of Moses Austin particularly during the years immediately after the Louisiana Purchase.

Eberstadt Collection. Eugene C. Barker Texas History Center, University of Texas at Austin. Includes a promissory note of Moses Austin.

Etting-Gratz Crogan. Papers. Pennsylvania Historical Society, Philadelphia. These papers of business associates of Stephen Austin illuminate aspects of his business career.

Executive Papers. Virginia State Archives, Richmond. The Governor's correspondence concerns both the Chiswell Lead Mine and the roofing of the capitol.

Fuller, Benjamin. Papers. Pennsylvania Historical Society, Philadelphia. Fuller's books of outgoing letters concern business and family affairs regarding both Moses and Mary Brown Austin.

Gamble, Hamilton R. Papers. Missouri Historical Society, St. Louis. The Gamble Papers contain documents regarding title to Mine a Breton.

Goodrich, Elizur. Account Book. Connecticut Historical Society, Hartford. The minister of the Durham Congregation kept a detailed account of births, deaths, and marriages.

Hempstead County, Arkansas, Court of Common Pleas. Judgments. Typescripts in Southwest Arkansas Regional Archives, Washington, Arkansas. The record includes cases concerning Stephen F. Austin and James Bryan.

Henrico County, Virginia. Deeds. Virginia State Archives, Richmond. The records document real estate transactions of Moses Austin.

————. Personal Property Taxes. Virginia State Archives, Richmond. The tax records illuminate Moses Austin's rising wealth.

Hustings Order Books. See: ["Richmond City, Virginia"].

Jefferson County, Missouri. Deed Books. County Courthouse, Hillsboro. The volumes document Moses Austin's land transactions in Herculaneum.

————. Circuit Court Record Book No. 1. County Courthouse, Hillsboro. Entries in the book document Moses Austin's failing financial condition.

————. Circuit Court Cases. County Courthouse, Hillsboro.

Jester, Beauford. Papers. Texas State Archives, Austin. The Moses Austin file concerns the proposal to move Austin's body to the Texas State Cemetery.

Judicial Records of the Spanish Cabildo. Louisiana Historical Center, Louisiana State Museum, New Orleans. Document No. 180105271 holds the papers of Moses Austin vs. Pasqual Detchemendy, 1803.

Knight, John E. Papers. Arkansas History Commission, Little Rock. This body of material contains documents from the earliest years of Little Rock.

Lamar, Mirabeau Buonaparte. Papers. Texas State Archives, Austin. A historian of Texas, Lamar collected data from the Austin family for a history of Texas that he never wrote.

Lesueur, Charles Alexandre. Drawings. Museum d'Histoire Naturelle du Havre, Le Harve, France. Lesueur's exquisite sketches provide a picture of the mine region of the 1820s.

Lewis, Ira Randolph. Papers. Eugene C. Barker Texas History Center, University of Texas at Austin. Contains an Austin account of 1814.

Link, T.C. Papers. Missouri Historical Society, St. Louis. Included are documents concerning the dissolution of the Bank of St. Louis.

[Louisiana Lead Company]. Petition and Original Bill. 11th and 12th Congresses, RG 46, Records of the United States Senate, National Archives, Washington, D.C. These documents both describe the proposed Louisiana Lead Company and chart its legislative history.

Lucas, John B.C. Collection. Missouri Historical Society, St. Louis. Lucas's notes on court cases document legal and business engagements of Moses Austin.

Merieult, John Francis, vs. Moses Austin. New Orleans City Archives, Louisiana Division, New Orleans Public Library, New Orleans, Louisiana. The case lays open one facet of the marketing of Moses Austin's Missouri lead.

Middletown, Connecticut. Land Records, Vol. 39. County Courthouse, Middle-
    town. Documents regarding Stephen Austin's bankruptcy were filed for
    record.
[Missouri]. Record of Land Titles. Missouri State Archives, Jefferson City. Volume
    A holds documents concerning both Moses Austin's title to Mine a Breton and
    Austin Survey No. 430 (Mine a Breton).
Mines Envelope. Missouri Historical Society, St. Louis. Contains, in particular, a
    document regarding Austin's dispute with French miners over possession of
    lead ashes.
Nacogdoches Archives. Texas State Archives, Austin. These records contain
    reports on Austin's visit to San Antonio.
Natchez Trace Collection. Eugene C. Barker Texas History Center, University of
    Texas at Austin. Holds documents concerning one of Moses Austin's boats on
    the Mississippi River, Stephen F. Austin in Arkansas, and the Texas Coloniza-
    tion project.
[New Orleans]. Records and Deliberations of the Cabildo. Louisiana Division, New
    Orleans Public Library. These records provide information on the career of
    John F. Merieult.
Papeles de Cuba. Archivo General de las Indias, Seville, Spain. Documenting
    Spanish government activity in the Mississippi Valley, these records illuminate
    Austin's first years at Mine a Breton.
Pedesclaux, Pedro. Acts. New Orleans Notary Archives, New Orleans Public
    Library, New Orleans, Louisiana. Pedesclaux recorded the documents he
    notarized, including ones by Moses Austin and ones by the Baron de Bastrop.
Perry, Halley Ballinger Bryan. Papers. Eugene C. Barker Texas History Center,
    University of Texas at Austin. Mrs. Perry gathered data on the Austin and
    related families.
Perry, James Franklin. Papers. Eugene C. Barker Texas History Center, University
    of Texas at Austin. Documents among the papers of the second husband of
    Emily Margaret Austin describe the efforts of the Austins to recover Durham
    Hall and illuminate Emily's later life.
Petitions. Virginia State Archives, Richmond. Petitions received by the General
    Assembly document business interests of Moses Austin.
Preston Papers. Virginia Historical Society, Richmond. A few documents concern
    Austin's mine operation at Austinville and his trip to Upper Louisiana.
Private Land Claims in Missouri. Division D, RG 49, Records of the Bureau of
    Land Management, General Land Office, National Archives, Washington,
    D.C. Volume 44 and the file on Missouri Private Land Claim #18 both contain
    testimony and significant documentation of Austin's claim to Mine a Breton.
[Richmond City, Virginia]. Hustings Order Books. Virginia State Archives, Rich-
    mond. These books record the disposition of court cases.
_____. Hustings Deed Book No. 1. Virginia State Archives, Richmond. Docu-
    ments Moses Austin's land transactions.
_____. Personal Property Tax Lists. Virginia State Archives, Richmond. Illu-
    minate Moses Austin's real estate holdings.
_____. Taxable Property. Virginia State Archives, Richmond. Displays Moses
    Austin's rising wealth.
Ross, Margaret Smith. Collection. University of Arkansas at Little Rock. Contains
    copies of documents regarding the early history of Little Rock, including the
    Amos Wheeler Papers.
Rutherford, Thomas. Letter Book. Virginia Historical Society, Richmond. Records
    the business climate in post-Revolution Richmond.

_____. "The Narrative of Thomas Rutherford, 1786-1852." Typescript. Valentine Museum, Richmond.

St. Louis, Missouri. Deed Books. Office of the Recorder of Deeds. Document Austin's land transactions in Herculaneum prior to the creation of Jefferson County.

St. Louis County, Missouri, Circuit Court. Minutes and Case Files. Twenty-second Judicial Circuit of Missouri, St. Louis. The records document several litigations in which Moses Austin was involved.

Ste. Genevieve Archives. Microfilm. Joint Collection: Western Historical Manuscript Collection and State Historical Society of Missouri Manuscripts, University of Missouri, Columbia. Records of the local government of Ste. Genevieve were compiled on film and illuminate the public business of the area.

Ste. Genevieve County, Missouri. Deed Books. County Courthouse, Ste. Genevieve, Missouri. The records document land transactions of Moses Austin.

Schoolcraft, Henry Rowe. Papers. Typescripts in Eugene C. Barker Texas History Center, University of Texas at Austin. These copies, made from originals in the Smithsonian Institution and the Library of Congress, concern principally Austin's proposed sale of the Mine a Breton tract.

Scranton, Mildred Mathewson. Old Houses of Connecticut: Historical and Technical Information in Regard to the Elias Austin House, Durham, Middlesex County. Manuscript produced for Connecticut Society of Colonial Dames of America. Connecticut State Library, Hartford.

Scrapbooks of Moses and Stephen F. Austin. Eugene C. Barker Texas History Center, University of Texas at Austin. Compiled long after their deaths, these volumes contain a variety of items concerning the two men.

Showalter, George W. Collection. In possession of George Showalter, Potosi, Missouri. Showalter has compiled an extensive collection of materials relating to the history of Potosi and Moses Austin.

Stoddard, Amos. Papers. Missouri Historical Society, St. Louis. Stoddard's letters to his mother describe St. Louis.

Streeter, Thomas W. Collection. Western Historical Manuscripts Collection, Yale University Library, New Haven, Connecticut. Streeter collected several items concerning Moses Austin.

Supreme Court of Missouri. Case Files. Missouri State Archives, Jefferson City. Moses Austin participated in several cases of this court, known in some years as the General Court of Missouri.

Thompson, Henry C. Collection. Joint Collection: Western Historical Manuscript Collection and State Historical Society of Missouri Manuscripts, University of Missouri, Columbia. In a talk, Thompson mentions in particular Moses Austin's burial on the Bryan Farm.

[Transylvania University]. University Records. Archives and Special Collections, Transylvania University, Lexington, Kentucky. Records document Stephen F. Austin's years at the University.

Trimble, Robert W. Collection. Arkansas History Commission, Little Rock. Trimble prepared a manuscript history of Arkansas which mentions the Austins.

United States Circuit Court, Virginia District, Middle Circuit. Case Files. Virginia State Library, Richmond. One case concerns business of Moses Austin.

Valle, Captain François. Collection. Missouri Historical Society, St. Louis. These papers document Austin's early years in Missouri.

Wadsworth, Jeremiah. Papers. Connecticut Historical Society, Hartford. Letters document the business activities of both Moses and his brother, Stephen.

Washington County, Missouri. Deed Books. County Courthouse, Potosi. Records in these volumes document Moses Austin's land transactions.

_____. Circuit Court Index. County Courthouse, Potosi. This volume records judgments affecting Moses Austin.

Wheeler, Amos. Papers. See: Ross, Margaret Smith, Papers.

Wilkinson, James. Papers. Missouri Historical Society, St. Louis. Contains documents regarding disputes at the Mine a Breton.

Wythe County, Virginia. Deed Books. Virginia State Archives, Richmond. These books document land transactions to which Moses Austin was a party.

_____. Land Tax Books. Virginia State Archives, Richmond. The records show Moses Austin's land holdings.

_____. Surveys. Virginia State Archives, Richmond. These records also document Moses Austin's land holdings.

Wythe County Court. Order Book. Virginia State Archives. This series of records documents the public offices Moses Austin held.

Wythe Lead and Zinc Mine Company. Abstract of Title. In possession of New Jersey Zinc Company, Austinville, Virginia. The document gives a history of the land at the lead mines in Virginia.

Interviews with

Clark, Edward, Houston, Texas, March 31, 1979.

Lang, Mr. and Mrs. Gregor, Suffield, Connecticut, October 22, 1978.

Mansfield, Mrs. Elizabeth, Durham, Connecticut, October 23, 1978.

Maps

Baldwin, R. *A Map of the Colonies of Connecticut and Rhode Island*. 1758. Connecticut Historical Society, Hartford.

Bates, Micajah. *Map of Richmond*. 1835. Virginia State Library, Richmond.

Covens and Murtier and Covens Junior. *Connecticut and Parts Adjacent*. 1780. Connecticut Historical Society, Hartford.

Latrobe, Benjamin Henry. Plan of Part of the City of Richmond. 1798. Library of Congress, Washington, D.C.

Map of the Mine a Breton. August, 1798. #198 Mapas y Planos, Archivo General de las Indias, Seville, Spain.

Melish, John. Map of the United States of America. 1820. Eugene C. Barker Texas History Center, University of Texas at Austin.

Plano de la Villa y Presidio de S. Antonio de Vejar. 1767. Texas State Archives, Austin.

Survey of Austin's Property. May, 1800. #260 Mapas y Planos, Archivo General de las Indias, Seville, Spain.

Publications

American State Papers, Public Lands. 4 vols. Washington: Gales and Seaton, 1834.

American State Papers, Finance. 5 vols. Washington: Gales and Seaton, 1832-1859.

Austin, Moses. *A Summary Description of the Lead Mines in Upper Louisiana: Also, An Estimate of Their Produce, For Three Years Past*. Document No. 3, Accompanying a Message from the President of the United States, November 8, 1804. Washington City: William Duane & Son, 1804.

Barker, Eugene C., ed. *The Austin Papers*. Annual Report of the American Historical Association for the Year 1919. 2 vols. Washington: Government Printing
Office, 1924.

Boyd, Julian P., ed. *The Papers of Thomas Jefferson*. Vol. 17. Princeton: Princeton
University Press, 1965.

Brackenridge, Henry Marie. *Recollections of Persons and Places in the West*. Philadelphia: James Kay, Jr., and Brother, 1834.

Bradbury, John. *Bradbury's Travels in the Interior of America, in the Years 1809,
1810, and 1811, Including a Description of Upper Louisiana Together with the
States of Ohio, Kentucky, Indiana, and Tennessee, with the Illinois Western Territories*. Vol. 5 in Reuben Gold Thwaites, *Early Western Travels, 1748-1846*.
Cleveland: Arthur H. Clark, Co., 1904.

Bryan, William J., et al., *vs.* Ferdinand B. Kennett, et al., *Transcript of Record*,
Supreme Court of the United States, October Term, 1883, No. 137. N.p.: n.p.,
n.d.

"Bryan, William J., et al., *v.* Kennett, Ferdinand B., et al.," *U.S. Reports 113*, October Term, 1884. New York: Banks and Brothers, 1885.

Byars, William Vincent, ed. *B. and M. Gratz, Merchants in Philadelphia, 1754-
1798: Papers of Interest to Their Posterity and the Posterity of Their Associates*.
Jefferson City, Missouri: Hugh Stephens Printing Co., 1916.

Carter, Clarence Edwin, comp. and ed. *The Territorial Papers of the United States*.
28 vols. Washington: U.S. Government Printing Office, 1934-1975.

Cole, Arthur Harrison, ed. *Industrial and Commerical Correspondence of Alexander
Hamilton Anticipating His Report on Manufactures*. Chicago: Business Historical Society, 1928.

Darby, John F. *Personal Recollections of Many Prominent People Whom I Have
Known, and of Events—Especially Those Relating to the History of St. Louis—
During the First Half of the Present Century*. St. Louis: G. I. Jones & Co.,
1880.

Delassus Deluzieres, Pierre Charles de Hault. *An Official Account of the Situation,
Soil, Produce, &c. of that part of Louisiana, Which lies between the Mouth of
the Missouri and New Madrid, or L'Anse a la Graise, and on the West Side of
the Mississippi, Together with an Abstract of the Spanish Government, &c.*
1796. In Frances L.S. Dugan and Jacqueline P. Bull, *An Epoch in Missouri
History*. Lexington: University of Kentucky Library Associates, 1958.

Dewees, W.B. *Letters From An Early Settler of Texas*. Compiled by Cara Cardelle.
2d. ed. Louisville: n.p., 1858.

Egle, William Henry, ed. *Pennsylvania Archives*. Third Series, Sixth Series. Har-
risburg, Pennsylvania: William Stanley Ray, 1894-1899, 1906-1907.

Featherstonhaugh, G.W. *Excursion Through the Slave States, From Washington on
the Potomac to the Frontier of Mexico; With Sketches of Popular Manners and
Geologic Notices*. New York: Harper and Brothers, 1844.

Flint, Timothy. *History and Geography of the Mississippi Valley*. 2 vols. Cincinatti:
E.H. Flint, 1833.

_____. *Recollections of the Last Ten Years In the Valley of the Mississippi*. Edited
by George R. Brooks. Carbondale: Southern Illinois University Press, 1968.

Garrison, George P., ed. "A Memorandum of M. Austin's Journey from the Lead
Mines in the County of Wythe in the State of Virginia to the Lead Mines in the
Province of Louisiana West of the Mississippi, 1796-1797." *American Histori-
cal Review* 5 (1900), 518-542.

Gracy, David B. II, ed. *Establishing Austin's Colony: The First Book Printed in*

Texas, With the Laws, Orders and Contracts of Colonization. Austin: Pemberton Press, 1970.

Hening, William Walter. *The Statutes at Large; Being a Collection of All the Laws of Virginia From the First Session of the Legislature in the Year 1619*. Vol. 1. Philadelphia: Thomas Desilver, 1823.

Hotten, John Camden, ed. *The Original Lists of Persons of Quality; Emigrants; Religious Exiles; Political Rebels; Serving Men Sold For a Term of Years; Apprentices; Children Stolen; Maidens Pressed; And Others Who Went From Great Britain to the American Plantations, 1600-1700*. 1874. Reprint. Baltimore: Genealogy Publishing Co., 1976.

Jefferson, Thomas. *Message from the President of the United States to Both Houses of Congress, 8th November, 1804*. Washington City: William Duane & Son, 1804.

_____. *Notes on the State of Virginia*. 1787. Reprint. Chapel Hill: University of North Carolina Press, 1955.

Jensen, Dana O., ed. "I at Home." *Bulletin of the Missouri Historical Society* 14 (October, 1957), 59-96.

Jordan, Helen. "Selections From the Military Correspondence of Colonel Henry Bouquet, 1756-1764." *Pennsylvania Magazine of History and Biography* 33 (1909), 216-227.

Journal of the House of Delegates of the Commonwealth of Virginia, 1789, 1790. Richmond: Thomas W. White, 1828.

Journal of the House of Delegates of the Commonwealth of Virginia, 1792, 1794. Richmond: Augustine David, 1792, 1794.

Laws of a Public and General Nature of the District of Louisiana, of the Territory of Louisiana, of the Territory of Missouri, and of the State of Missouri. Up to the Year 1824. Jefferson City: W. Lusk & Son, 1842.

"Letters to Jefferson Relative to the Virginia Capitol." *William and Mary Quarterly* Ser. 2, Vol. 5 (1925), 95-98.

McLean, Malcolm, comp. and ed. *Papers Concerning Robertson's Colony in Texas*. Vol. 1. Ft. Worth: Texas Christian University Press, 1974.

Macpherson's Directory for the City and Suburbs of Philadelphia. Philadelphia: Francis Bailey, 1785.

Marshall, Thomas Maitland, ed. *The Life and Papers of Frederick Bates*. 2 vols. St. Louis: Missouri Historical Society, 1926.

Missouri Land Claims. See: Report from the Commissioner of the General Land Office.

Morse, Jedidiah. *The American Universal Geography: Or a View of the Present State of All the Empires, Kingdoms, States and Republicks in the Known World, and of the United States of America in Particular*. 2 vols. Boston: J.T. Buckingham, 1805.

Official Letters of the Governors of the State of Virginia: The Letters of Thomas Jefferson. Richmond: Virginia State Library, 1928.

"An Old Virginia Correspondence." *Atlantic Monthly* 84 (1899), 535-549.

Palmer, William P., and Sherwin McRae, eds. *Calendar of Virginia State Papers and Other Manuscripts*. 11 vols. Richmond: Superintendent of Public Printing, 1875-1893.

[Parker, Laura Bryan, ed.] "A Letter from Mary (Mrs. Moses) Austin." *Quarterly of the Texas State Historical Association* 10 (1907), 343-346.

[Poultney, Joseph.] "A Letter of Joseph Poultney." *Pennsylvania Magazine of History and Biography* 52 (1928), 94-96.

"The Preston Papers Relating to Western Virginia." *Virginia Magazine of History and Biography* 26 (1918), 363-379.

Report from the Commissioner of the General Land Office, December 10, 1835. 24th Congress, 1st Session, Senate Document #16. Washington: Gates and Seaton, 1835. Reprinted as *Missouri Land Claims.* New Orleans: Polyanthos, 1976.

Schoolcraft, Henry Rowe. *The American Indians: Their History, Condition and Prospects, From Original Notes and Manuscripts.* Rochester: Wanzer, Foot and Co., 1851.

————. *Journal of a Tour into the Interior of Missouri and Arkansaw, from Potosi, or Mine a Burton, in Missouri Territory, in a South-West Direction, toward the Rocky Mountains; Performed in the Years 1818 and 1819.* London: Sir Richard Phillips and Co., 1821.

————. *Scenes and Adventures in the Semi-Alpine Region of the Ozark Mountains of Missouri and Arkansas.* Philadelphia: Lippincott, Grambo and Co., 1853.

————. *Travels in the Central Portions of the Mississippi Valley.* New York: Collins and Hannay, 1825.

————. *A View of the Lead Mines of Missouri: Including Some Observations on the Mineralogy, Geology, Geography, Antiquities, Soil, Climate, Population, and Productions of Missouri and Arkansaw, and Other Sections of the Western Country.* New York: Charles Wiley & Co., 1819.

Schultz, Christian. *Travels on an Inland Voyage Through the States of New York, Pennsylvania, Virginia, Ohio, Kentucky and Tennessee and Through the Territories of Indiana, Louisiana, Mississippi and New Orleans Performed in the Years 1807 and 1808, including a Tour of nearly 6000 Miles.* 2 vols. New York: Isaac Riley, 1810.

Smither, Harriet, ed. *The Papers of Mirabeau Buonaparte Lamar.* 6 vols. Austin: Texas Library and Historical Commission, 1921-1927.

Stoddard, Amos. *Sketches, Historical and Descriptive, of Louisiana.* Philadelphia: Mathew Carey, 1812.

Tariff Acts Passed By the Congress of the United States From 1789 to 1909. 61st Congress, 2nd Session, House Document #671. Washington: Government Printing Office, 1909.

Taylor, Virginia H. *The Letters of Antonio Martínez, Last Spanish Governor of Texas, 1817-1822.* Austin: Texas State Library, 1957.

Tinkcom, Harry M. "Sir Augustus in Pennsylvania: The Travels and Observations of Sir Augustus J. Foster in Early Nineteenth-Century Pennsylvania." *Pennsylvania Magazine of History and Biography* 75 (1957), 369-399.

Toulmin, Harry. *The Western Country in 1793, Reports on Kentucky and Virginia.* Edited by Tinling, Marion, and Godfrey Davies. San Marino, California: ————, 1948.

Weld, Isaac, Jr. *Travels Through the States of North America and the Provinces of Upper and Lower Canada During the Years 1795, 1796, and 1797.* 1807. Reprint. New York: Johnson Reprint Corp., 1968.

Wetmore, Alphonso, comp. *Gazetteer of the State of Missouri.* St. Louis: C. Keemle, 1837.

Woodruff, Mrs. Howard W. "Original Baptismal Register, 1759-1811: The Church of Ste. Genevieve." *Missouri Miscellany* 9 (March, 1980), 1-44.

The Wyllys Papers: Correspondence and Documents Chiefly of Descendants of Gov. George Wyllys of Connecticut, 1590-1796. Collections of the Connecticut Historical Society, vol. 21. Hartford: Connecticut Historical Society, 1924.

Newspapers

Arkansas Gazette (Little Rock), 1819-1821, 1959.
Austin *American-Statesman*, 1946.
Connecticut Courant (Hartford), 1768-1788.
Dallas *Morning News*, 1941.
Gazette of the United States (Philadelphia), 1792.
Missouri Gazette (St. Louis), 1808-1821.
The News (Lynchburg, Virginia), 1953.
Kansas City *Star*, 1949.
Pennsylvania Journal (Philadelphia), 1791.
Potosi *Journal*, 1895, 1897, 1904, 1906.
Potosi *Independent Journal*, 1935, 1938, 1941, 1949, 1962, 1968.
Potosi *Weekly Independent*, 1878.
St. Louis *Daily Globe Democrat*, 1889.
St. Louis *Globe Democrat*, 1925, 1938.
St. Louis *Post-Dispatch*, 1938, 1949.
San Antonio *Express*, 1938, 1939.
Tennessee Gazette (Nashville), 1804.
Virginia Gazette and General Advertiser (Richmond), 1791-1797.
Virginia Gazette or the American Advertiser (Richmond), 1785-1786.

SECONDARY WORKS

Abernethy, Thomas Perkins. *The South in the New Nation*. Vol. 4. A History of the South. Baton Rouge: Louisiana State University Press, 1961.

Alcorn, Robert Hayden. *The Biography of a Town: Suffield, Connecticut, 1670-1970*. Suffield: Three Hundreth Anniversary Committee of the Town of Suffield, 1970.

Austin, Eugene K. "The Austin Family in America, 1638-1908." Manuscript. New York Public Library, New York.

Austin, Paul R. *Austins to Wisconsin*. Wilmington, Delaware: William N. Cann, Inc., 1964.

"Austinville Mine Completes Two Centuries." *Commonwealth* 23, No. 12 (December, 1956), 53-55.

Bacarisse, Charles A. "The Baron de Bastrop: Life and Times of Philip Hendrik Nering Bogel, 1759 to 1827." Ph.D. dissertation, University of Texas, 1955.

_____. "Baron de Bastrop." *Southwestern Historical Quarterly* 58 (January, 1955), 319-330.

_____. "Why Moses Austin Came to Texas." *Southwestern Social Science Quarterly* 40 (June, 1959), 16-27.

"Bank of the United States." *Virginia Magazine of Biography and History* 8 (January, 1907), 287-295.

Barber, John Warner. *Connecticut Historical Collections*. New Haven: John W. Barber, 1836.

Barker, Eugene C. *The Life of Stephen F. Austin, Founder of Texas, 1793-1836: A Chapter in the Westward Movement of the Anglo-American People*. Nashville: Cokesbury Press, 1925.

Basler, Lucille. *A Tour of Old Ste. Genevieve*. N.p.: Lucille Basler and Wehmeyer Printing Co., 1975.

_____. *Ste. Genevieve: Mother of the West, 1725*. N.p.: n.p., 1978.

Beveridge, Albert J. *The Life of John Marshall*. 4 vols. Boston: Houghton Mifflin Co., 1916-1919.

Billington, Ray Allen. *Westward Expansion: A History of the American Frontier*. 2d. ed. New York: The Macmillan Co., 1966.

Billion, Frederick L. *Annals of St. Louis in its Early Days under the French and Spanish Dominations*. St. Louis: G. I. Jones & Co., 1886.

————. *Annals of St. Louis in its Territorial Days, 1804-1821*. St. Louis: n.p., 1888.

Bishop, J. Leander. *A History of American Manufactures from 1608 to 1860*. 3 vols. Philadelphia: Edward Young & Co., 1868.

Bissell, Charles S. *Antique Furniture in Suffield, Connecticut, 1670-1956*. Hartford: Connecticut Historical Society and Suffield Historical Society, 1956.

Bridenbaugh, Carl, and Jessica Bridenbaugh. *Rebels and Gentlemen: Philadelphia in the Age of Franklin*. New York: Reynal and Hitchcock, 1942.

Bryan, Carter Royston, comp. "DeBrienne-Bryan." Manuscript in possession of P.H. Bell, Houston, Texas.

Bryant, William Cullen, ed. *Picturesque America; or, The Land We Live In*. 2 vols. New York: D. Appleton and Co, 1874.

Buehler, H.A. "The Wythe Lead Mines." Joint Collection: Western Historical Manuscript Collection and State Historical Society of Missouri Manuscripts, University of Missouri, Columbia.

Burke, Harry R. "Texas' Attempt to Obtain Moses Austin's Body Parallels Mining Pioneer's Own Tactics." St. Louis *Globe-Democrat*, May 6, 1938.

Bushman, Richard L. *From Puritan to Yankee: Character and the Social Order in Connecticut, 1690-1765*. 1967. New York: W.W. Norton & Co., 1970.

Cable, John Ray. *The Bank of the State of Missouri*. Volume 102, No. 2. Columbia University Studies in History, Economics and Public Law. New York: Columbia University, 1923.

Campbell County, Virginia, Bicentennial Commission, Historical Committee, comp. *Lest It Be Forgotten: A Scrapbook of Campbell County, Virginia*. N.p.: Altavista Printing Co., 1976.

Carter, Clarence E. "The Burr-Wilkinson Intrigue in St. Louis." *Bulletin of the Missouri Historical Society* 10 (July, 1954), 447-464.

Castañeda, Carlos E. *Our Catholic Heritage in Texas, 1519-1936*. Vol. 4: *The Transition Period: The Fight for Freedom, 1810-1836*. Austin: Von Boeckmann-Jones Co., 1950.

Chalkley, Lyman. "Before the Gates of the Wilderness Road: The Settlement of Southwestern Virginia." *Virginia Magazine of Biography and History* 30 (1922), 183-188.

Christian, W. Asbury. *Richmond: Her Past and Present*. Richmond: L.H. Jenkins, 1912.

Clark, Victor S. *History of Manufactures in the United States*. 2 Vols. New York: McGraw-Hill Book Co., 1929.

Clokey, Richard M. *William H. Ashley*. Norman: University of Oklahoma Press, 1980.

Collins, Richard H. *History of Kentucky*. 2 Vols. Covington, Kentucky: Collins & Co., 1874.

Crofut, Florence S. Mary. *Guide to the History and the Historic Sites of Connecticut*. 2 Vols. New Haven: Yale University Press, 1937,

"Crossing the Atlantic in 1638: Passengers Aboard the Ship Bevis." *The Second Boat* 1 (May, 1980), 12-15.

Currier, L.W. *Zinc and Lead Region of Southwestern Virginia*. Virginia Geological

Survey Bulletin No. 43. Richmond: Division of Purchase and Printing, 1935.

Curtis, Janet Austin. "Southside Virginia Austins." *Virginia Genealogist* 5 (1961), 147-154.

Dabney, Virginius. *Richmond: The Story of a City*. Garden City, New York: Doubleday & Co., 1976.

Deckler, Edna Perry, comp. "Austin-Perry Memorandum." *Stirpes* 7-9 (June, 1967-September, 1969).

Denslow, William R. *10,000 Famous Freemasons*. Trenton, Missouri: Missouri Lodge of Research, ca. 1957.

Destler, Chester McArthur. "Barnabas Deane and Barnabas Deane & Company." Manuscript. Chester McArthur Destler Papers, Connecticut Historical Society, Hartford.

————. "Barnabas Deane and Barnabas Deane & Company." *Connecticut Historical Society Bulletin* 35 (January, 1970), 7-19.

"Director's Notebook." *Bulletin of the Missouri Historical Society* 18 (April, 1962), 274-276.

Dodson, E. Griffith. *The Capitol of the Commonwealth of Virginia at Richmond*. 2d. ed. Richmond: E. Griffith Dodson, 1938.

Douglass, Robert Sidney. *History of Southeast Missouri*. 2 vols., 1912. Reprint (2 vols. in 1). Cape Giradeau: Ramfre Press, 1961.

Drumm, Stella M. "Samuel Hammond." *Missouri Historical Society Collections* 4 (1923), 402-422.

Duvall, Rezin Fenton. "Philadelphia's Maritime Commerce with the British Empire, 1783-1789." Ph.D. dissertation, University of Pennsylvania, 1960.

East, Robert A. *Business Enterprise in the American Revolution Era*. New York: Columbia University Press, 1938.

"The Dr. Aaron Elliott House (1805)." Typescript in possession of Mrs. Garighity, Ste. Genevieve, Missouri.

Ellyson, Louise. *Richmond on the James*. Santa Fe: Press of the Territorian, 1970.

Field, David D. *Centennial Address*. Middletown, Connecticut: Wm. B. Casey, 1853.

Foley, William E. *A History of Missouri, 1673-1820*. Columbia: University of Missouri Press, 1971.

————. "Territorial Politics in Frontier Missouri, 1804-1820." Ph.D. dissertation, University of Missouri, 1967.

Fowler, William Chauncey. *History of Durham, Connecticut: From the First Grant of Land in 1662 to 1866*. 1866. Reprint. Durham, Connecticut: n.p., 1970.

Franzwa, Gregory M. *The Story of Old Ste. Genevieve*. St. Louis: Patrice Press, Inc., 1967.

Gardner, James Alexander. *Lead King: Moses Austin*. St. Louis: Sunrise Publishing Co., 1980.

————. "The Life of Moses Austin." Ph.D. dissertation, Washington University, 1963.

Geib, George Winthrop. "A History of Philadelphia, 1776-1789." Ph.D. dissertation, University of Wisconsin, 1969.

Gracy, David B. II. "George Washington Littlefield: A Biography in Business." Ph.D. dissertation, Texas Tech University, 1971.

Green, James Albert. *William Henry Harrison: His Life and Times*. Richmond: Garrett and Massie, 1941.

Gwathmey, H.H. *Historical Register of Virginians in the Revolution*. Richmond: Dietz Press, 1938.

H., F.M. "Biography of Dr. Matthew Cunningham." *The Arkansas Pioneers* Vol. 1, No. 1 (September, 1912), 7-8.

Hammond, Bray. *Banking and Politics in America: From the Revolution to the Civil War*. Princeton: Princeton University Press, 1957.

Hart, Charles Henry. "Colonel John Nixon." *Pennsylvania Magazine of History and Biography* 1 (1877), 188-201.

Hatcher, Mattie Austin. *The Opening of Texas to Foreign Settlement, 1801-1821*. University of Texas Bulletin No. 2714. Austin: University of Texas, 1927.

Hecht, Arthur. "Lead Production in Virginia During the Seventeenth and Eighteenth Centuries." *West Virginia History* 25 (April, 1964), 173-184.

Herndon, Dallas T. *The Centennial History of Arkansas*. 3 Vols. Chicago: S.J. Clarke Publishing Co., 1922.

_____. *Why Little Rock Was Born*. Little Rock: Central Printing Co., 1933.

Higginbotham, Valle. *John Smith T: Missouri Pioneer*. N.p.: n.p., 1968.

_____. "John Smith T." De Soto (Missouri) *Press*, January___, 1964.

History of Franklin, Jefferson, Washington, Crawford and Gasconade Counties, Missouri. 1888. Reprint. Cape Giradeau: Ramfre Press, 1970.

History of Middlesex County, Connecticut, With Biographical Sketches of Its Prominent Men. New York: J.B. Beers and Co., 1884.

Hogan, William R. "Life and Letters of Henry Austin." Ph.D. dissertation, University of Texas, 1932.

Houck, Louis. *A History of Missouri From the Earliest Explorations and Settlements Until the Admission of the State into the Union*. 3 Vols. Chicago: R.R. Donnelley & Sons Co., 1908.

Howe, Henry. *Historical Collections of Virginia*. Charleston, South Carolina: William R. Babcock, 1856.

Hutson, Alice. *From Chalk to Bronze: A Biography of Waldine Tauch*. Austin: Shoal Creek Publishers, [1978?].

Ingalls, Walter Renton. *Lead and Zinc in the United States: Comprising An Economic History of the Mining and Smelting of the Metals and the Conditions Which Have Affected the Development of the Industries*. New York: Hill Publishing Company, 1908.

Jacobs, James Ripley. *Tarnished Warrior: Major-General James Wilkinson*. New York: The MacMillan Company, 1938.

John, Elizabeth A.H. *Storms Brewed in Other Men's Worlds: The Confrontation of Indians, Spanish, and French in the Southwest, 1540-1795*. College Station: Texas A & M University Press, 1975.

Jones, Breckinridge. "One Hundred Years of Banking in Missouri, 1820-1920." *Missouri Historical Review* 15 (January, 1921), 345-392.

[Jones, J. Wyman.] *A History of the St. Joseph Lead Company From Its Organization in 1864 to January 1, 1892*. N.p.: n.p., [1892].

Jones, Robert L., and Pauline H. "Stephen F. Austin in Arkansas." *Arkansas Historical Quarterly* 25 (Winter, 1966), 336-353.

Kegley, Frederick B. "A Sentinel of the Southwest: The Old Shot Tower at Jackson's Ferry on New River." Manuscript in possession of New Jersey Zinc Company, Austinville, Virginia.

_____. "Shot Tower at Jackson's Ferry." *Journal of the Roanoke Historical Society* Vol. 3, No. 1 (Summer, 1966), 1-7.

Kegley, Mary B. "The First Settlers." *Wythe County Historical Review* 1 (July, 1971), 17-18.

Kelly, John Frederick. *Early Domestic Architecture of Connecticut*. New York: Dover Publishers, 1963.

Kirkpatrick, Robert Lawhead. "History of St. Louis, 1804-1816." M.A. thesis, Washington University, 1947.

Kohler, William. "The Lead Mines." Manuscript. University of Virginia Library, Charlottesville.

Lee, Rebecca Smith. *Mary Austin Holley: A Biography*. Austin: University of Texas Press, 1962.

Little, John P. *History of Richmond*. Richmond: Dietz Printing Co., 1933.

Lomask, Milton. *Aaron Burr: The Conspiracy and Years of Exile, 1805-1836*. New York: Farrar, Straus, Giroux, 1982.

Loomis, Noel M., and Abraham P. Nasatir. *Pedro Vial and the Roads to Santa Fe*. Norman: University of Oklahoma Press, 1967.

Luchowski, Linda Susan. "Sunshine Soldiers: New Haven and the American Revolution." Ph.D. dissertation, State University of New York at Buffalo, 1976.

Lutz, Frances Earle. *Chesterfield—An Old Virginia County*. Richmond: William Byrd Press, [c. 1954].

"Lynch Law." *William and Mary Quarterly* Series 1, Vol. 13 (1905), 203-205.

McReynolds, Edwin C. *Missouri: A History of the Crossroads State*. Norman: University of Oklahoma Press, 1962.

Marion, John Francis. *Bicentennial City: Walking Tours of Historic Philadelphia*. Princeton: Pyne Press, 1974.

Martin, Joseph. *A New and Comprehensive Gazetteer of Virginia and the District of Columbia*. Charlottesville: Joseph Martin, 1835.

Martin, Margaret E. *Merchants and Trade of the Connecticut River Valley, 1750-1820*. Smith College Studies in History Volume 16. Northampton, Massachusetts: Smith College, October, 1938-July, 1939.

The Mattabesset Silver Lead Mining Co.: Reports of James G. Percival, et al., with the By-laws of the Company. Middletown: Charles H. Pelton, 1857.

Medearis, Mary. *Washington, Arkansas: History on the Southwest Trail*. 2d. ed. Hope, Arkansas: Etter Printing Co., 1978.

Middlebrook, Louis F. *History of Maritime Connecticut During the American Revolution, 1775-1783*. 2 vols. Salem, Massachusetts: Essex Institute, 1925.

Miller, John C. *The Federalist Era, 1789-1801*. 1960. Reprint. New York: Harper and Row, 1963.

————. *Triumph of Freedom, 1775-1783*. Boston: Little, Brown and Co., 1948.

Moore, Adella Breckenridge. "They Gathered There ...." *Lead Belt News* (Flat River), May 8, 1953.

————. "Moses Austin and the Lure of Lead." *Congressional Record*, 81st Congress, 1st Session, March 21, 1949.

Moore, Edith Austin, and William Allen Day, comps. *The Descendants of Richard Austin of Charlestown, Massachusetts, 1638*. N.p.: n.p., n.d.

Mordecai, Samuel. *Richmond in By-Gone Days: Being Reminiscences of an Old Citizen*. Richmond: George M. West, 1856.

Morrison, A.J. "Joseph H. Hawkins." *Tyler's Quarterly Historical and Genealogical Magazine* 3 (1922), 20-22.

Niles, Blair. *The James: From Iron Gate to the Sea*. New York: Farrar & Rinehart, 1945.

Oberholtzer, Ellis Paxon. *Philadelphia: A History of the City and Its People, A Record of 225 Years*. 4 vols. Chicago: S.J. Clarke Publishing Co., 1911.

Osborn, Norris Galpin. *History of Connecticut*. 5 vols. New York: States History Company, 1925.

P., J.H. "The Wythe Lead Mines." Manuscript. Joint Collection: Western Historical Manuscript Collection and State Historical Society of Missouri Manuscripts, University of Missouri, Columbia.

Pankey, George Edward. *John Pankey of Manakin Town, Virginia, and His Descendants*. Ruston, Louisiana: G.E. Pankey, 1969.

Parker, Laura Bryan. "Facts Concerning Moses Austin, His Family, and Forebears." Typescript. Laura Bryan Parker Papers, Eugene C. Barker Texas History Center, University of Texas at Austin.

Peters, Samuel. *General History of Connecticut*. 1781. Reprint. Upper Saddle River, New Jersey: Literature House, 1970.

Potter, Dorothy T., and Clifton W. Potter, Jr. *Lynchburg: "The Most Interesting Spot"*. Lynchburg: Progress Publishing Corp., 1976.

Presgraves, James S., ed. *Wythe County Chapters*. Wytheville: James S. Presgraves, 1972.

Pulsifer, William H. *Notes for a History of Lead and an Inquiry into the Development of the Manufacture of White Lead and Lead Oxides*. New York: D. Van Nostrand, 1888.

Purcell, Richard J. *Connecticut in Transition: 1775-1818*. 1918. Reprint. Middletown: Wesleyan University Press, 1963.

Raistrick, Arthur, and Bernard Jennings. *A History of Lead Mining in the Pennines*. London: Longman's Green and Company, Ltd., 1965.

Ramsdell, Charles. *San Antonio: A Historical and Pictorial Guide*. Austin: University of Texas Press, 1959.

Rhodes, Marylou. *Landmarks of Richmond: Places to Know and See in the Nation's Most Historic City*. Richmond: Garrett and Massie, 1938.

Richeson, Paul R. "The Perrys of Potosi: A Time to Triumph." Photocopy of typescript, in possession of the author.

Riley, Agnes Graham Sanders. "James Newell, 1749-1823." The Historical Society of Washington County, Virginia, *Publications* Series 2, No. 8 (July, 1970), 16-34.

Rosenberry, Lois Kimbell Mathews. *Migrations from Connecticut Prior to 1800*. Tercentenary Series No. 28. New Haven: Yale University Press, 1934.

Ross, Margaret. *Arkansas Gazette: The Early Years, 1819-1866: A History*. Little Rock: Arkansas Gazette Foundation, 1969.

————. "From First, The Little Rock Site Favored; Old Settler Speaks of His Fellow Pioneers," *Arkansas Gazette* (Little Rock), January 11, 1959.

Scharf, J. Thomas, and Thomas Westcott. *History of Philadelphia, 1609-1884*. 3 Vols. Philadelphia: L.H. Everts & Co., 1884.

Scruggs, Philip Lightfoot. *Lynchburg, Virginia*. Lynchburg: J.P. Bell Co., 1978.

Shearer, Ernest C. "Moses Austin: Let Him Rest in Peace." West Texas Scientific and Historical Society Publication No. 18. *Sul Ross State College Bulletin*, Vol. 43, No. 3 (September, 1963), 106-120.

Sheldon, H.S. *Documentary History of Suffield, 1670-1749*. Springfield, Massachusetts: Clark W. Bryan Co., 1888.

————. *Suffield and the Lexington Alarm in April, 1775*. Hartford: Case, Lockwood & Brainard Co., 1881.

Shoemaker, Floyd Calvin. "Fathers of the State." *Missouri Historical Review* 10 (October, 1915), 1-32.

————. "Herculaneum Shot Tower." *Missouri Historical Review* 20 (January, 1926), 214-216.

————. "Judge John Rice Jones: The Living Chronicle of Passing Times." Typescript in possession of George W. Showalter, Potosi, Missouri.

————. *Missouri and Missourians: Land of Contrasts and People of Achievements*. 2 Vols. Chicago: Lewis Publishing Co., 1943.

_____. *Missouri's Struggle for Statehood, 1804-1821*. Jefferson City: Hugh Stephens Printing Co., 1916.

_____. "Six Periods of Missouri History." *Missouri Historical Review* 9 (July, 1915), 221-240.

Showalter, George W. *Potosi, Missouri: A Bicentennial Scrapbook, 1763-1963*. Potosi: Independent Journal, 1975.

Simpson, Henry. *The Lives of Eminent Philadelphians, Now Deceased*. Philadelphia: William Brotherhead, 1859.

Southwark, Moyamensing, Weccacoe, Passyunk, Dock Ward for Two Hundred and Seventy Years. Philadelphia: Quaker City Publishing Co., 1892.

Starnes, George T. *Sixty Years of Branch Banking in Virginia*. New York: MacMillan Co., 1931.

Stevens, Walter B. *Centennial History of Missouri (The Center State): One Hundred Years in the Union, 1820-1921*. 2 Vols. St. Louis: S.J. Clarke Publishing Co., 1921.

Talbot, Gayle. "John Rice Jones." *Southwestern Historical Quarterly* 35 (October, 1931), 146-150.

Taussig, F.W. *The Tariff History of the United States*. 8th Edition. New York: G.P. Putnam's Sons, ca. 1931.

"Texas Collection." *Southwestern Historical Quarterly* 42 (July, 1953), 125.

"Texas Would Honor Moses Austin." *Missouri Historical Review* 24 (1930), 469-470.

Thompson, Ernest Trice. *Presbyterians in the South, 1607-1861*. 3 Vols. Richmond: John Knox Press, 1963.

Thompson, Henry C. *Our Lead Belt Heritage*. Flat River, Missouri: The News-Sun, ca. 1955.

Trevelyan, George Macaulay. *England Under The Stuarts*. London: Methuen & Co., Ltd., 1904.

Trumbull, James Hammond, ed. *Memorial History of Hartford County, Connecticut, 1633-1844*. 2 Vols. Boston: Cambridge University Press, 1886.

Tubbs, Walter Louis. "Elder Joseph L. Bays, A Pioneer Texas Baptist Preacher." M.A. thesis, Southwestern Baptist Theological Seminary, 1916.

Van Dusen, Albert E. *Connecticut*. New York: Random House, 1961.

_____. *Middletown and the American Revolution*. Middletown: Rockfall Corporation of Middletown and Middlesex County Historical Society, 1950.

_____. "The Trade of Revolutionary Connecticut." Ph.D. dissertation, University of Pennsylvania, 1948.

Vernon, Walter N. *William Stevenson: Riding Preacher*. Dallas: Southern Methodist University Press, 1964.

Victor, William B. *Life and Events*. Cincinatti: Applegate & Co., 1859.

Viles, Jonas. "Missouri in 1820." *Missouri Historical Review* 15 (October, 1920), 36-52.

_____. "Population and Extent of Settlement in Missouri Before 1804." *Missouri Historical Review* 5 (July, 1911), 189-207.

Violette, Eugene Morrow. "Early Settlements in Missouri." *Missouri Historical Review* I (October, 1906), 38-52.

_____. *A History of Missouri*. Reprint. Cape Giradeau: Ramfre Press, 1951.

The Virginia State Capitol, Richmond, Virginia. Richmond: Division of Engineering and Building, 1974.

Ward, Harry M., and Harold E. Greer, Jr. *Richmond During the Revolution, 1775-1783*. Charlottesville, Virginia: University Press of Virginia, 1977.

Warner, Sam Bass, Jr. *The Private City: Philadelphia in Three Periods of Its Growth*. Philadelphia: University of Pennsylvania Press, 1968.

Webb, Walter Prescott, and H. Bailey Carroll, eds. *The Handbook of Texas*. 2 Vols. Austin: Texas State Historical Association, 1952.

Wettereau, James O. "Branches of the First Bank of the United States." *Journal of Economic History* 2 (December, 1942), 66-100.

Whitaker, Arthur P. "Reed and Forde: Merchant Adventurers of Philadelphia." *Pennsylvania Magazine of History and Biography* 41 (July, 1937), 237-262.

Whited, Milton H. *Durham's Heritage: Men and Homes of Early Durham*. Durham: Town of Durham, 1976.

————. "Elias Austin, 1718-1776," Typescript in possession of Milton Whited, Meriden, Connecticut.

Willms, Welton Lyle. "Lead Mining in Missouri, 1700-1811." M.A. thesis, Washington University, 1935.

Wooten, Dudley G., ed. *A Comprehensive History of Texas, 1685 to 1897*. 2 Vols. Dallas: William G. Scarff, 1898.

Yancey, Rosa Faulkner. *Lynchburg and Its Neighbors*. Richmond: J.W. Fergusson & Sons, 1935.

Young, John Russell. *Memorial History of the City of Philadelphia From Its First Settlement to the Year 1895*. 2 Vols. New York: New York History Co., 1895.

INDEX
by
Linda K. Fetters

This index is designed to serve two purposes. One is to assist the user in locating specific items of information in the text. The other, essential because the chapters are untitled and thus provide no indication of the breaks in Moses Austin's life, is to give the reader a means of plotting the course of his career. To save space, abbreviations have been used for geographical place names and for the two principals, Moses Austin (MA) and Stephen F. Austin (SFA).

About the Author

DAVID B. GRACY II is the Governor Bill Daniel Professor in Archival Enterprise in the Graduate School of Library and Information Science, The University of Texas at Austin. Formerly on the staff of the Texas State Historical Association, 1963-66, and Director of the Texas State Archives, 1977-1986, Gracy has written a considerable number of works, including *Littlefield Lands: Colonization on the Texas Plains, 1912-1920* (University of Texas Press, 1968), which received the Award of Merit from the American Association for State and Local History, and *Establishing Austin's Colony* (Pemberton Press, 1970). His many articles have appeared in major historical and archival journals.

Gracy received his B.A. and M.A. in history from The University of Texas at Austin and his Ph.D. in history from Texas Tech University. During his distinguished career, he has received many honors and awards, the most recent being the Texas Excellence in Teaching Award, Graduate School of Library and Information Science, The University of Texas at Austin, and the first Distinguished Alumnus of the Department of History, Texas Tech University. He served as President of the Society of American Archivists, 1983-84.

Currently Gracy serves on the Board of the National Archives of the Episcopal Church and is the United States Representative to the Archives Committee of the Pan American Institute of Geography and History.

Trinity University Press would take note of the production of this volume. The author submitted the manuscript to the publisher on disks. Through a cooperative effort among author, publisher, and printer, this project was edited and processed onto the printer's system, using the author's disks.

The printer is Best Printing Company, Inc.
The typeface is Century Old Style.
The jacket design is by Jerry Tokola.
The binding is by Custom Bookbinders.